THE ART OF Rock COVERS

“Vinyl is the real deal. I’ve always felt like, until you buy the vinyl record, you don’t really own the album. And it’s not just me or a little pet thing or some kind of retro romantic thing from the past. It is still alive.”

Jack White

Composer, Music Producer & Football Player

‘That looks dangerous indeed,’ my dentist said. As if something unpleasant could crawl up his arm, he held out the album Fun House by Iggy Pop’s band The Stooges with the tips of his fingers. It was 1971, and I was 17 years old. Before going to the dentist, I had bought three LPs and now he was curious to see what was in my plastic bag. I don’t remember what the other two LPs were, but the sight of five wild-looking guys you could barely make out on the red, yellow and black cover left me in no doubt: I had to have that record. And fortu-nately, the music delivered what the cover promised – wicked rock ‘n’ roll that no other band was playing at the time. With so little pocket money, it was a risky strategy to buy records based on their covers. A few years later, the hairstyles no longer provided any clues: there was every possibility the long-haired blokes would be the sort that gently strum their acoustic guitars, while the guys with short hair could blow their amps. It was hard work to keep up with everything. Sure, there were music magazines – the revered Sounds was always a reliable guide. But what could you listen to? Helpful radio shows were a rarity; the records in the shop were sealed. There was only the shop near me where the man behind the counter would graciously put a record on the turntable for you while you listened with headphones. But by the time the second track kicked in, he’d yank up the tone arm and ask, ‘Is that the one you want then?’ As my disposable income grew larger, so too did my record collection over time. Today, my collection is arranged in alphabetical order in wooden boxes. And as only the 366 covers in this calendar can show – there is no world more colourful than that of record sleeves. Milestones in music and imagery are covered here: the simple three letters on NEU!’s first album, members of The Clash loitering menacingly on their debut release, the baby diving after a dollar bill on Nirvana’s Nevermind – every record takes the listener on a wonderful journey as soon as the needle sinks into the groove. Above my shelf, there is a picture frame which features a different record from time to time. I think it’s time to remove Let It Bleed by The Rolling Stones and replace it with Fun House.

Alf Burchardt

Book/music author (HH Calling, Sounds of Hamburg with Bernd Jonkmanns) and travel journalist; record collector since the age of 15.

Hamburg, January 2023

In memory of our friend, editor and photographer
Bernd Jonkmanns (1966–2025),
whose passion for vinyl records made this project
possible and lives on in this calendar.

SCAN & LISTEN

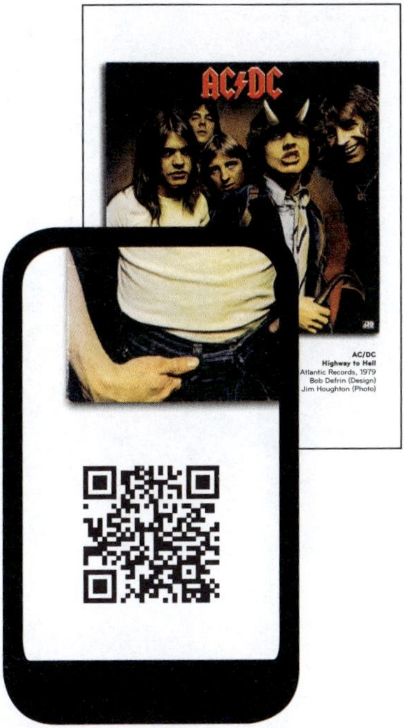

1. SCAN THE QR CODE

Open the camera app on your smartphone and point it at the QR code.

2. CHOOSE YOUR STREAMING SERVICE

You will be redirected to a page where you can select your preferred platform.

3. FIND THE ALBUM

Your streaming service will show the album in the search results. Select it to start listening!

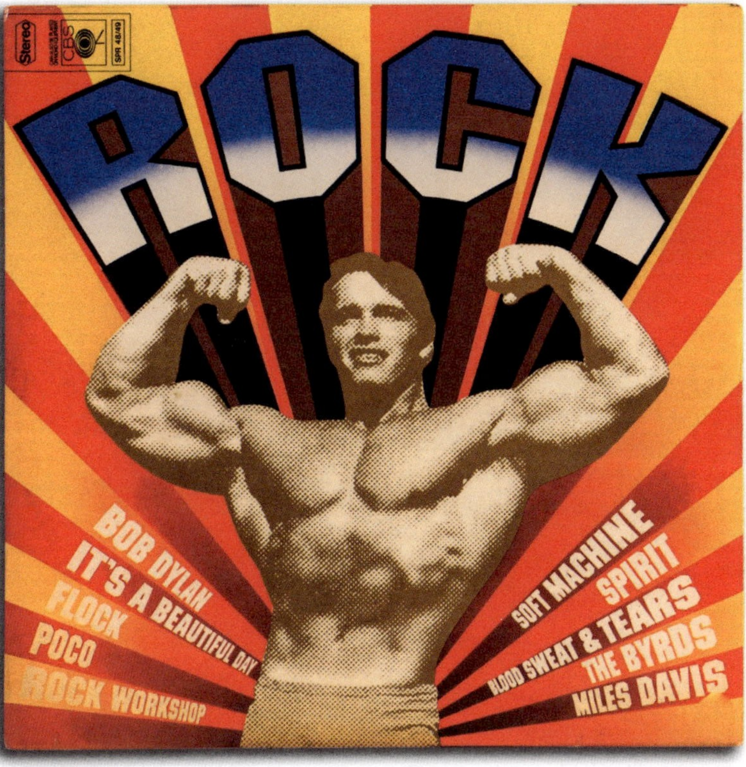

Various Artists
Rock Buster
CBS Records, 1970
Arthur Bayes Associatio1970 (Design)
Weider Ltd. (Photo)

01 JAN

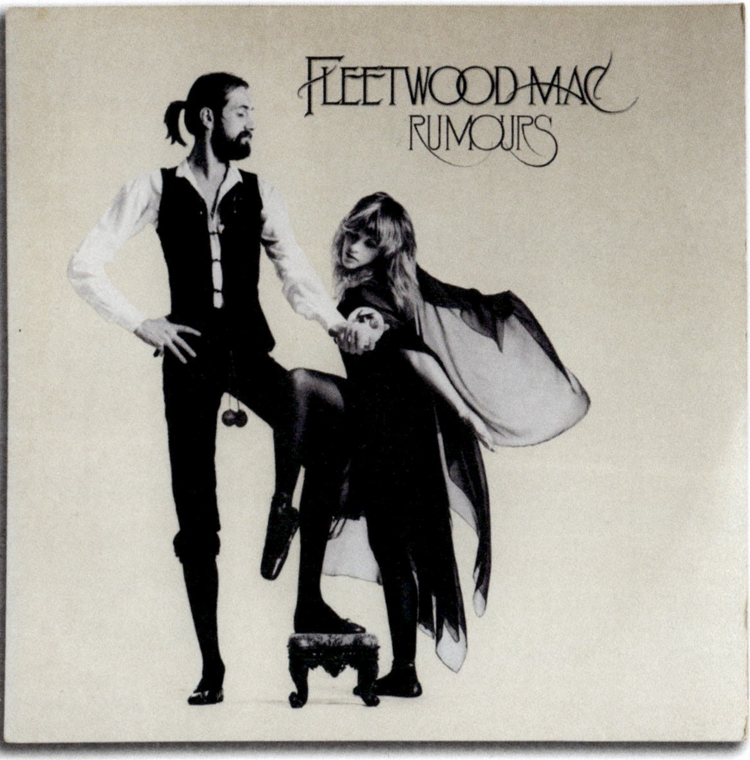

Fleetwood Mac
Rumours
Warner Bros. Records, 1977
Herbert Worthington (Photo)

02 JAN

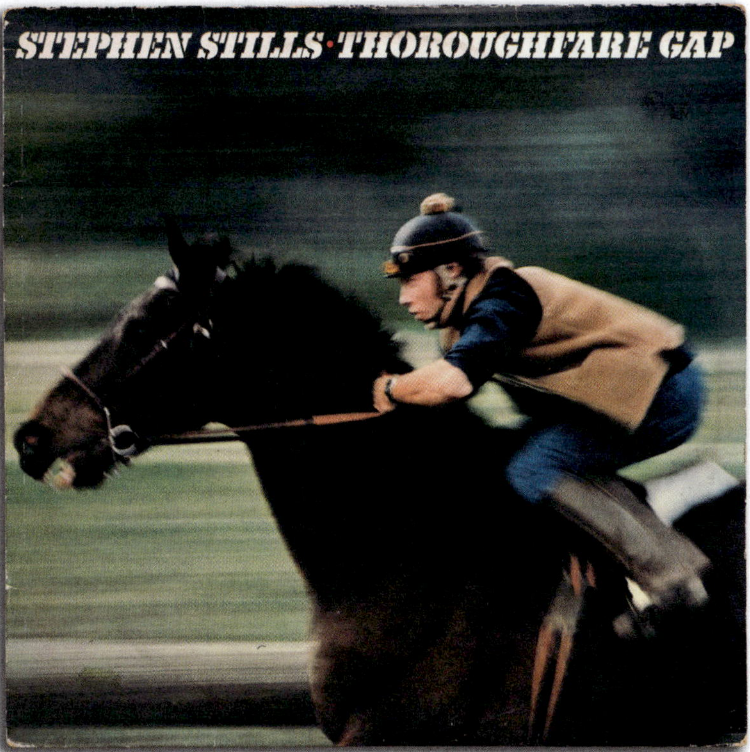

Steven Stills
Thoroughfare Gap
CBS Records, 1978
Stephen Stills, John Berg (Design)

* Jan 3rd, 1945
Steven Stills
Dallas (Texas)

03 JAN

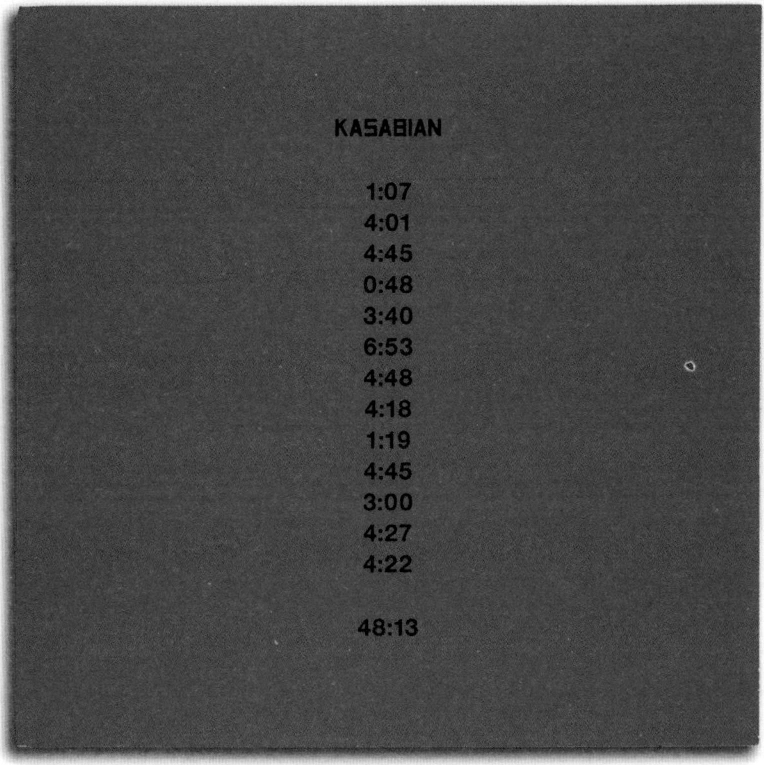

Kasabian
48:13
Columbia, 2014
Aitor Throup (Design)

04 JAN

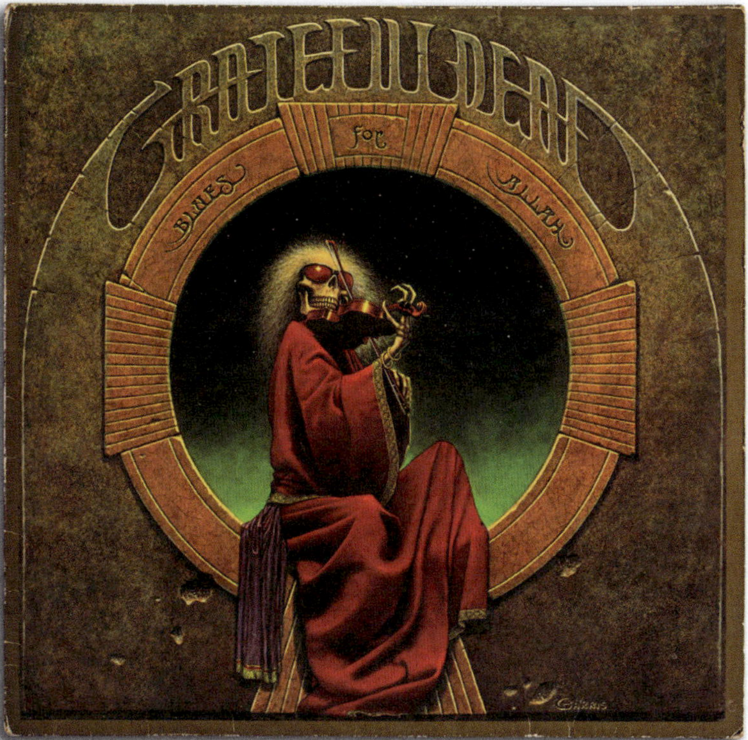

Grateful Dead
Blues For Allah
United Artists Records, 1975
Philip Garris (Illustration)

05 JAN

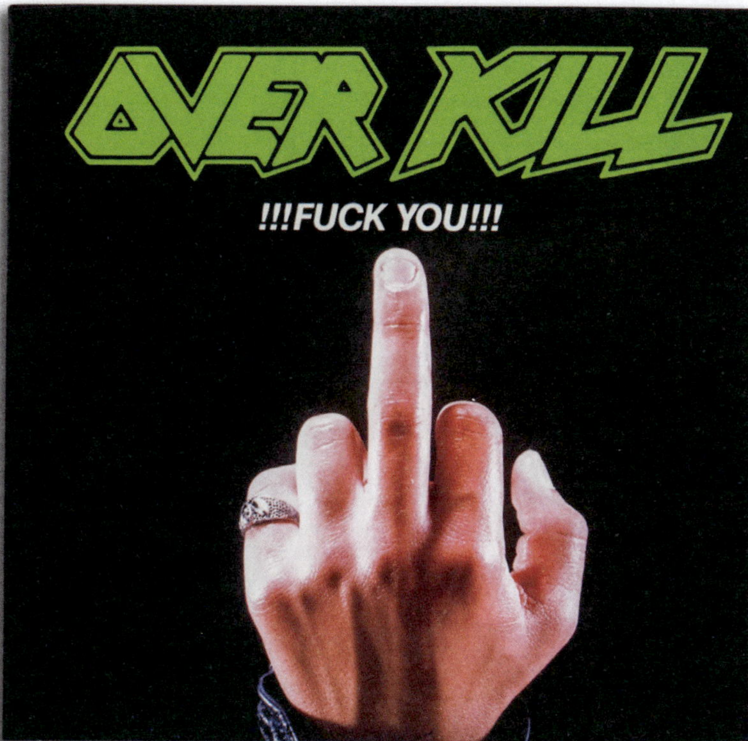

Over Kill
!!! Fuck You !!!
Atlantic Records, 1987
Danny Muro & Pat Celello (Design)
Danny Muro (Photo)

06 JAN

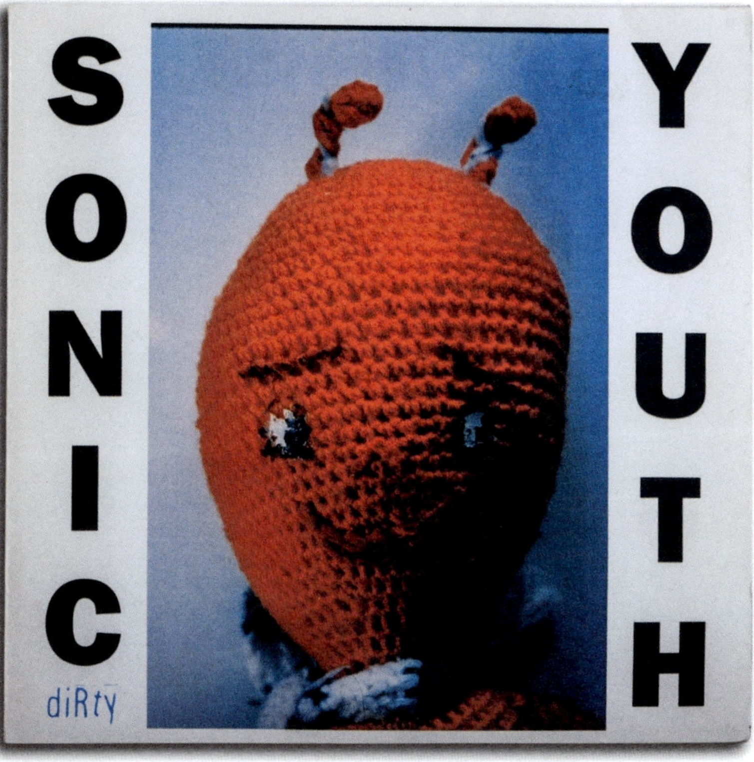

Sonic Youth
Dirty
Geffen Records, 1992
Kevin Reegan (Design)
Mike Kelley (Photo)

07 JAN

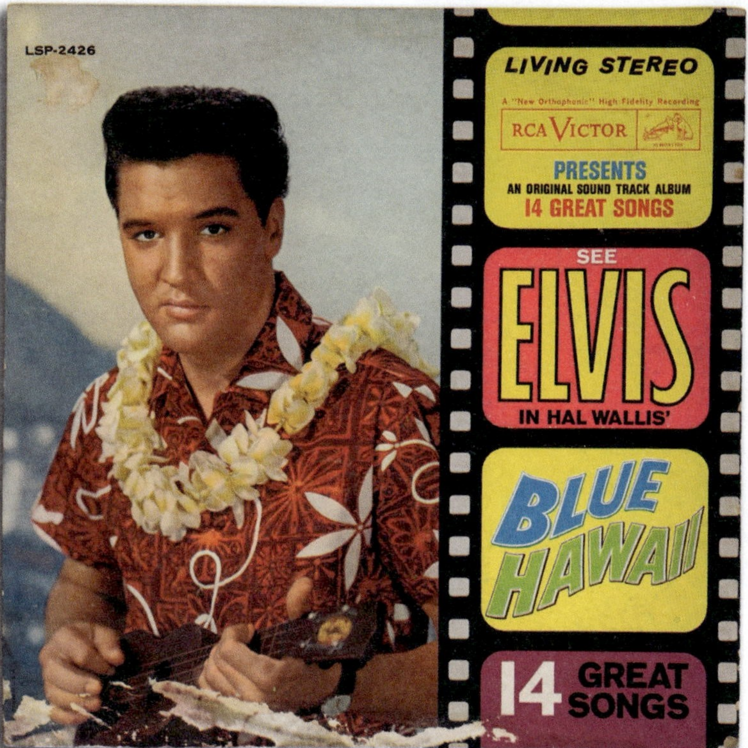

Elvis Presley
Blue Hawaii (Soundtrack)
RCA, 1961
Cover Artists Unknown

08 JAN

* Jan 8th, 1935
Elvis Aaron Presley
Tupelo (Mississippi)

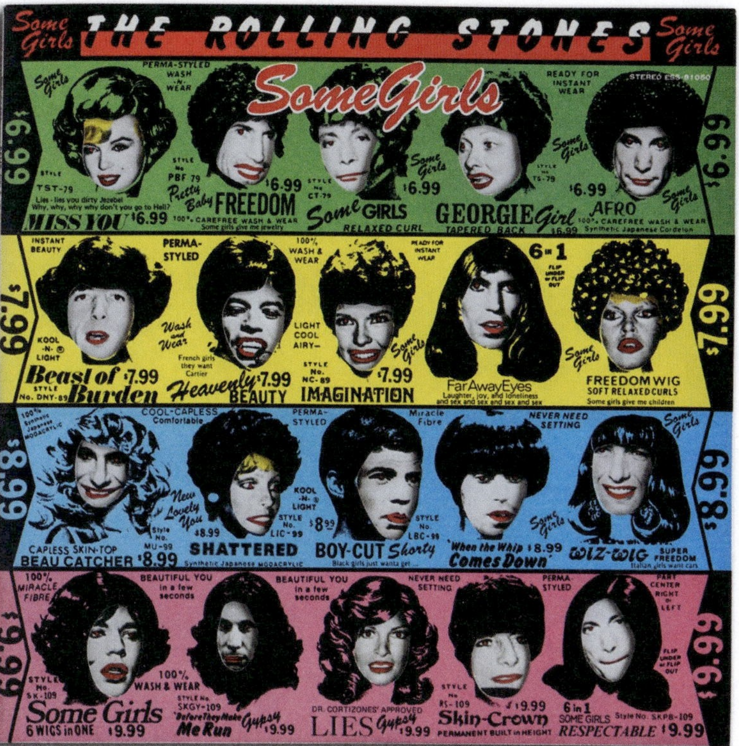

The Rolling Stones
Some Girls
Toshiba EMI, 1978
Peter Corriston (Design)

09 JAN

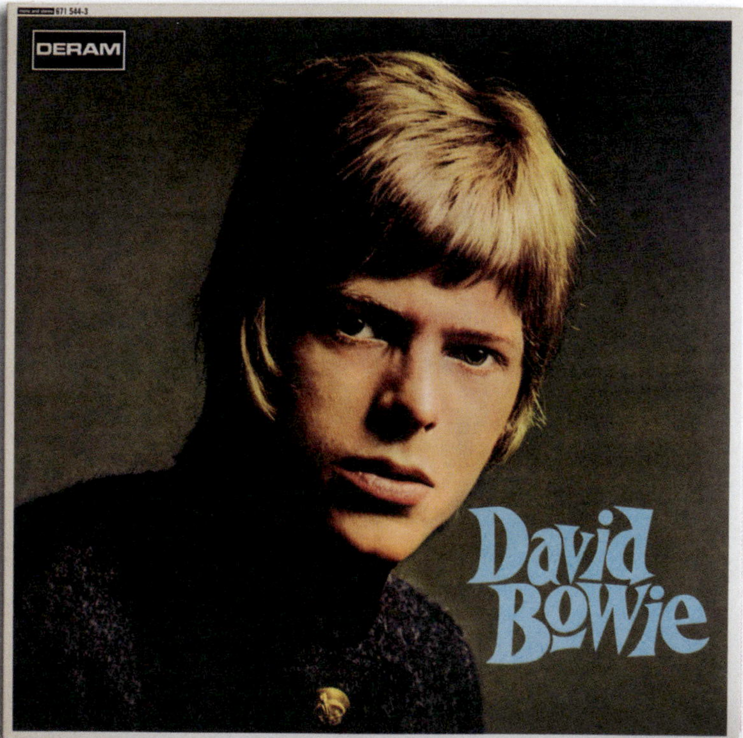

David Bowie
Deram, 1967
Gerald Fearnley (Photo)

10 JAN

† Jan 10th, 2016
David Bowie
New York City

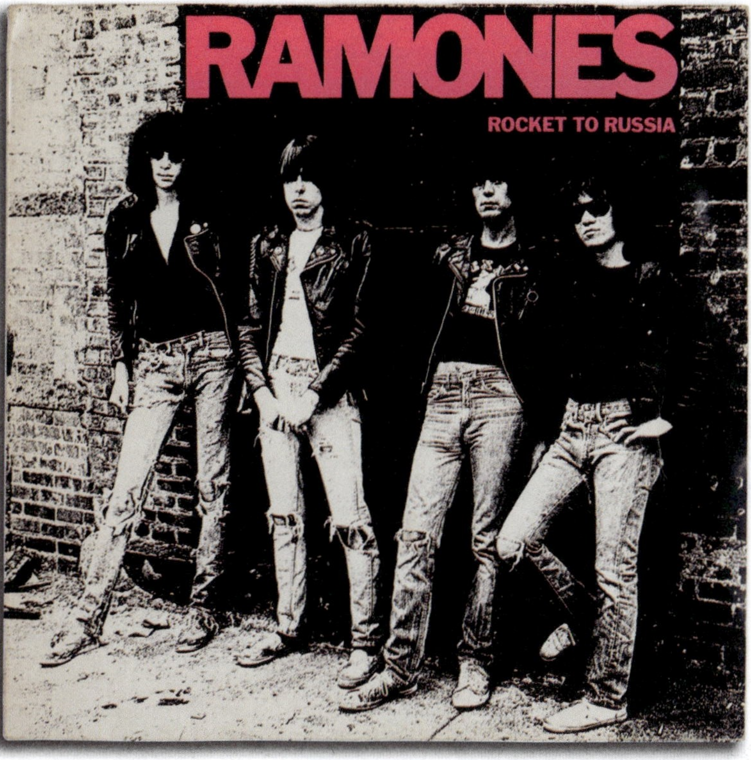

Ramones
Rocket To Russia
Philips, 1977
John Gillespie (Design)
Danny Fields (Photo)

11 JAN

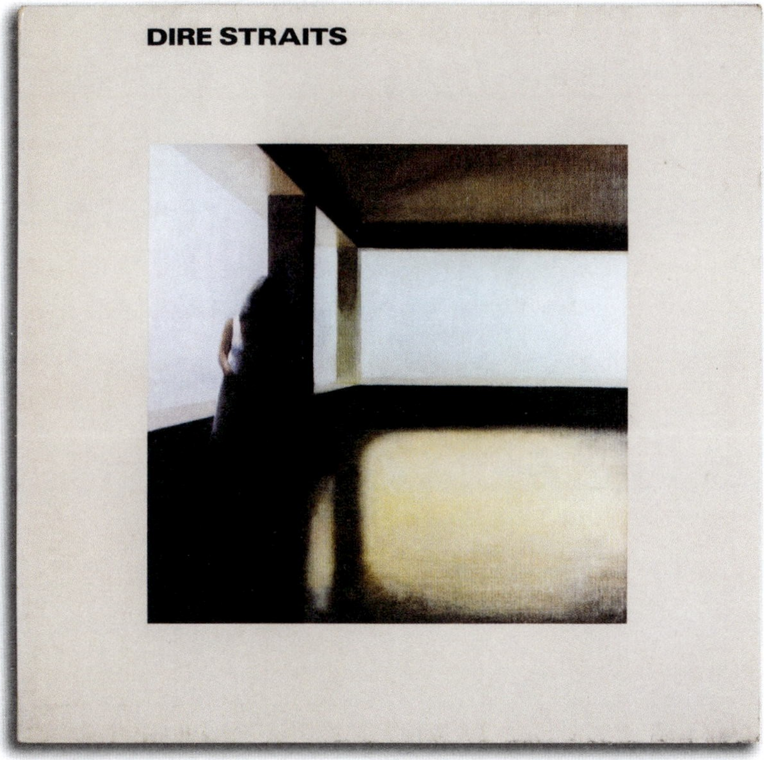

Dire Straits
Phonogram, 1978
Hothouse (Design)
Chuck Loyola (Photo)

12 JAN

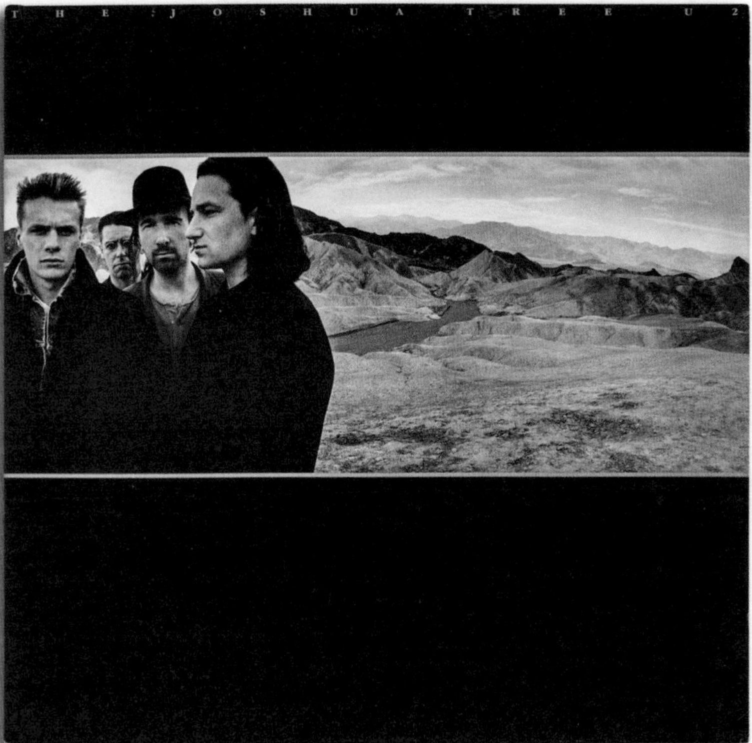

U2
The Joshua Tree
Island Records, 1987
Steve Averill (Design)
Anton Corbijn (Photo)

13 JAN

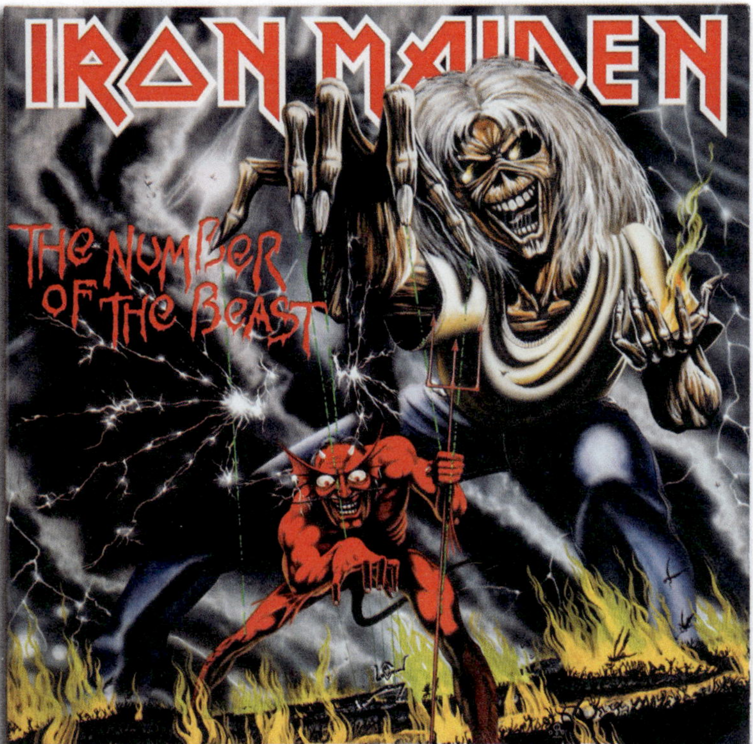

Iron Maiden
The Number Of The Beast
EMI Records, 1982
Cream (Design)
Derek Riggs (Illustration)

14 JAN

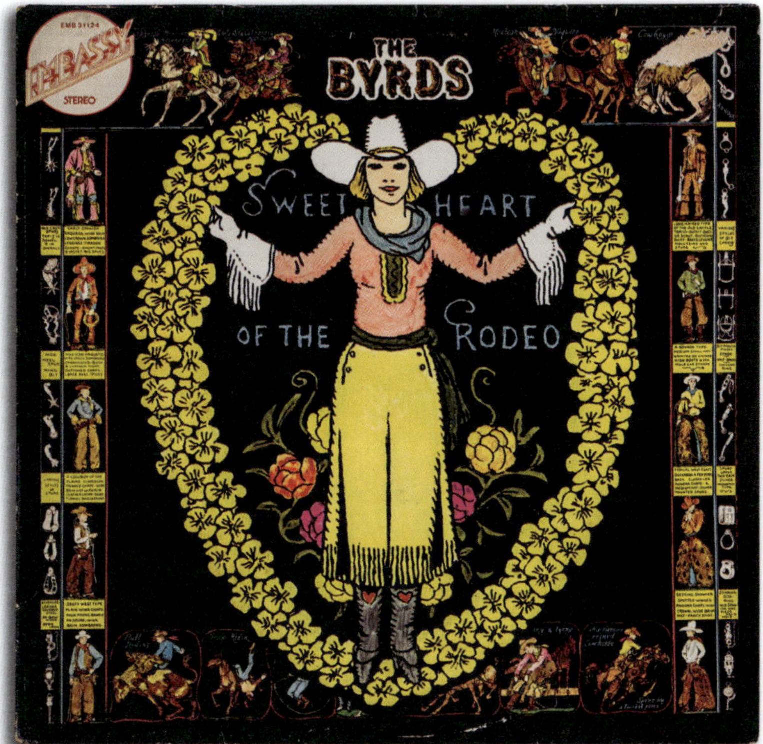

The Byrds
Sweetheart Of The Rodeo
Columbia Records, 1968
Geller And Butler Advertising (Design)
Jo Mora (Illustration)

15 JAN

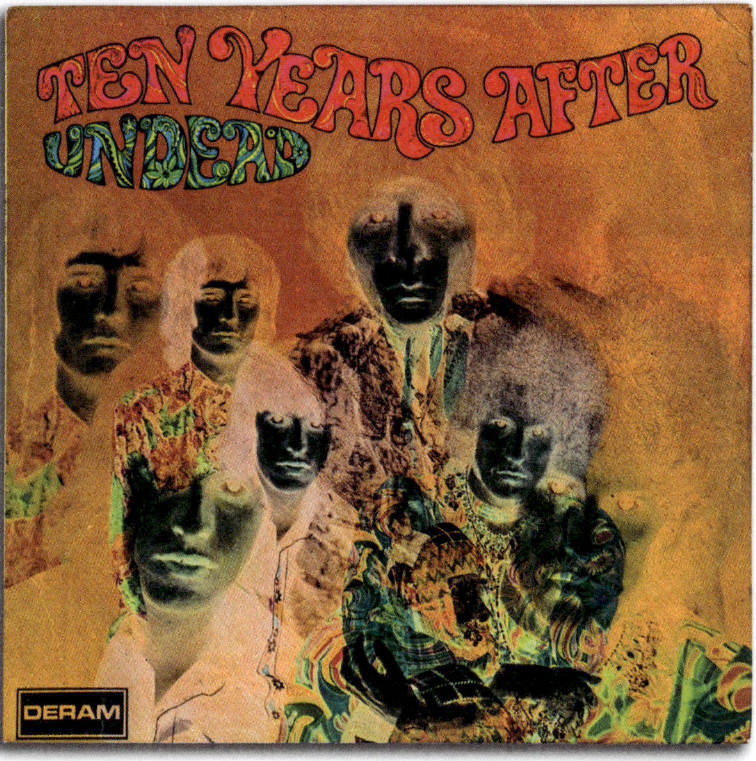

Ten Years After
Ten Years After Undead
Deram, 1968
John Fowley (Photo)

16 JAN

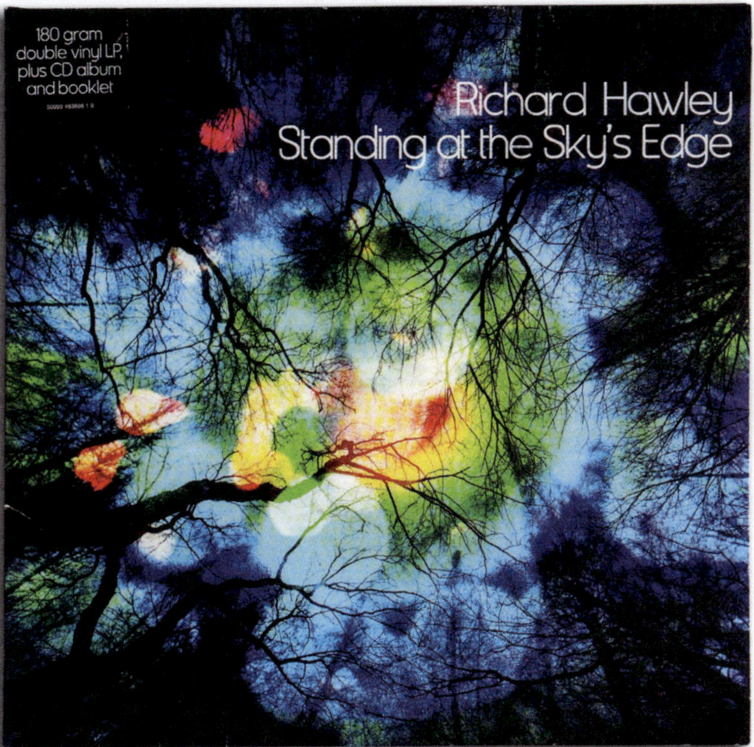

Richard Hawley
Standing At The Sky's Edge
Parlophone, 2012
Nick Philipps (Design)
Richard Tailby (Photo)

* Jan 17th, 1967
Richard Willis Hawley
Sheffield (UK)

17 JAN

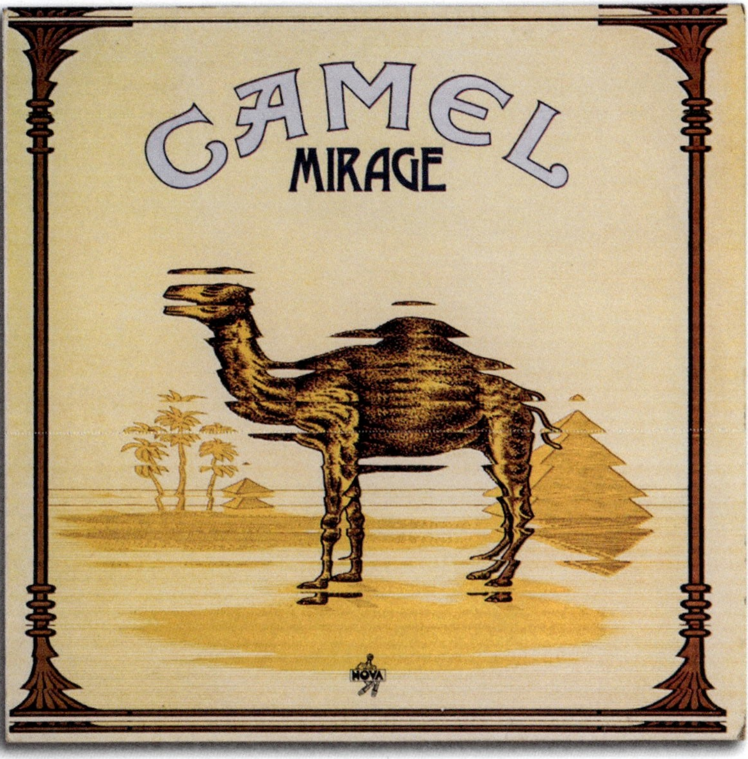

Camel
Mirage
Nova Records, 1975
Modula (Photo)

18 JAN

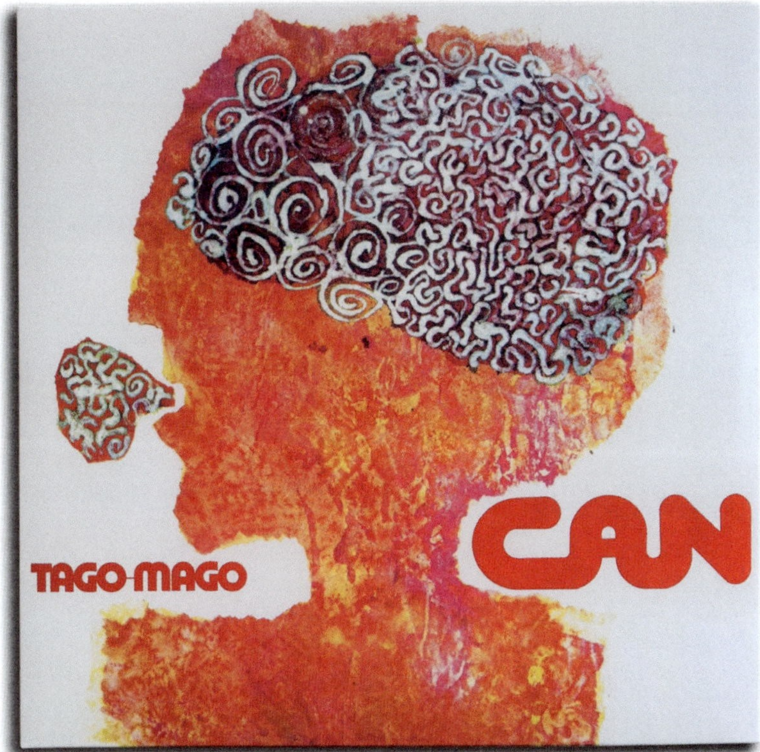

Can
Tago Mago
Spoon Records, 1971
U.Eichberger (Design)

19 JAN

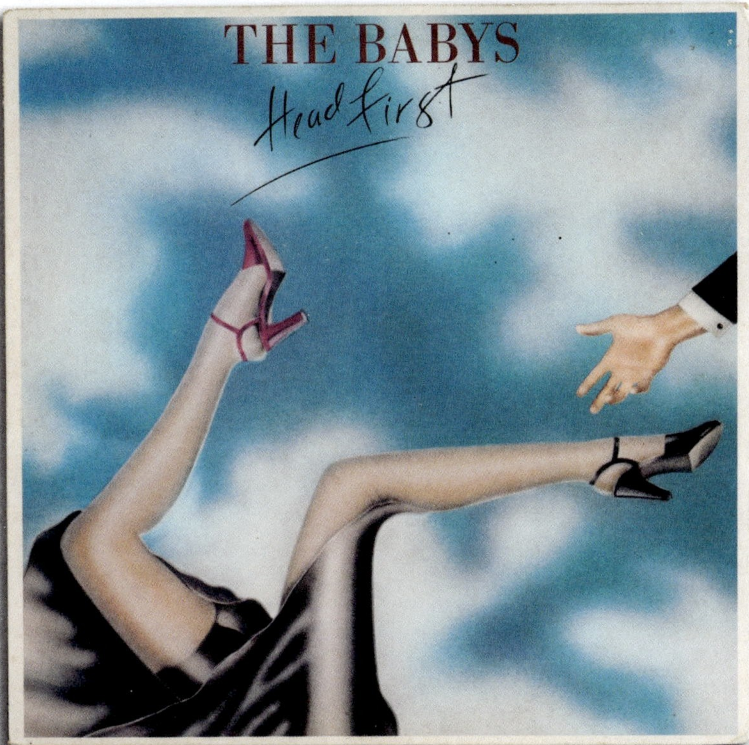

The Babys
Head First
Chrysalis, 1978
Bill Murphy, Rod Dyer Inc. (Design)

20 JAN

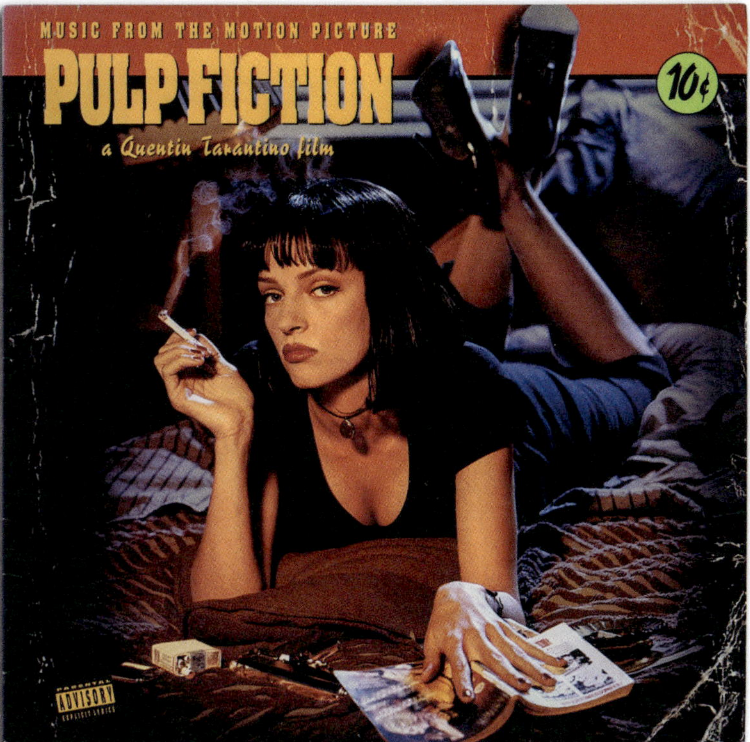

Various Artists Soundtrack
Pulp Fiction
MCA Records, 1994
Tim Stedmann (Design)

21 JAN

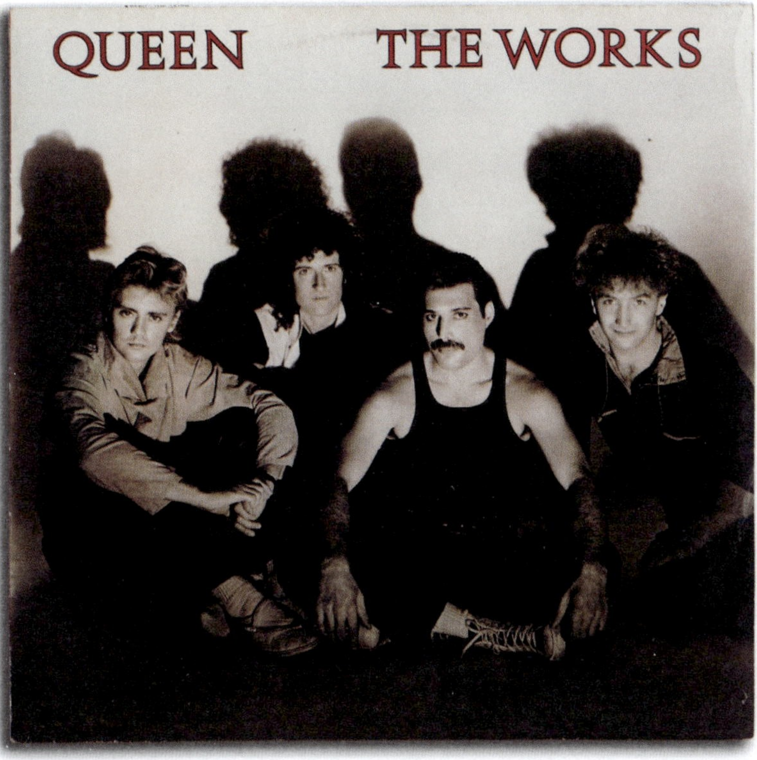

Queen
The Works
EMI Records, 1984
Bill Smith (Design)
George Hurrell (Photo)

22 JAN

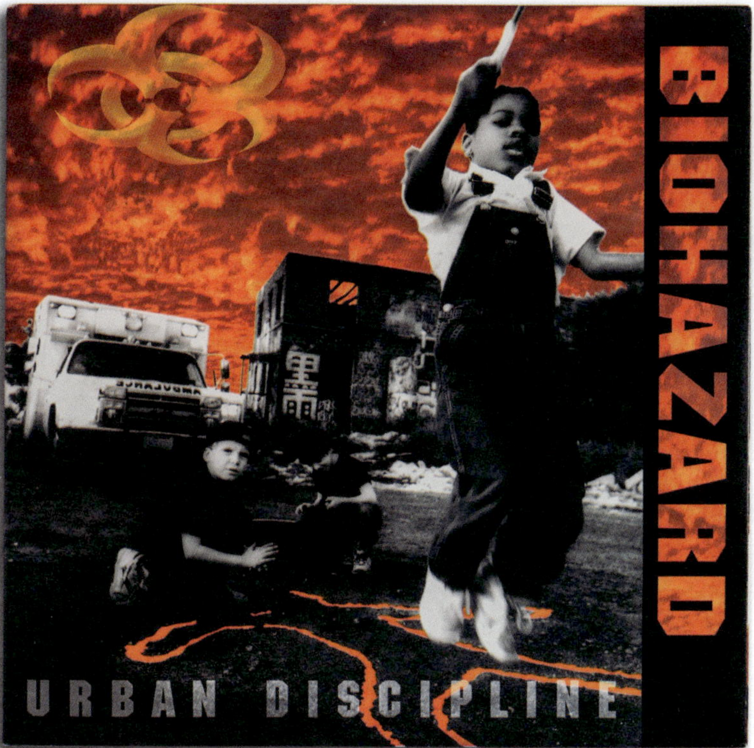

Biohazard
Urban Discipline
Roadrunner Records, 1992
Bryan Thatcher (Design)
Ursula Kojote (Photo)

23 JAN

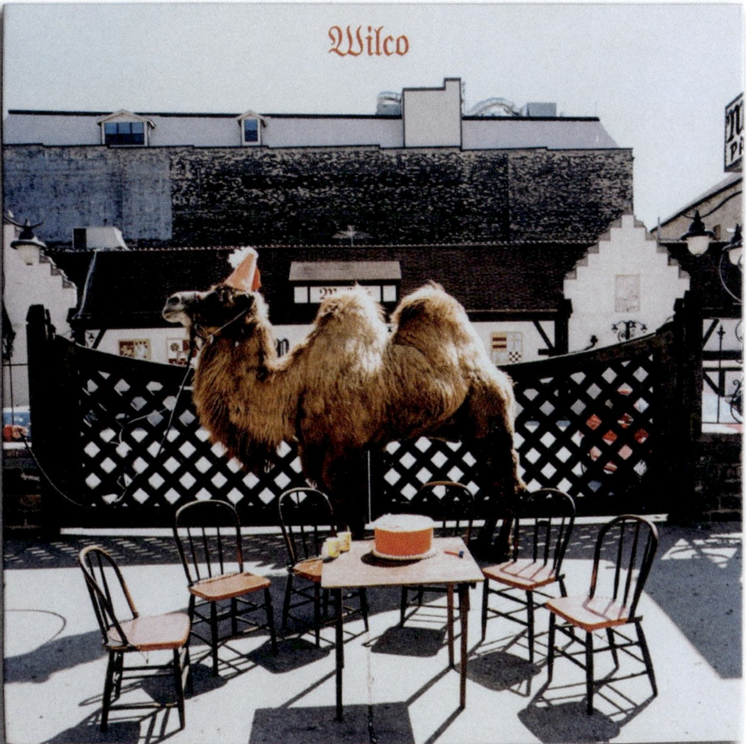

Wilco
Wilco The Album
Nonesuch Records, 2009
Jeff Tweedy, Lawrence Azerrad (Design)
Autumn de Wilde (Photo)

24 JAN

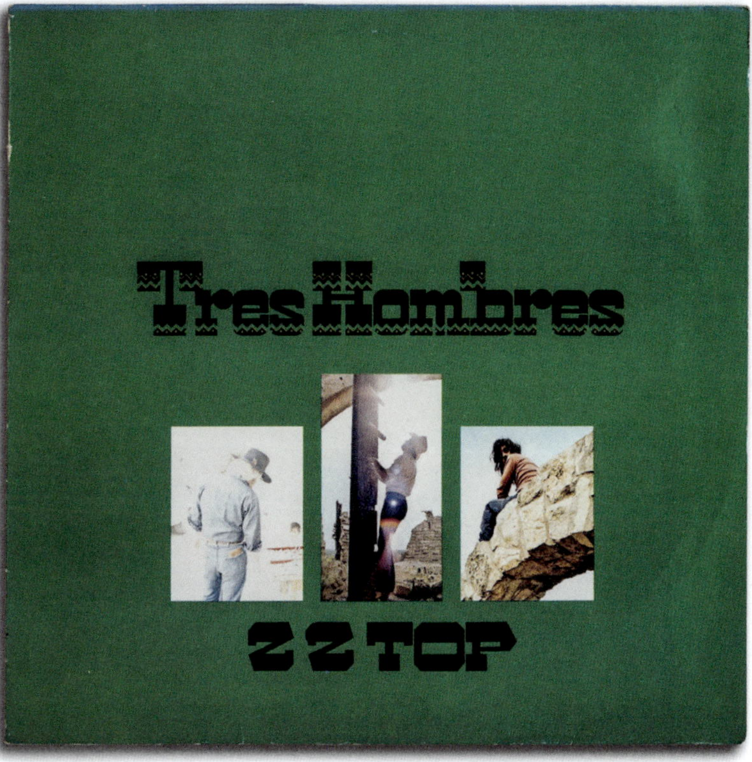

ZZ Top
Tres Hombres
London Records, 1973
Bill Narum (Design)
Galen Scott (Photo)

25 JAN

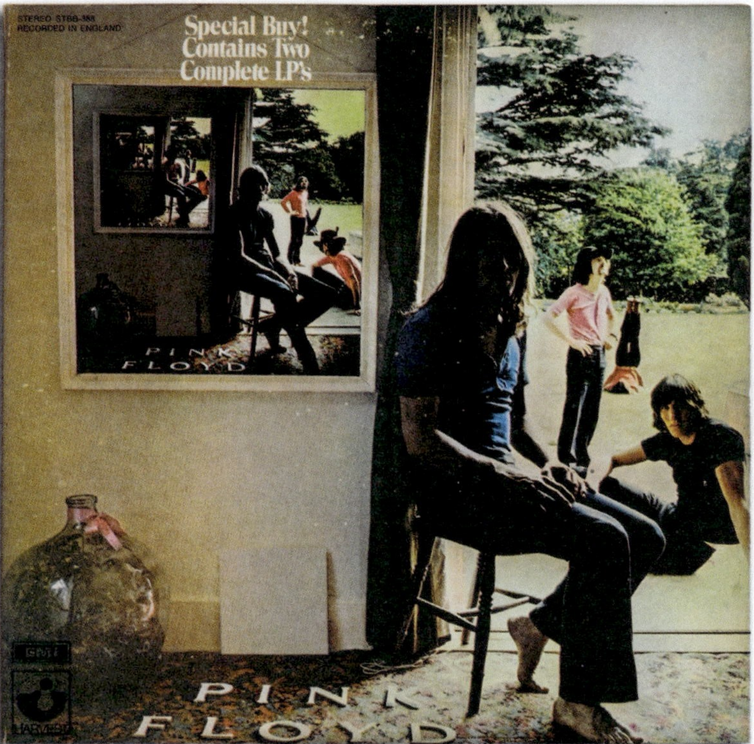

Pink Floyd
Ummagumma
Harvest, 1969
Hipgnosis (Design)
Hipgnosis (Photo)

26 JAN

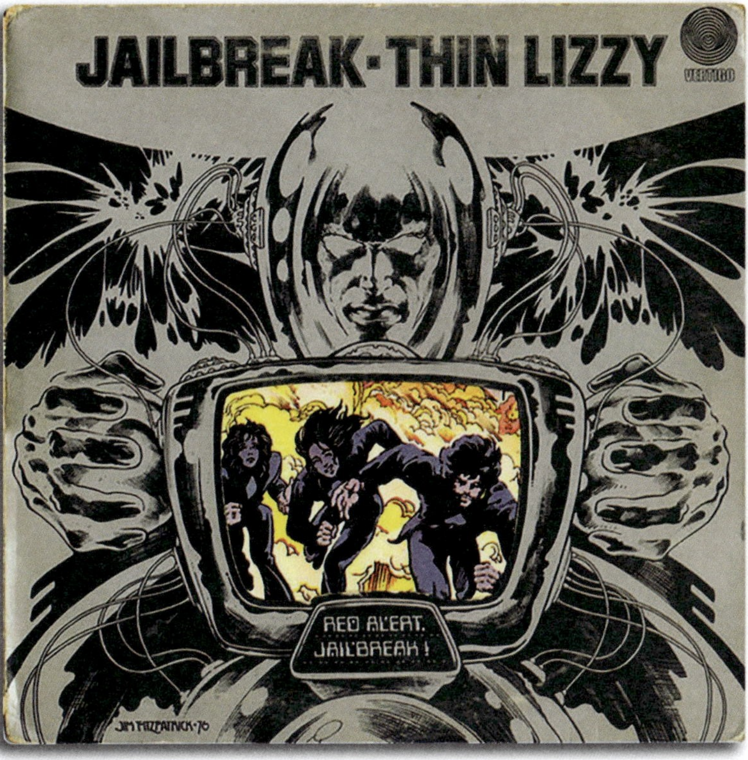

Thin Lizzy
Jailbreak
Vertigo Records, 1976
Jim Fitzpatrick (Photo)

27 JAN

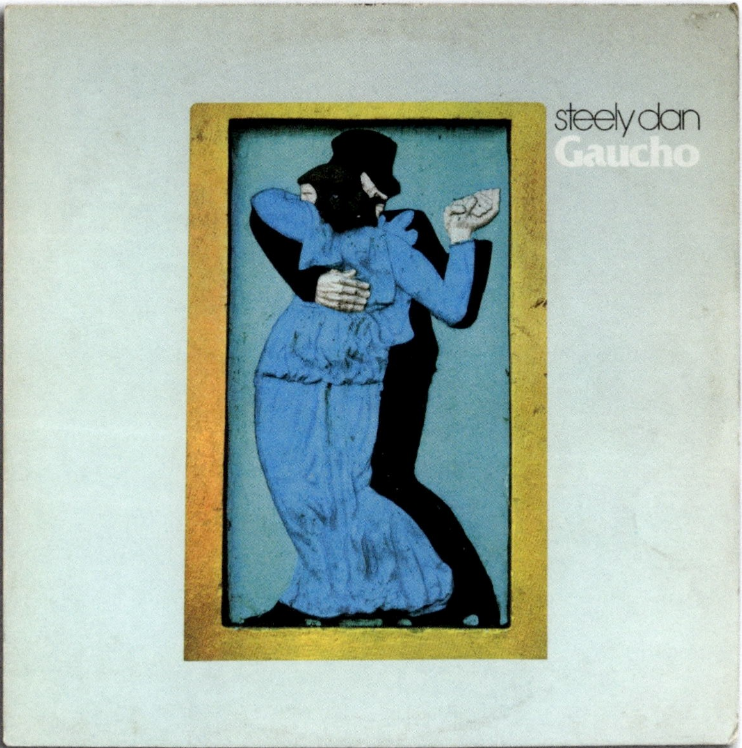

Steely Dan
Gaucho
MCA Records, 1980
Susanne Walsh (Design)

28 JAN

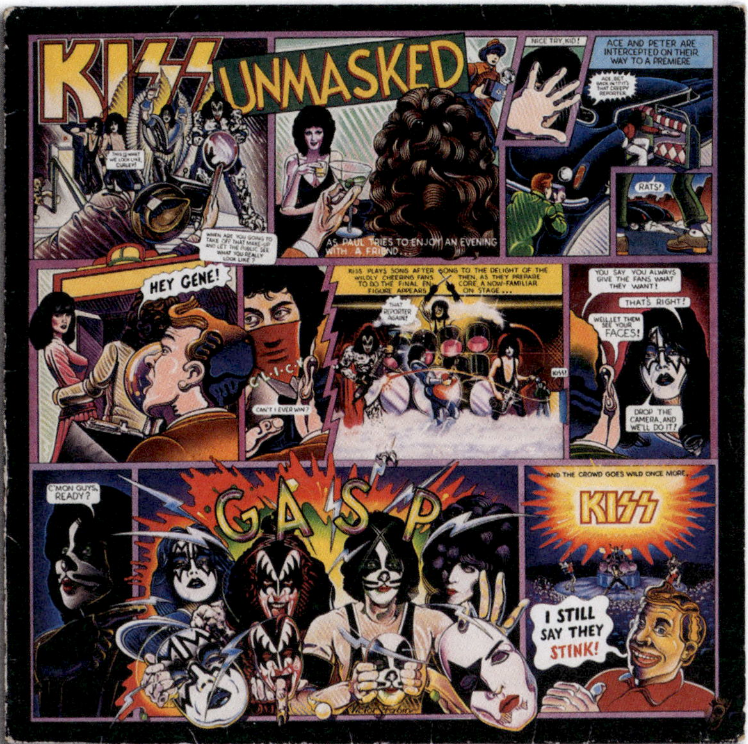

Kiss
Unmasked
Casablanca Records, 1980
Victor Stabin & Mark Samuels & Jose Rivero (Illustration)

29 JAN

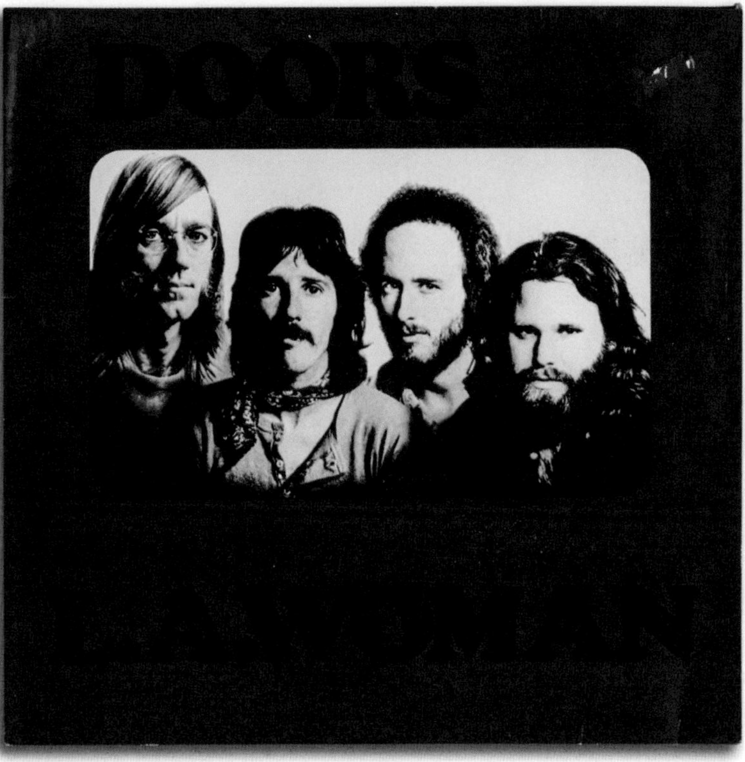

Doors
L.A. Woman
Elektra Records, 1971
Carl Cossick (Design)
Wendell Hamick (Photo)

30 JAN

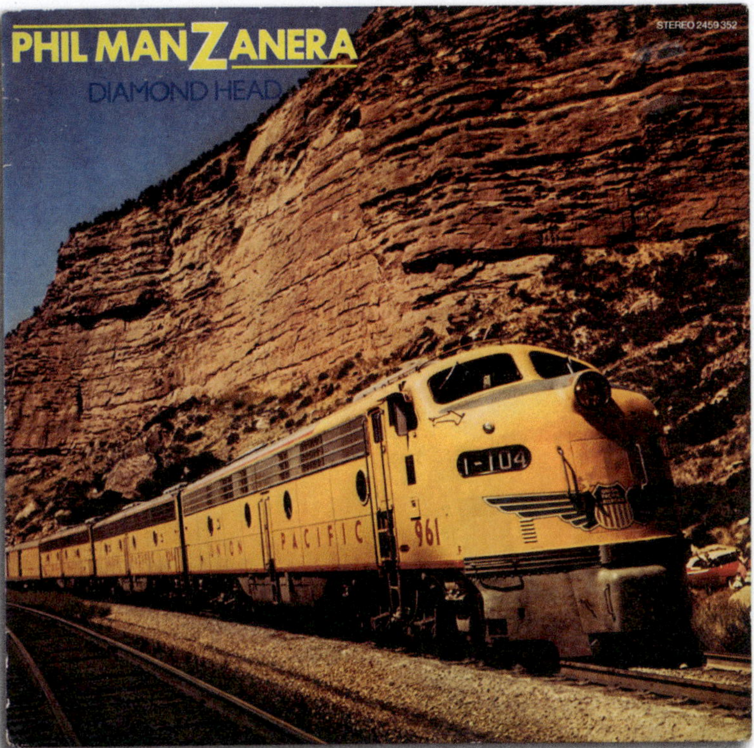

Phil Manzanera
Diamond Head
ATCO Records, 1975
Jon Prew (Photo)

* Jan 31st, 1951
Philip Geoffrey Targett-Adams
Sheffield (UK)

31 JAN

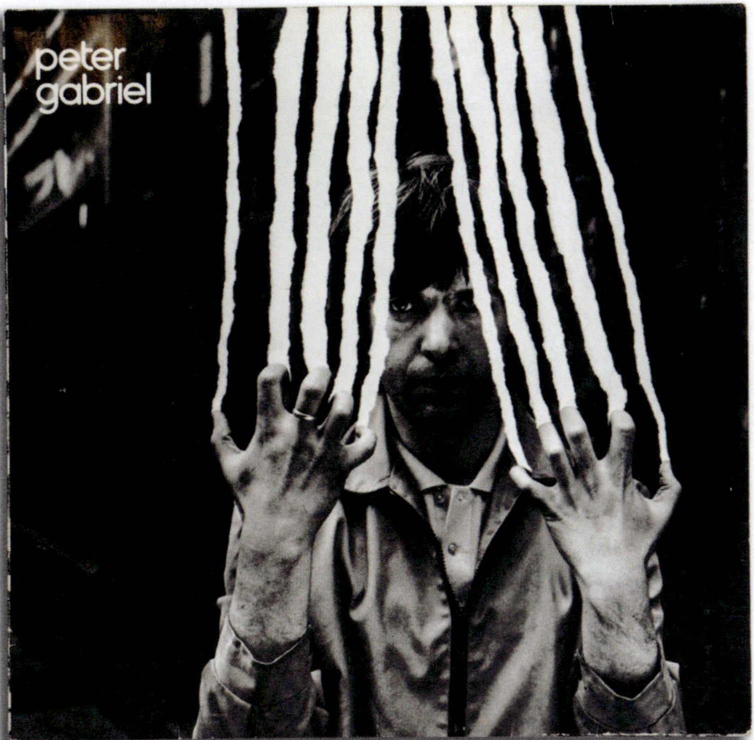

Peter Gabriel
Charisma, 1978
Hipgnosis (Photo)

01 FEB

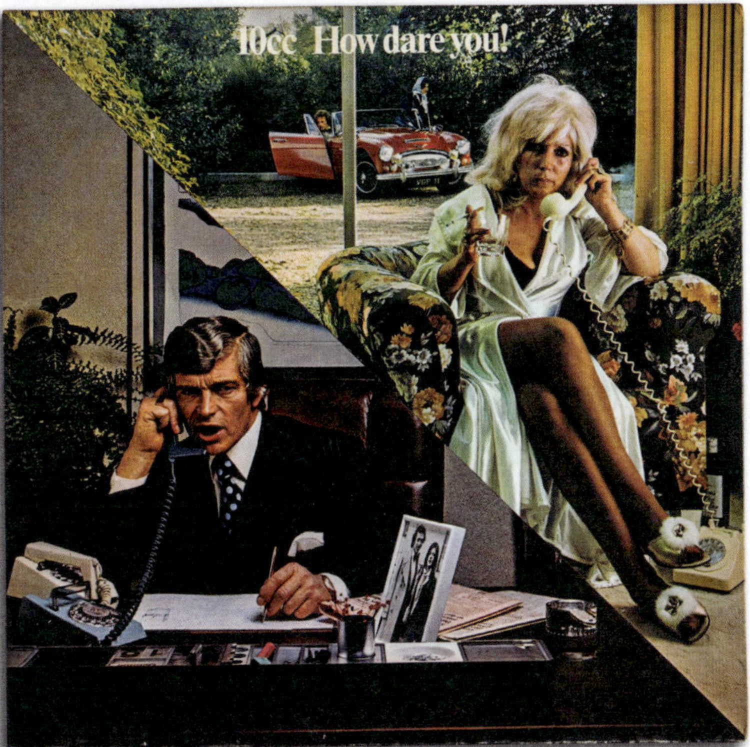

10CC
How Dare You!
Mercury Records, 1975
Hipgnosis (Design)
Hipgnosis (Photo)

02 FEB

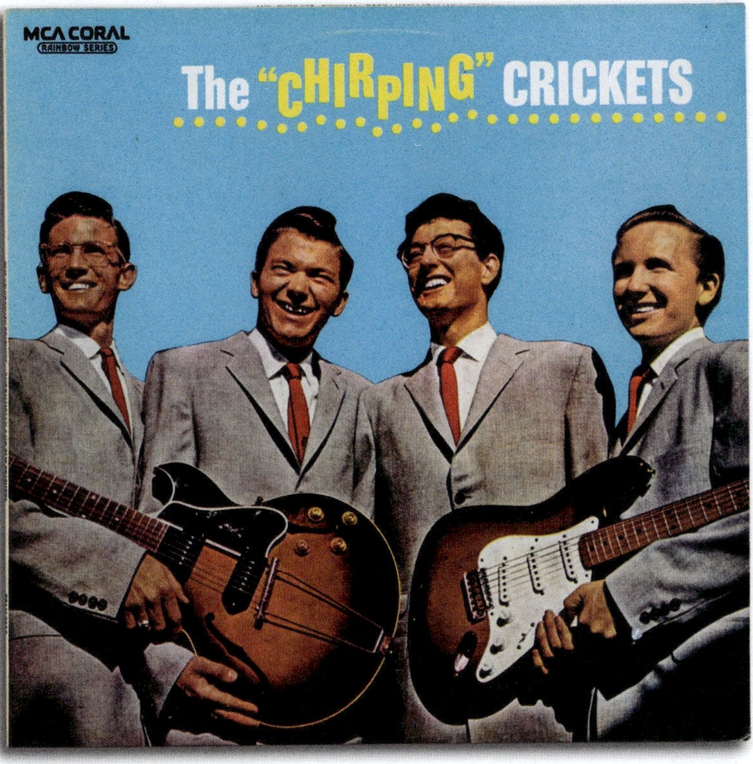

Buddy Holly & The Crickets
The "Chirping" Crickets
MCA Records, 1973
Cover Artists Unknown

† Feb 3rd, 1959
Buddy Holly
Mason City (Iowa)

03 FEB

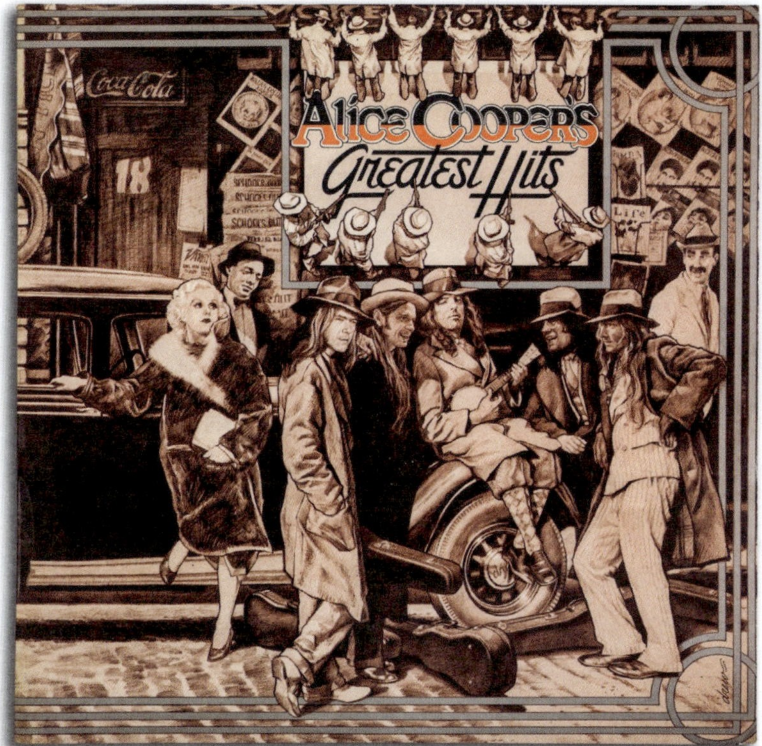

Alice Cooper
Greatest Hits
Warner Brothers, 1974
Pacific Eye & Ear (Design)
Bill Garland, Drew Struzan (Illustration)

* Feb 4th, 1948
Vincent Damon Furnier
Detroit (Michigan)

04 FEB

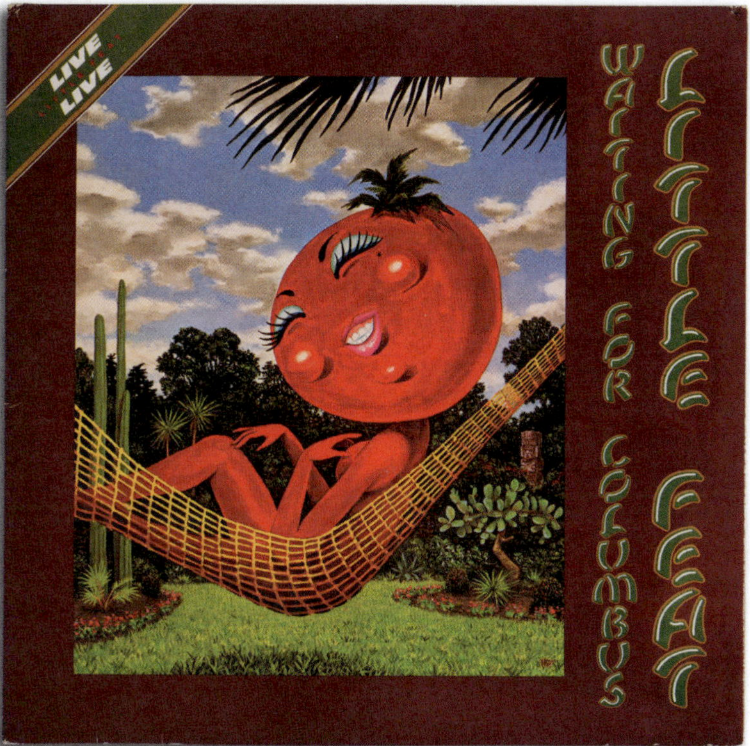

Little Feat
Waiting For Columbus
Warner Bros. Records, 1978
Neon Park (Illustration)

05 FEB

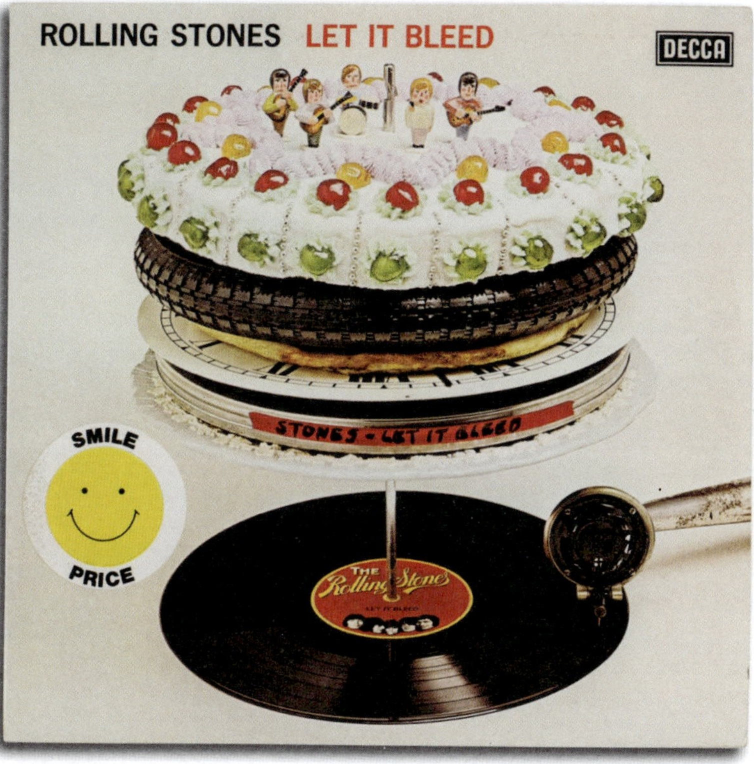

Rolling Stones
Let It Bleed
Decca Records, 1969
Victor Kahn (Design)
Don McAllester (Photo)

06 FEB

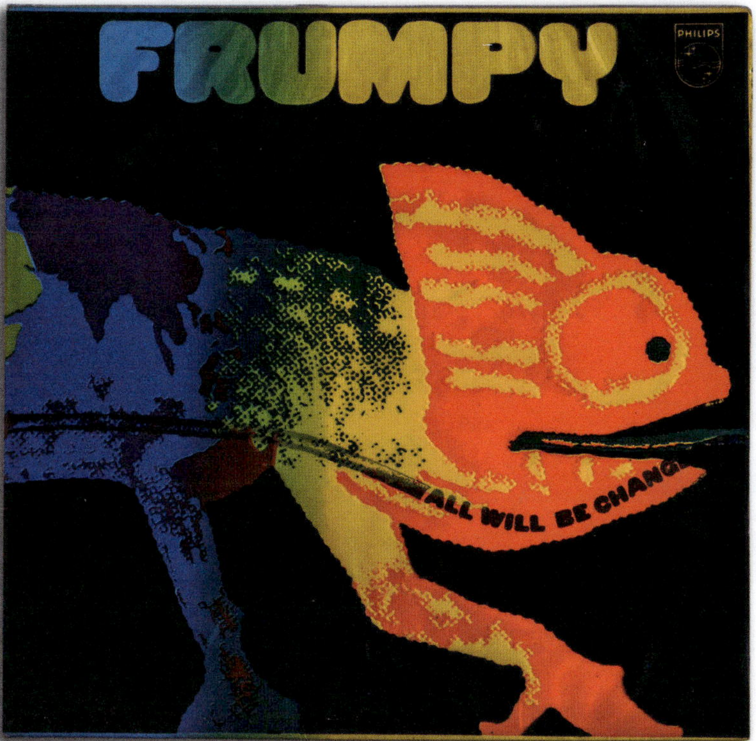

Frumpy
All Will Be Changed
Philips, 1970
Klaus Witt (Design)

07 FEB

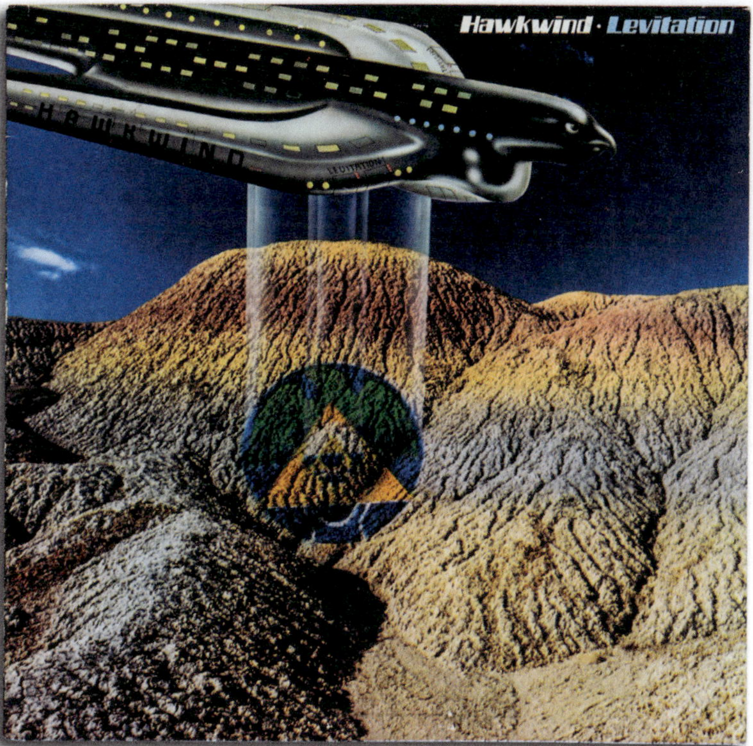

Hawkwind
Levitation
Bronze, 1980
Linda Curry (Photo)

08 FEB

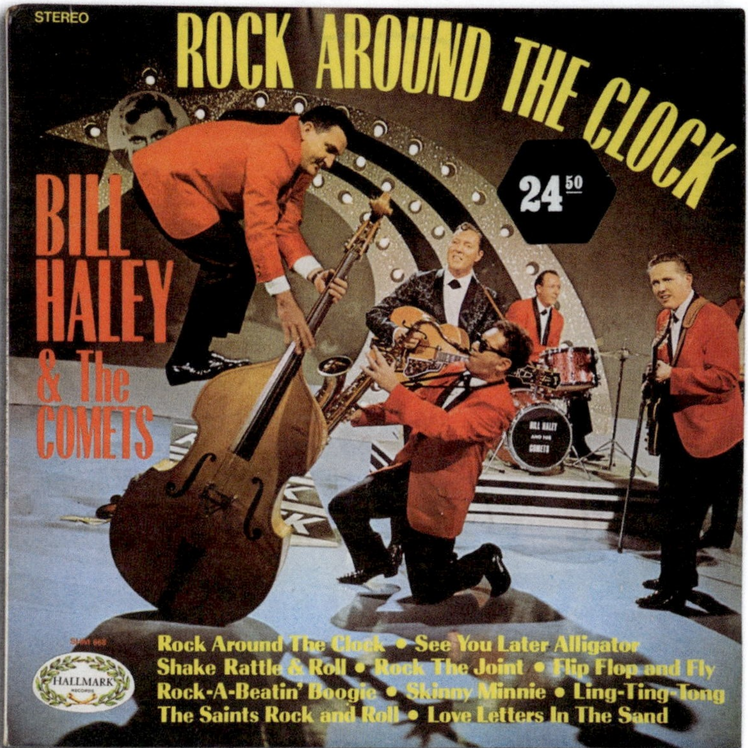

Bill Haley & The Comets
Rock Around The Clock
Hallmark Records, 1968
Cover Artists Unknown

09 FEB

† Feb 9th, 1981
Bill Haley
Harlington (Texas)

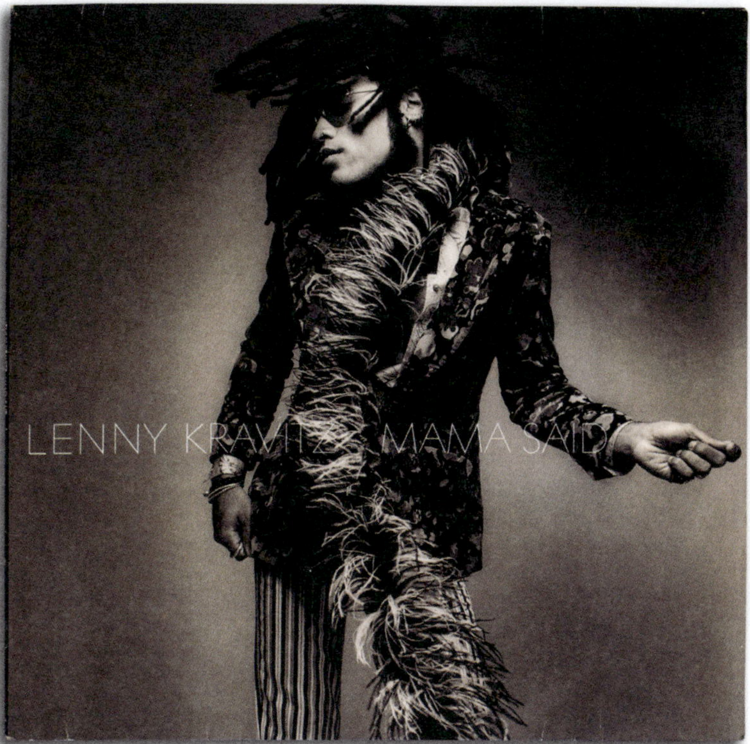

Lenny Kravitz
Mama Said
Virgin Records, 1991
Melanie Nissen (Design)
James Calderaro (Photo)

10 FEB

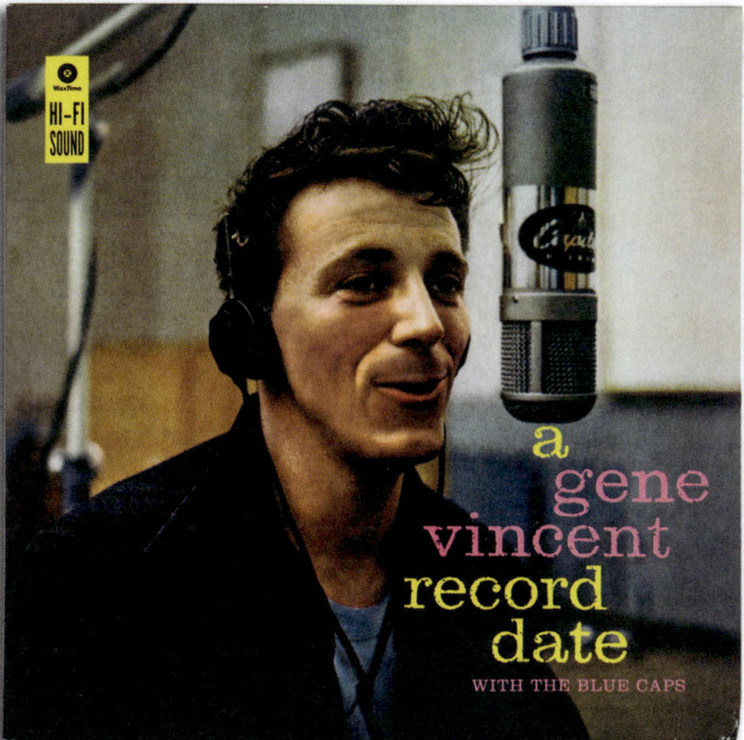

Gene Vincent
A Gene Vincent Record Date With The Blue Caps
Capitol Records, 1958
Cover Artists Unknown

11 FEB

* Feb 11th, 1935
Gene Vincent
Norfolk (Virginia)

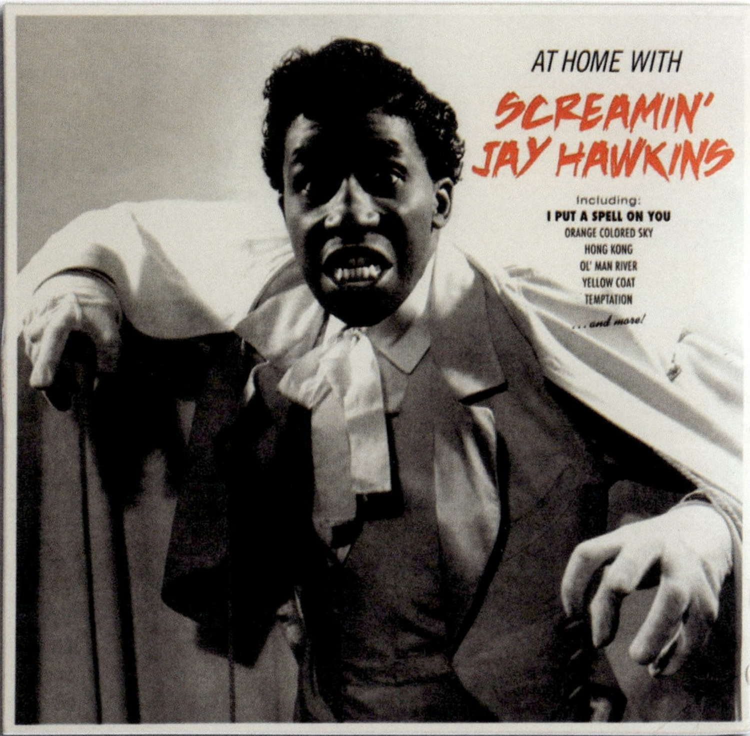

Screamin' Jay Hawkins
At Home With
Wax Time, 2016
Cover Artists Unknown

12 FEB

† Feb 12th, 2000
Jalacy "Jay" Hawkins
Neuilly-sur-Seine (France)

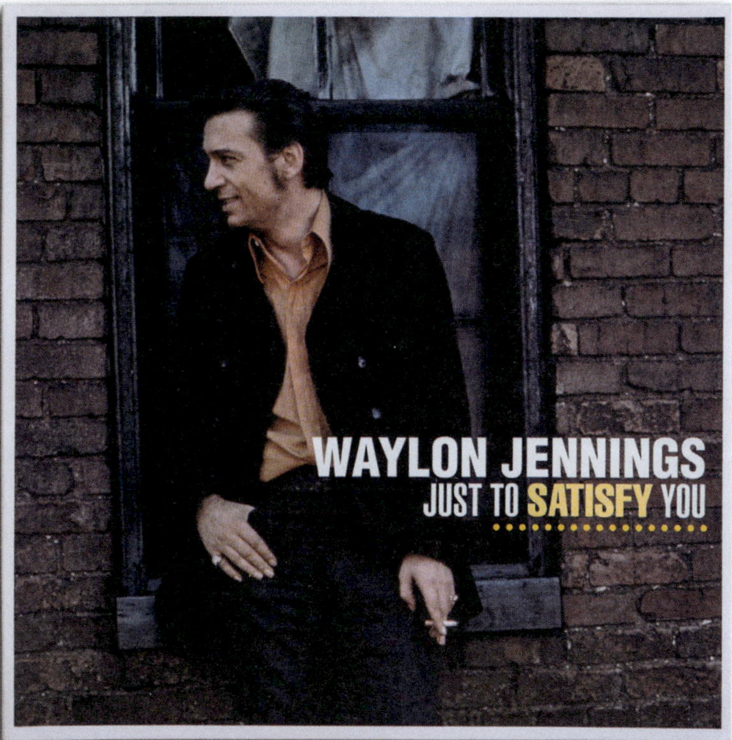

Waylon Jennings
Just To Satisfy You
Bear Family Prod., 2014
Cover Artists Unknown

13 FEB

† Feb 13th, 2002
Waylon Arnold Jennings
Chandler (Arizona)

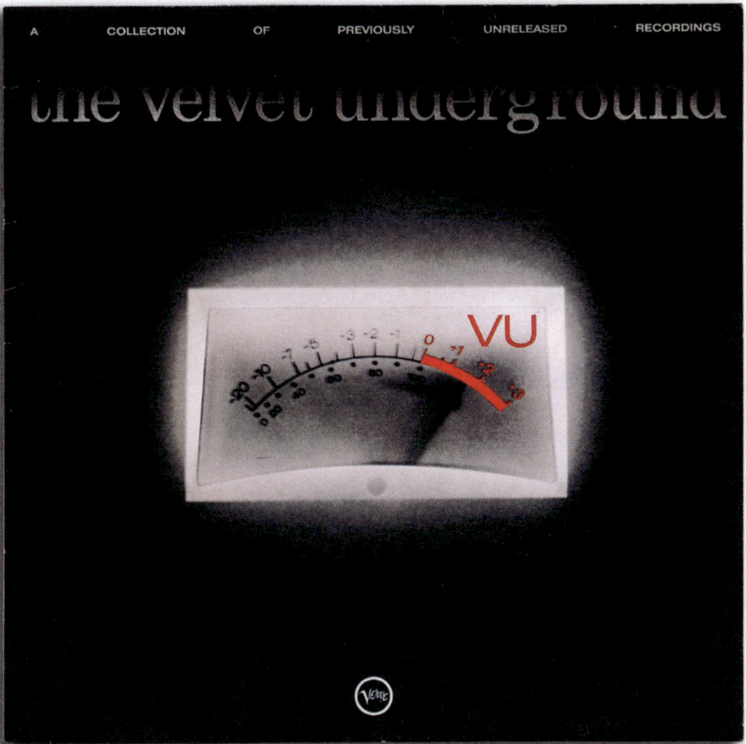

The Velvet Underground
VU
Verve Records, 1984
Larry Kazal (Design)
Tobi Seftel (Photo)

14 FEB

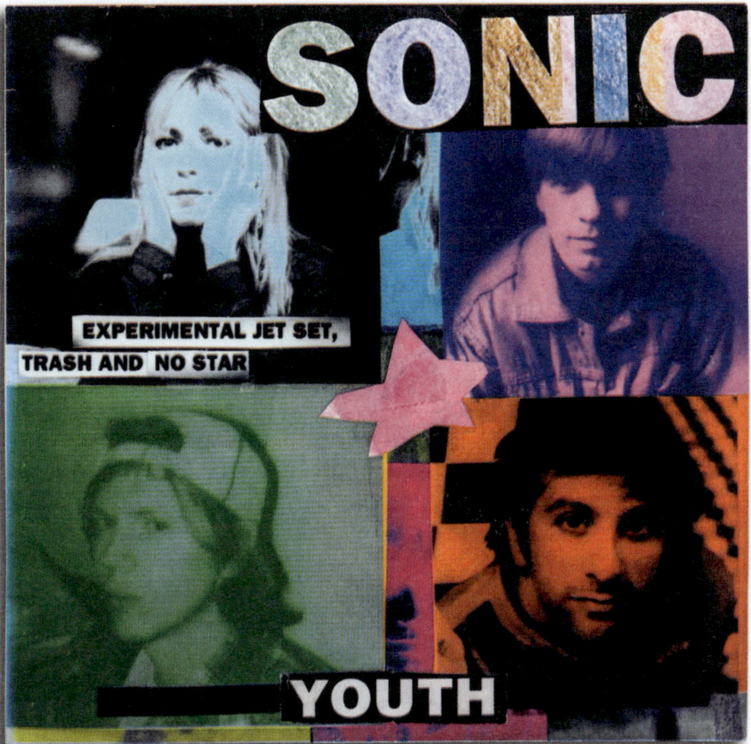

Sonic Youth
Experimental Jet Set, Trash And No Star
Geffen Records, 1994
Kevin Reagan (Design)
Catherine Lewis (Photo)

15 FEB

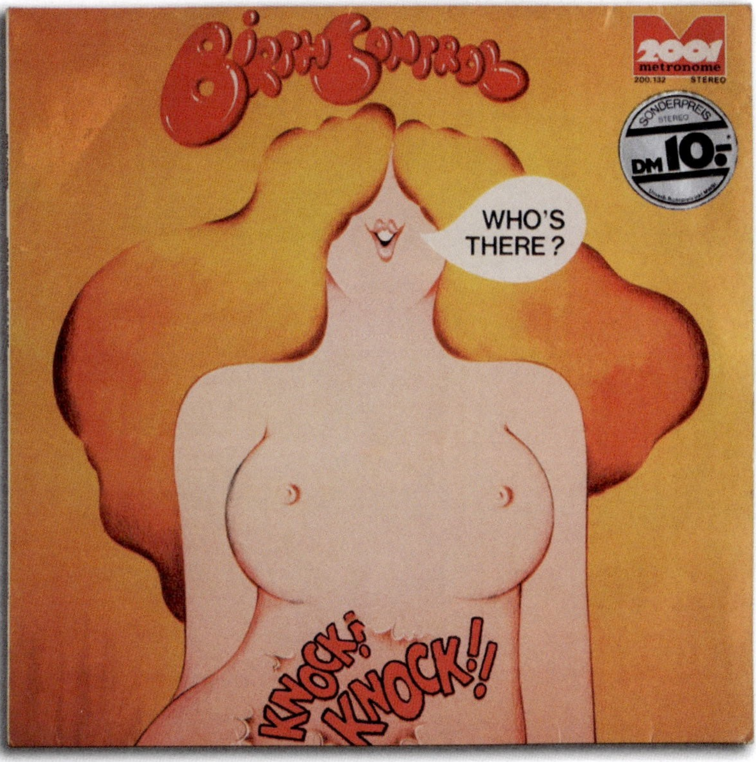

Birth Control
Knock! Knock!! Who's There ?
Metronome 2001, 1973
Heinz Dofflein (Design)
Heinz Dofflein (Illustration)

16 FEB

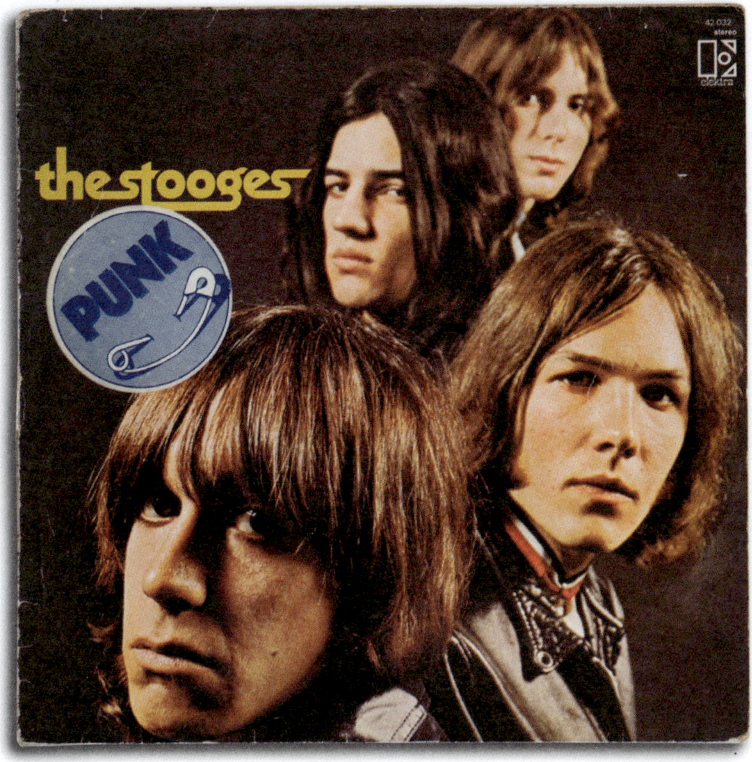

The Stooges
Elektra, 1969
William S. Harvey (Design)
Joel Brodsky (Photo)

17 FEB

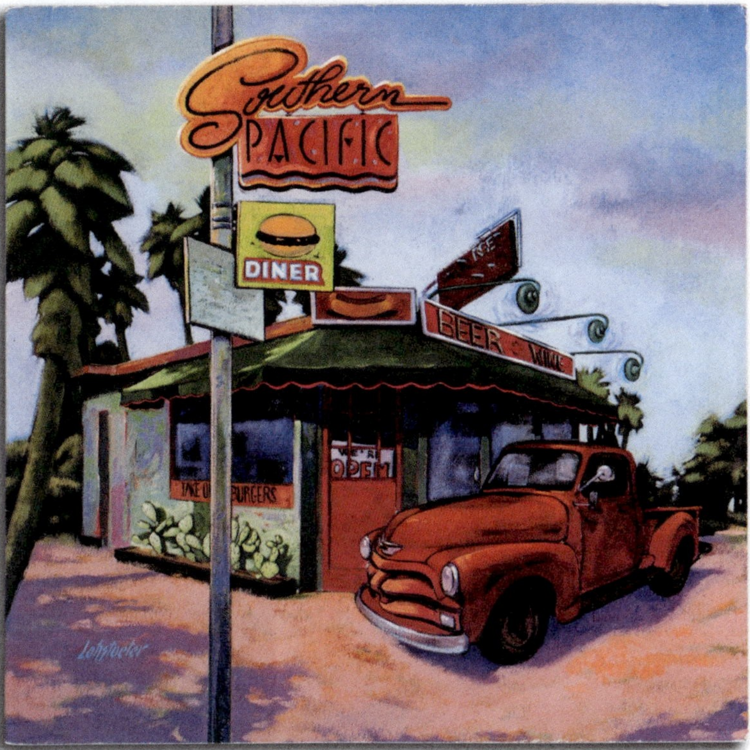

Southern Pacific
Warner Bros. Records, 1985
Gabrielle Raumberger (Design)
Lori Lohstoeter (Illustration)

18 FEB

Scorpions
Fly To The Rainbow
RCA Victor, 1974
Wandrey's Studio (Design)

19 FEB

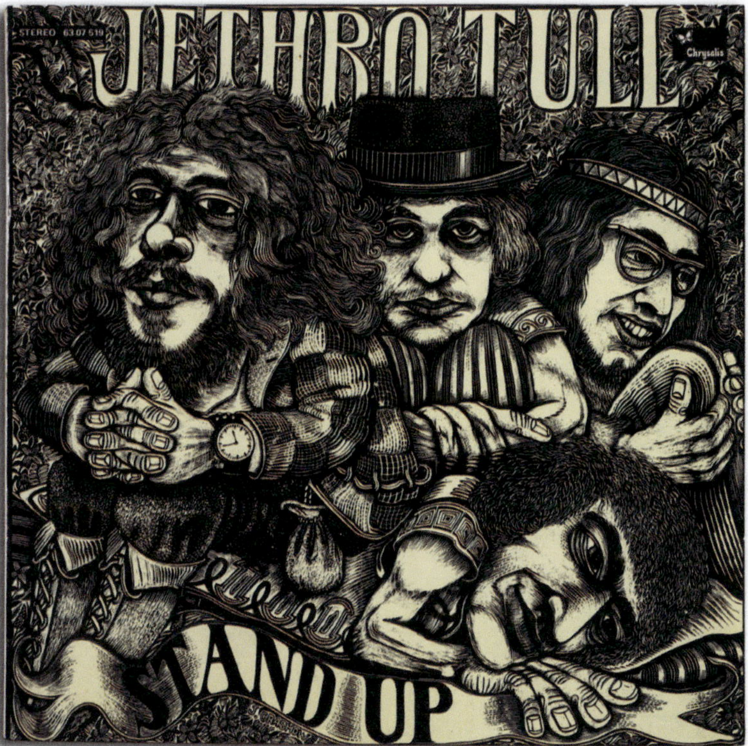

Jethro Tull
Stand Up
Chrysalis Records, 1969
John Williams Terry Ellis (Design)
Jimmy Grashow (Illustration)

20 FEB

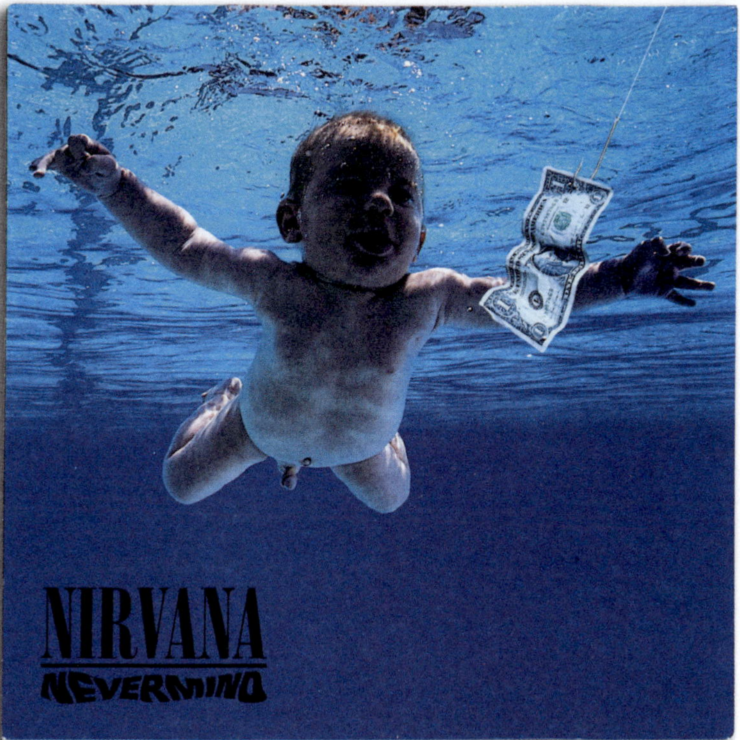

Nirvana
Nevermind
David Geffen Company, 1991
Robert Fisher (Design)
Kirk Weddle (Photo)

21 FEB

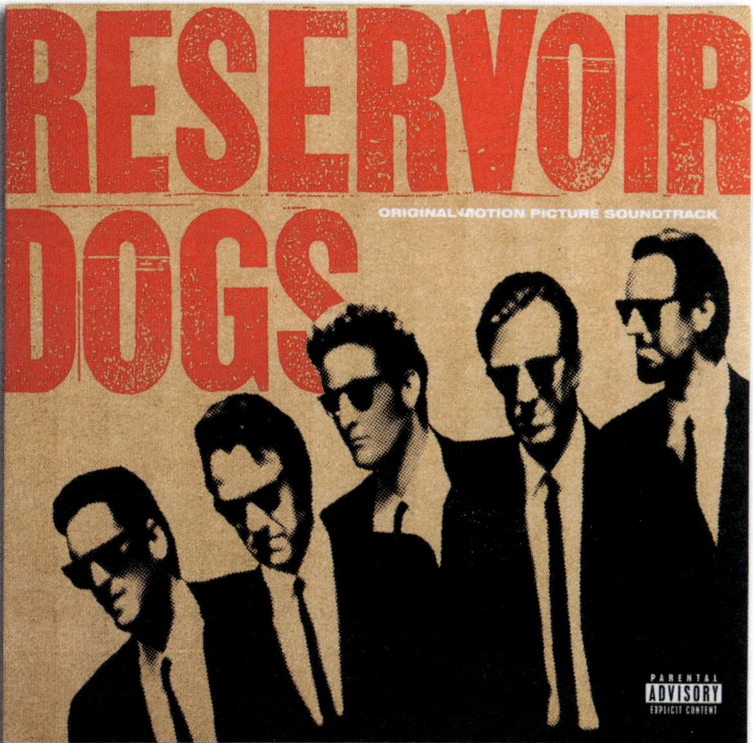

Various Artists – Soundtrack
Reservoir Dogs
Geffen Records, 1992
Vartan Design (Design)

22 FEB

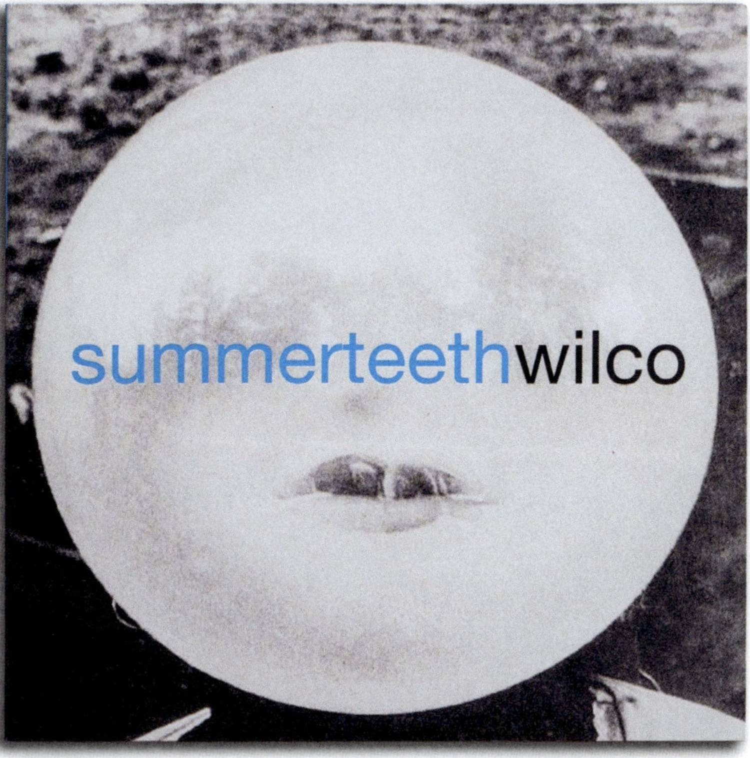

Wilco
Summerteeth
Nonesuch Records, 2009
Laurence Azerrad (Design)
Justine Parsons (Photo)

23 FEB

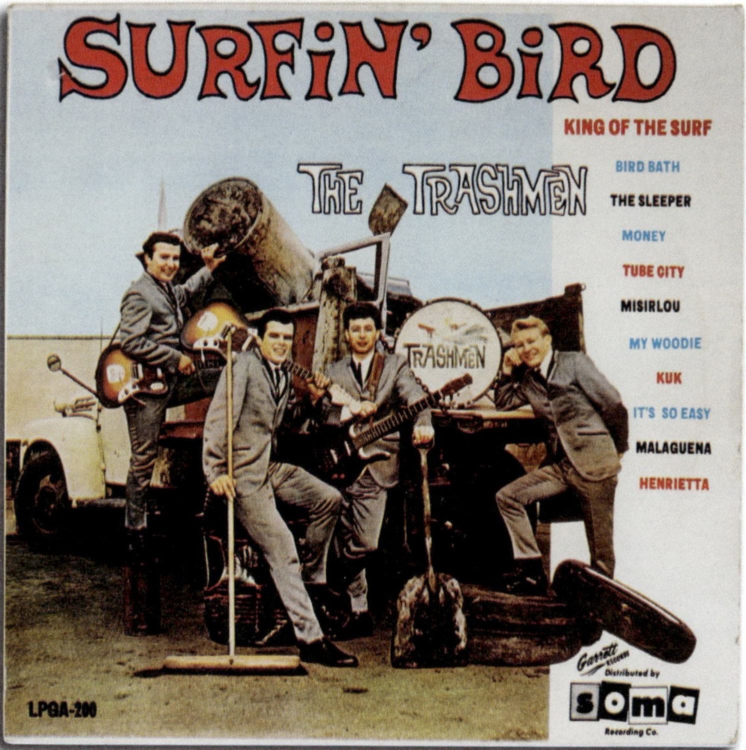

The Trashmen
Surfin' Bird
Garrett Records, 1964
Phil Howard (Photo)

24 FEB

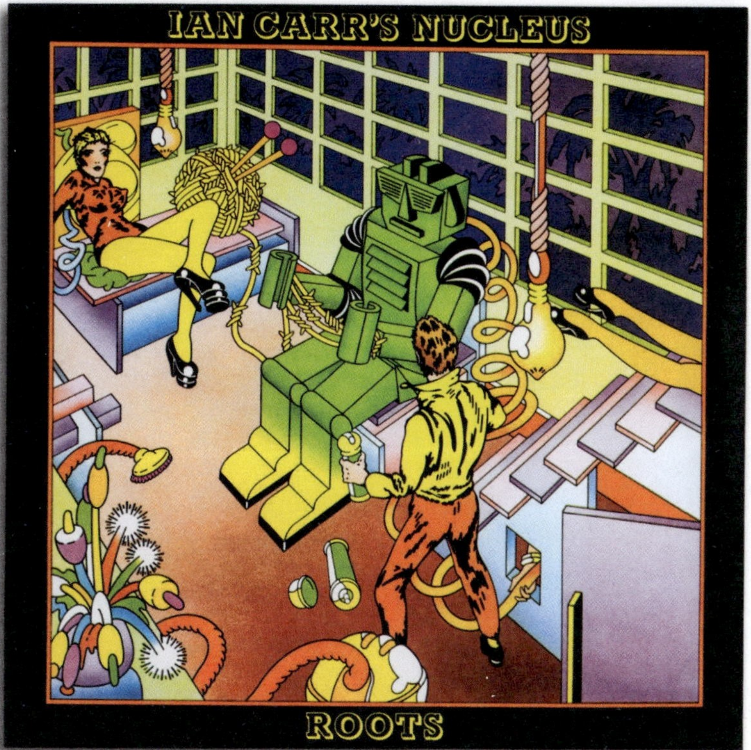

Ian Carr's Nucleus
Roots
Vertigo Records, 1973
Keith Davis (Design)

† Feb 25th, 2009
Ian Henry Randell Carr
London (UK)

25 FEB

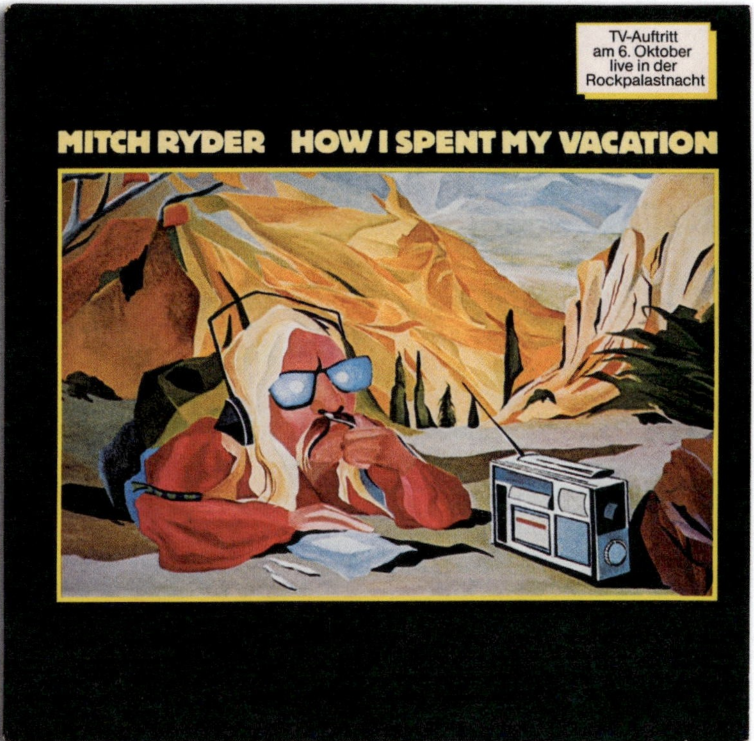

Mitch Ryder
How I Spent My Vacation
Line Records, 1979
Mitch Ryder & Renee Gougeon (Design)
William S. Levise (Illustration)

* Feb 26th, 1945
Mitch Ryder
Hamtramck (Michigan)

26 FEB

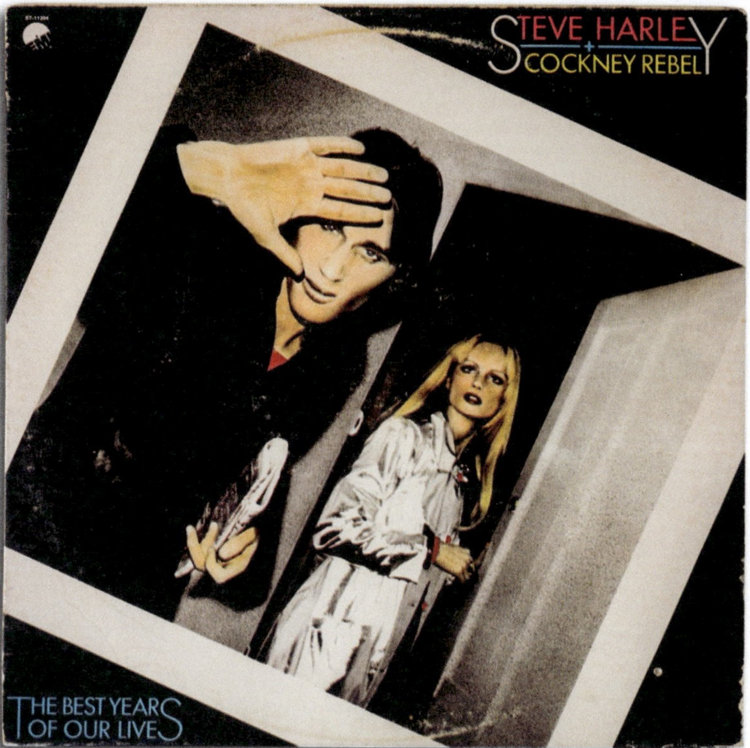

Steve Harley & Cockney Rebel
The Best Year Of Our Lives
EMI, 1975
Mick Rock (Design)
Mick Rock (Photo)

* Feb 27th, 1951
Steve Harley
London (UK)

27 FEB

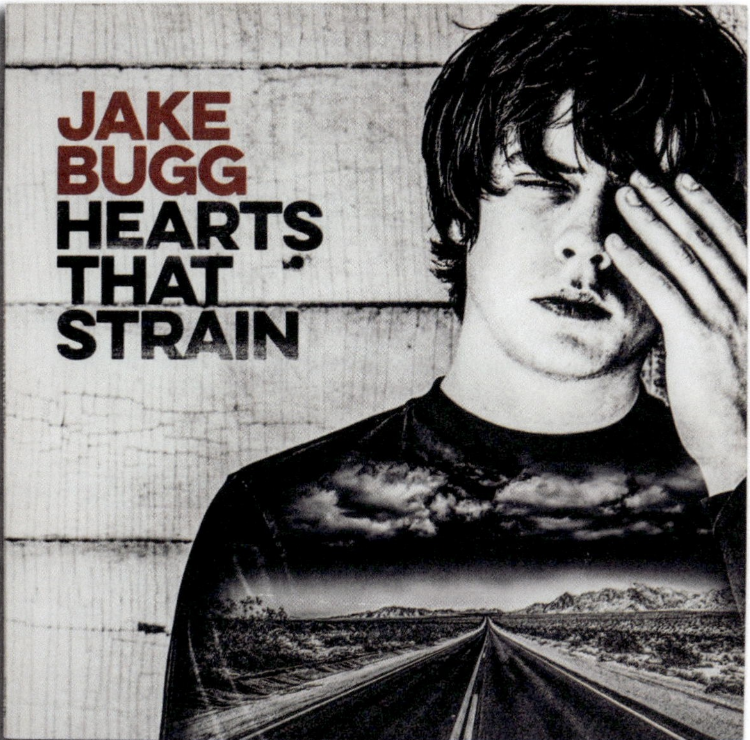

Jake Bugg
Hearts That Strain
Virgin Records, 2017
The Magnificient Pete Barrett, Esq (Design)
Jesse Lirola (Photo)

* Feb 28th, 1994
Jake Bugg as Jake Edwin Charles Kenned
Nottingham (UK)

28 FEB

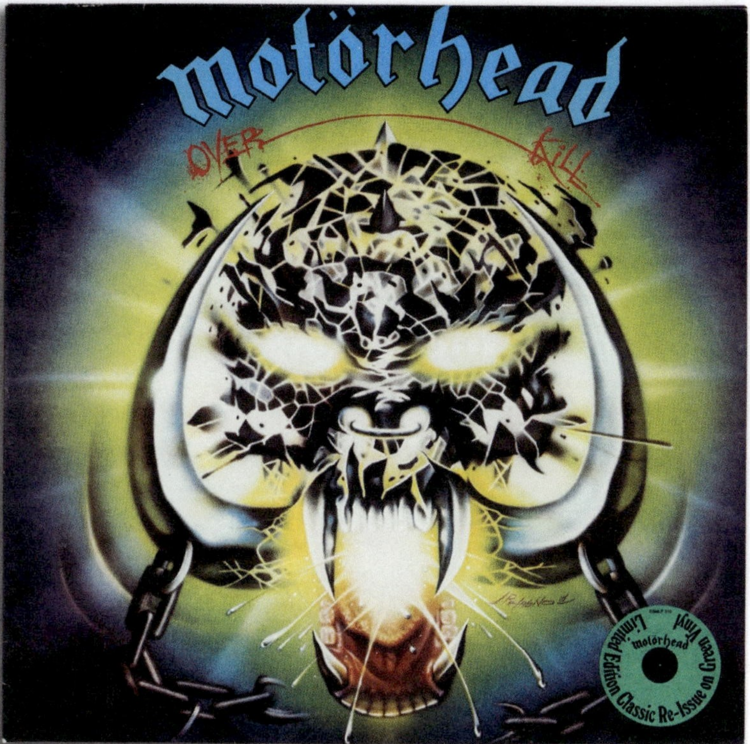

Motörhead
Over Kill
Cvastle Music Ltd., 1979
Joe Pentagon (Design)

29 FEB

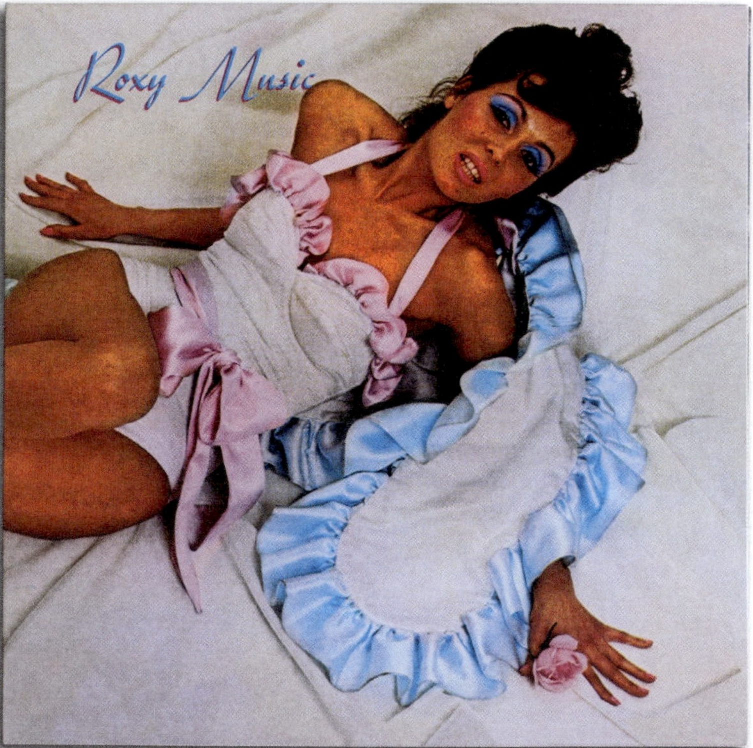

Roxy Music
Island Records, 1972
CCS (Design)
Karl Stoecker (Photo)

01 MAR

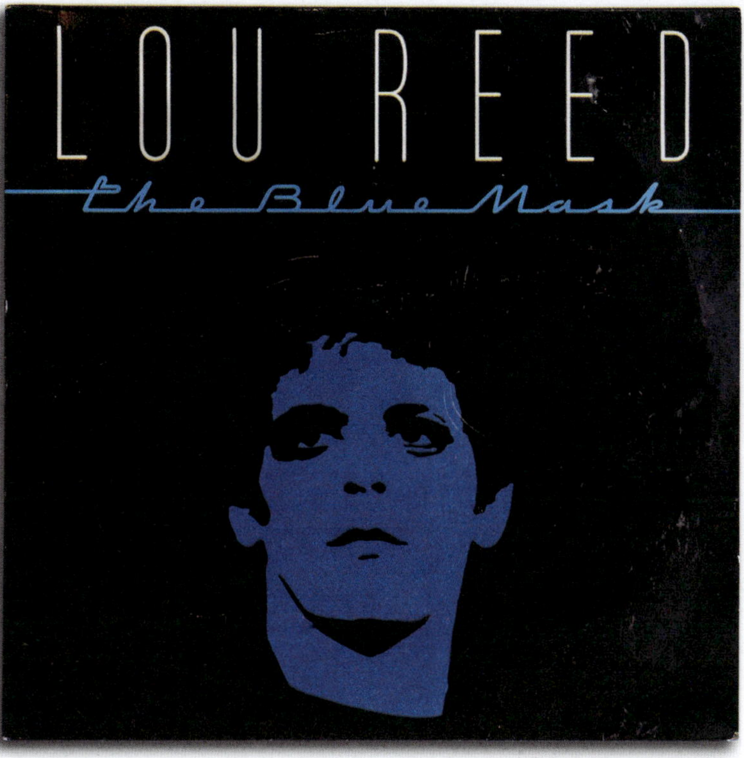

Lou Reed
The Blue Mask
RCA Records, 1982
Josef J. Stelmach (Design)
Mick Rock (Photo)

* Mar 2nd, 1942
Lewis Allan "Lou" Reed
New York

02 MAR

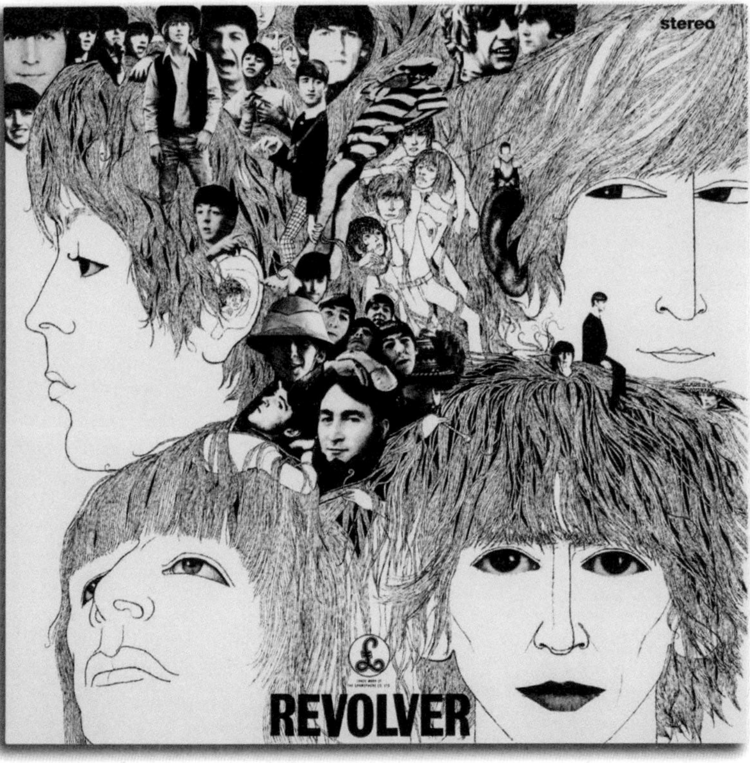

The Beatles
Revolver
Parlophone, 1966
Klaus Voormann (Illustration)

03 MAR

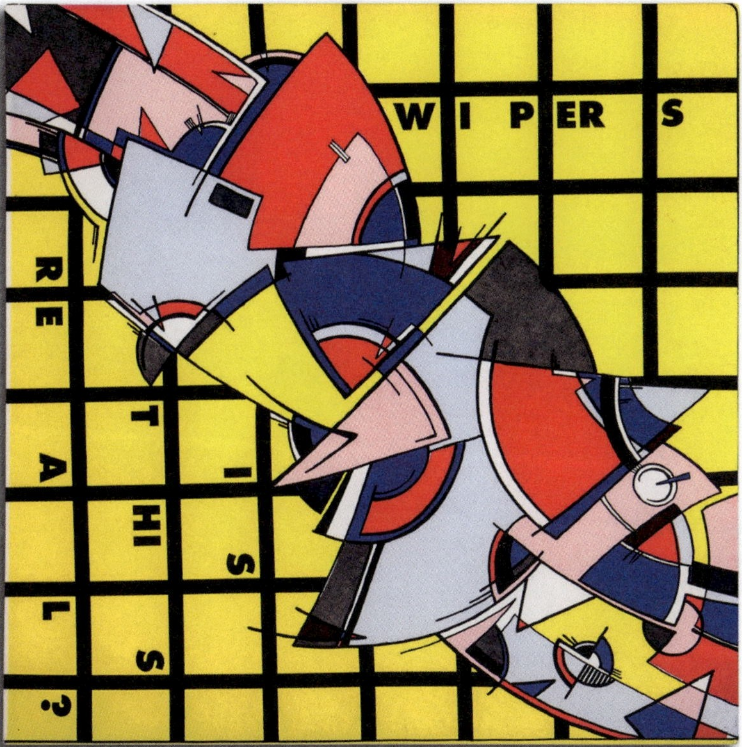

Wipers
Is This Real?
Park Avenue Records, 1979
M.X.King (Design)
Mark Helm (Illustration)

04 MAR

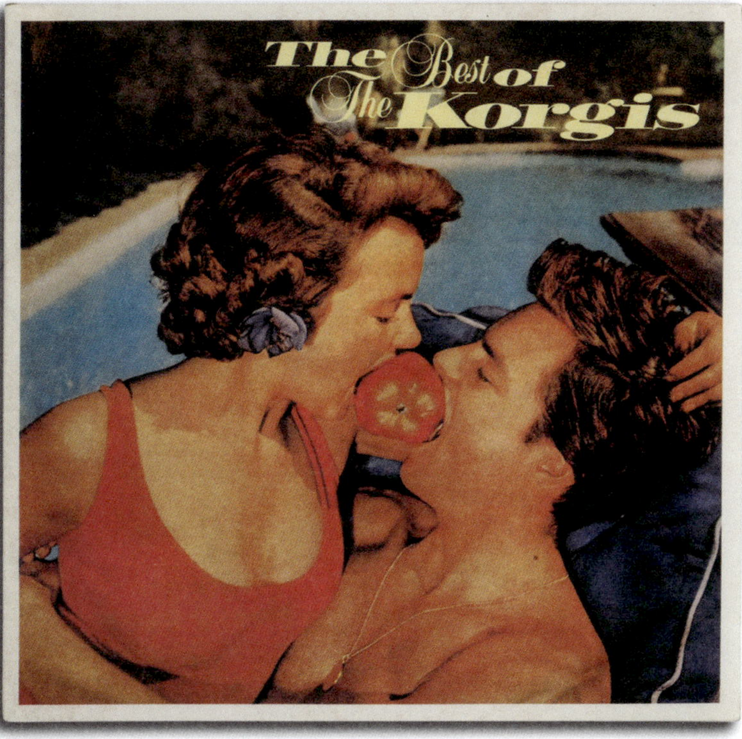

Korgis
The Best Of
Rialto, 1983
George Rowbottom (Design)

05 MAR

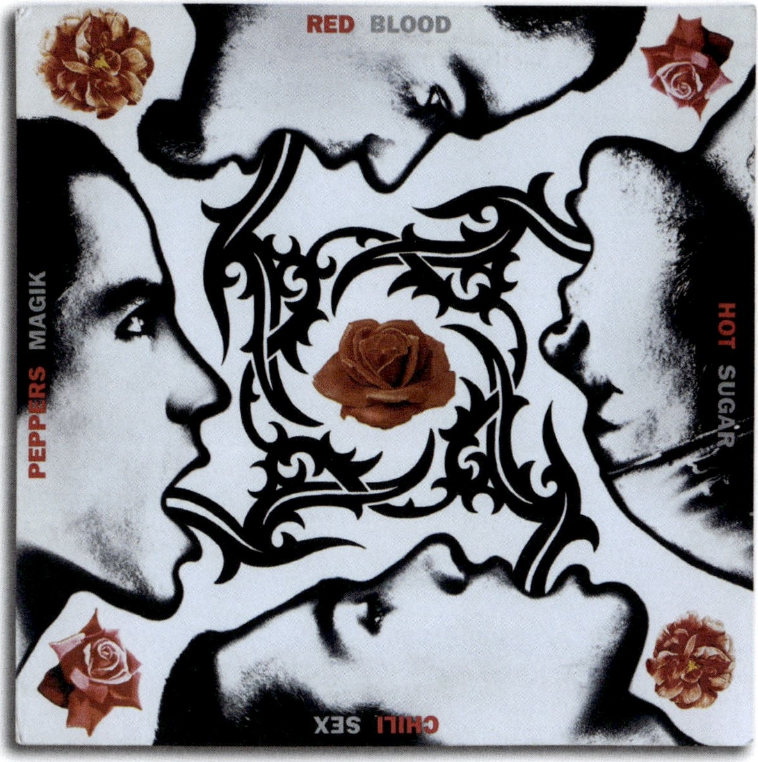

Red Hot Chili Peppers
Blood Sugar Sex Magik
Warner Bros. Records, 1991
Henky Penky (Design)
Gus Van Zant (Photo)

06 MAR

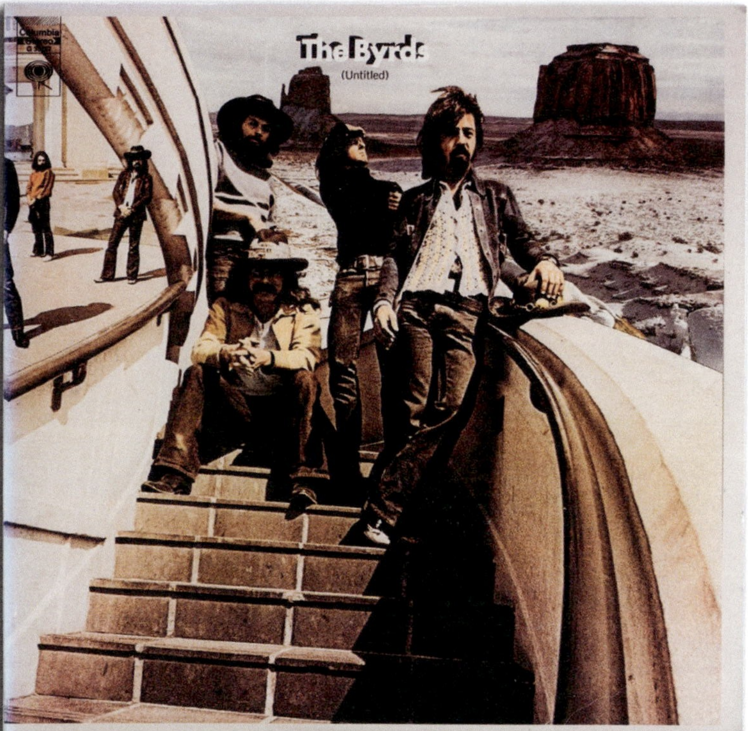

The Byrds
(Untitled)
Columbia Records, 1970
The Cafe Society Dancing Band (Design)
Nancy Chester (Photo)

07 MAR

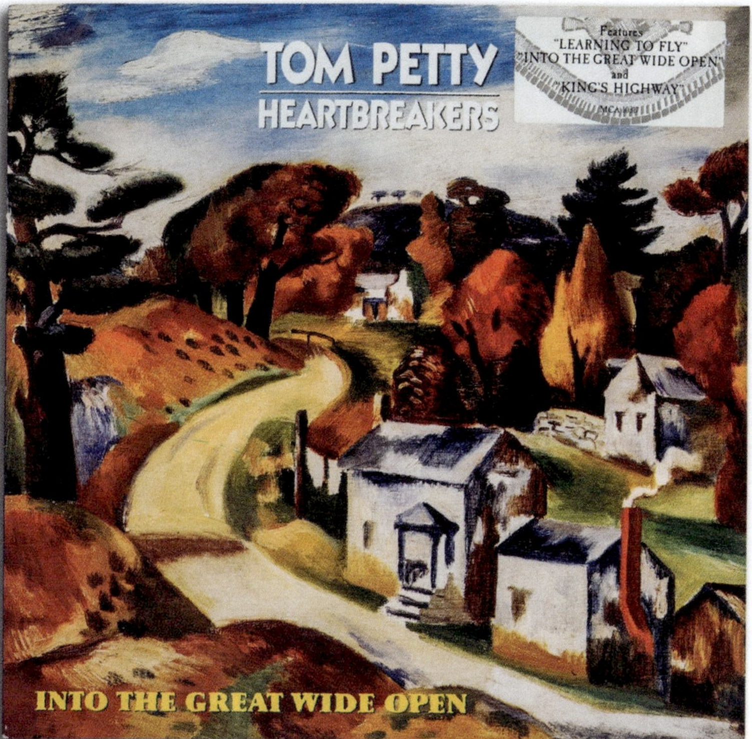

Tom Petty & The Heartbreakers
Into The Great Wide Open
MCA Records, 1991
Awest, Tiny Bouchet (Design)
Jan Matulka (Illustration)

08 MAR

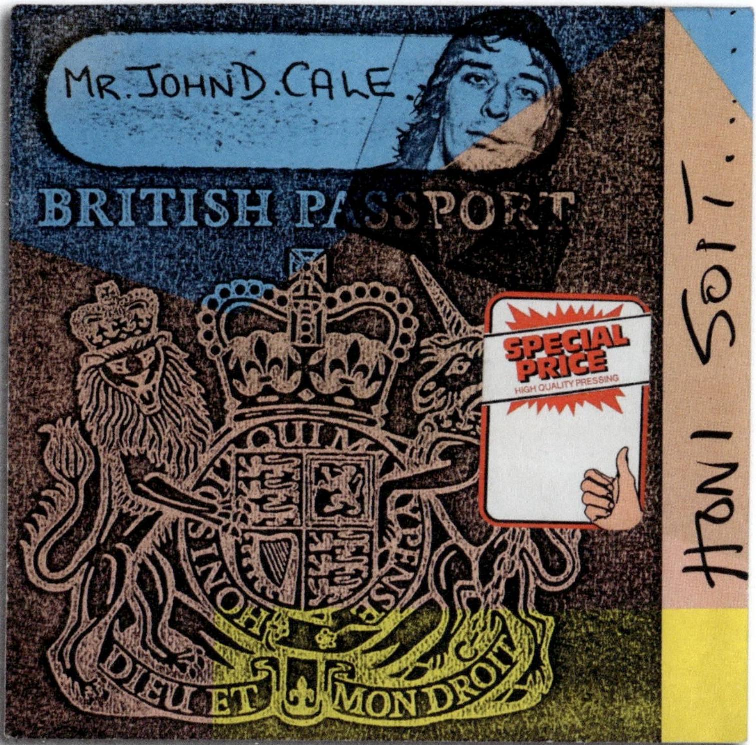

John Cale
Honi Soit
A&M Records, 1981
Andy Warhol (Design)
Fred Lorery (Photo)

* Mar 9th, 1942
John Cale
Garnant (UK)

09 MAR

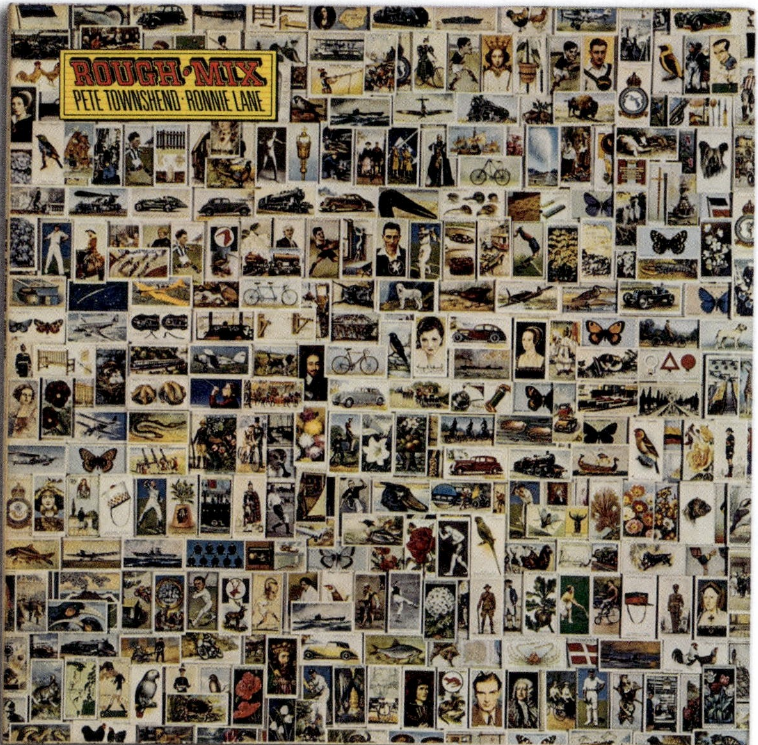

Pete Townshend / Ronnie Lane
Rough Mix Ronnie Lane
Polydor Records, 1977
Jo Mirowski (Design)
Martin Cook (Photo)

10 MAR

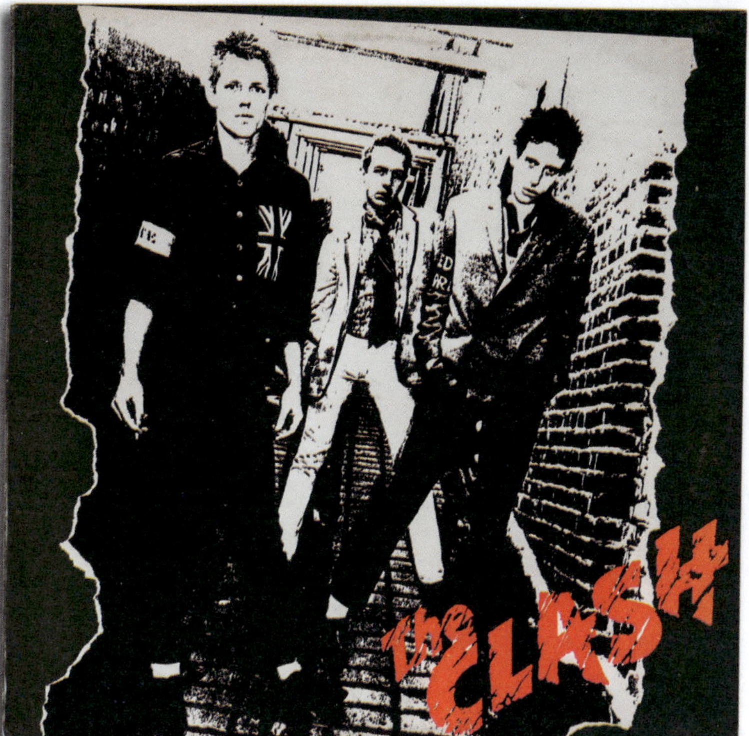

The Clash
CBS Records, 1977
Rostaw Szaybo (Design)
Kate Simon (Photo)

11 MAR

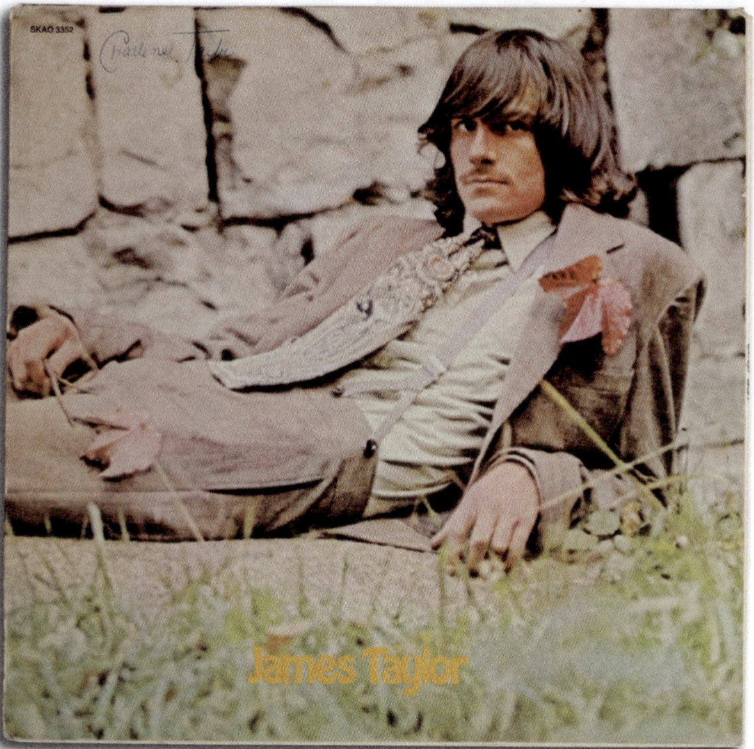

James Taylor
Apple Records, 1968
Richard Imrie (Photo)

12 MAR

* Mar 12th, 1948
James Vernon Taylor
Boston (Massachusetts)

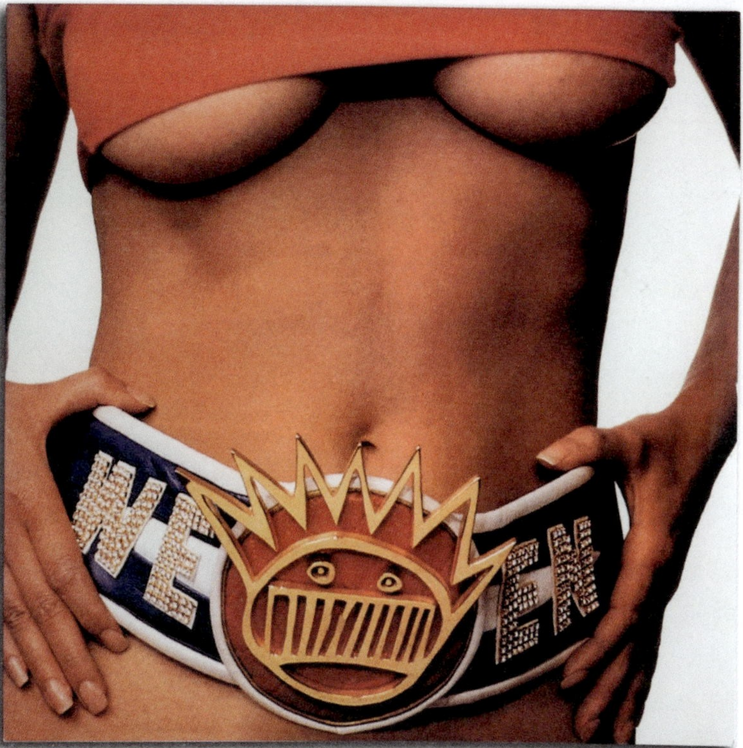

Ween
Chocolate and Cheese
Grand Royal, 1994
Reiner Design Consultants, Inc. (Design)
John Kuczala (Photo)

13 MAR

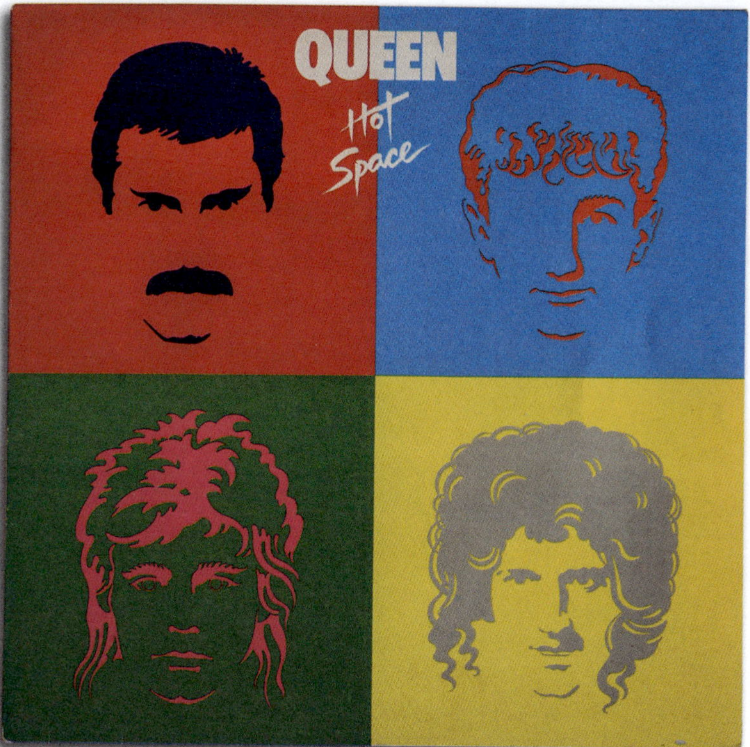

Queen
Hot Space
EMI, 1982
Freddie Mercury (Design)
John Barr, Norm Ung, Steve Miller (Photo)

14 MAR

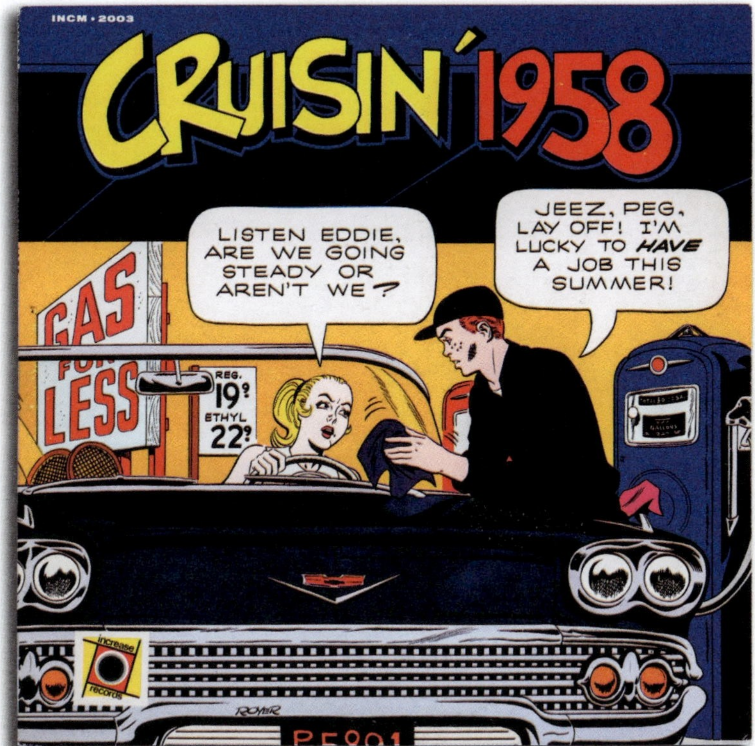

Various Artists
Cruisin' 1958
Increase Records, 1970
Mike Royer (Design)

15 MAR

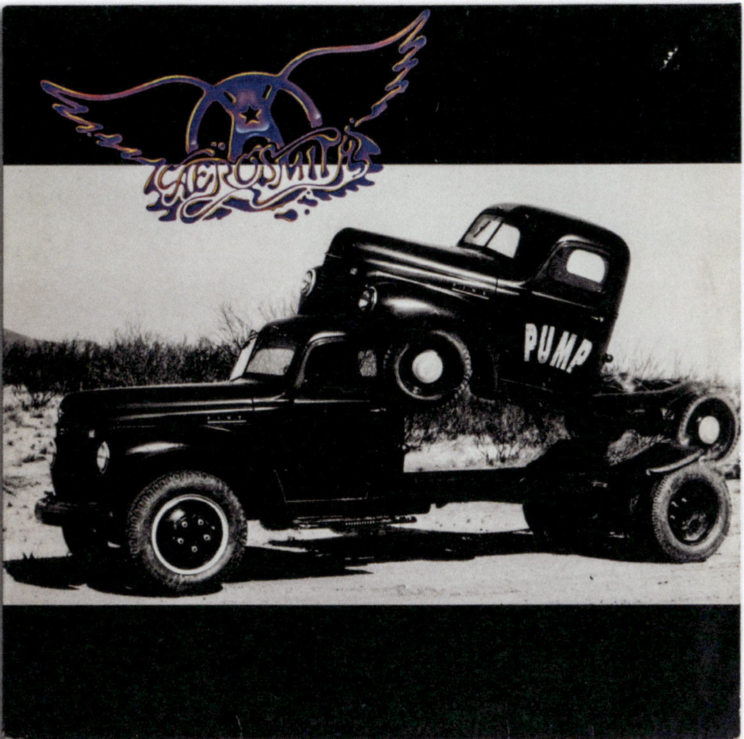

Aerosmith
Pump
Geffen Records, 1989
Gabrielle Raumberger (Design)
Sol Libsohn (Photo)

16 MAR

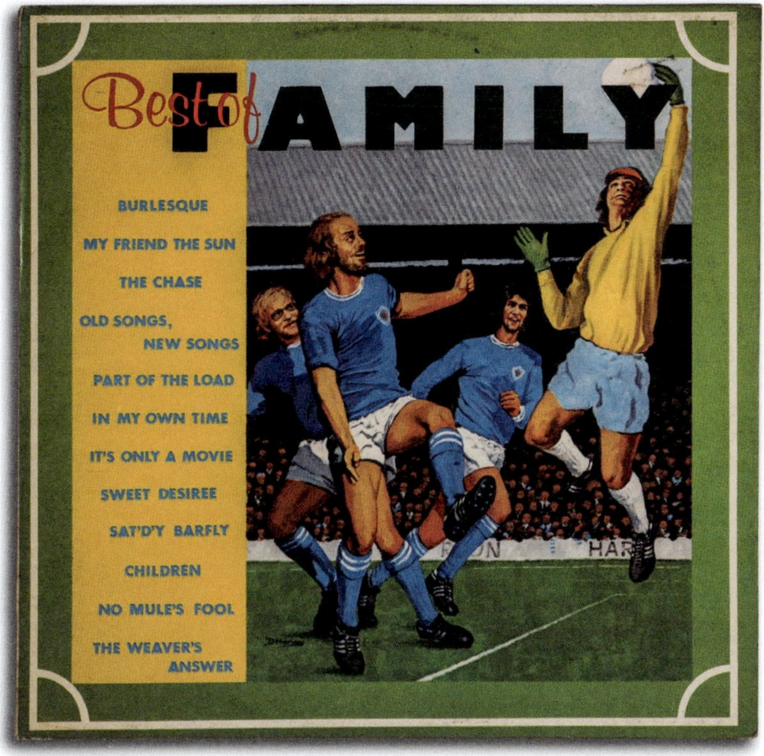

Family
Best Of Family
Reprise Records, 1974
Bryan Harvey (Illustration)

17 MAR

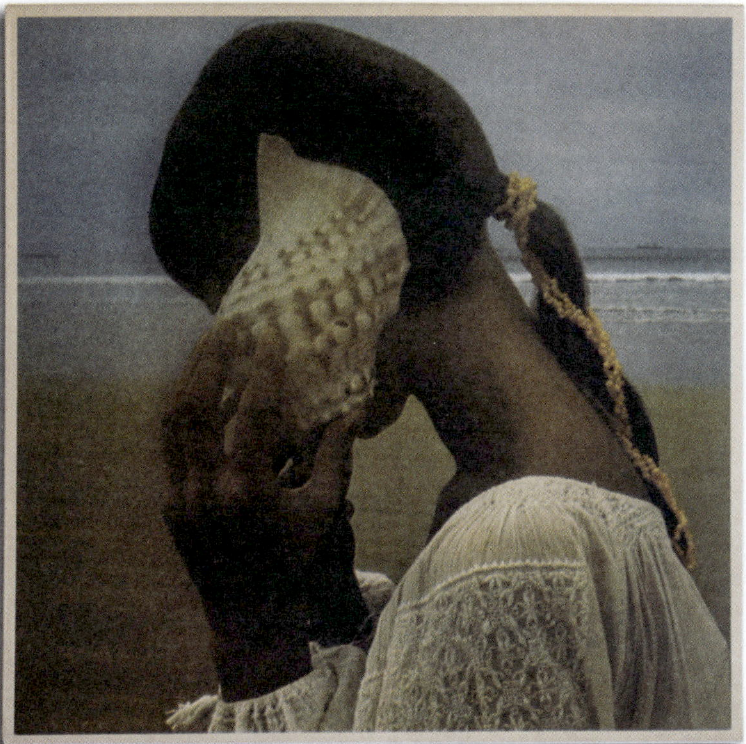

Allah-Las
Innovative Leisure Records, 2012
Matthew Correia, Robbie Smith (Design)
David Hamilton (Photo)

18 MAR

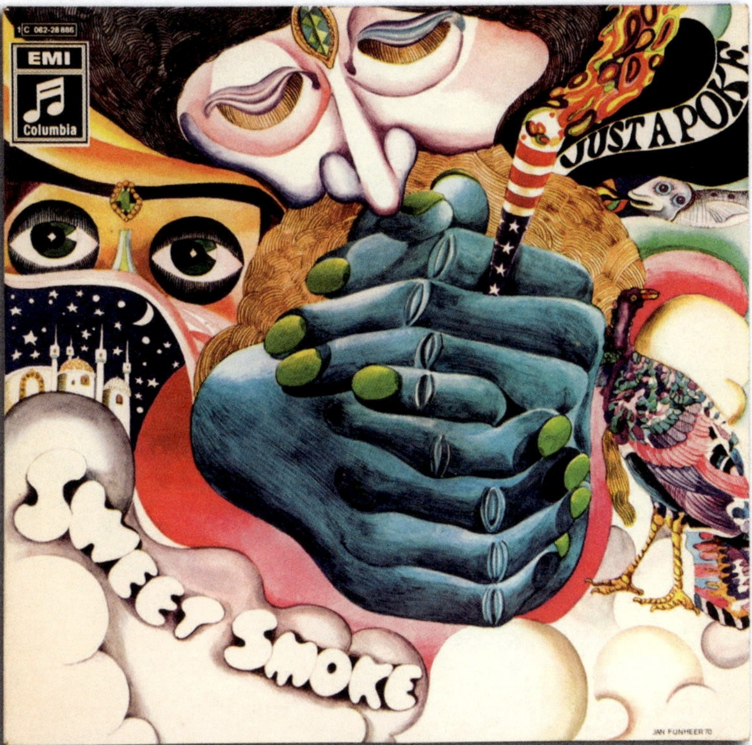

Sweet Smoke
Just A Poke
Columbia Records, 1970
Jan Fijnheer (Illustration)

19 MAR

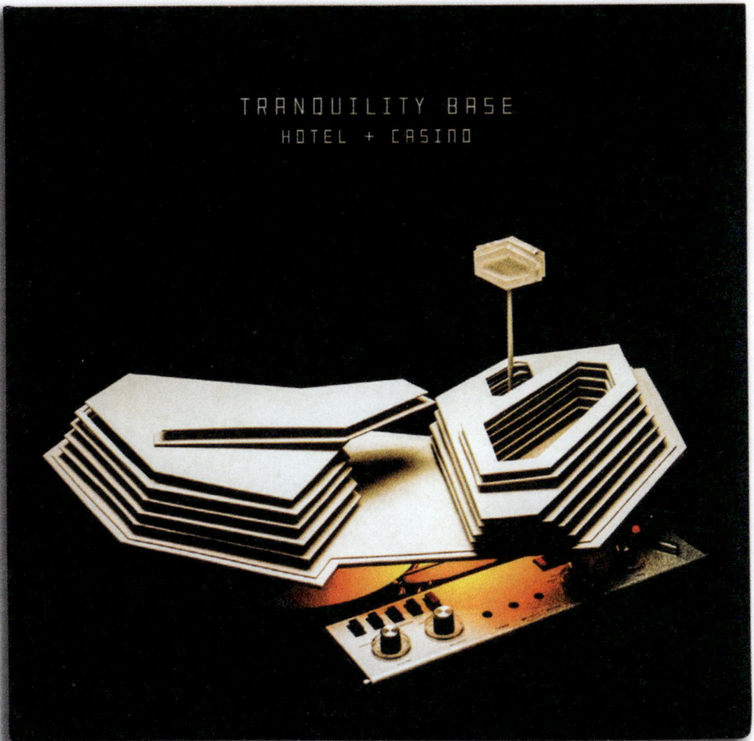

Arctic Monkeys
Tranquilty Base Hotel + Casino
Domino Records, 2018
Alex Turner (Design)
Zackery Michael (Photo)

20 MAR

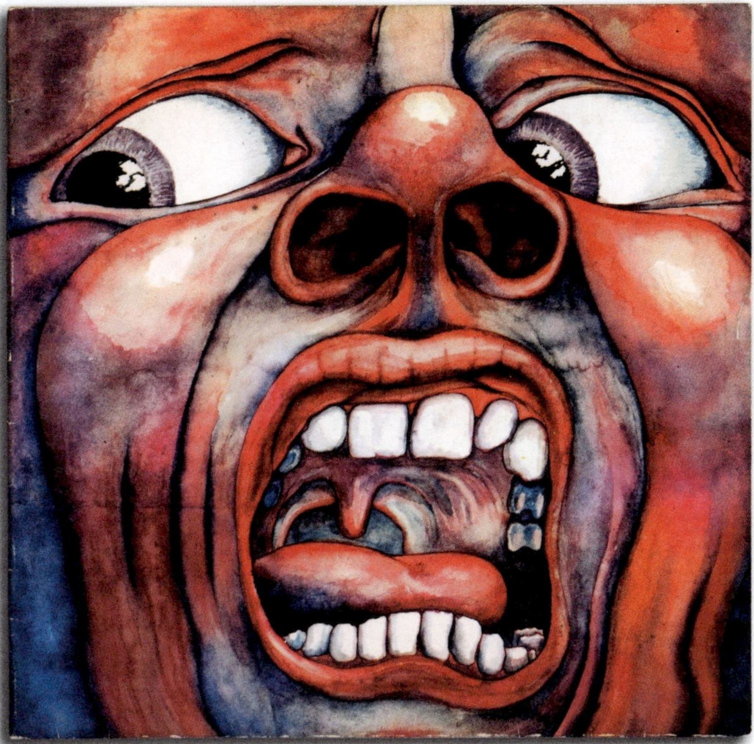

King Crimson
In The Court Of The Crimson King
Island Records, 1969
Barry Godber (Illustration)

21 MAR

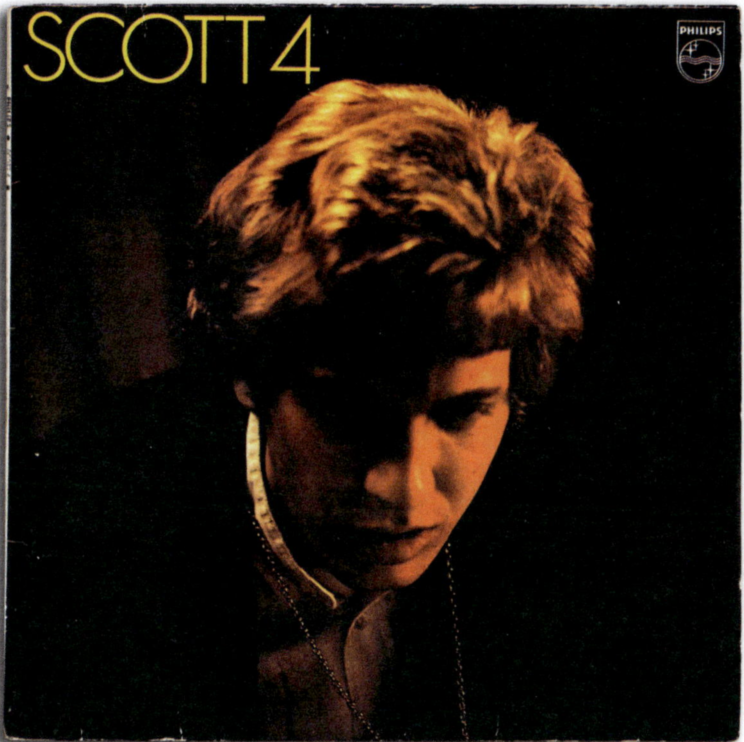

Scott Walker
Scott 4
Philips, 1969
John Constable (Photo)

† Mar 22nd, 2019
Noel Scott Engel Junior
London (UK)

22 MAR

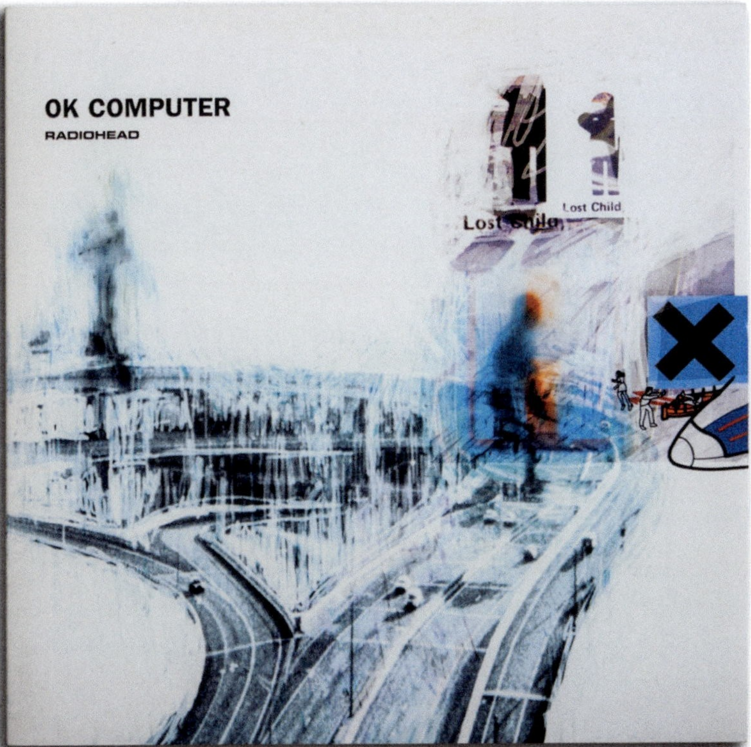

Radiohead
OK Computer
Parlophone, 1997
Hubdesign, Matt Bale, Mr. Barry, The Whole Hog (Design)
Stanley Donwood, The White Chocolate Farm (Photo)

23 MAR

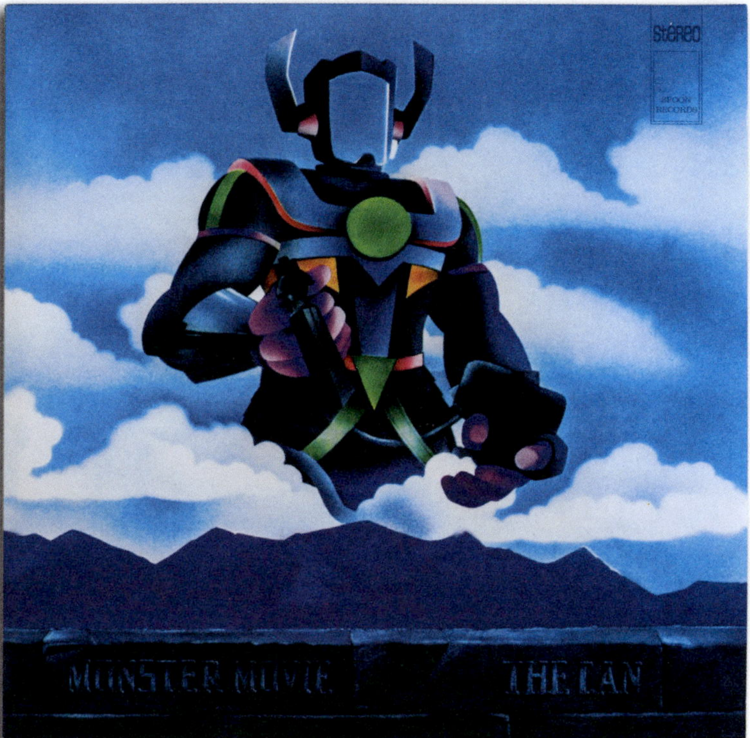

The Can
Monster Movie
Spoon Records, 1980
Wandrey's Studio (Design)

24 MAR

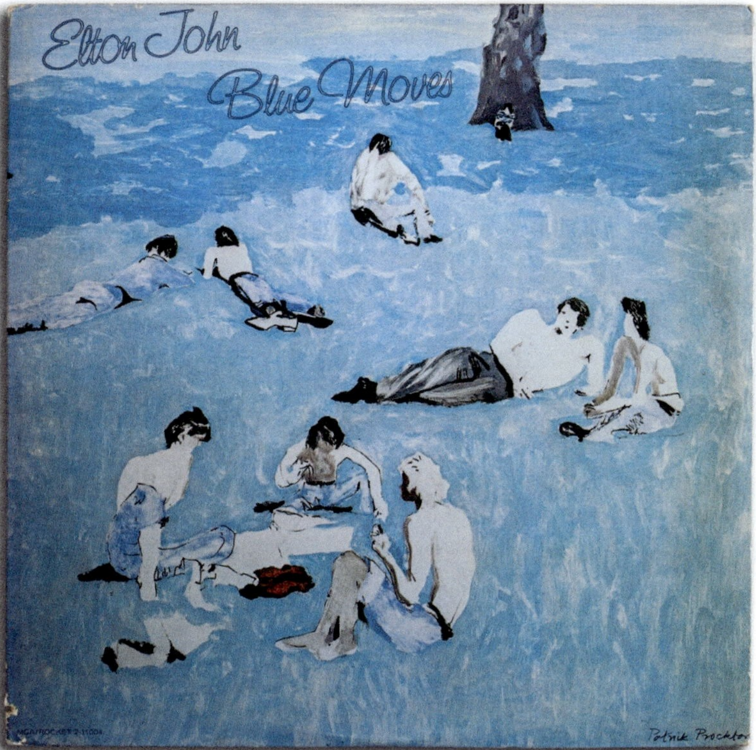

Elton John
Blue Moves
MCA Records, 1976
David Costa (Design)
The Guardian Readers by Patrick Procktor (Illustration)

* Mar 25th, 1947
Reginald Kenneth Dwigh
Pinner (UK)

25 MAR

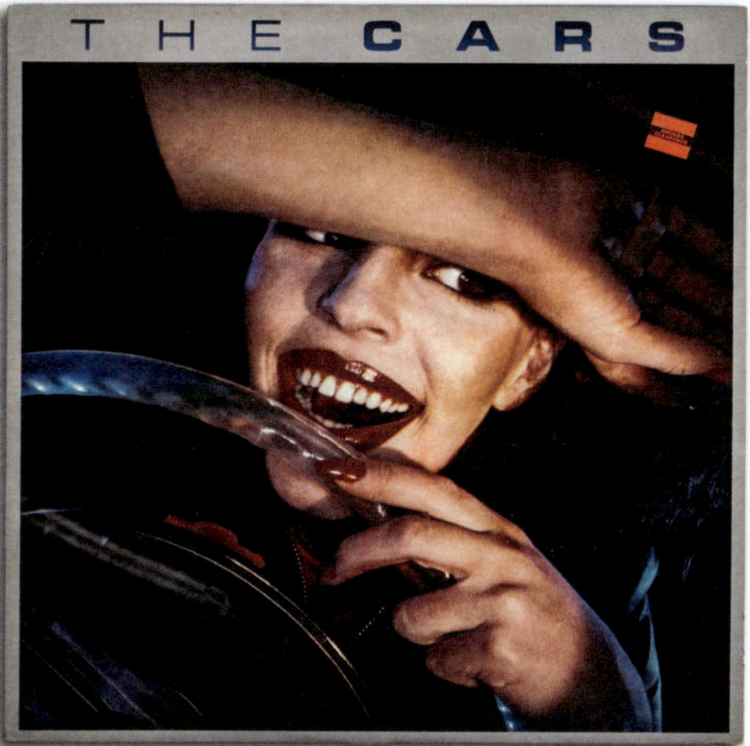

The Cars
Elektra Records, 1978
Ron Coro (Design)
Elliot Gilbert (Photo)

26 MAR

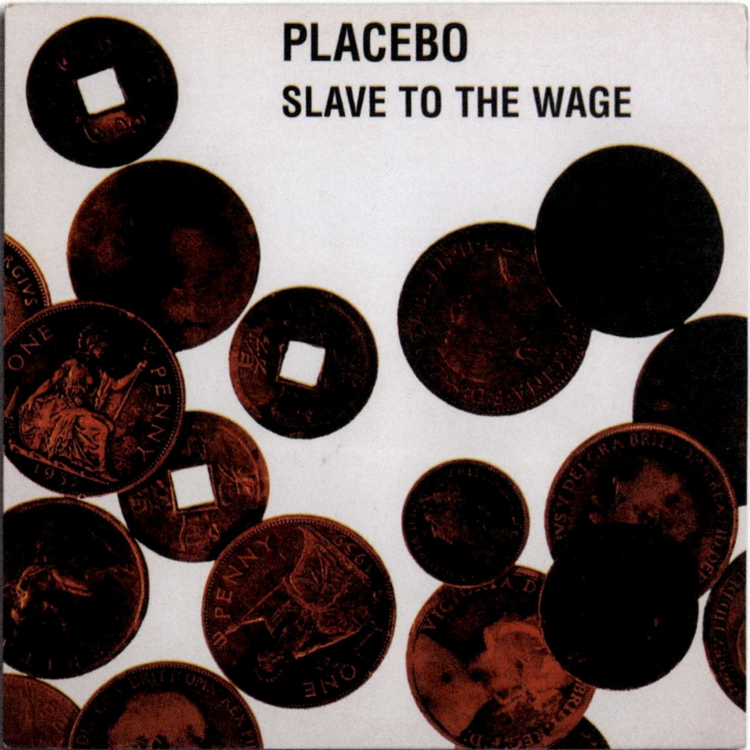

Placebo
Slave To The Wage
Elevator Music, 2000
Kevin Westenberg (Photo)

27 MAR

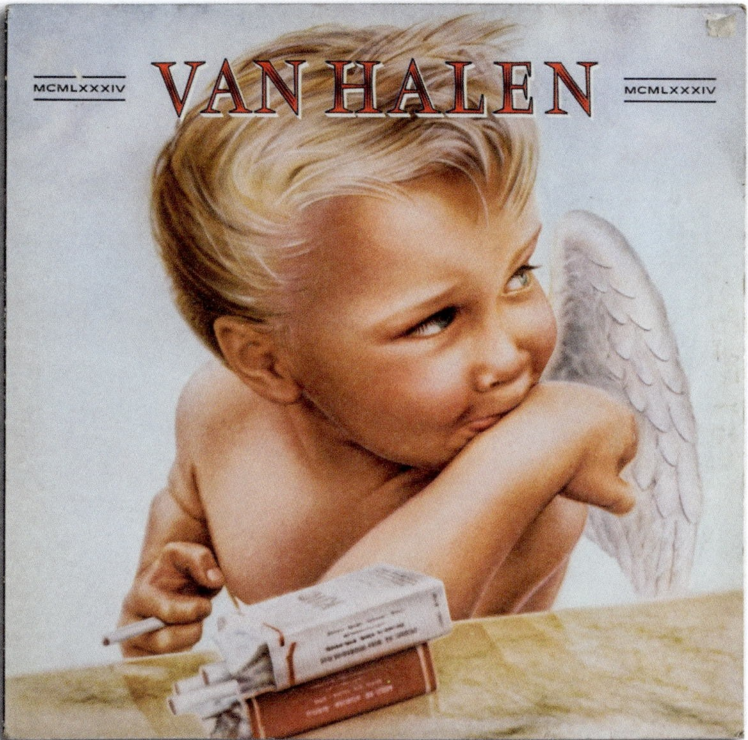

Van Halen
1984
Warner Bros. Records, 1984
David Jellison, Pete Angelus, Richard Seireeni (Design)
Margo Zafer Nahas (Illustration)

28 MAR

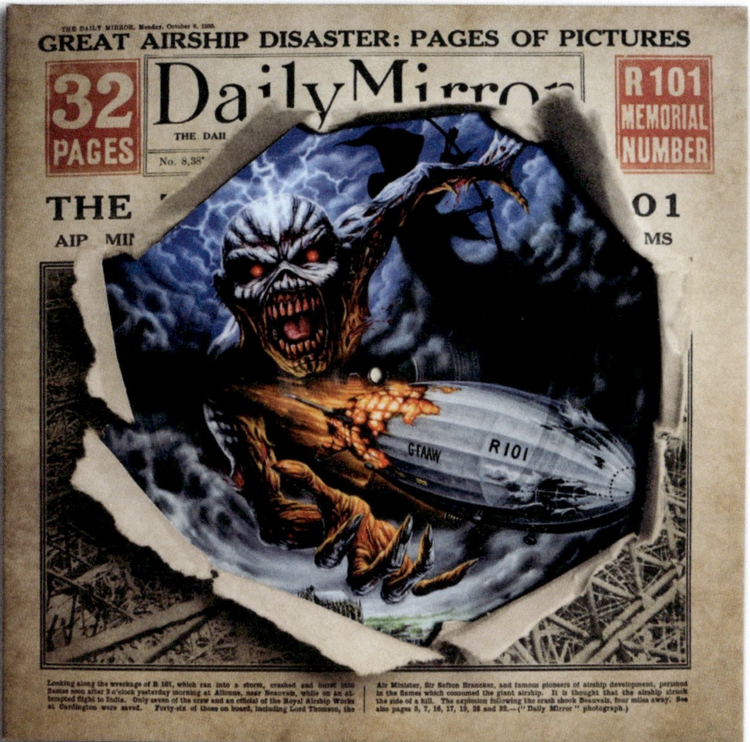

Iron Maiden
Empire of The Clouds
Parlophone, 2016
Herve Monjeaud (Illustration)

29 MAR

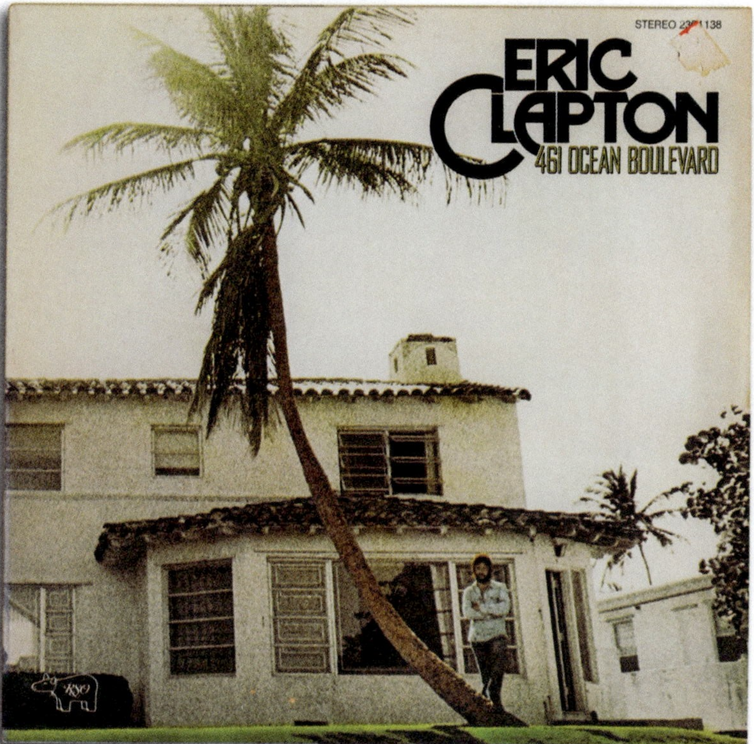

Eric Clapton
461 Ocean Boulevard
RSO, 1974
Bob Defrin (Design)
David Gahr (Photo)

* Mar 30th, 1945
Eric Patrick Clapton
Ripley (Borough of Guildford)

30 MAR

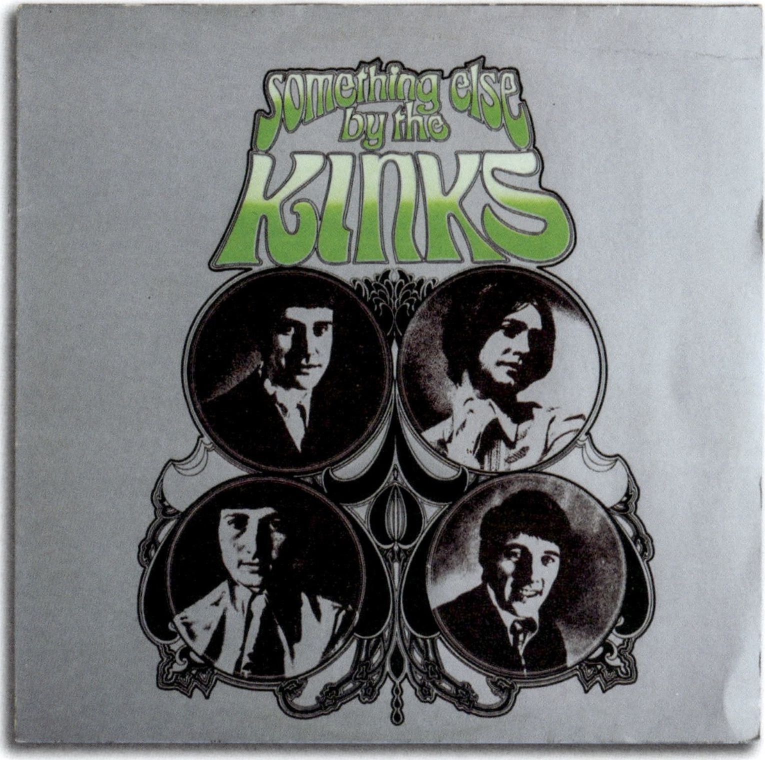

The Kinks
Something Else
Pye Records, 1967
Cover Artists Unknown

31 MAR

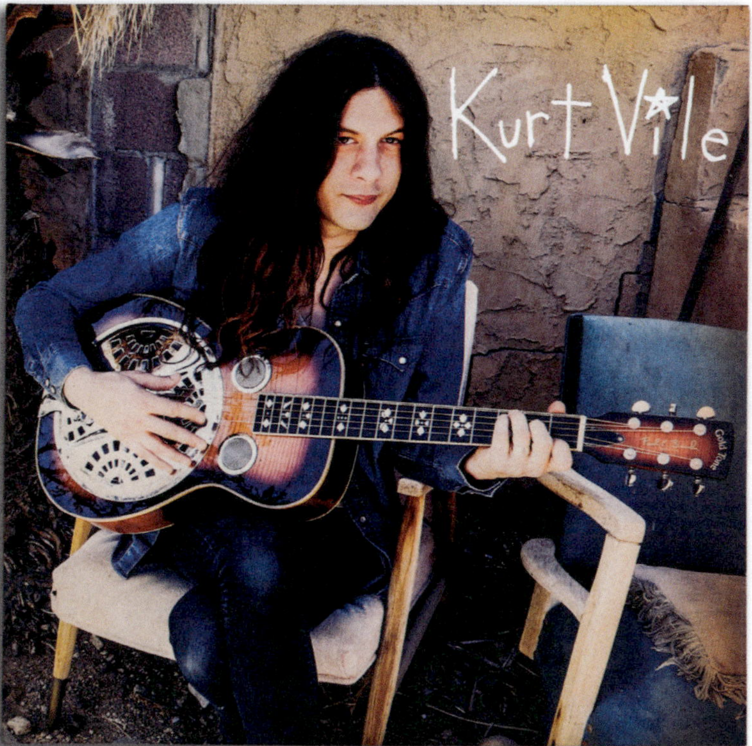

Kurt Vile
B'lieve I'm Goin Down...
Matador Records, 2015
Gary Burden & Jenice Heo (Design)
Henry Diltz (Photo)

01 APR

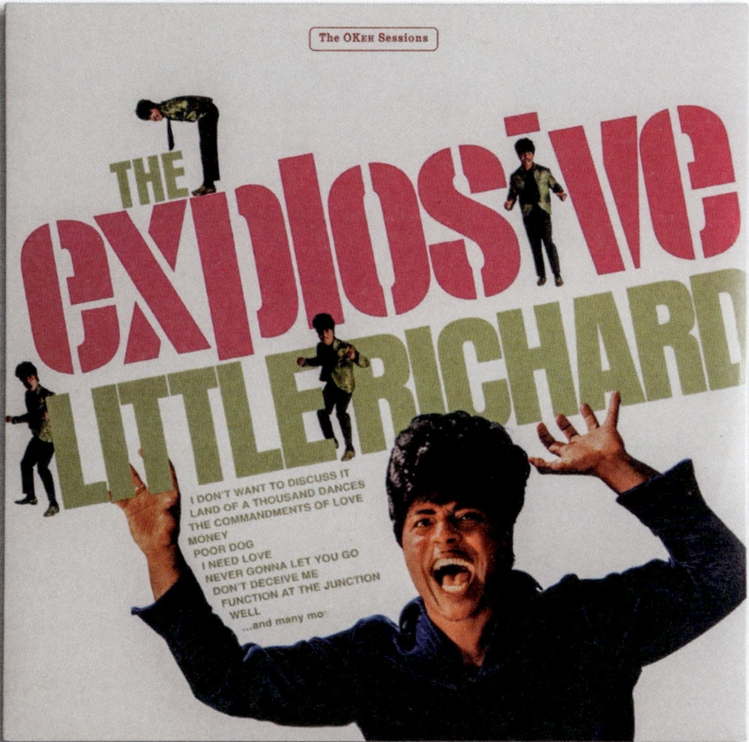

Little Richard
The Explosive Little Richard
Okeh, 1967
Cover Artists Unknown

02 APR

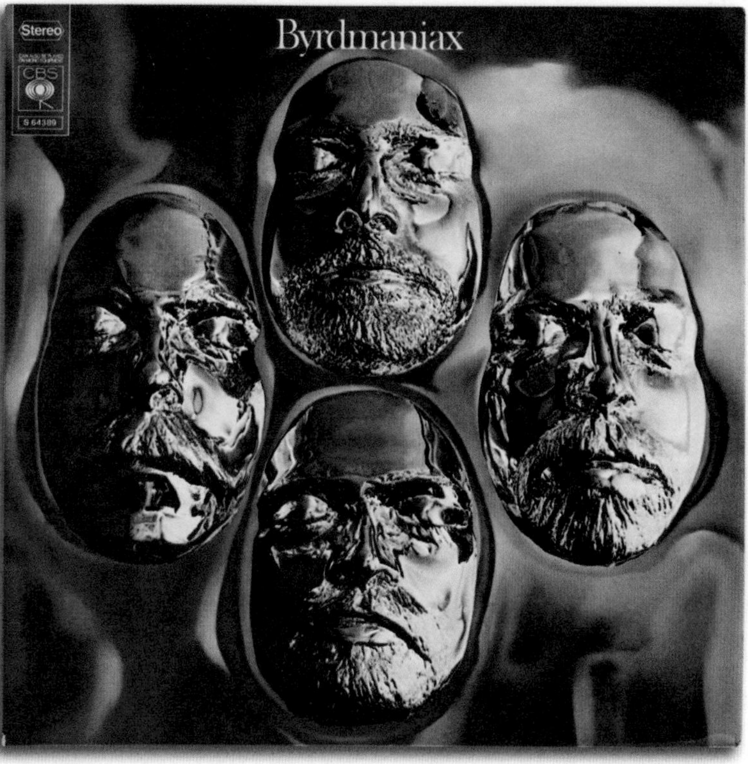

The Byrds
Byrdmaniax
CBS Records, 1971
Virginia Team & John Berg (Design)
Don Jim (Photo)

03 APR

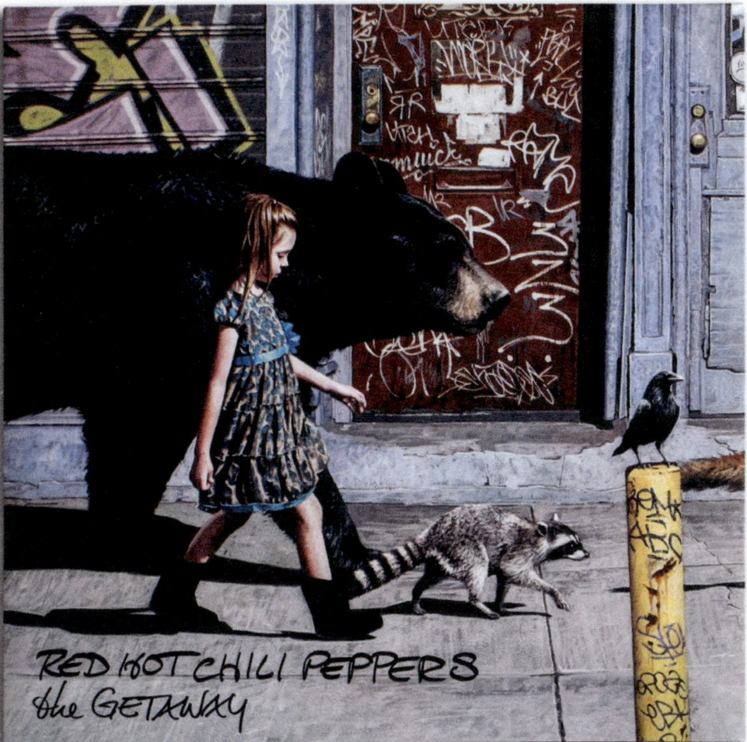

Red Hot Chili Peppers
The Getaway
Warner Bros. Records, 2016
Red Hot Chili Peppers (Design)
Kevin Peterson (Illustration)

04 APR

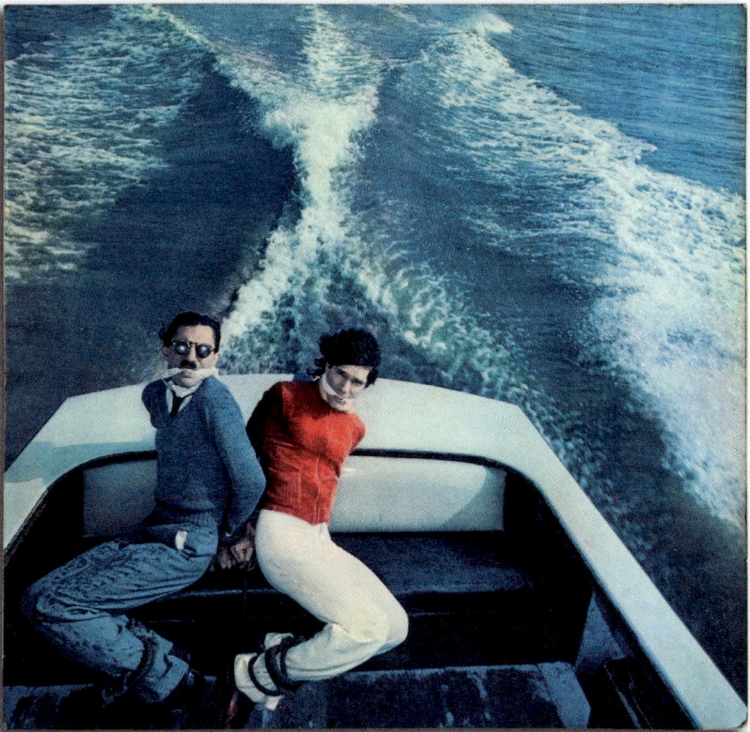

Sparks
Propaganda
Island Records, 1974
Monty Coles (Photo)

05 APR

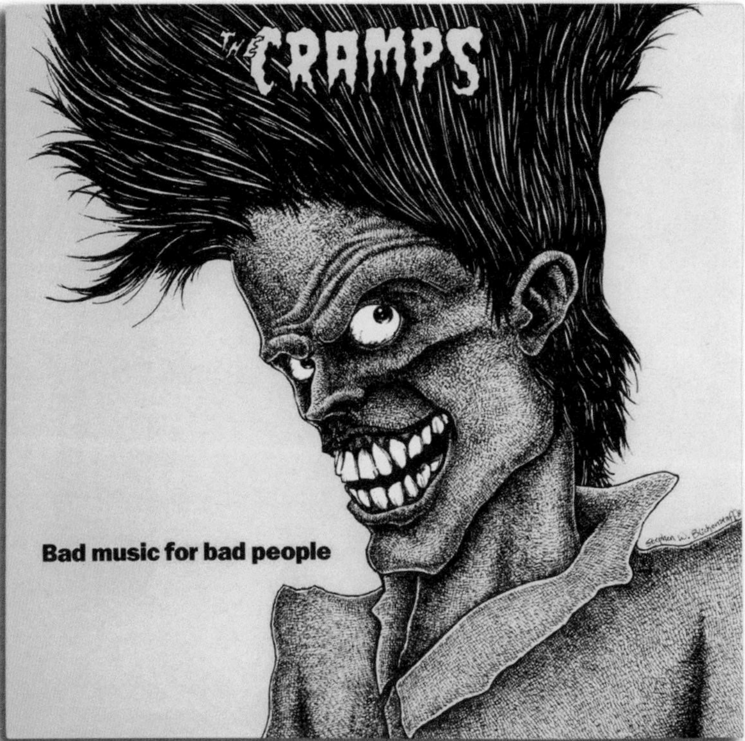

The Cramps
Bad Music for Bad People
I.R.S. Records, 1984
Stephen Blickenstaff (Design)
Stephen Blickenstaff (Illustration)

06 APR

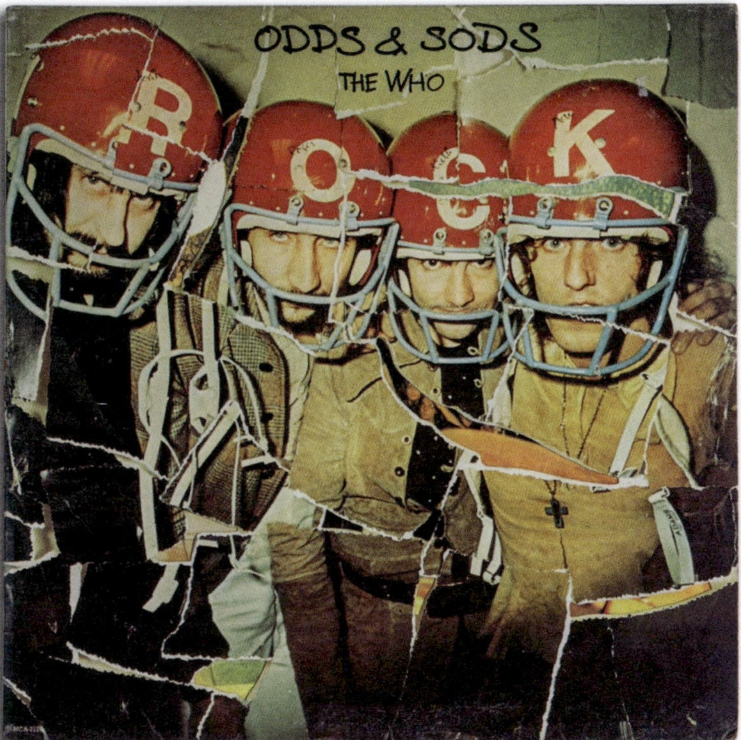

The Who
Odds & Sods
Track Records, 1974
Roger Daltrey (Design)
Graham Hughes (Photo)

07 APR

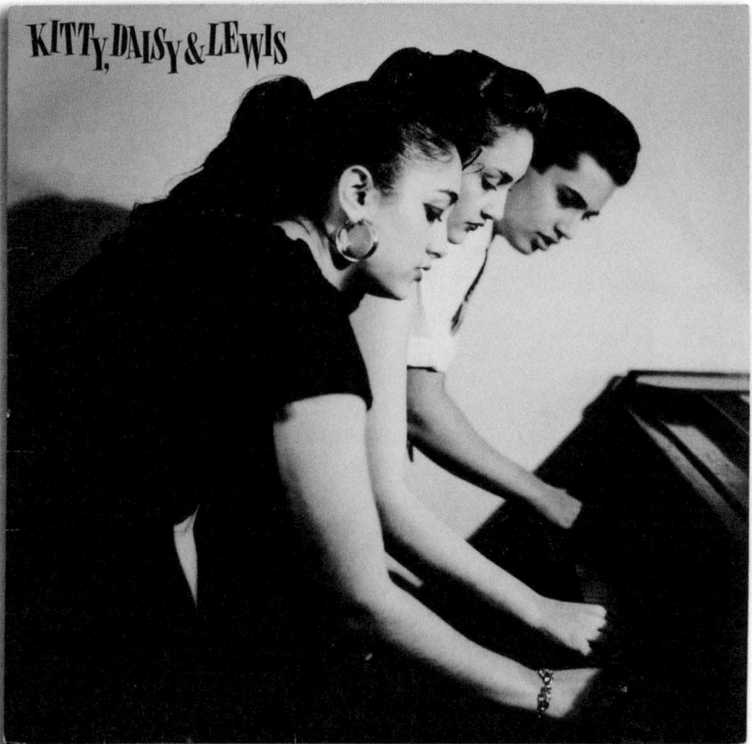

Kitty, Daisy & Lewis
Sunday Best Recordings, 2008
G. Durham, I.Weiss, K,D,L (Photo)

08 APR

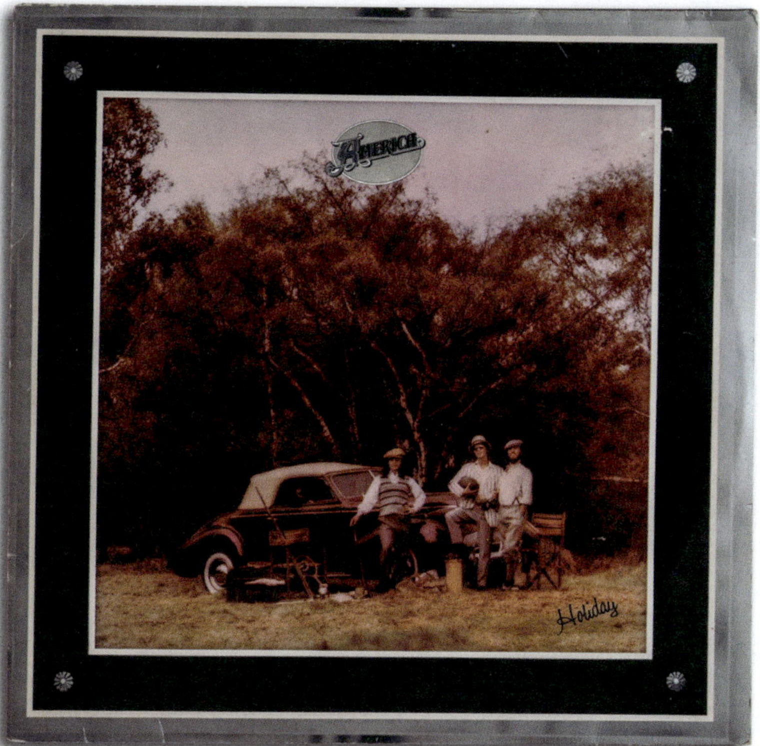

America
Holiday
Warner Bros. Records, 1974
Gary Burden (Design)
Gered Mankowitz (Photo)

09 APR

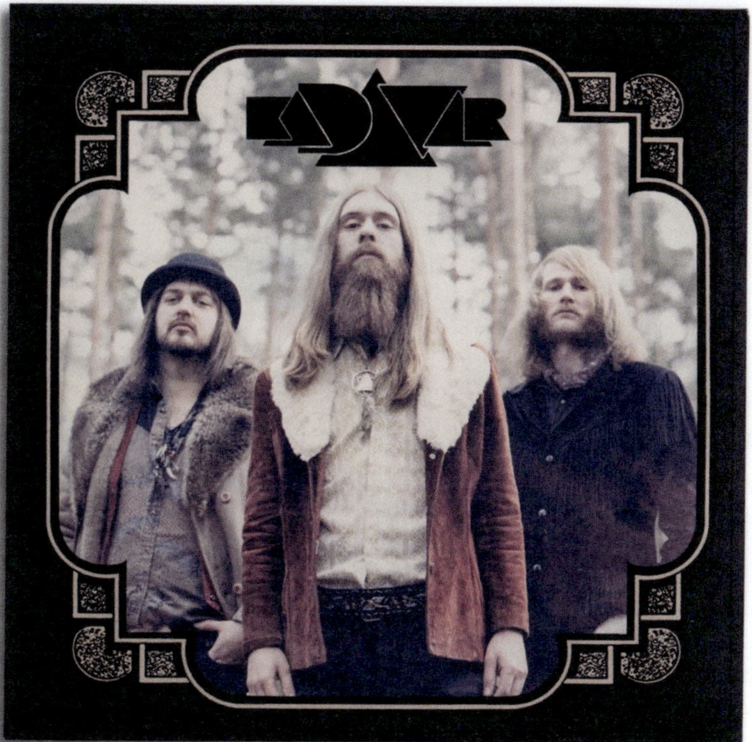

Kadaver
This Charming Man Records, 2012
Christoph Lindemann (Design)
Joe Dilworth (Photo)

10 APR

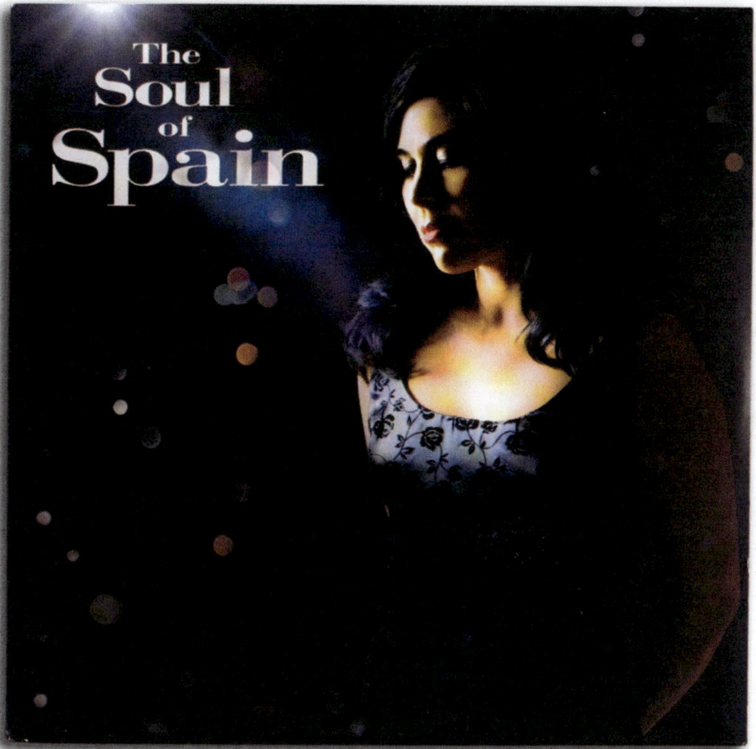

Spain
The Soul of Spain
Glitterhouse Records, 2012
Andrea Morgenstern (Design)
Dave Naz (Photo)

11 APR

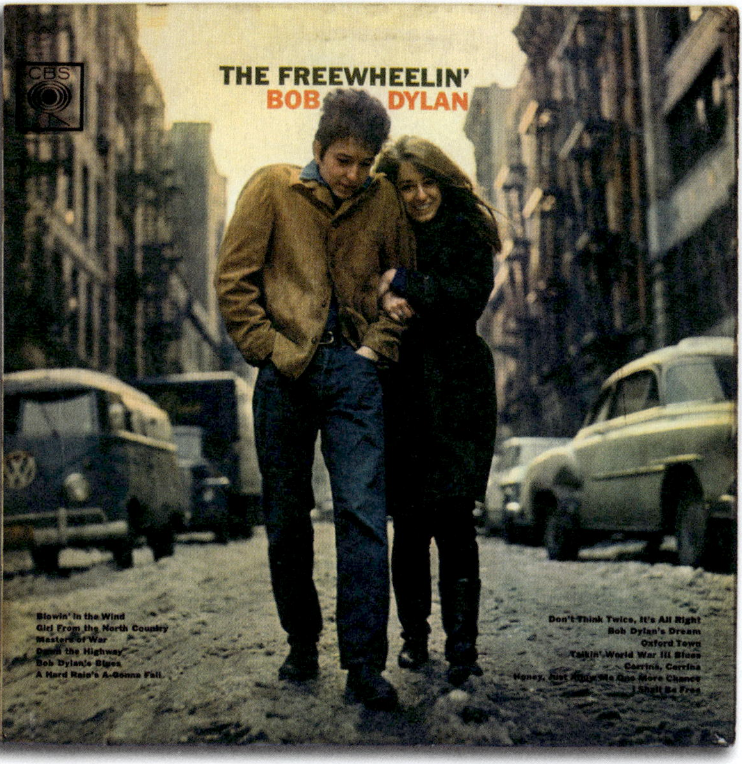

Bob Dylan
The Freewheelin'
CBS Records, 1963
Don Hunstein (Photo)

12 APR

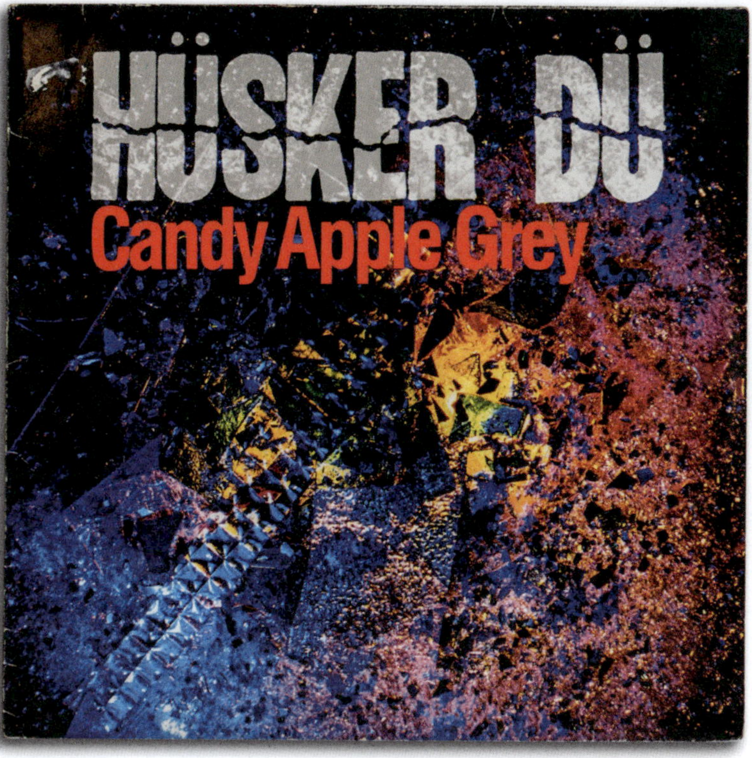

Hüsker Dü
Candy Apple Grey
Warner Brothers, 1986
Daniel Corrigan (Photo)

13 APR

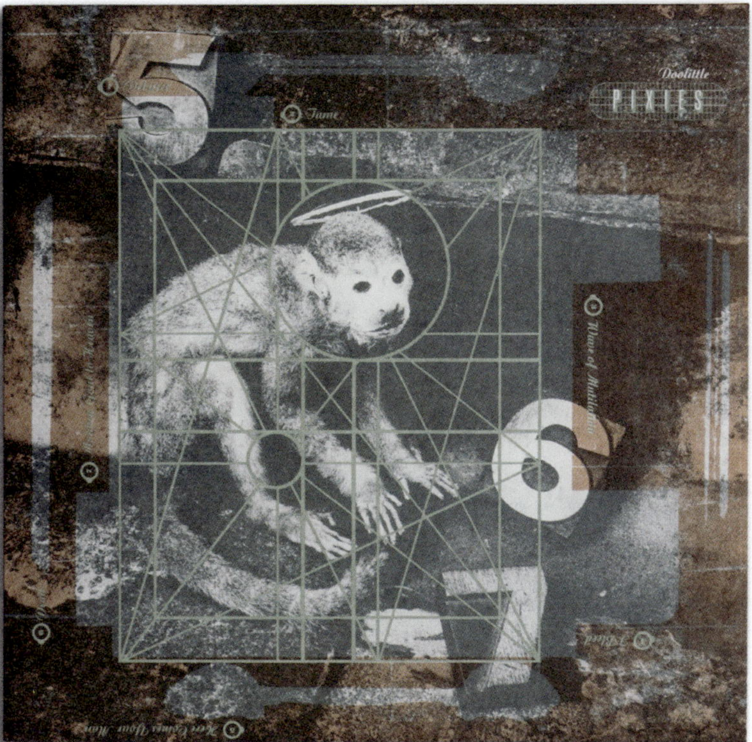

Pixies
Doolittle
4 AD, 1989
Vaughan Oliver (Design)
Simon Larbalestier (Illustration)

14 APR

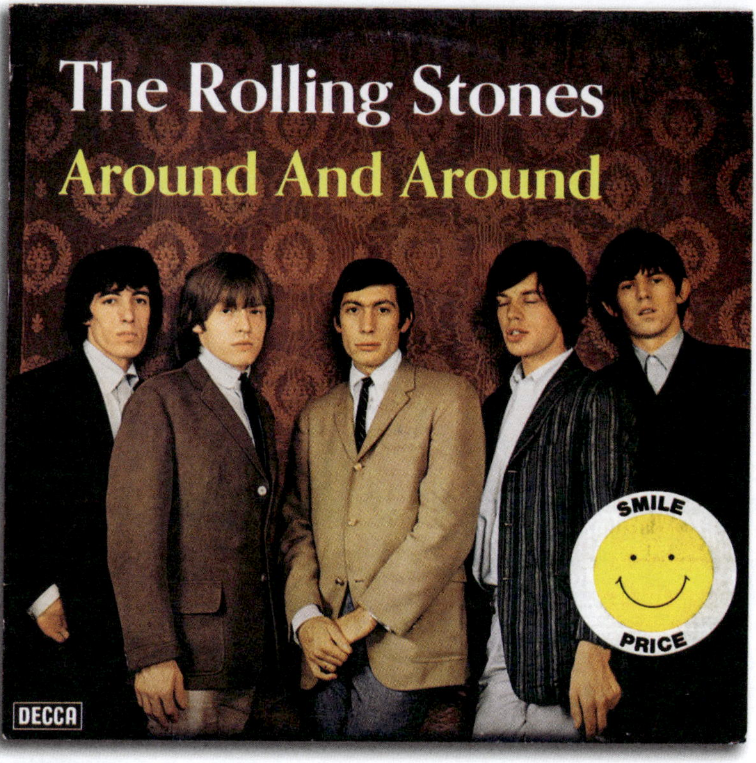

The Rolling Stones
Around And Around
Decca Records, 1964
Cover Artists Unknown

15 APR

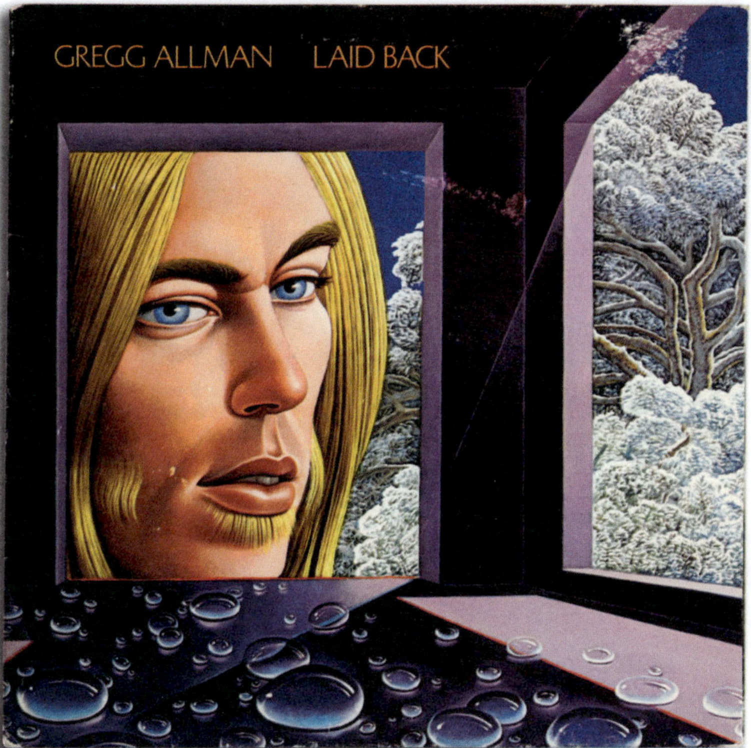

Gregg Allman
Laid Back
Capricorn Records, 1973
Abdul Mati Klarwein (Illustration)

16 APR

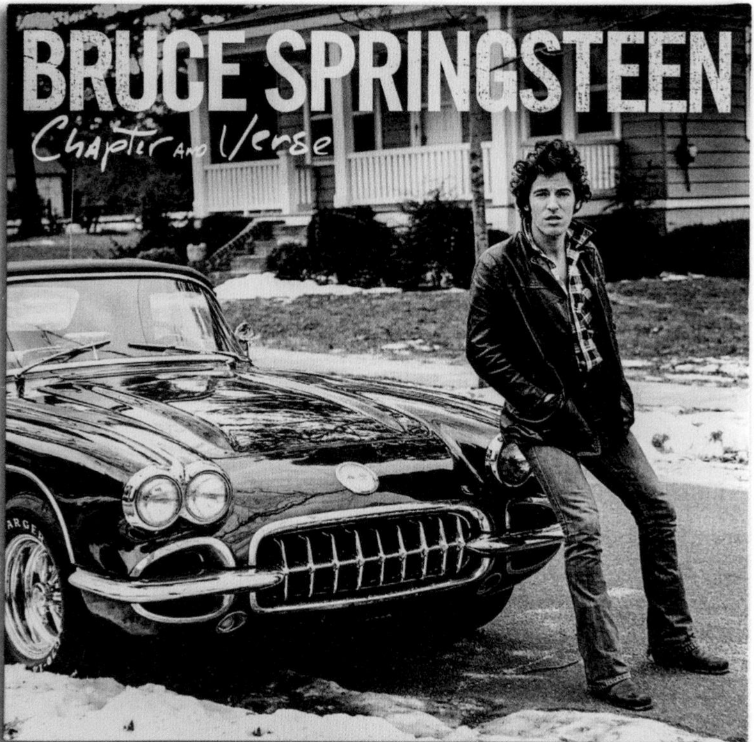

Bruce Springsteen
Chapter And Verse
Columbia, 2016
Michael Holme (Design)
Frank Stefanko (Photo)

17 APR

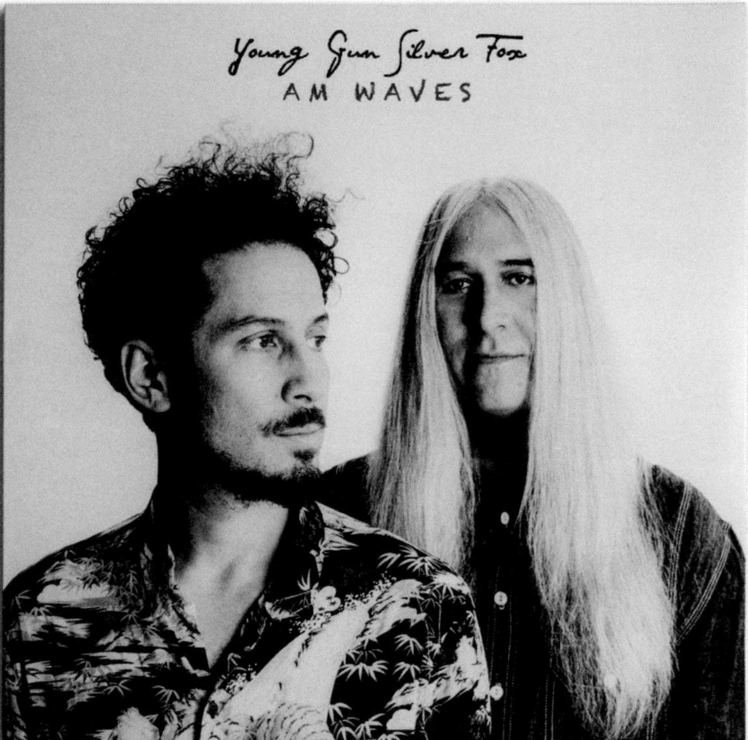

Young Gun Silver Fox
AM Waves
Légère Recordings, 2018
Andy Platts (Design)
Dan Massie (Photo)

18 APR

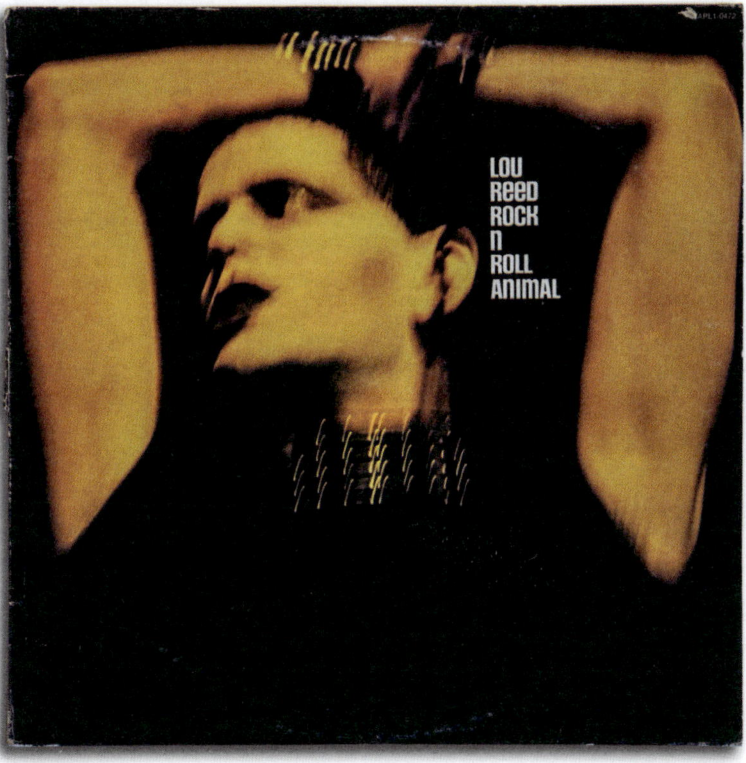

Lou Reed
Rock'n Roll Animal
RCA Victor, 1974
Acy R. Lehman (Design)
Dalrymple (Photo)

19 APR

Black Keys
Turn Blue
Nonesuch Records, 2014
Michael Carney (Design)
Ghoulardi (Illustration)

20 APR

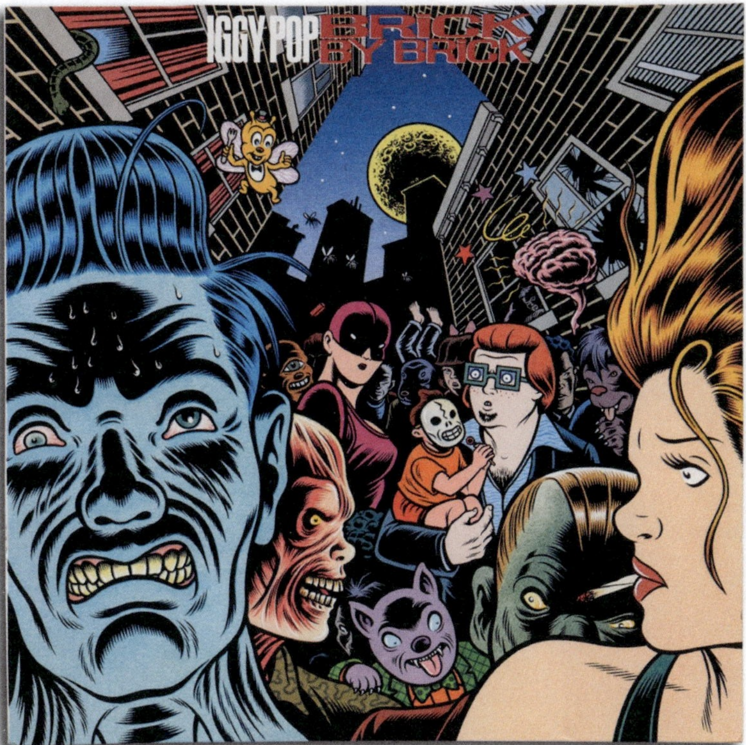

Iggy Pop
Brick By Brick
Virgin Records, 1990
Melanie Nissen (Design)
Charles Burns (Illustration)

* Apr 21st, 1947
James Newell Osterberg
Muskegon (Michigan)

21 APR

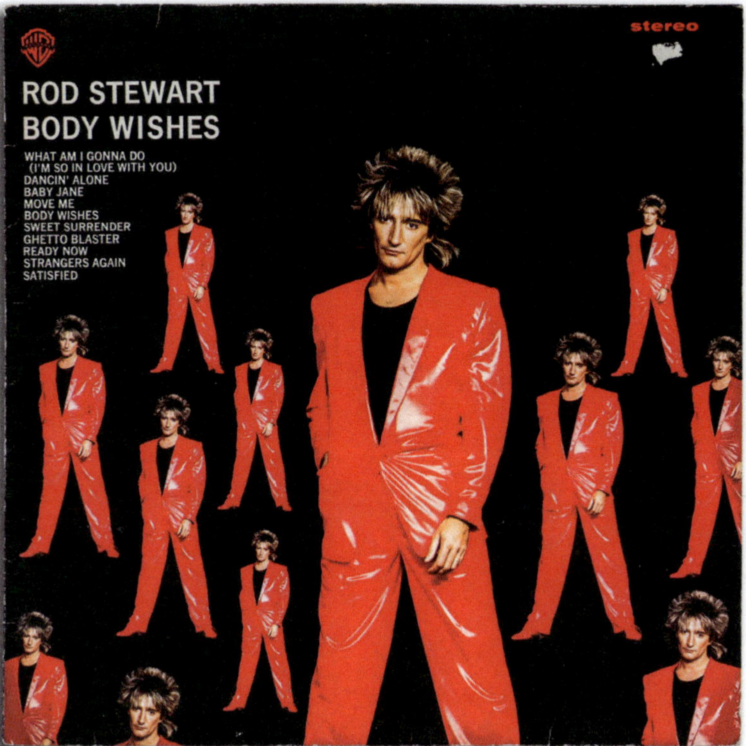

Rod Stewart
Body Wishes
Warner Bros. Records, 1983
Kosh & Ron Larson (Design)
Leon Lecash (Photo)

22 APR

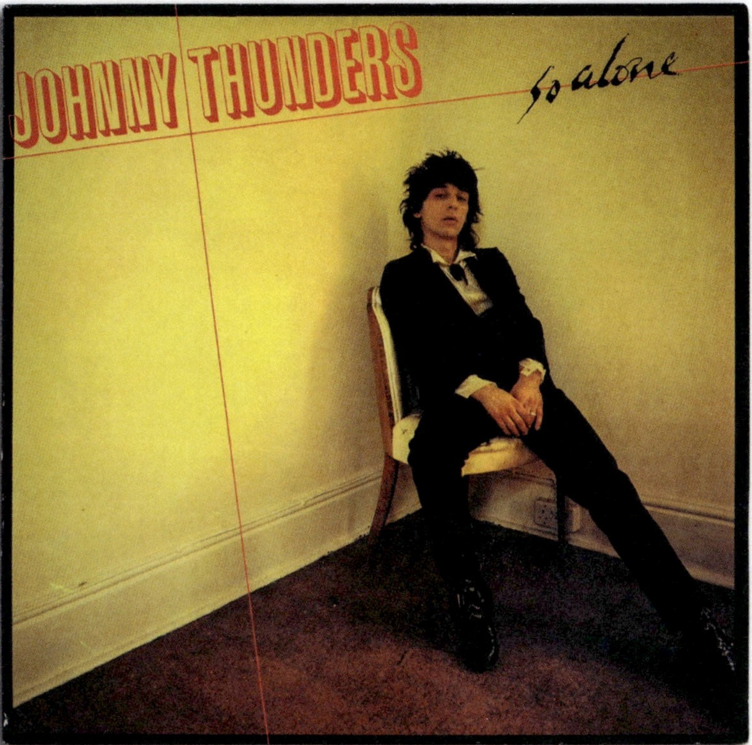

Johnny Thunders
So Alone
Real Records, 1978
Bill Smith (Design)
Peter Gravelle (Photo)

† Apr 23rd, 1991
Johnny Thunders, birth name John Anthony Genzale Jr
New Orleans (Louisiana)

23 APR

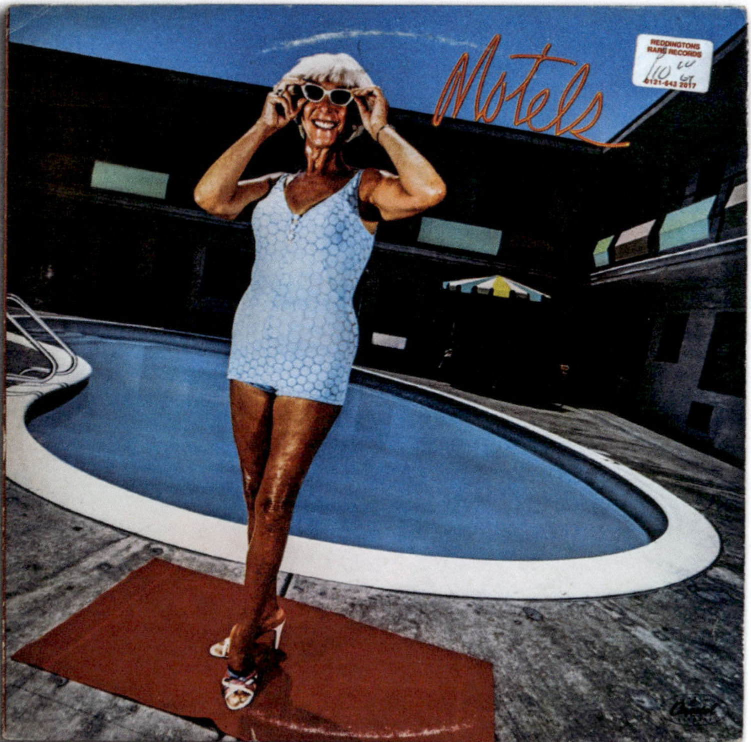

Motels
Capitol Records, 1979
Henry Marquez, Ray Kohara (Design)
Elliot Gilbert (Photo)

24 APR

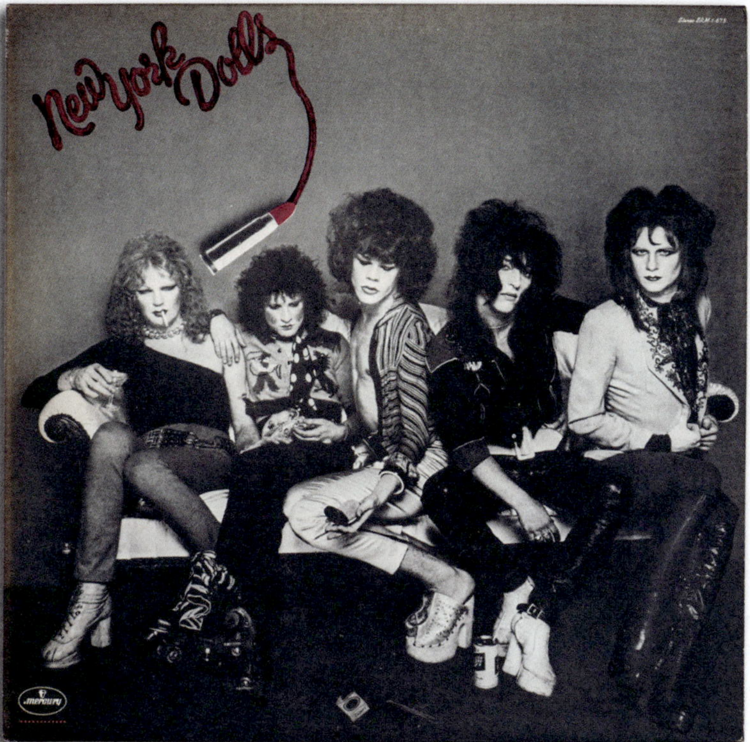

New York Dolls
Mercury Records, 1973
Album Graphics, Inc. (Design)
Toshi (Photo)

25 APR

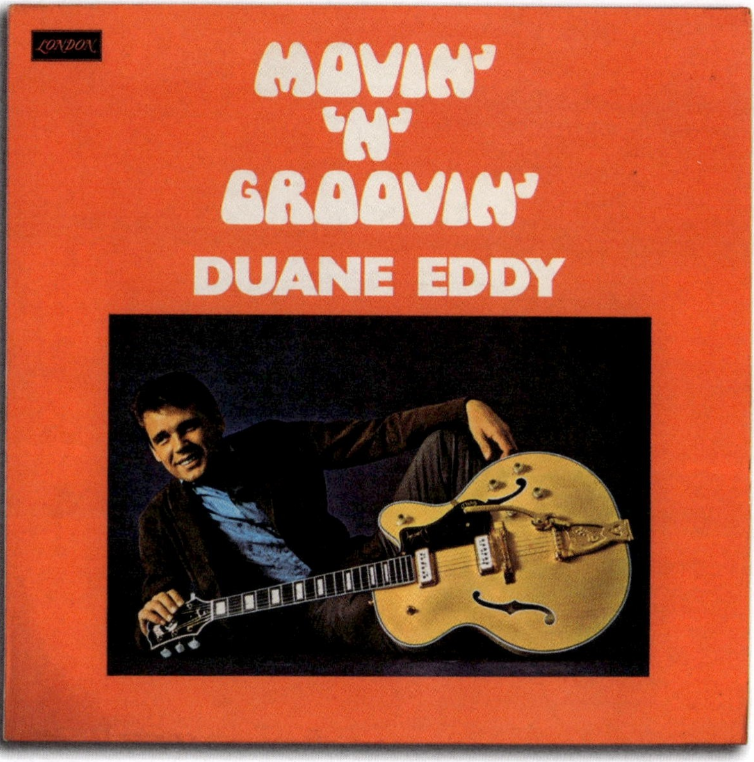

Duane Eddy
Movin'n' Groovin'
London Records, 1970
Cover Artists Unknown

26 APR

* Apr 26th, 1938
Duane Eddy
Coring (New York)

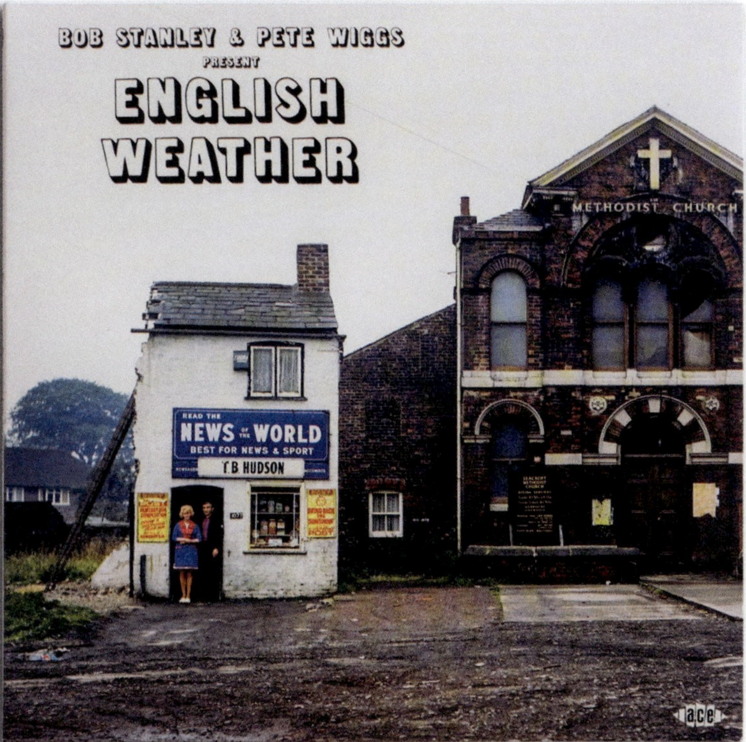

Various Artists
Bob Stanley & Pete Wiggs Pres. English Weather
ACE Records, 2017
Neil Dell at 9thPlanetDesign (Design)
Peter Mitchell (Photo)

27 APR

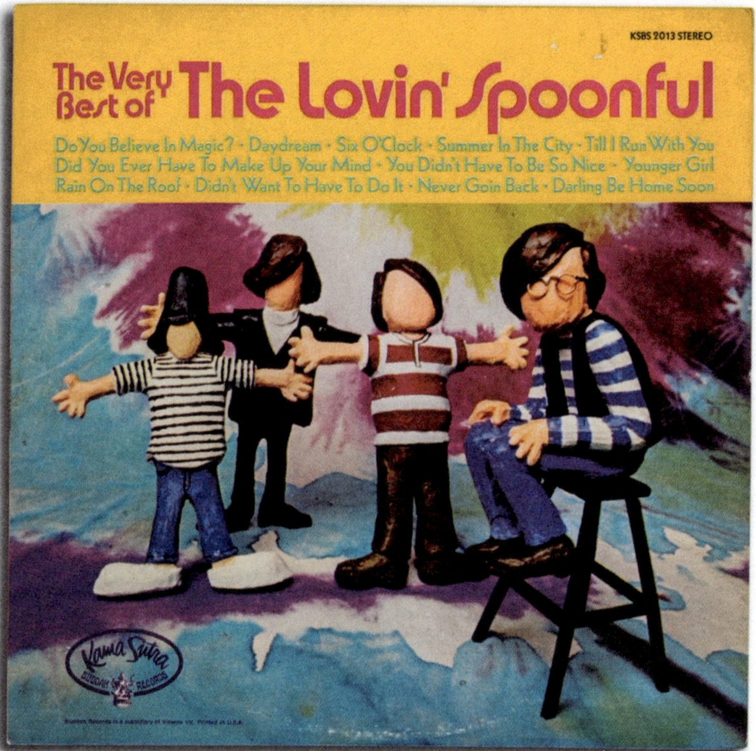

The Lovin' Spoonful
The Very Best Of The Lovin' Spoonful
Kama Sutra, 1970
Silver & Morris (Design)
Ollie Alpert (Photo)

28 APR

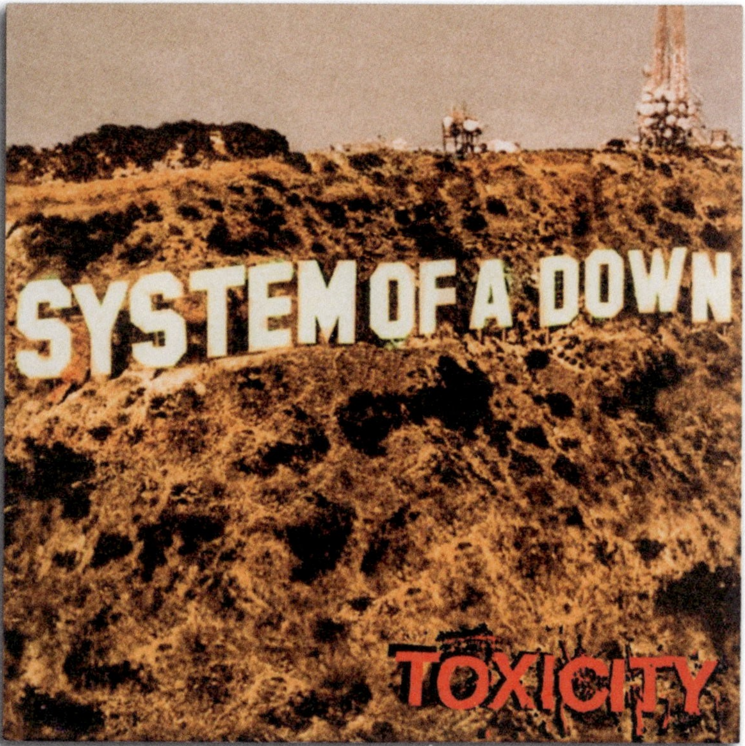

System Of A Down
Toxicity
Columbia Records, 2001
Brandy Flower, Shavo Odadjian (Design)
Mark Wakefield (Photo)

29 APR

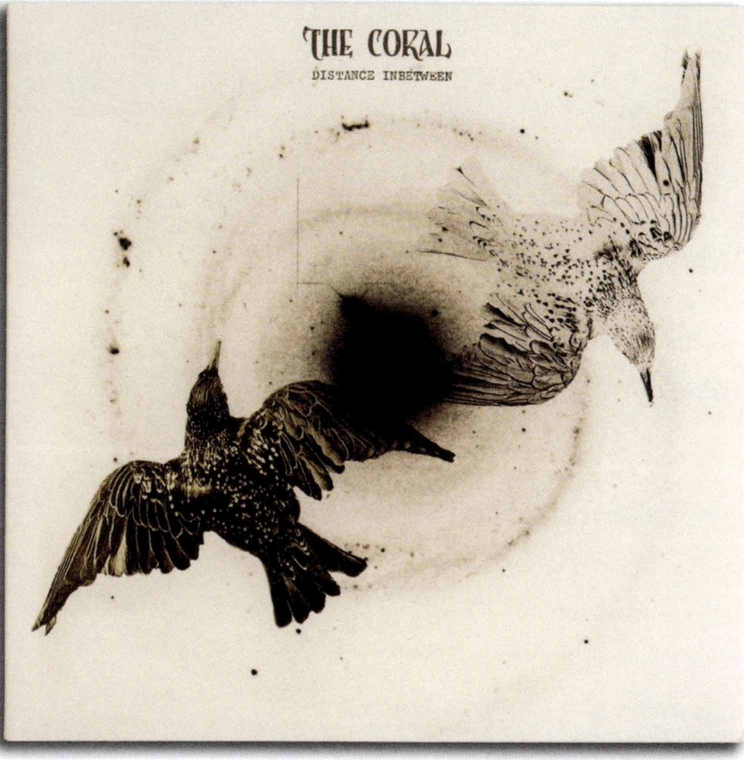

The Coral
Distance In Between
Ignition Records Ltd., 2016
Mike Snowdon (Design)
Ian Skelly & Anna Benson (Photo)

30 APR

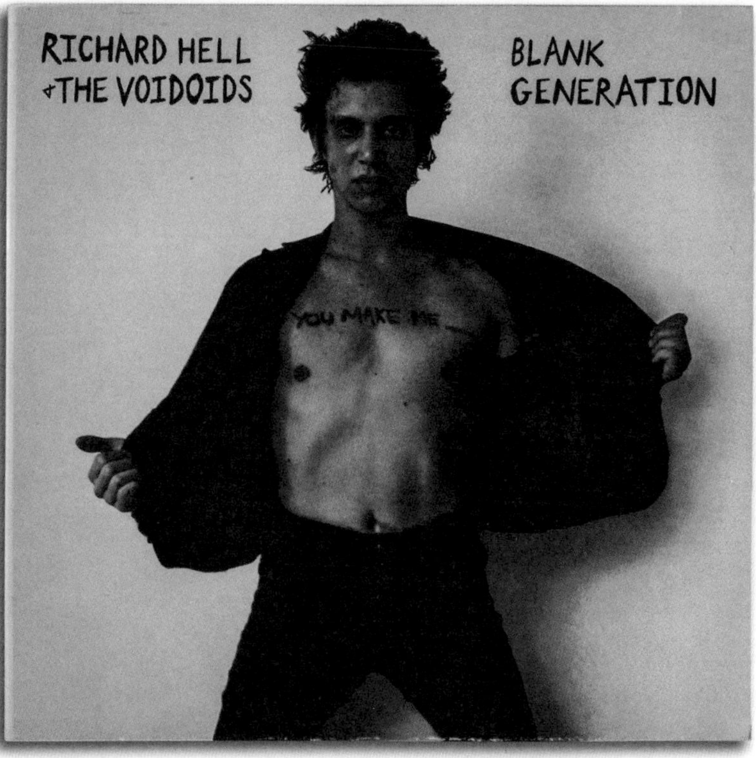

Richard Hell & The Voidoids
Blank Generation
Sire Records, 1977
John Gillespie & Richard Hell (Design)
Robert Bayley (Photo)

01 MAY

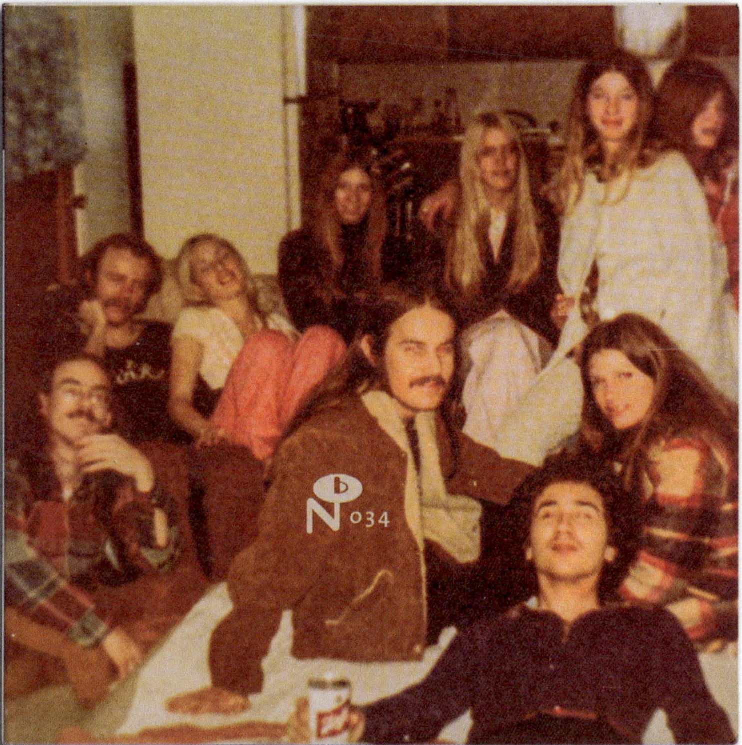

Various Artists
Local Customs: Lone Star Lowlands
Numero Group, 2010
Cover Artists Unknown

02 MAY

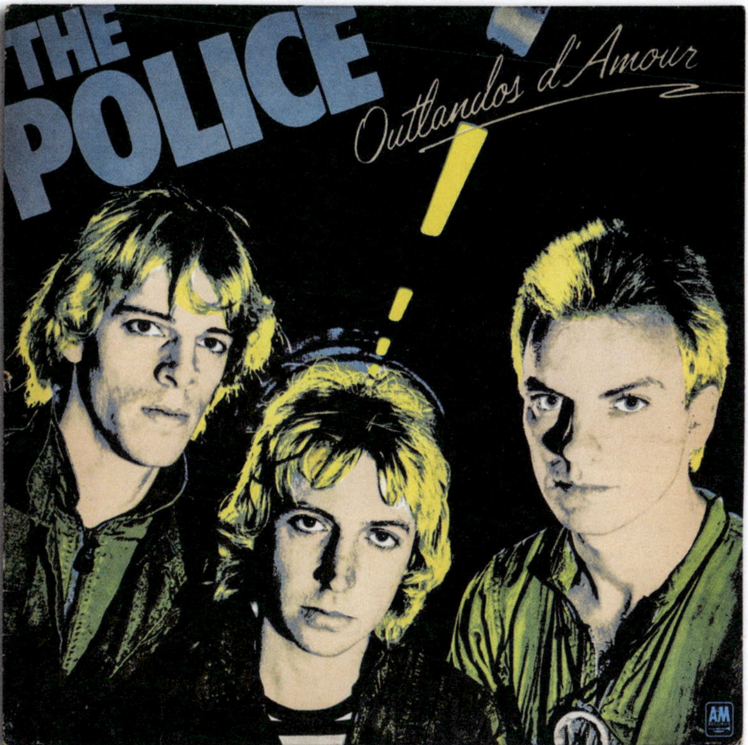

The Police
Outlandos D'Amour
A&M Records, 1978
Michael Ross (Design)
Janette Beckman (Photo)

03 MAY

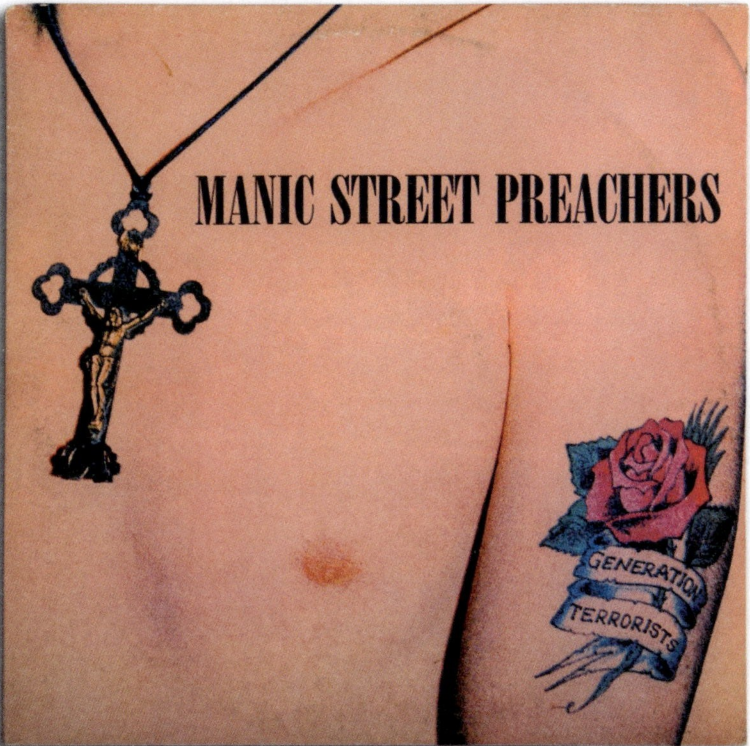

Manic Street Preachers
Generation Terrorists
Columbia Records, 1992
Manic Street Preachers (Photo)

04 MAY

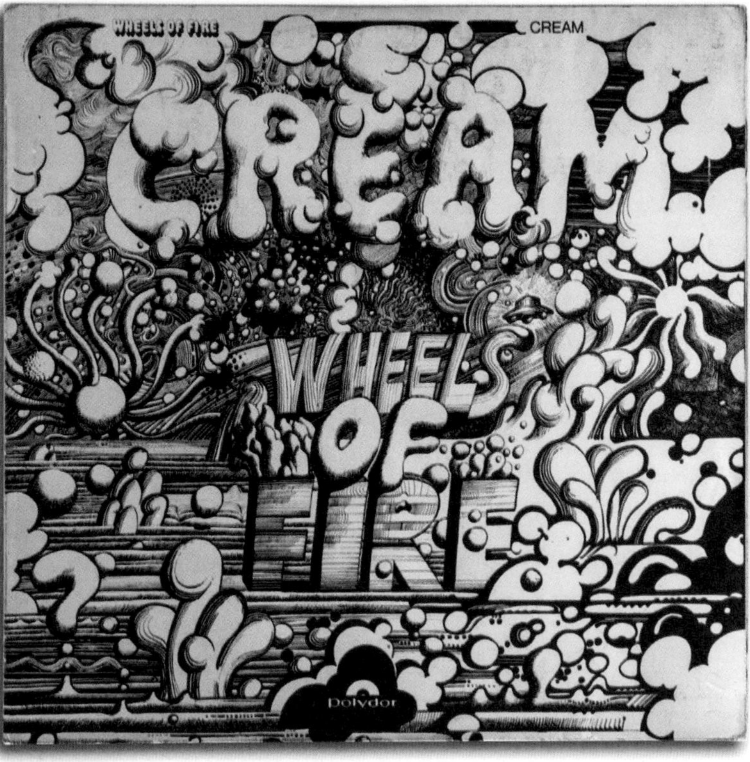

Cream
Wheels Of Fire
Polydor, 1968
Marton Sharp (Design)

05 MAY

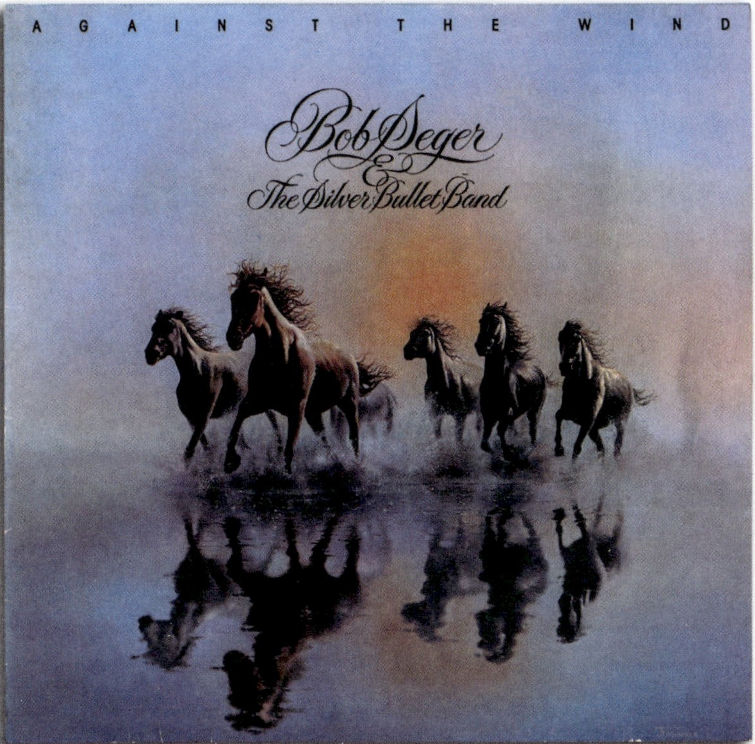

Bob Seger & The Silver Bullet Band
Against The Wind
Capitol Records, 1980
Roy Kohara (Design)
Jim Warren (Illustration)

* May 6th, 1945
Robert Clark Bob Seger
Detroit (Michigan)

06 MAY

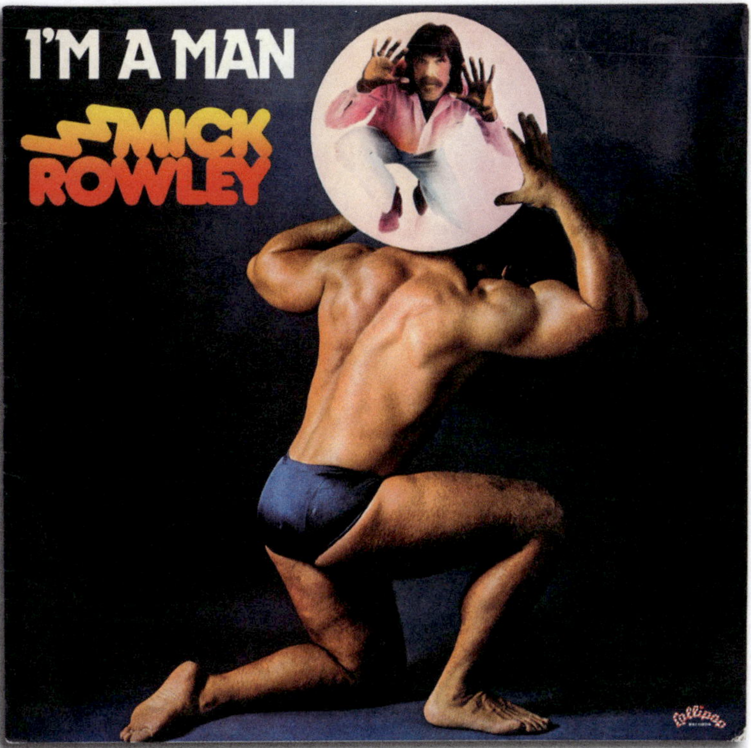

Mick Rowley
I'm A Man
Lollipop Records, 1978
Fessel + Hoffmann (Design)
Falk und Rogner (Photo)

07 MAY

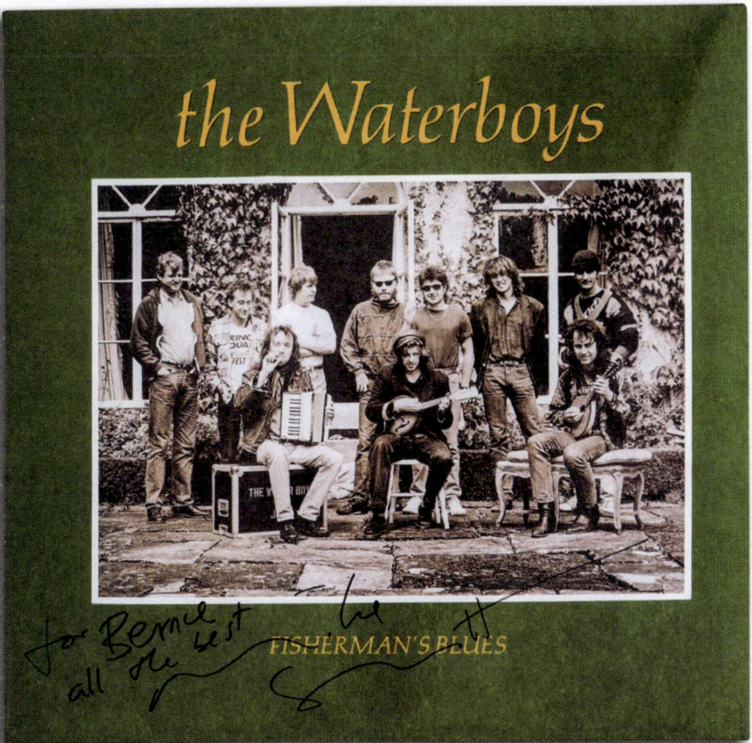

The Waterboys
Fisherman's Blues
Chrysalis Records, 1988
Steve Meany (Photo)

08 MAY

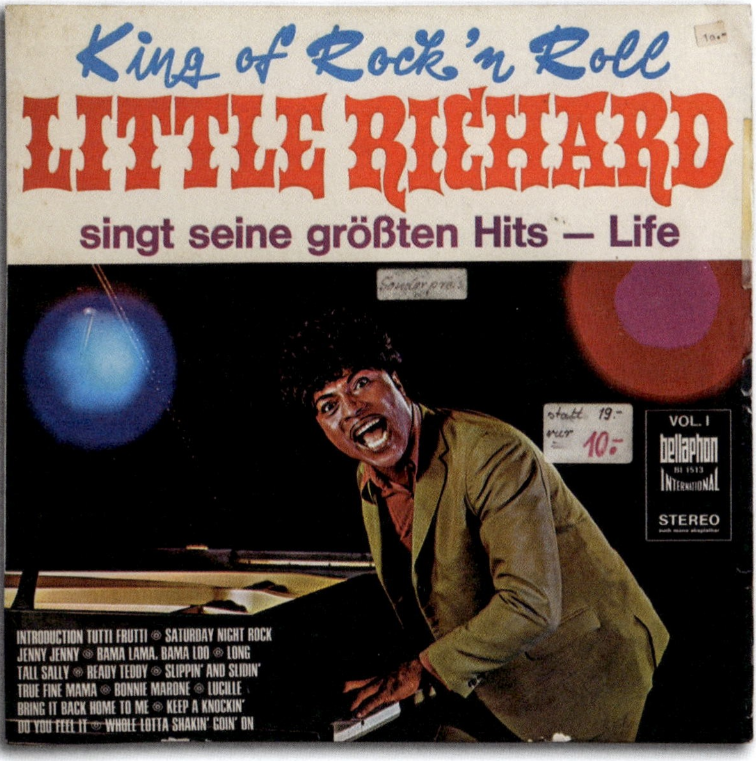

Litte Richard
King of Rock'n Roll
Bellaphon, 1970
Hartmut Wenske (Design)

† May 9th, 2020
Richard Wayne Penniman
Tullahoma (Tennessee)

09 MAY

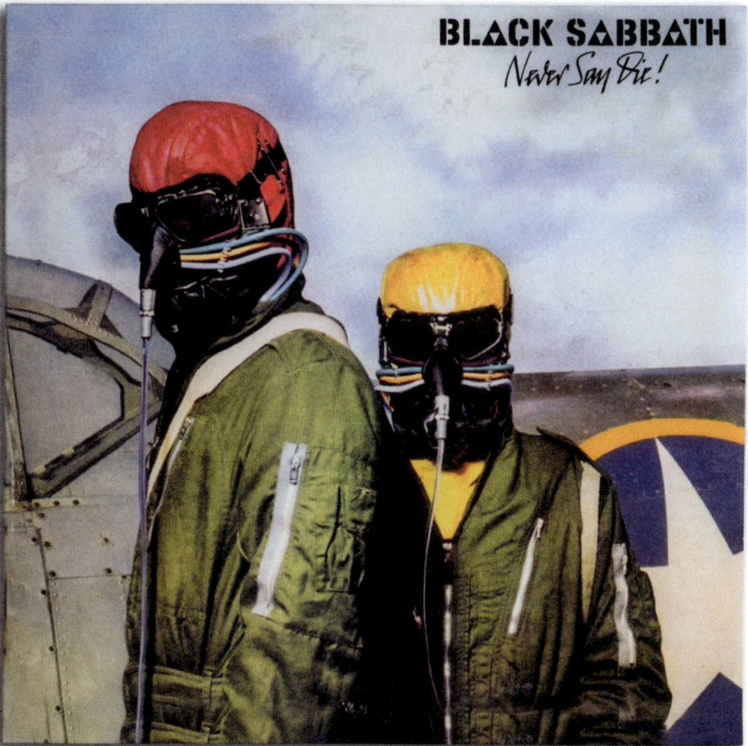

Black Sabbath
Never Say Die!
Sanctuary Records, 1978
Hipgnosis (Design)
Hipgnosis (Photo)

10 MAY

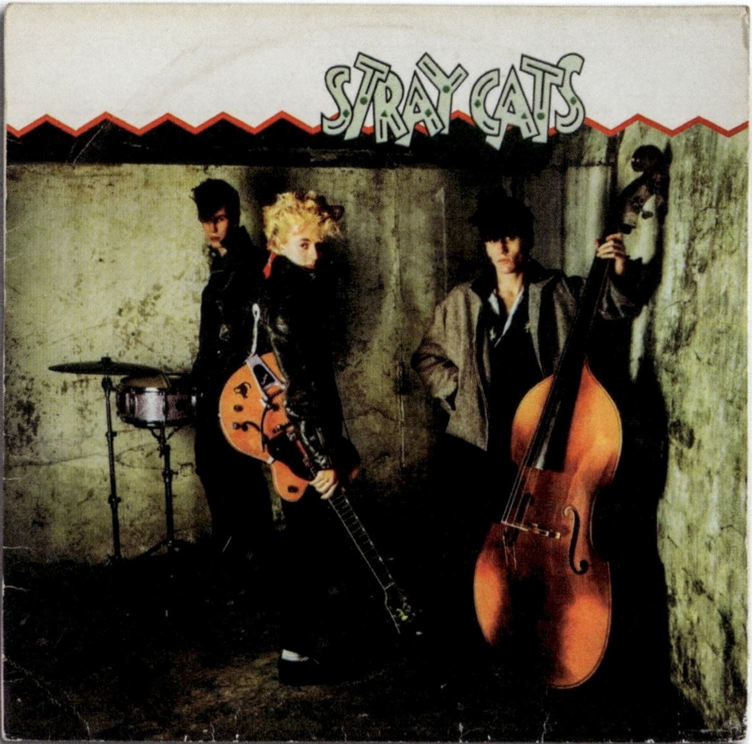

Stray Cats
Arista Records, 1981
Malcolm Garret (Design)
Gavin Cochrane (Photo)

11 MAY

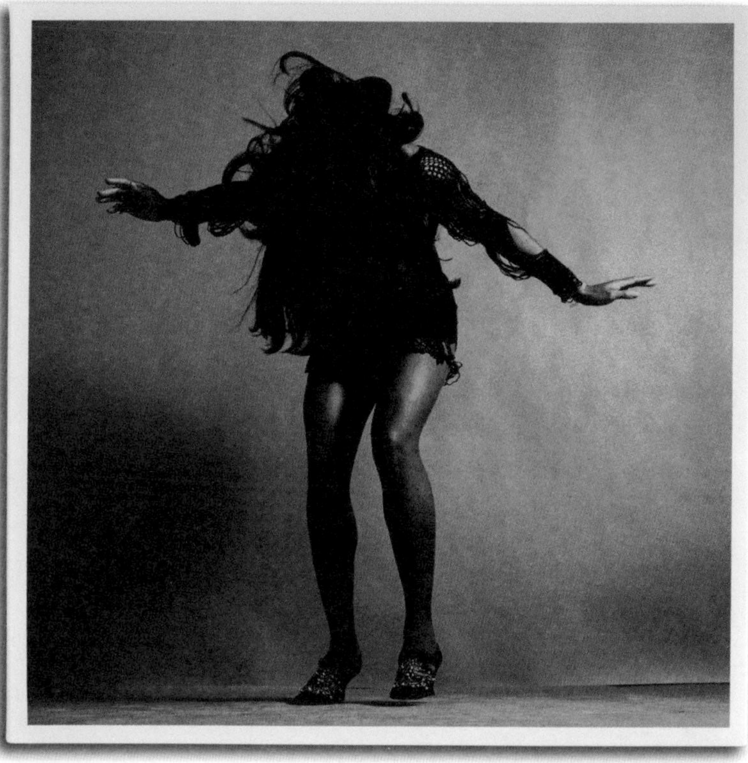

The Last Shadow Puppets
Everything You've Come To Expect
Domino Records, 2016
Matthew Cooper (Design)
Jack Robinson (Photo)

12 MAY

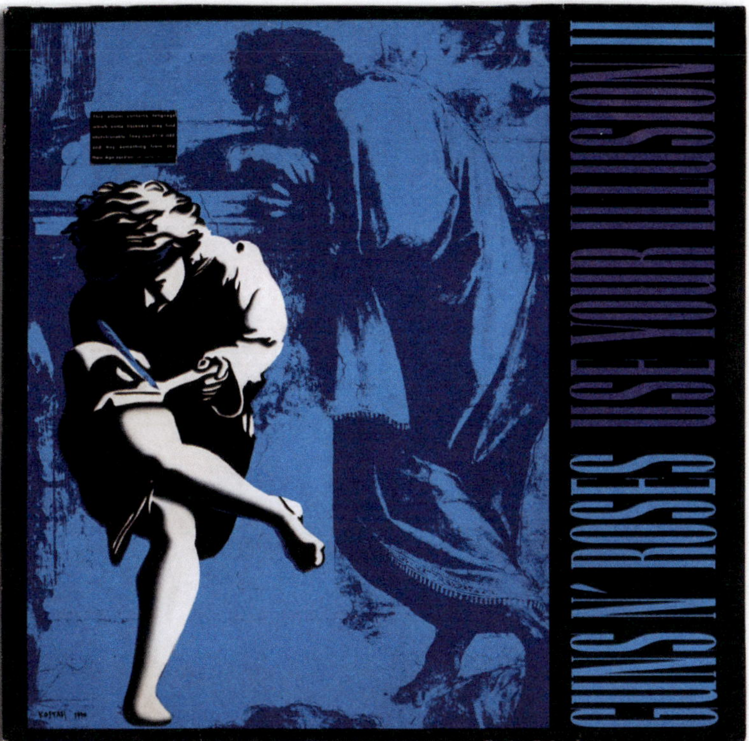

Guns N'Roses
Use Your Illusion II
Geffen Records, 1991
Kevin Reagan (Design)
Mark Kostabi (Illustration)

13 MAY

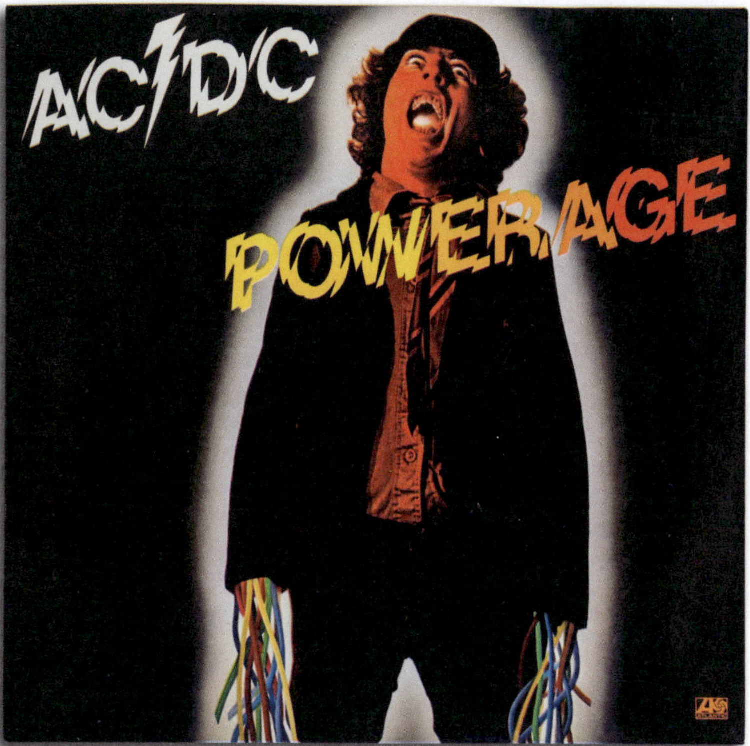

AC/DC
Powerage
Atlantic Records, 1978
Bob Defrin (Design)
Jim Houghton (Photo)

14 MAY

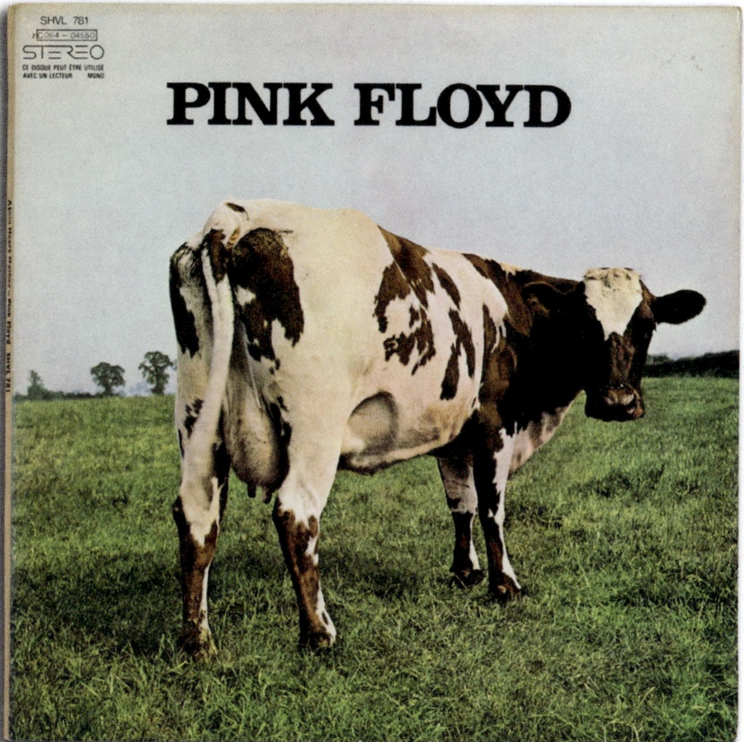

Pink Floyd
Atom Heart Mother
E.M.I. Records, 1970
Hipgnosis (Design)
Hipgnosis (Photo)

15 MAY

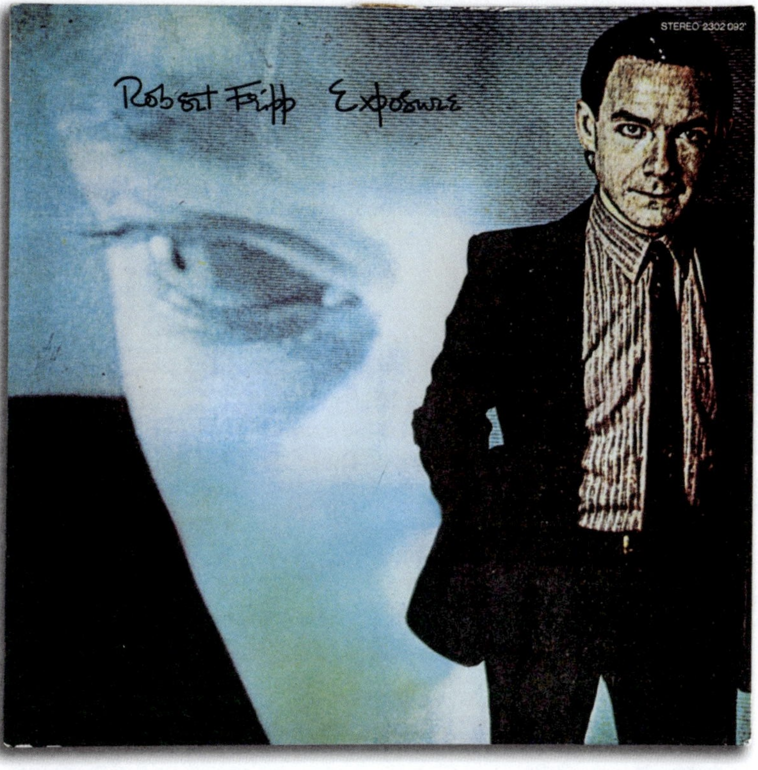

Robert Fripp
Exposure
Polydor, EG Records, 1979
Chris Stein (Design)
Chris Stein (Photo)

* May 16th, 1946
Robert Fripp
Wimborne Minster (Dorset)

16 MAY

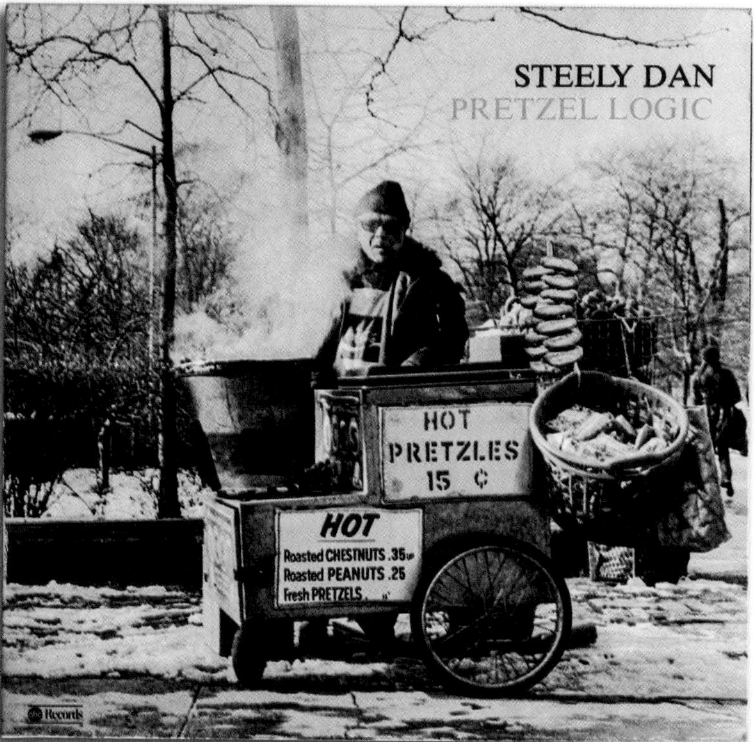

Steely Dan
Pretzel Logic
ABC Records, 1974
Ed Caraeff (Design)
Raenne Rubenstein (Photo)

17 MAY

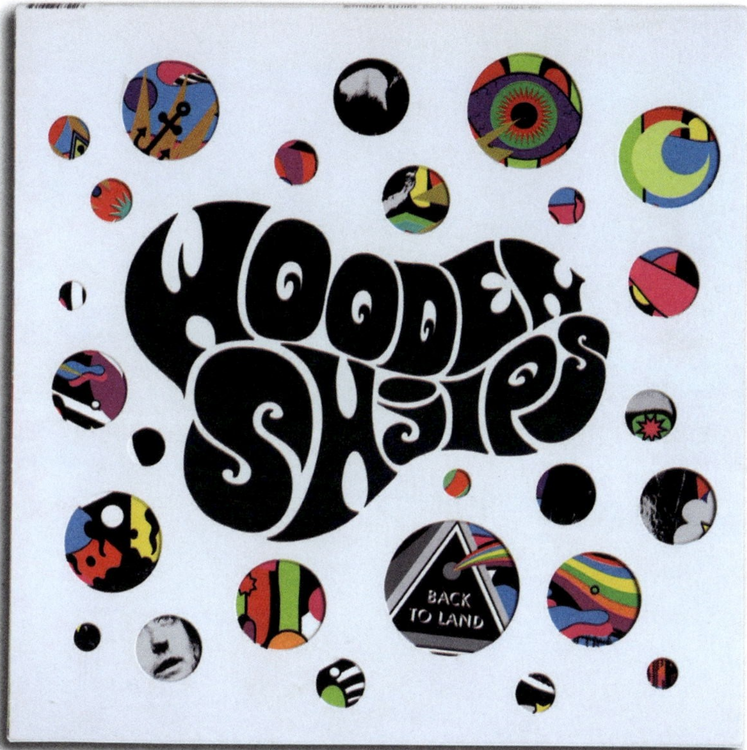

Wooden Shjips
Back to Land
Thrill Jockey Records, 2013
Oliver Hibert (Design)

18 MAY

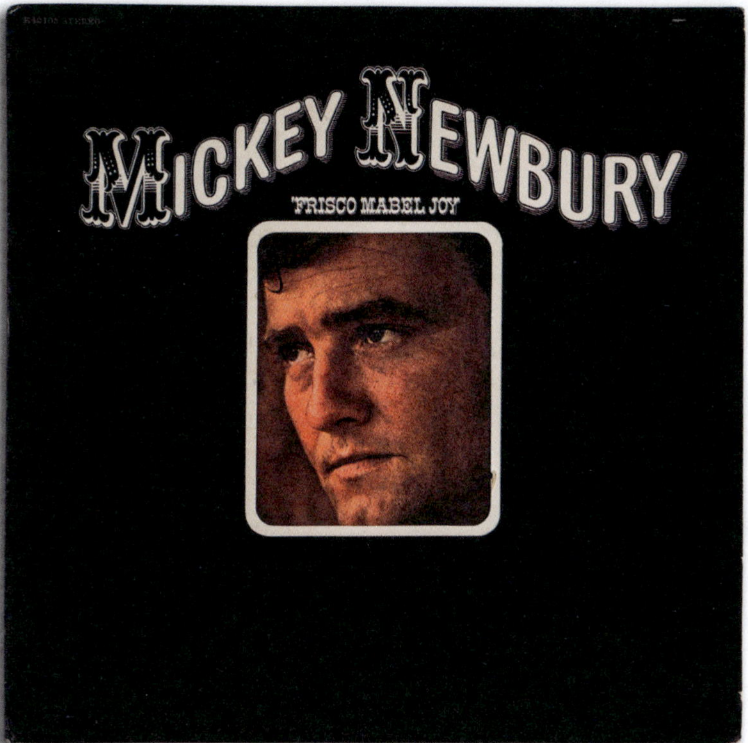

Mickey Newbury
Frisco Mabel Joy
Elektra Record, 1971
Robert L. Heimall (Design)

19 MAY

* May 19th, 1940
Milton Sims "Mickey" Newbury Jr.
Houston (Texas)

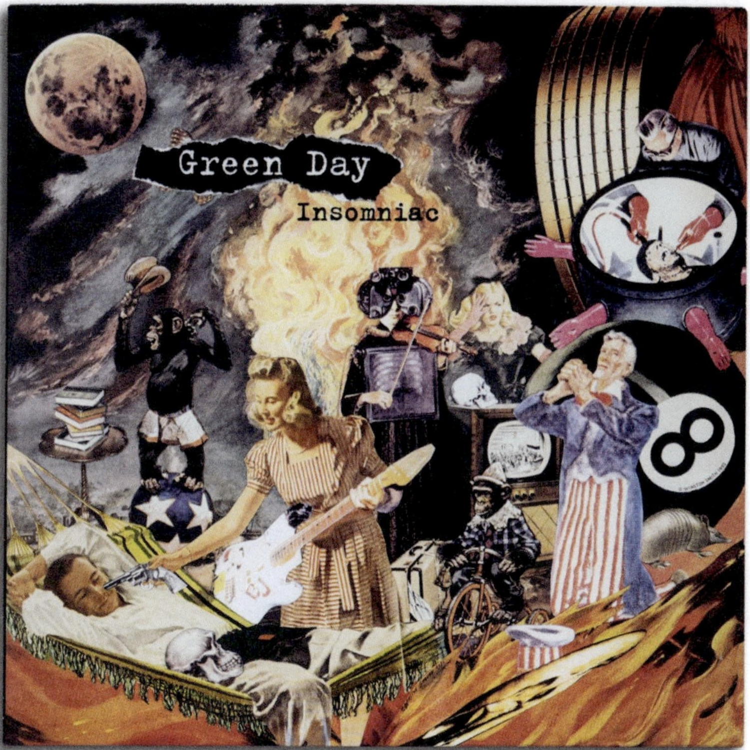

Green Day
Insomniac
Reprise Records, 1995
Dirk Walter (Design)
Winston Smith (Illustration)

20 MAY

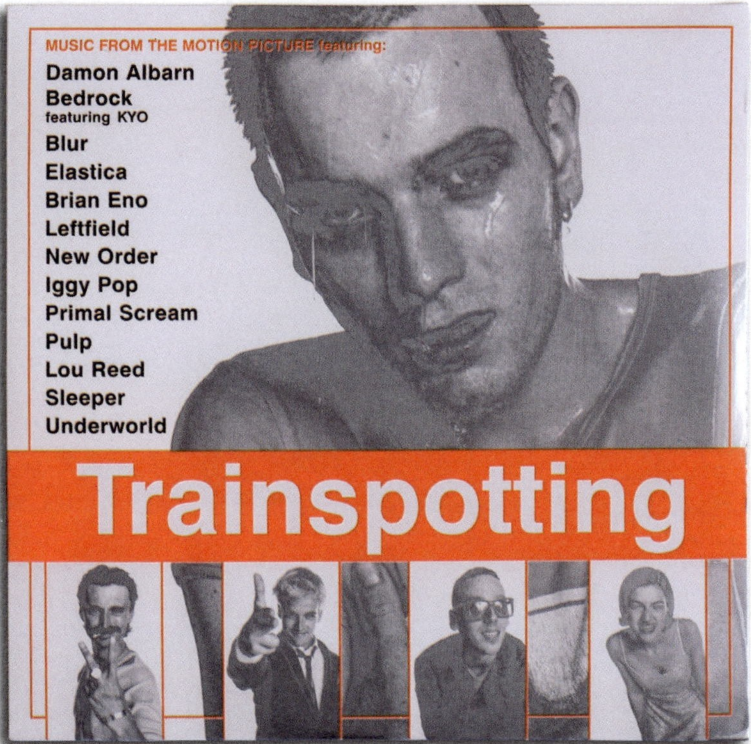

Various Artists – Soundtrack
Trainspotting
EMI Records, 1996
Cover Artists Unknown

21 MAY

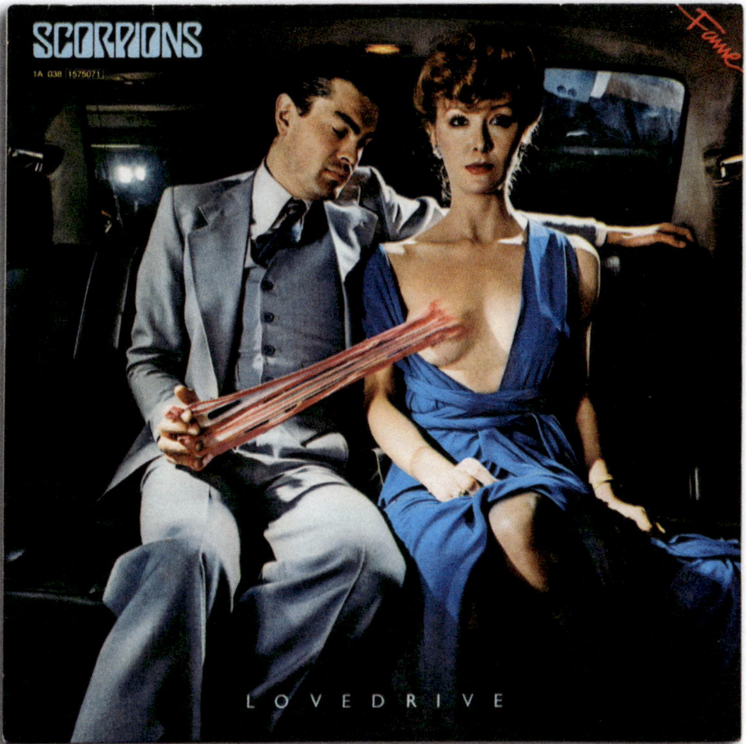

Scorpions
Lovedrive
Harvest, 1979
Hipgnosis (Design)
Hipgnosis (Photo)

22 MAY

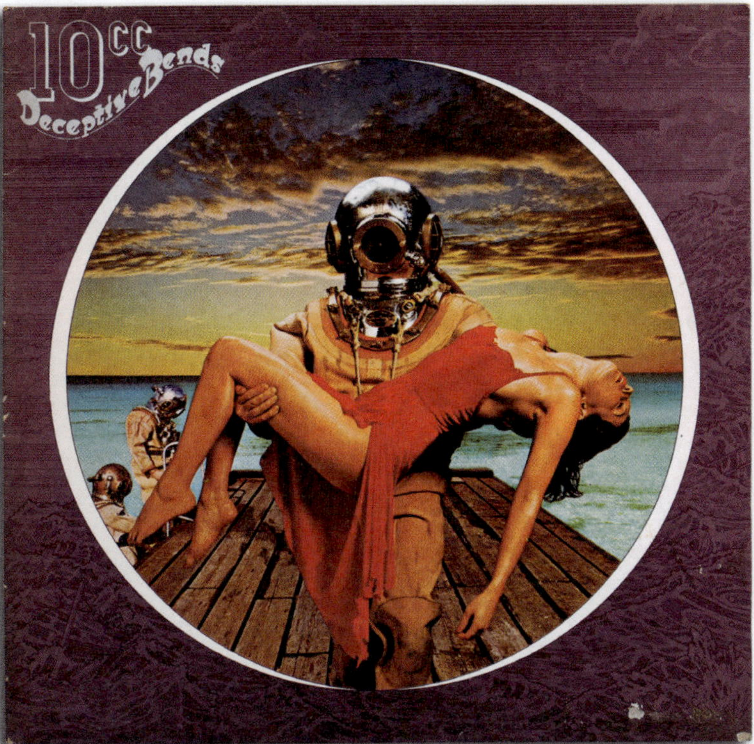

10cc
Deceptive Bends
Mercury Records, 1977
Hipgnosis (Design)
Hipgnosis (Photo)

23 MAY

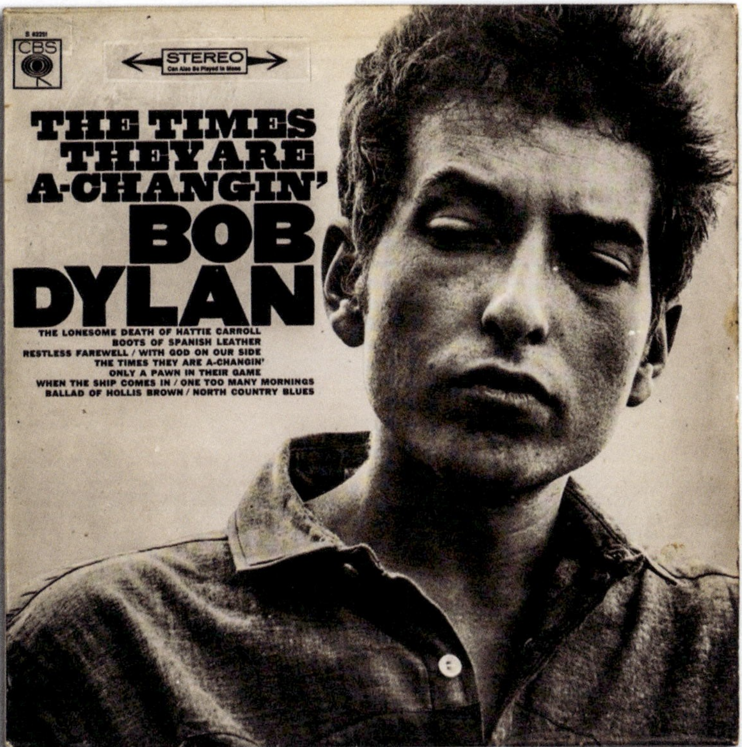

Bob Dylan
The Times They Are A-Changin'
CBS Records, 1964
Barry Feinstein (Photo)

* May 24th, 1941
Bob Dylan
Duluth (Minnesota)

24 MAY

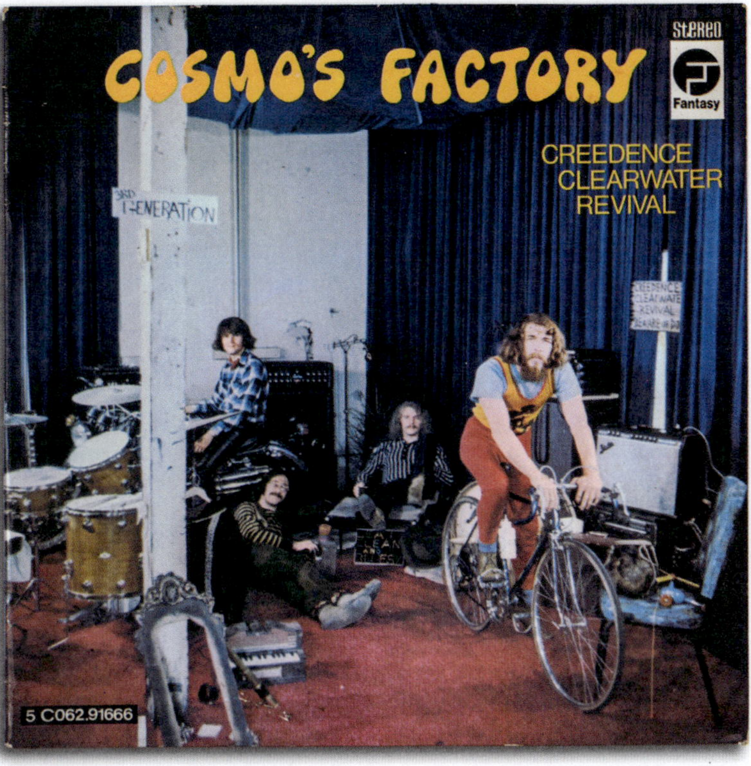

Creedence Clearwater Revival
Cosmo's Factory
Liberty, 1970
Richard Taddel (Design)
Bob Fogerty (Photo)

25 MAY

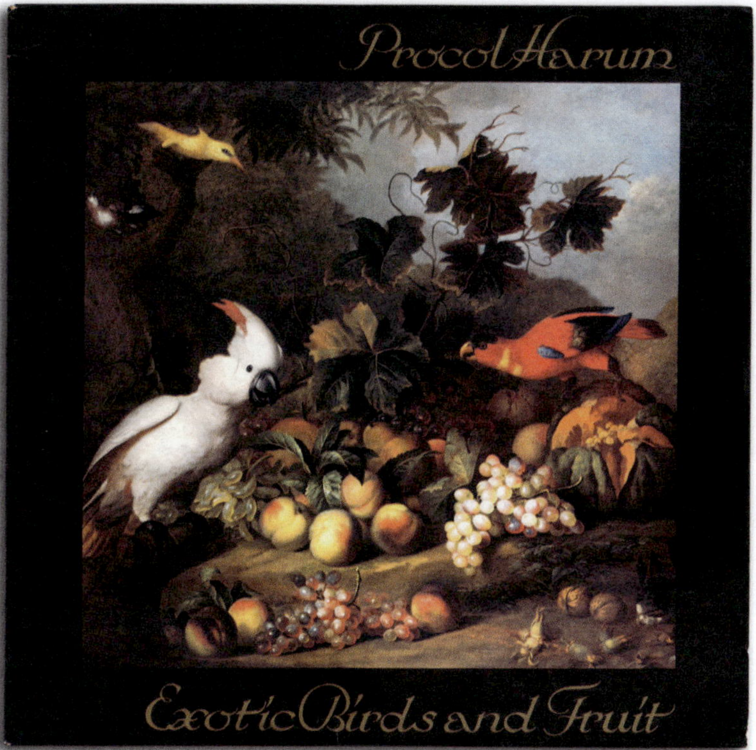

Procol Harum
Exotic Birds and Fruit
Chrysalis Records Ltd., 1974
Jakob Bogdani 1670–1724 (Painting)

26 MAY

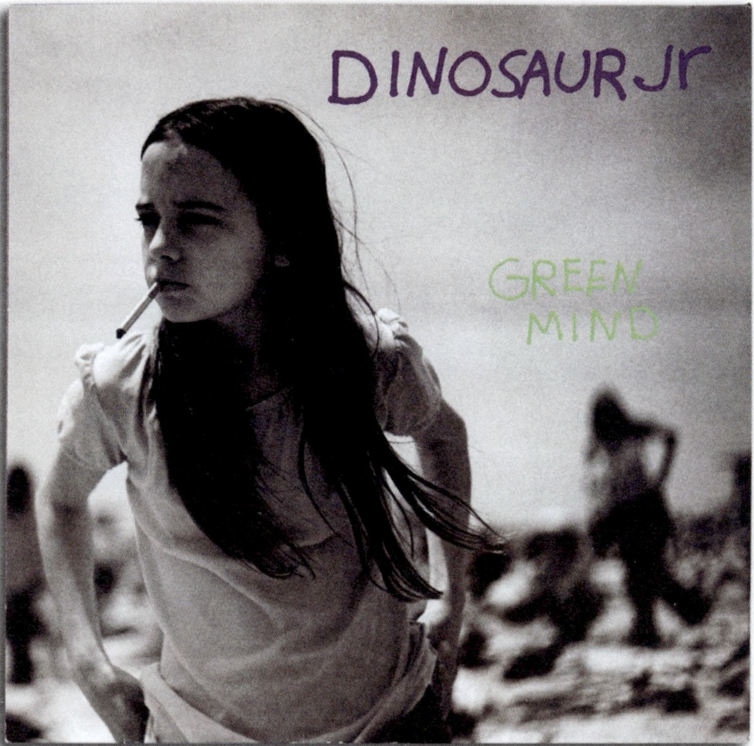

Dinosaur Jr.
Green Mind
Blanco Y Negro, 1991
Joseph Szabo (Photo)

27 MAY

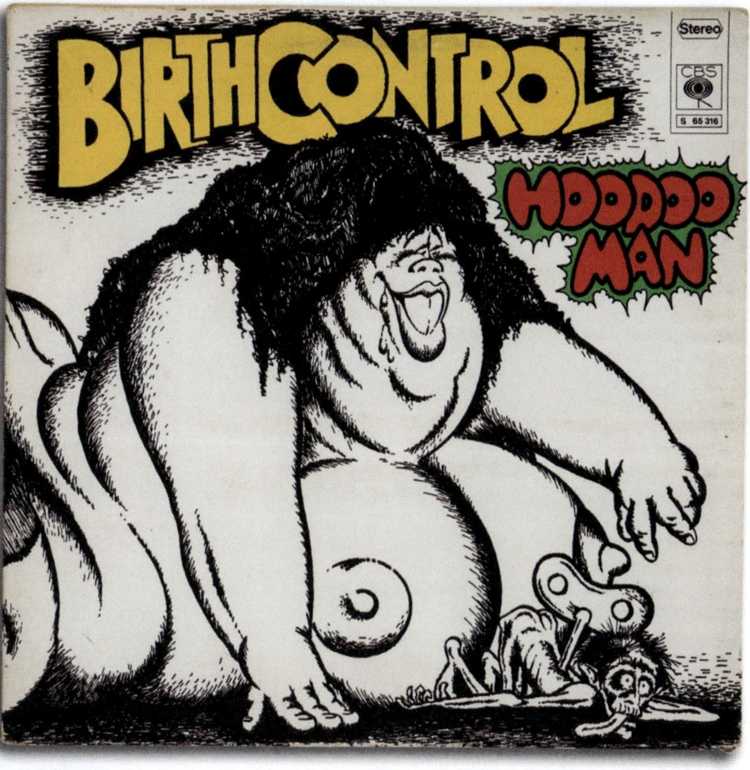

Birth Control
Hoodoo Man
CBS Records, 1973
Heinz Dofflein (Design)

28 MAY

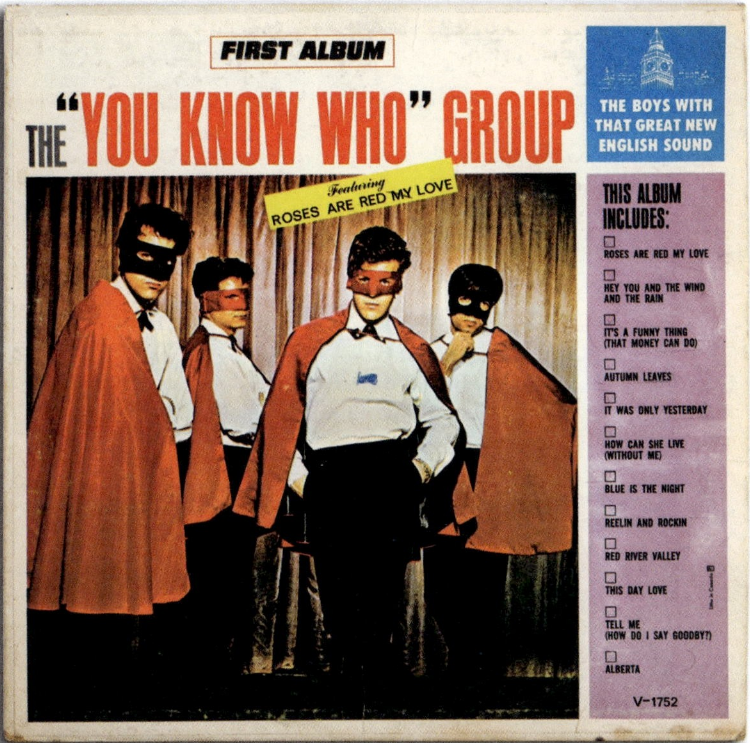

"The Know Who" Group
First Album
Quality Records Ltd., 1965
Cover Artists Unknown

29 MAY

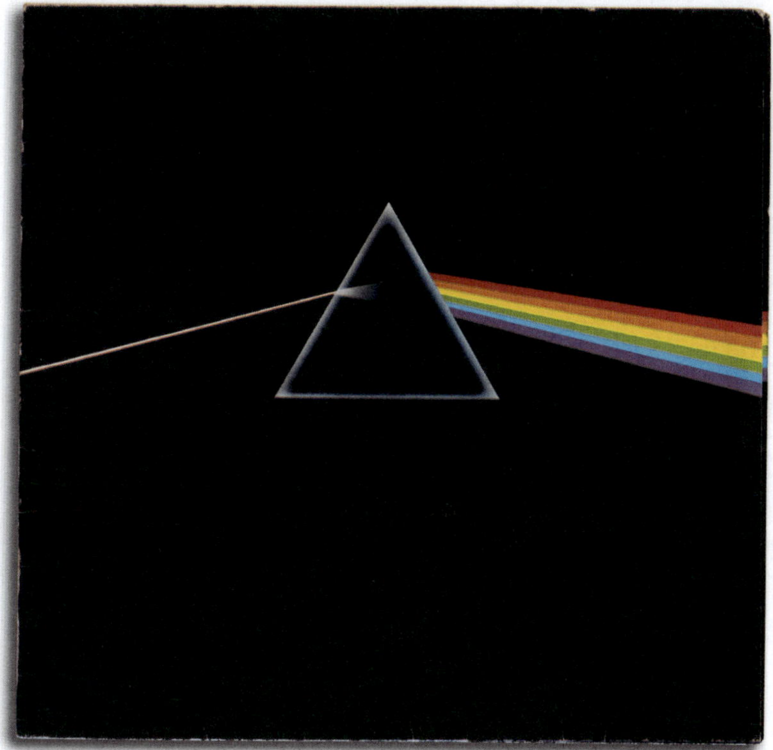

Pink Floyd
The Dark Side Of The Moon
EMI Electrola, 1973
Hipgnosis (Design)

30 MAY

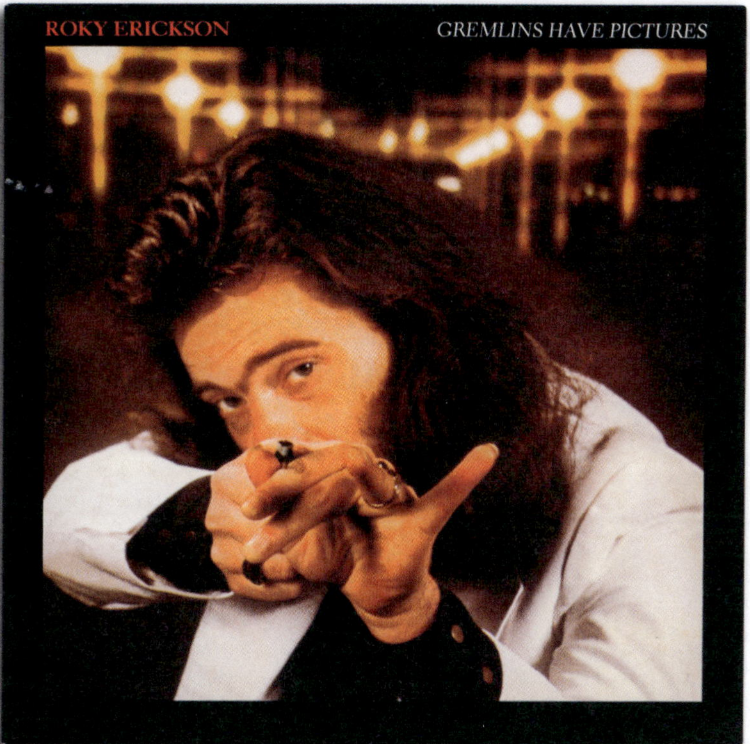

Roky Erikson
Gremlins Have Pictures
Demon Records, 1986
Michael Krage (Design)

31 MAY

† May 31st, 2019
Roger Kynard "Roky" Erickson
Austin (Texas)

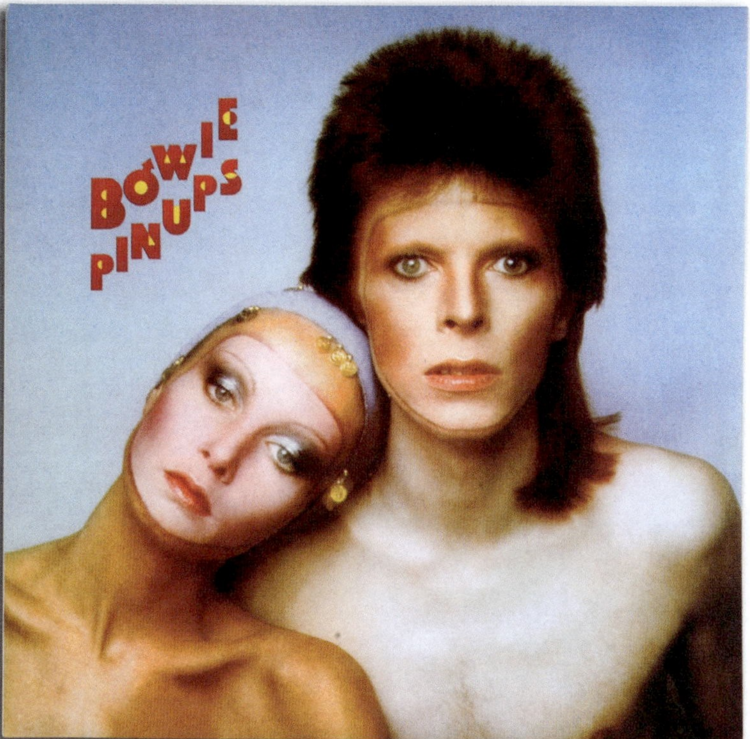

David Bowie
Pinups
RCA Victor, 1973
Pierre Laroche (Design)
Justin De Villeneuve (Photo)

01 JUN

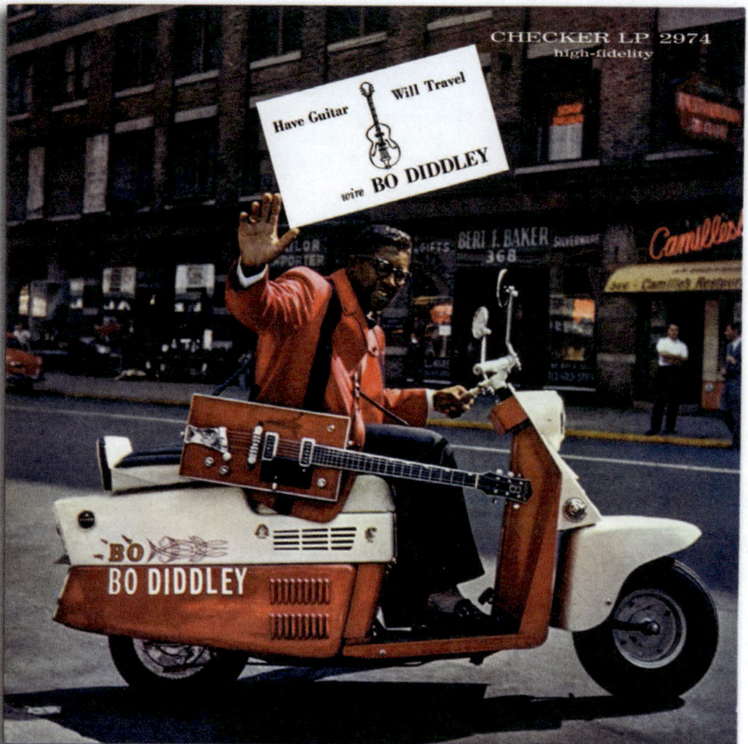

Bo Diddley
Have Guitar Will Travel
Checker Record Corp., 1960
Cover Artists Unknown

† Jun 2nd, 2008
Ellas McDaniel
Archer (Florida)

02 JUN

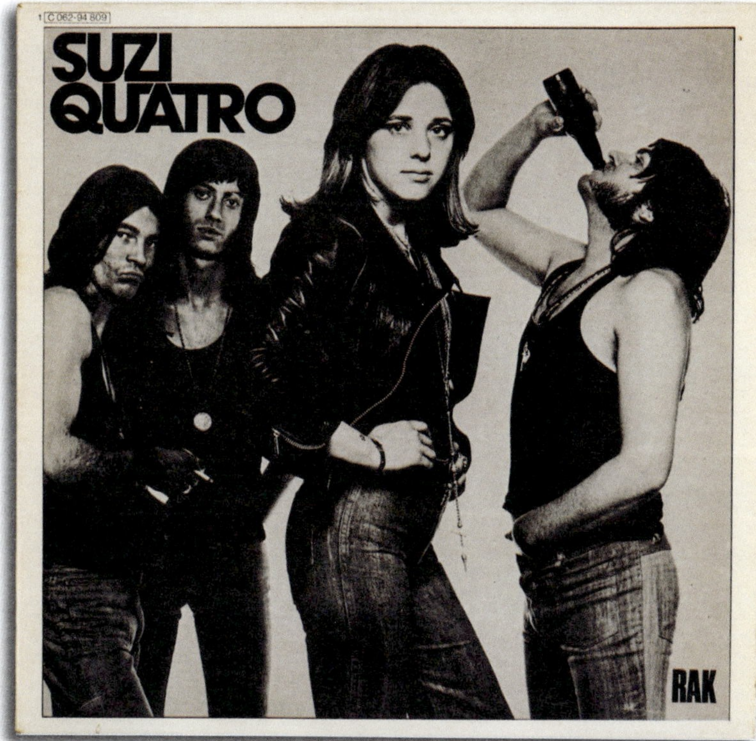

Suzi Quatro
RAK, 1973
Gered Mankowitz (Photo)

03 JUN

* Jun 3rd, 1950
Susan "Suzi" Kay Quatro
Detroit (Michigan)

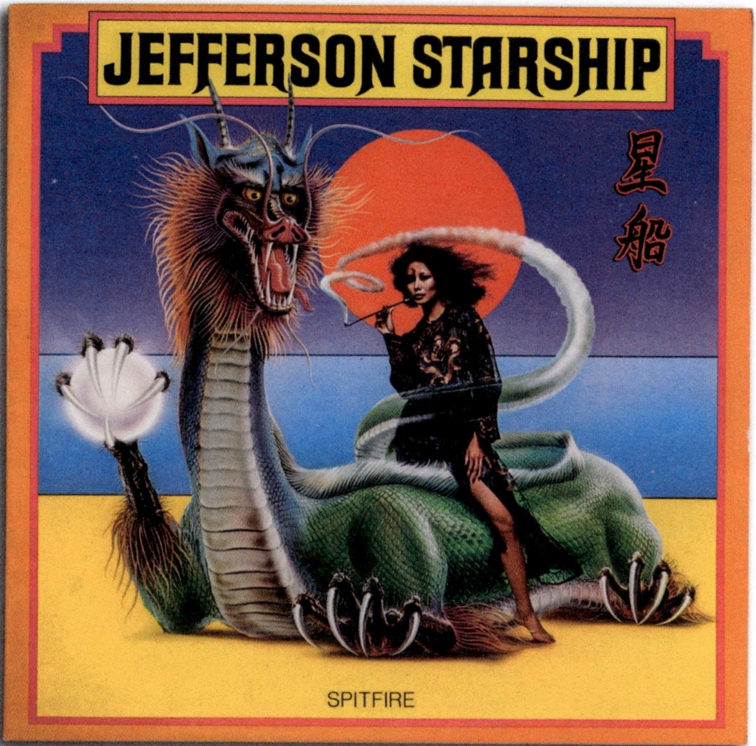

Jefferson Starship
Spitfire
RCA Records, 1976
John Langdon (Design)
Shusei Nagoka (Illustration)

04 JUN

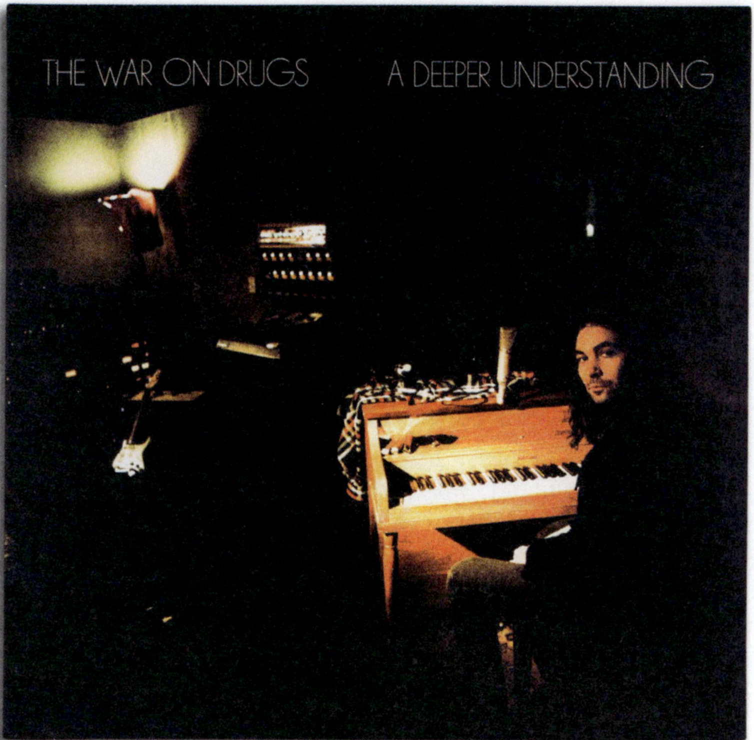

The War on Drugs
A Deeper Understanding
Atlantic Records, 2017
Adam Granduciel & Rob Carmichael (Design)
Dusdin Condren (Photo)

05 JUN

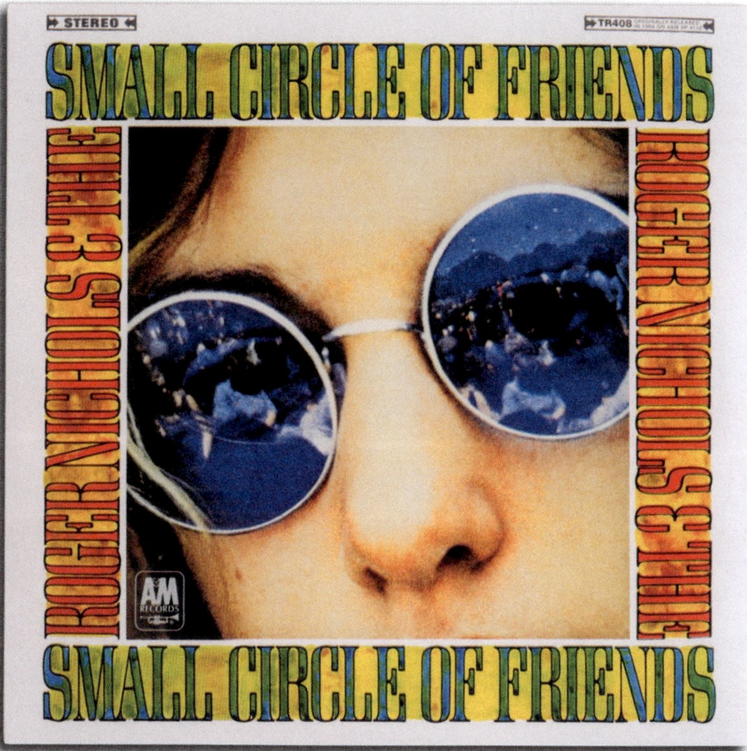

Roger Nichols & The Small Circle Of Friends
Tapete Records, 2018
Tom Wilkes (Design)

06 JUN

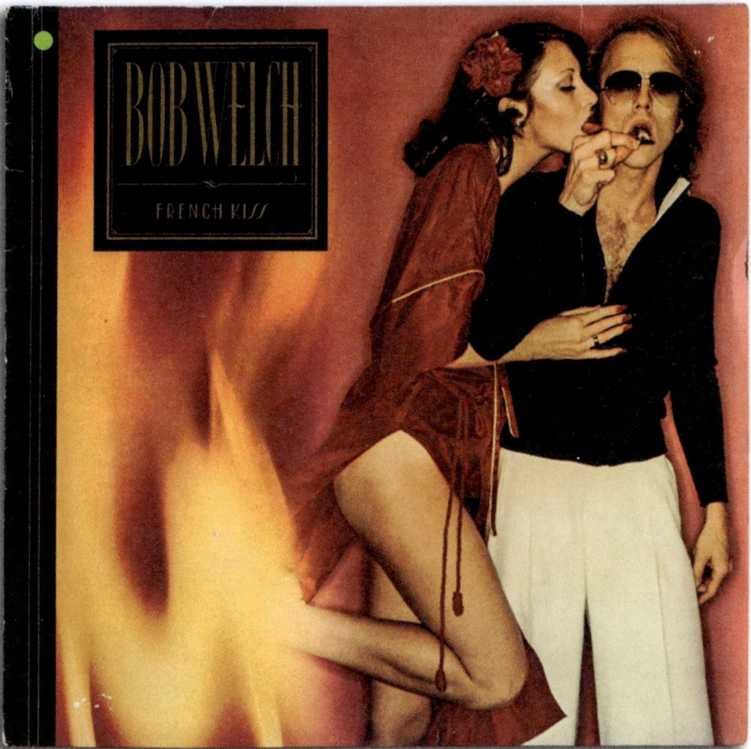

Bob Welch
French Kiss
Capitol Records, 1977
Roy Kohara (Design)
Olivier Ferrand / Daniel Catherine (Photo)

† Jun 7th, 2012
Bob Welch
Nashville (Tennessee)

07 JUN

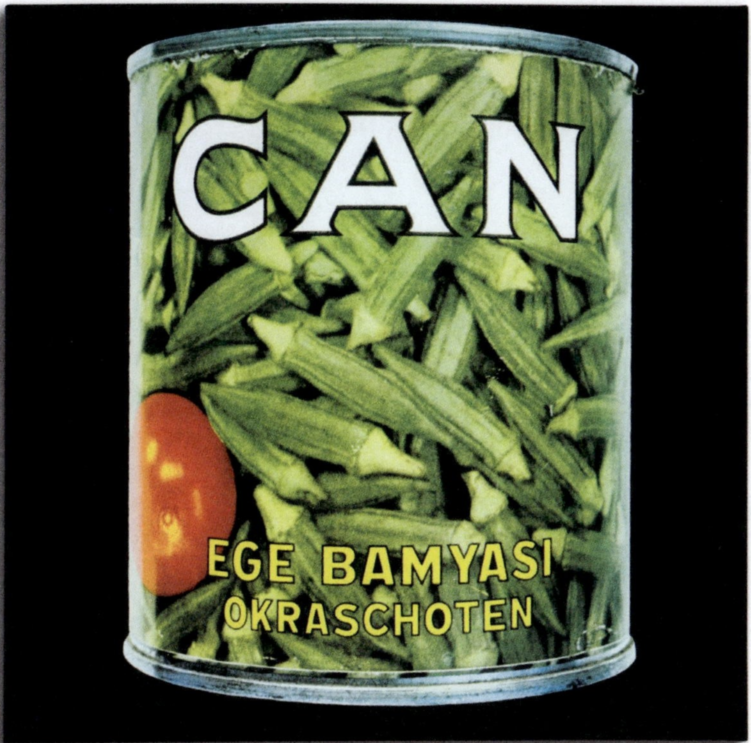

CAN
Ege Bamyasi
Spoon Records, 1972
Ingo Trauer & Richard J. Rudow (Design)

08 JUN

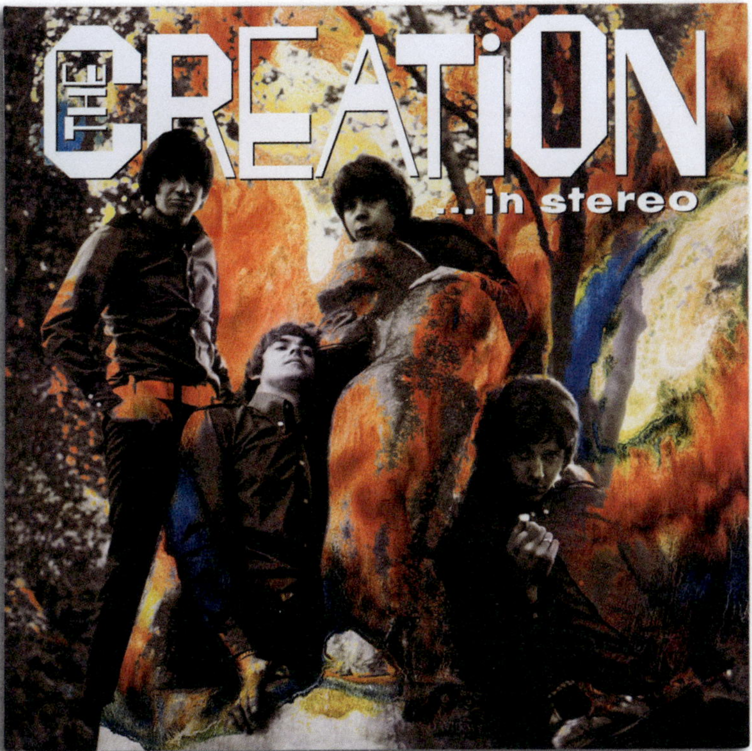

The Creation
In Stereo
Demon Records, 2021
Phil Smee (Design)

09 JUN

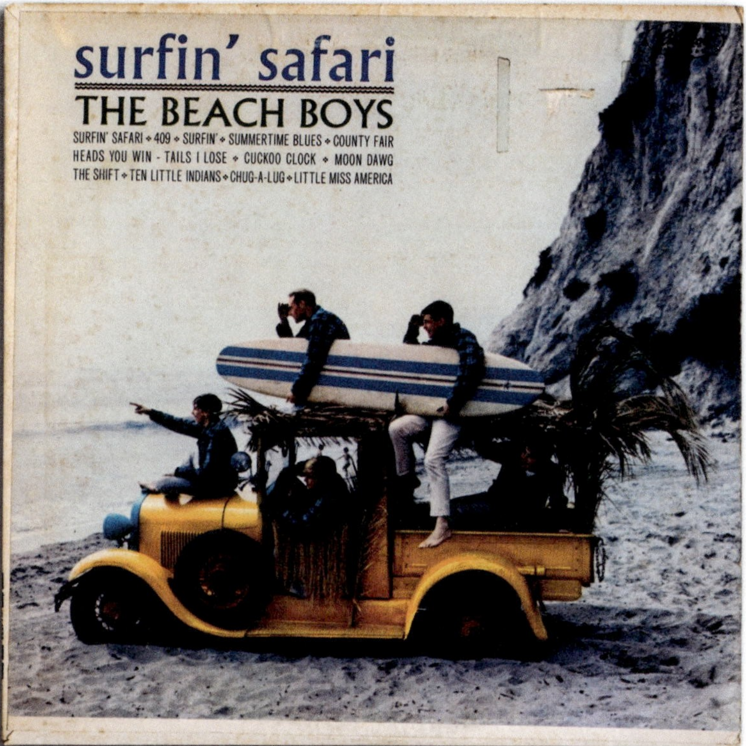

The Beach Boys
Surfin' Safari
Capitol Records, 1962
Ken Veeder, Capitol Photo Studio (Photo)

10 JUN

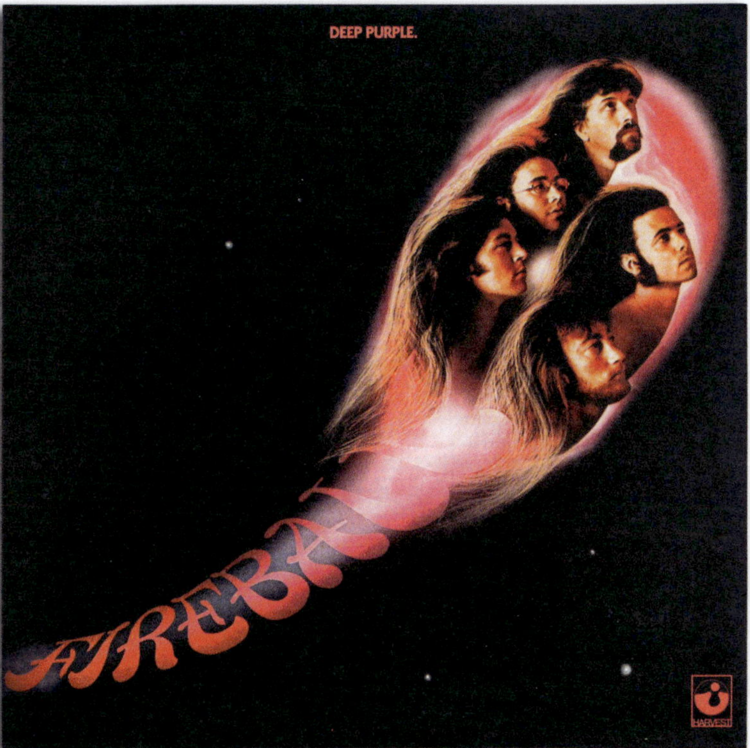

Deep Purple
Fireball
Harvest, 1971
Castle, Chappell & Partners Limited (Design)
Tony Burrett (Photo)

11 JUN

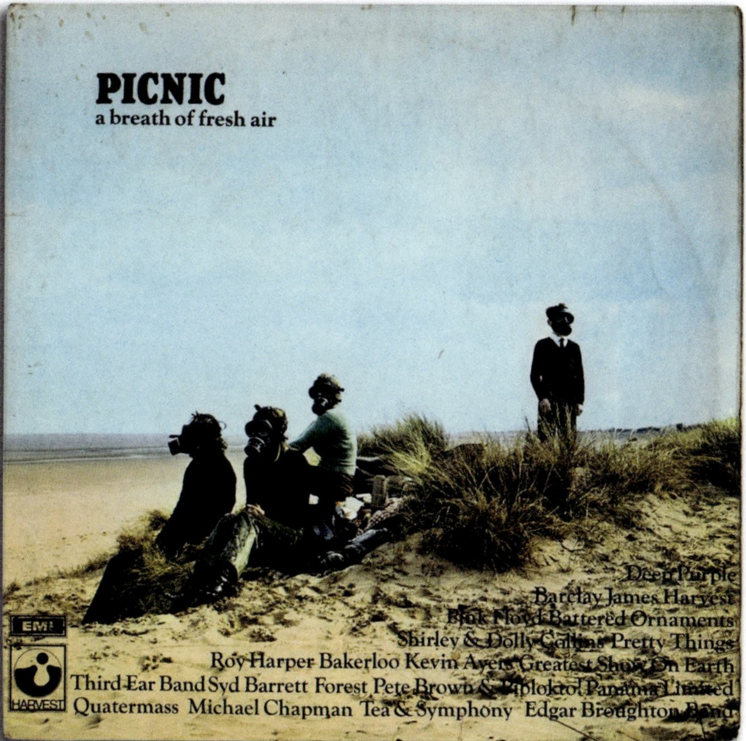

Various Artists
Picnic A Breath Of Fresh Air
Harvest, 1970
Hipgnosis (Design)
Hipgnosis (Photo)

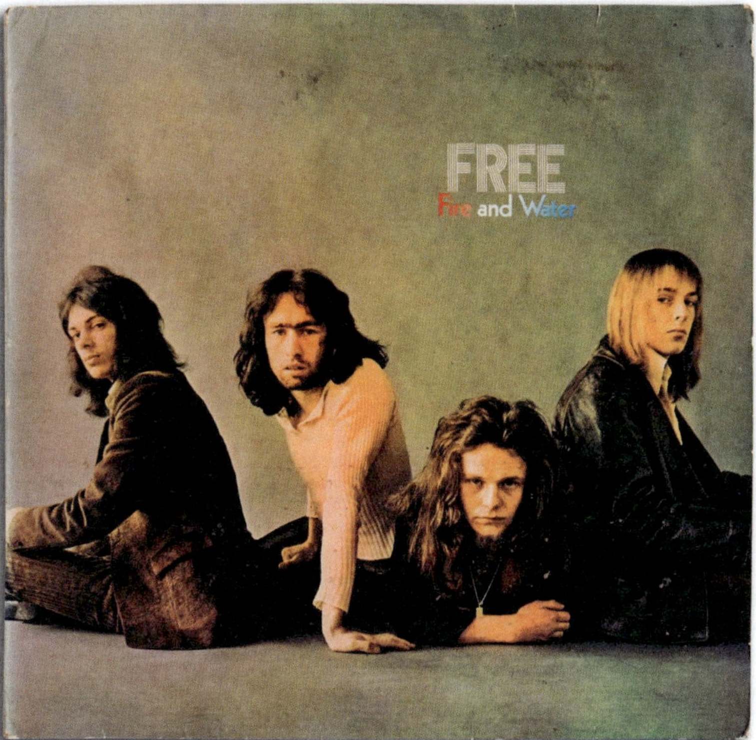

Free
Fire And Water
Island Records Ltd., 1970
Mike Sida (Design)
Hiroshi / Richard Polak (Photo)

13 JUN

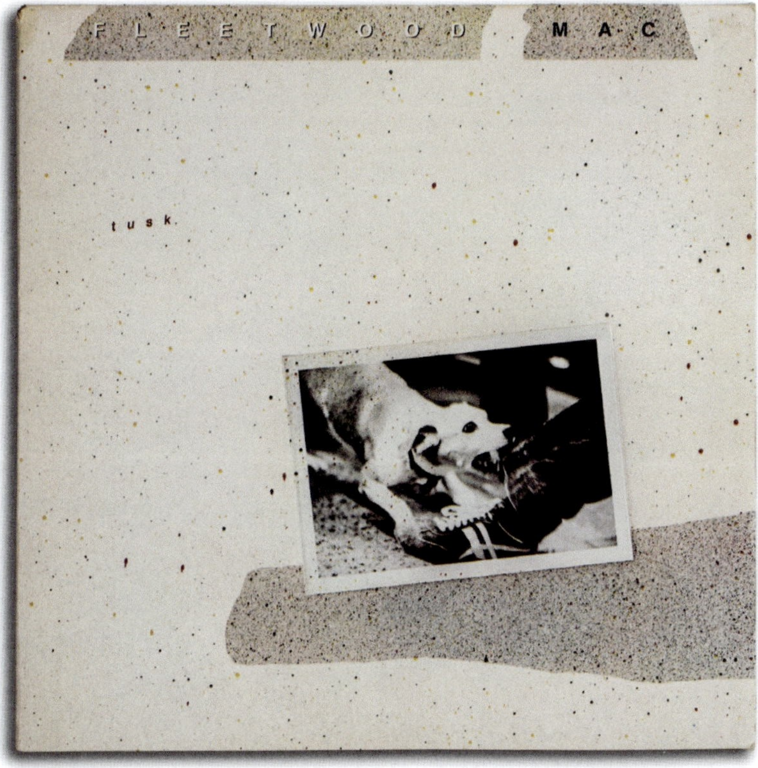

Fleetwood Mac
Tusk
Warner Bros. Records, 1979
Vigon Nahas Vigon (Design)
Norman Seef (Photo)

14 JUN

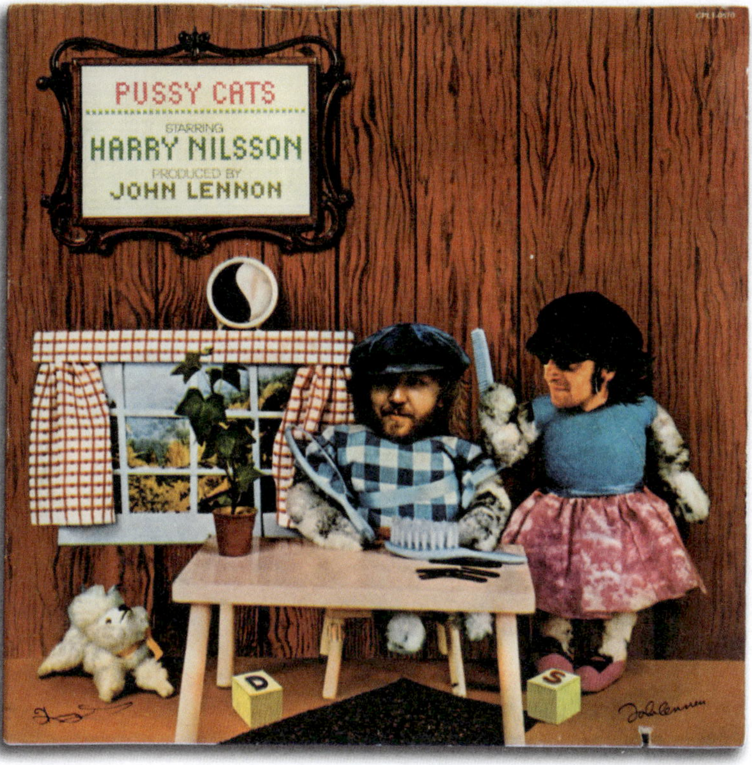

Harry Nilsson produced by John Lennon
Pussy Cats
RCA Victor, 1974
Acy R. Lehman (Design)

15 JUN

* Jun 15th, 1941
Harry Nilsson
Brooklyn (New York)

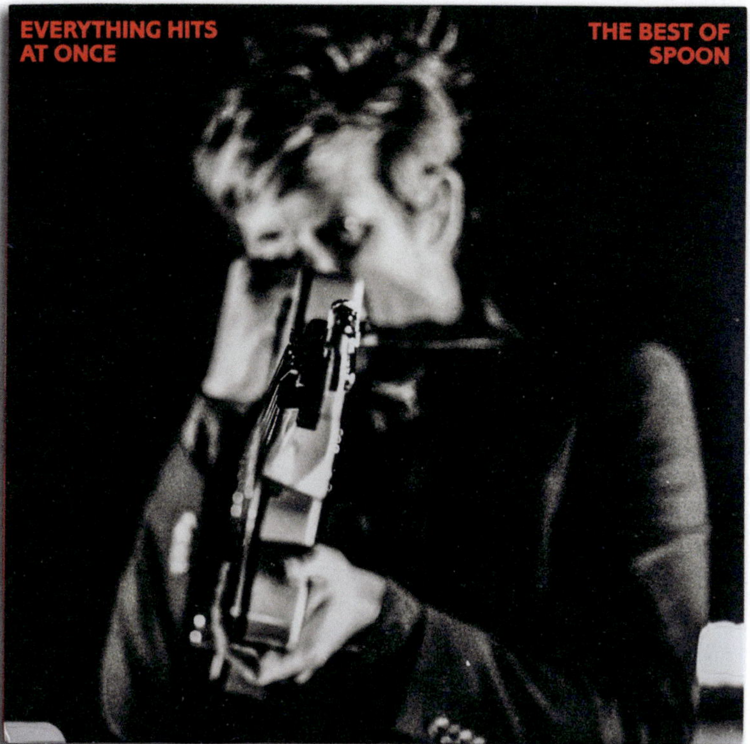

Spoon
Everything Hits at Once – The Best Of Spoon
Matador, 2019
Mike Krol (Design)
Sam Watson (Photo)

16 JUN

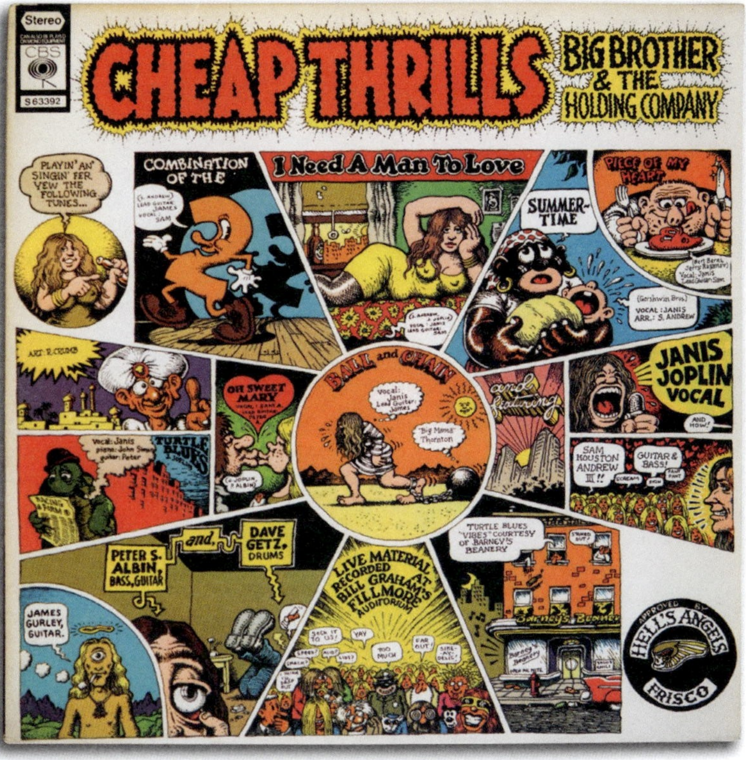

Big Brother & The Holding Company
Cheap Thrills
Columbia Records, 1968
Robert Crumb (Illustration)

17 JUN

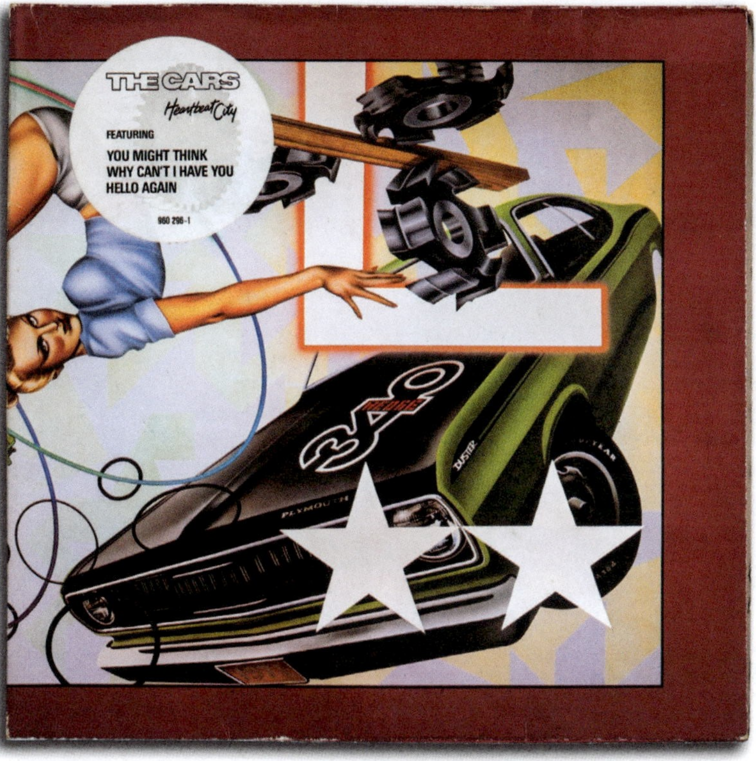

The Cars
Heartbeat City
Elektra, 1984
Cathey Henszey (Design)
Peter Philips (Illustration)

18 JUN

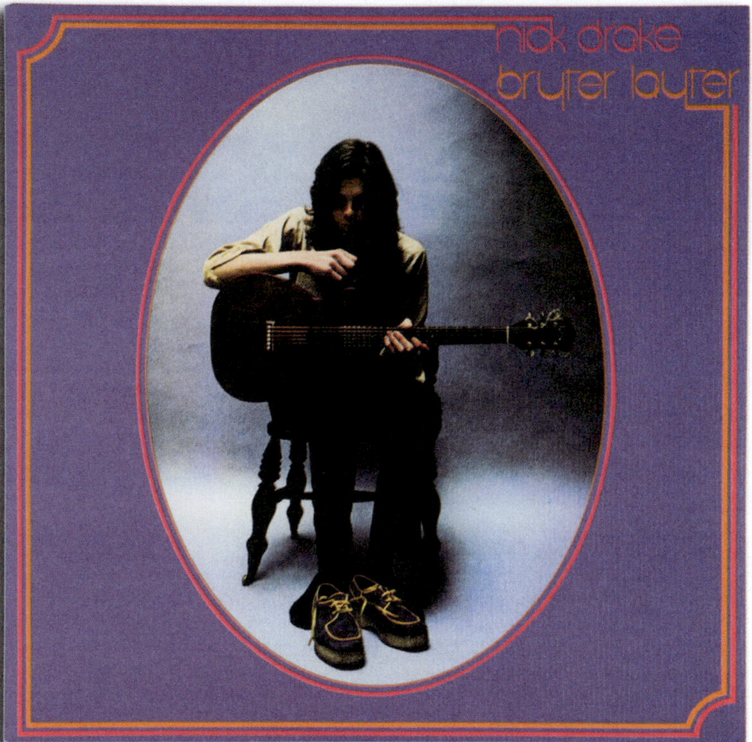

Nick Drake
Bryter Layter
Island Records, 1970
Nigel Waymouth (Design)
Nigel Wamouth (Photo)

* Jun 19th, 1948
Nicolas Rodney Drake
Rangun (Birma)

19 JUN

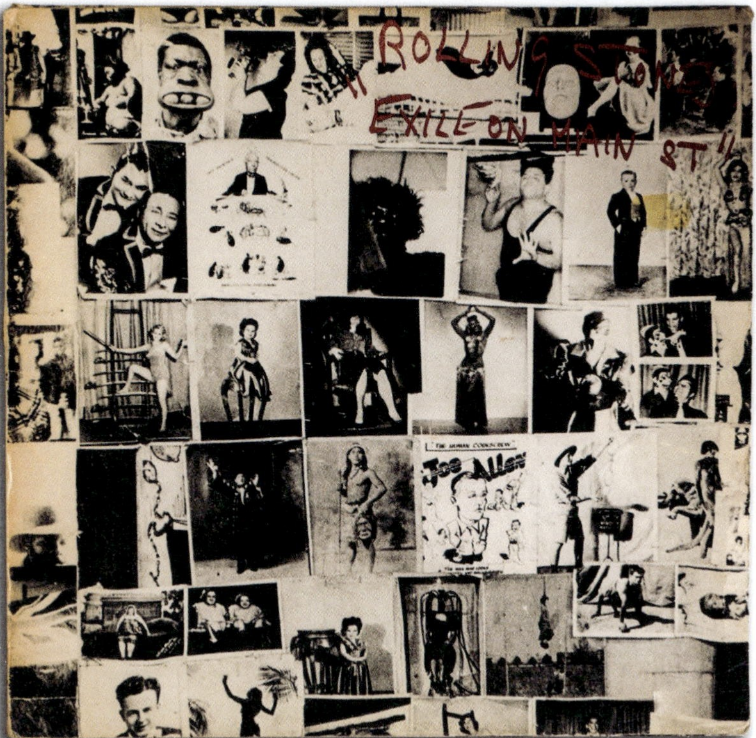

Rolling Stones
Exile On Main St.
Rolling Stones Records, 1972
John van Hamersveld, Norman Seef (Design)
Robert Frank (Photo)

20 JUN

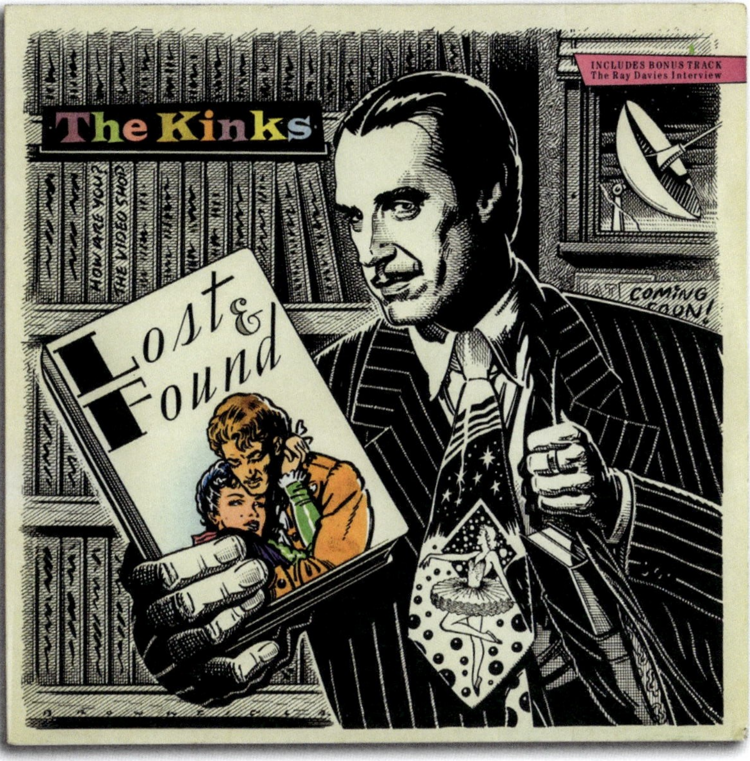

The Kinks
Lost & Found
London Records, 1987
Stylorouge (Design)
Mick Brownfield (Illustration)

21 JUN

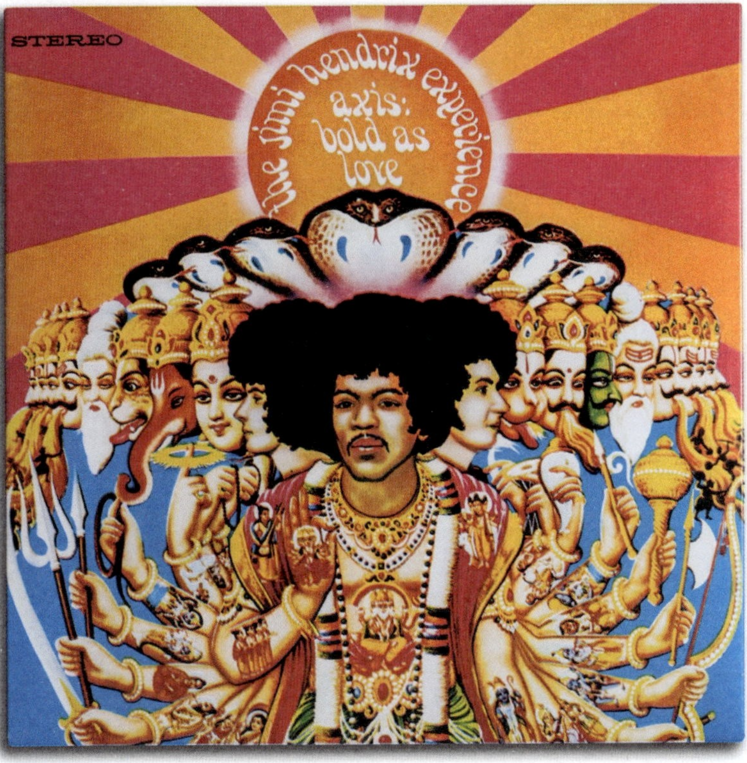

The Jimi Hendrix Experience
Axis: Bold As Love
Track Record, 1967
David King, Roger Law (Design)
Donald Silverstein (Illustration)

22 JUN

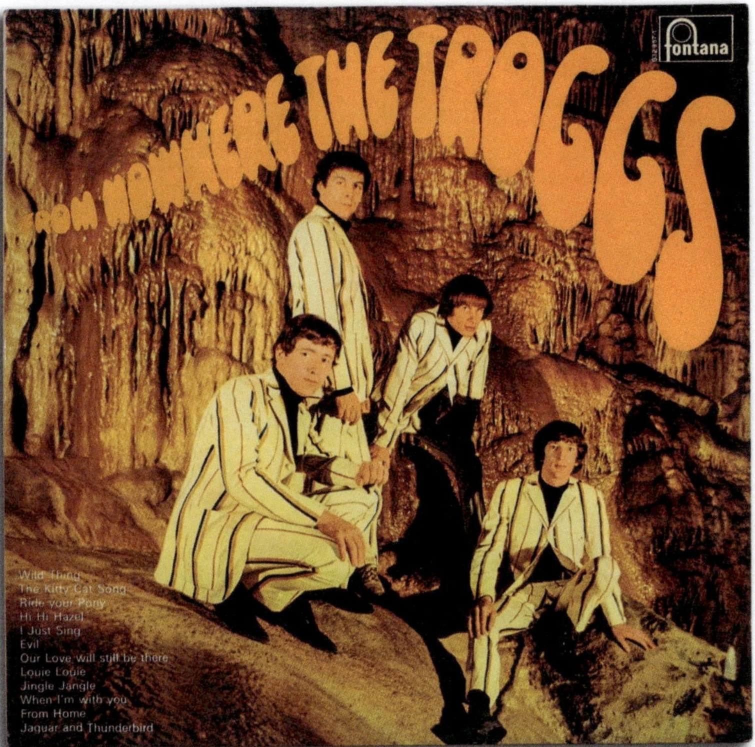

The Troggs
From Nowhere
Fontana, 1966
Cover Artists Unknown

23 JUN

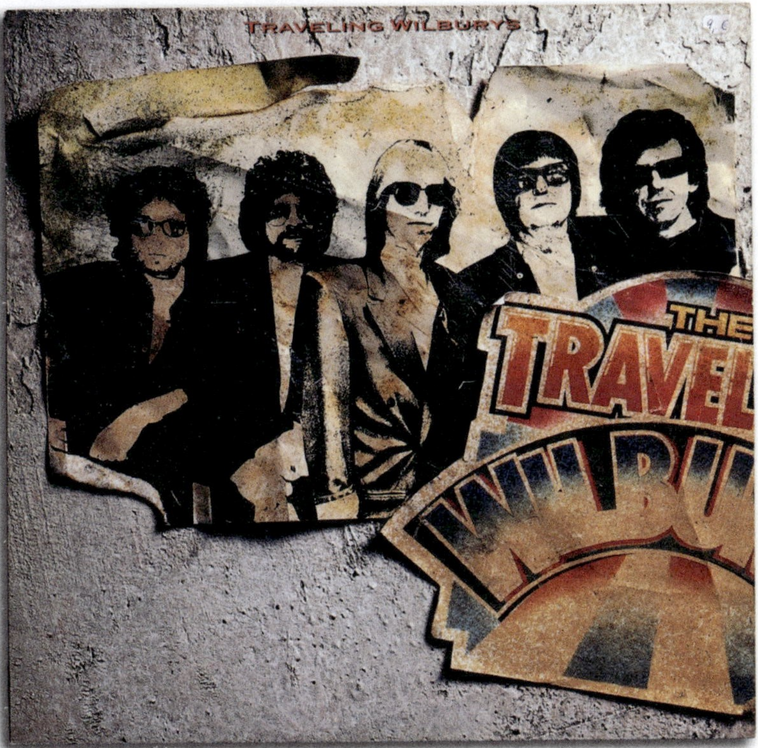

The Traveling Wilburys Volume One
Wilbury Records, 1988
David Costa (Design)
Neal Preston (Photo)

24 JUN

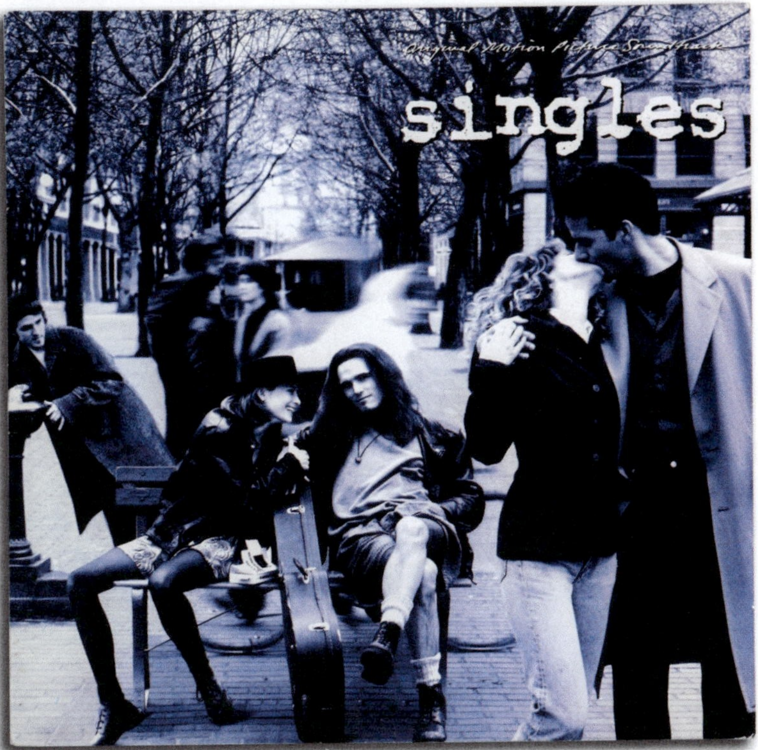

Various Artists – Soundtrack
Singles
EPIC Records, 1992
David Coleman, Nancy Donald (Design)
Steve Nilsson (Photo)

25 JUN

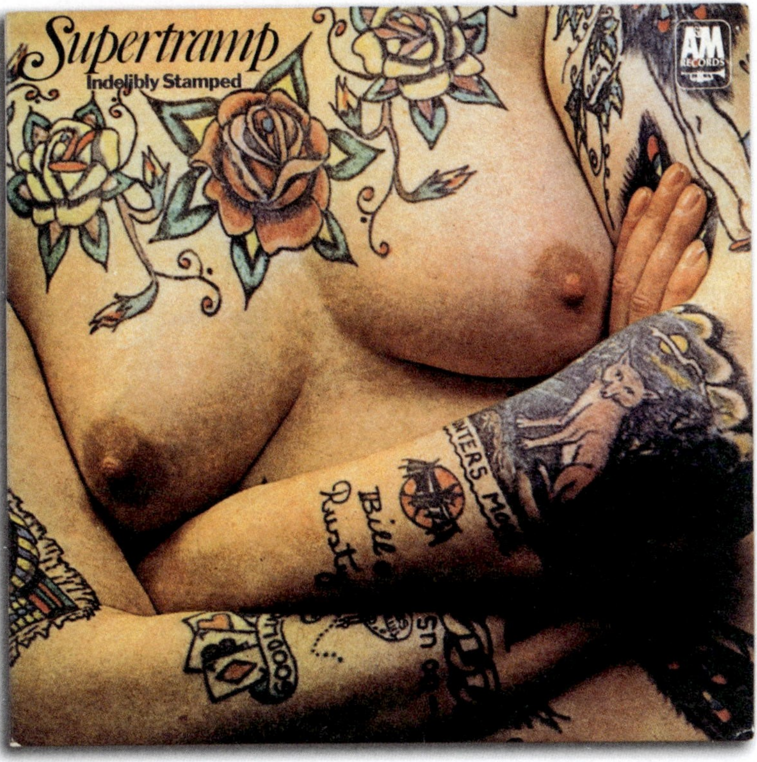

Supertramp
Indelibly Stamped
A&M Records, 1971
Bob Hook (Design)
Keith Morris (Photo)

26 JUN

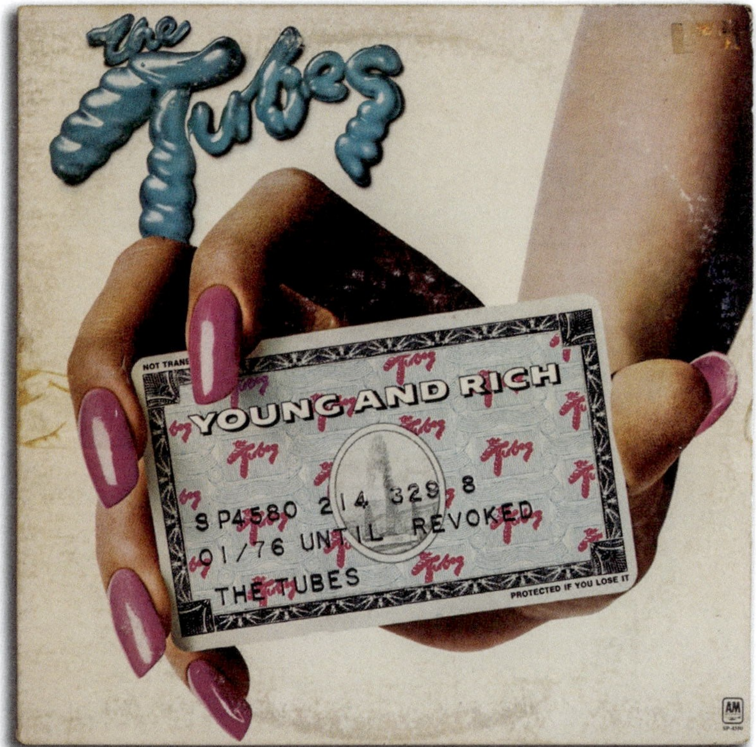

The Tubes
Young And Rich
A&M Records, 1976
Michael Cotten, Prairie Prince (Design)

27 JUN

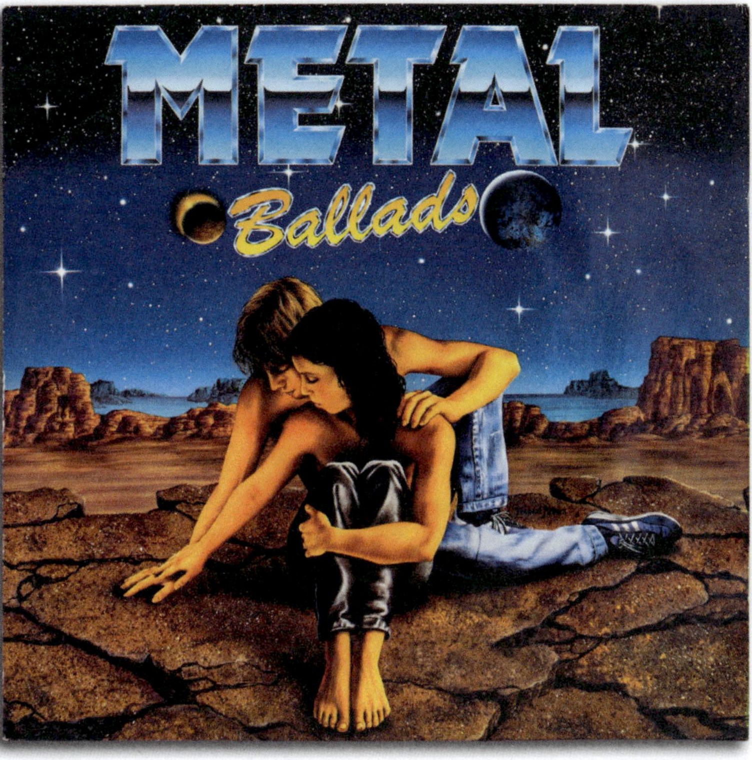

Various Artists
Metal Ballads
RCA Bertelsmann Club, 1988
Michael Albers (Illustration)

28 JUN

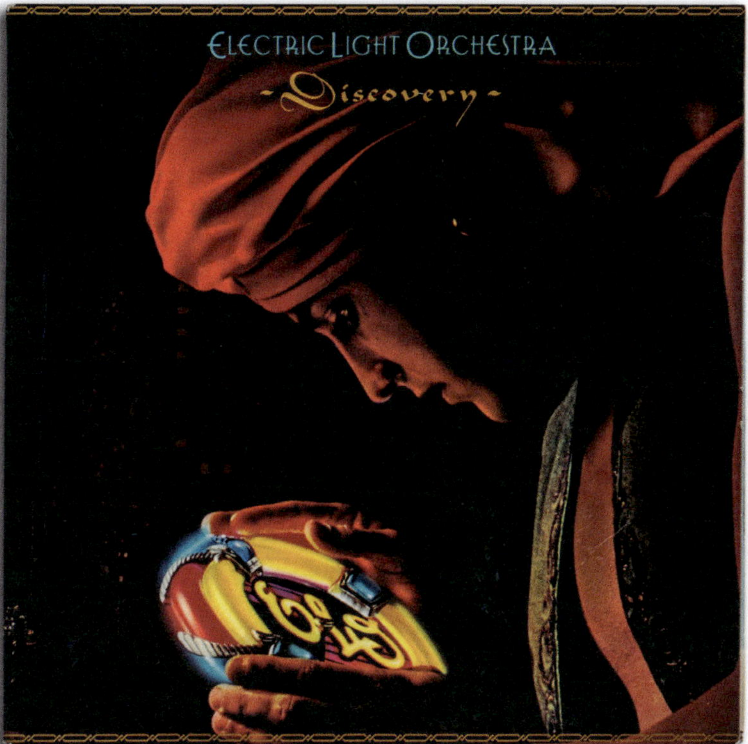

Electric Light Orchestra
Discovery
Jet Records, 1979
Norman Moore, Paul Gross (Design)
Jim Shea (Photo)

29 JUN

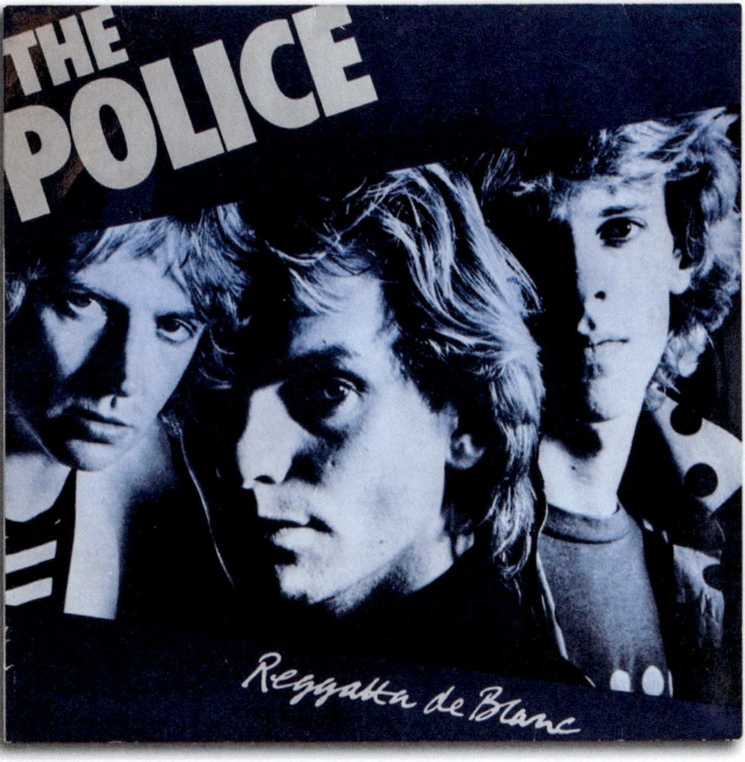

The Police
Regatta De Blanc
A&M Records, 1979
Michael Ross (Design)
James Wedge (Photo)

30 JUN

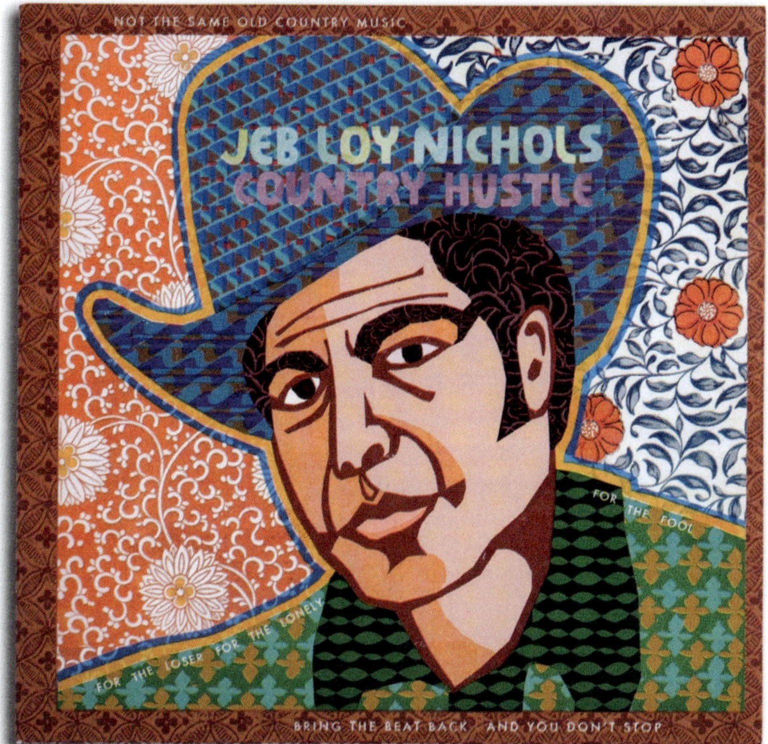

Jeb Loy Nichols
Country Hustle
City Country Hustle, 2017
Cover Artists Unknown

01 JUL

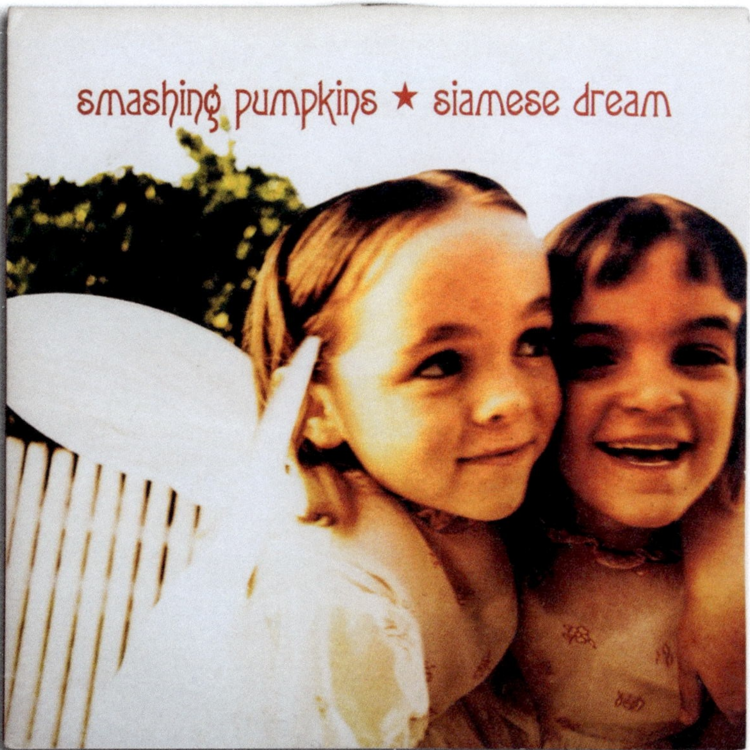

Smashing Pumpkins
Siamese Dreams
Caroline Records, 1993
Len Peltier (Design)
Melodie McDaniel (Photo)

02 JUL

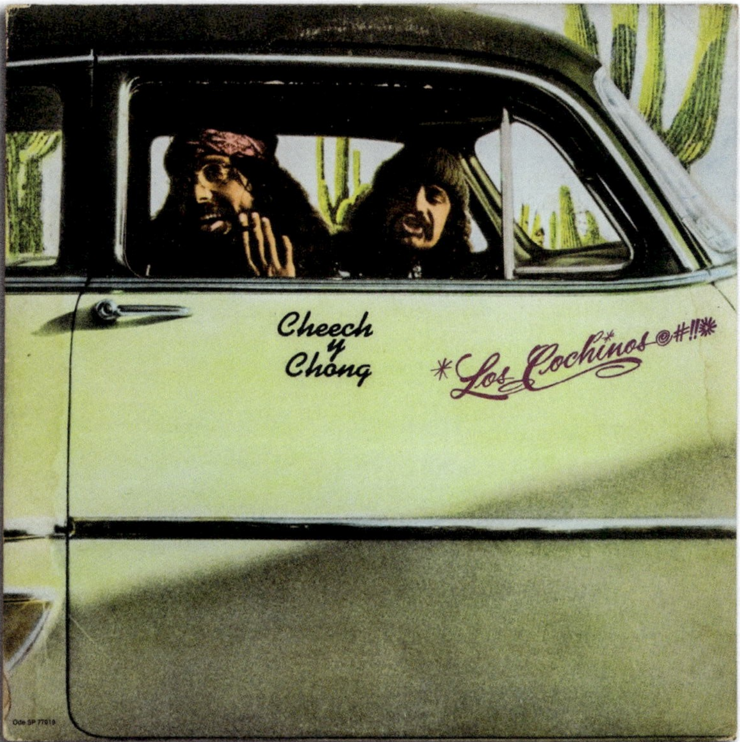

Cheech Y Chong
Los Cochinos
Ode Records, 1973
Paul Zammit (Design)
Ed Caraeff (Photo)

03 JUL

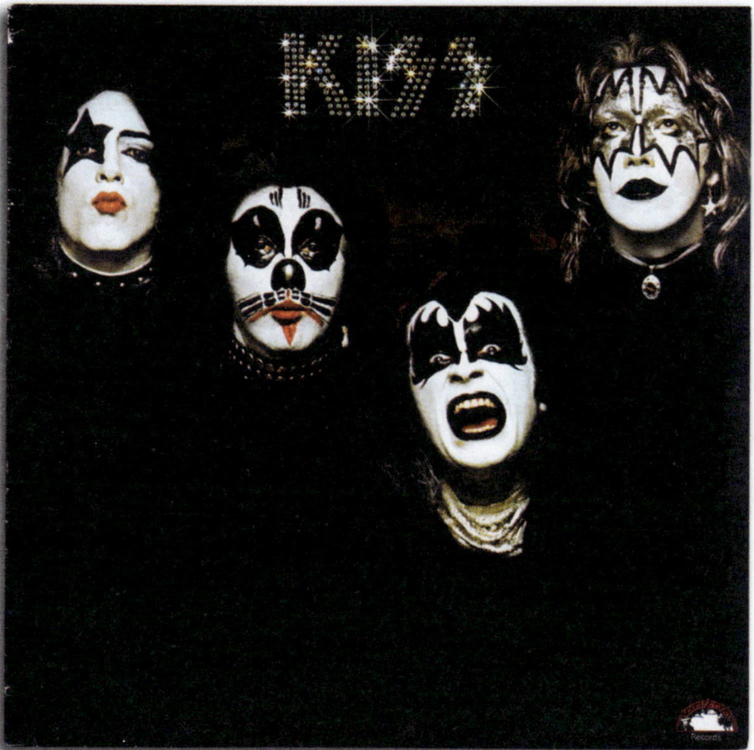

Kiss
Casablanca Records, 1974
Robert Lockart (Design)
Joel Brodsky (Photo)

04 JUL

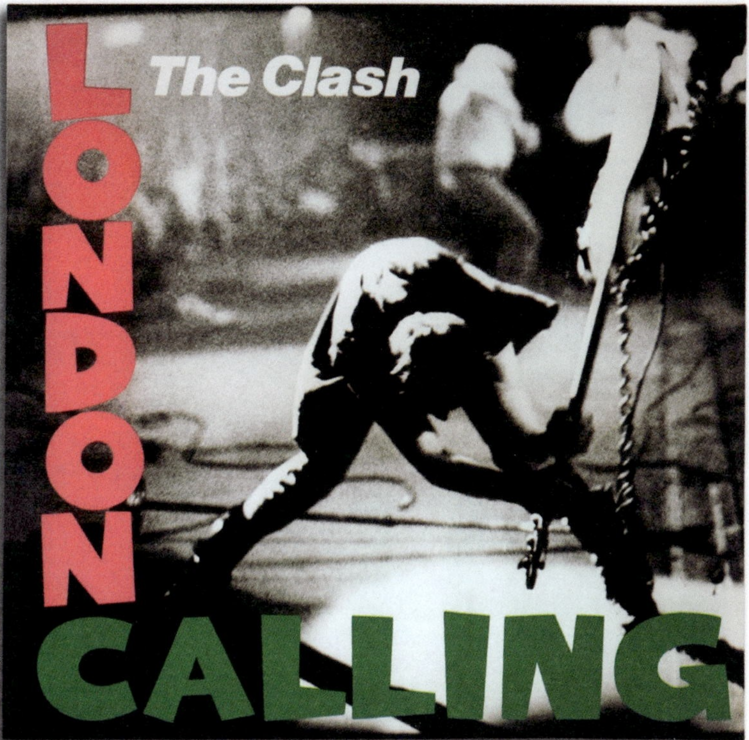

The Clash
London Calling
Columbia Records, 1979
Ray Lowry (Design)
Pennie Smith (Photo)

05 JUL

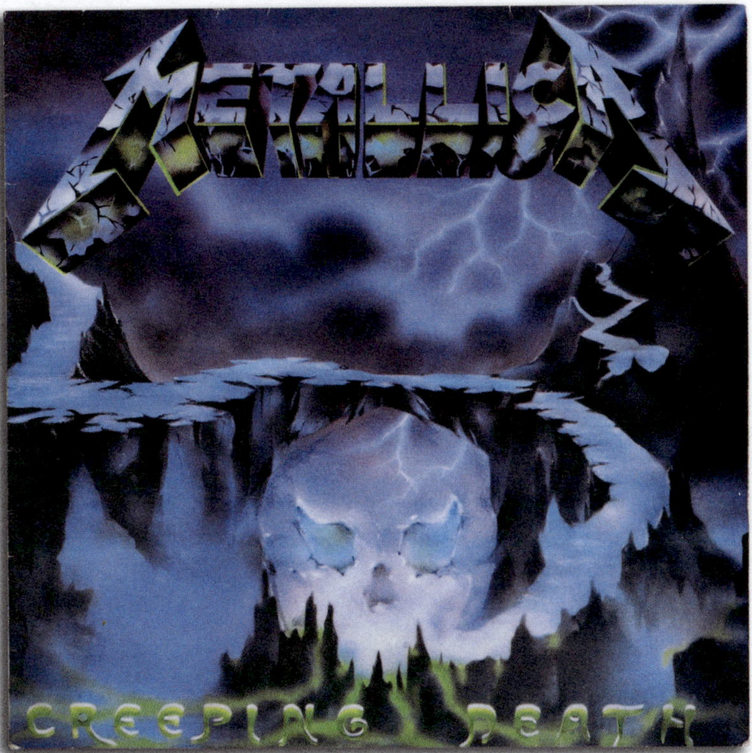

Metallica
Creeping Death
Music For Nations, 1984
Alvin Petty (Illustration)

06 JUL

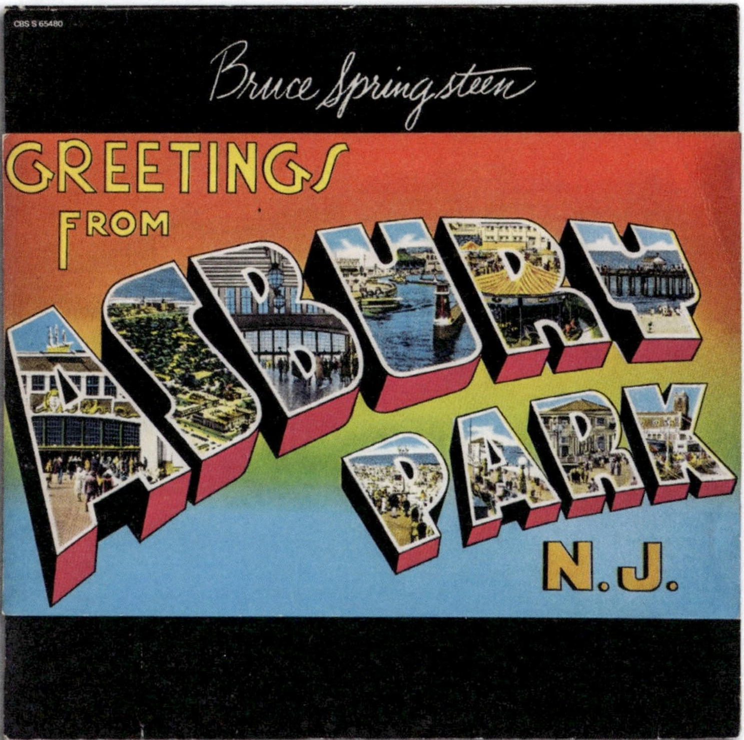

Bruce Springsteen
Greetings from Ashbury Park, N.J.
CBS Records, 1973
John Berg (Design)

07 JUL

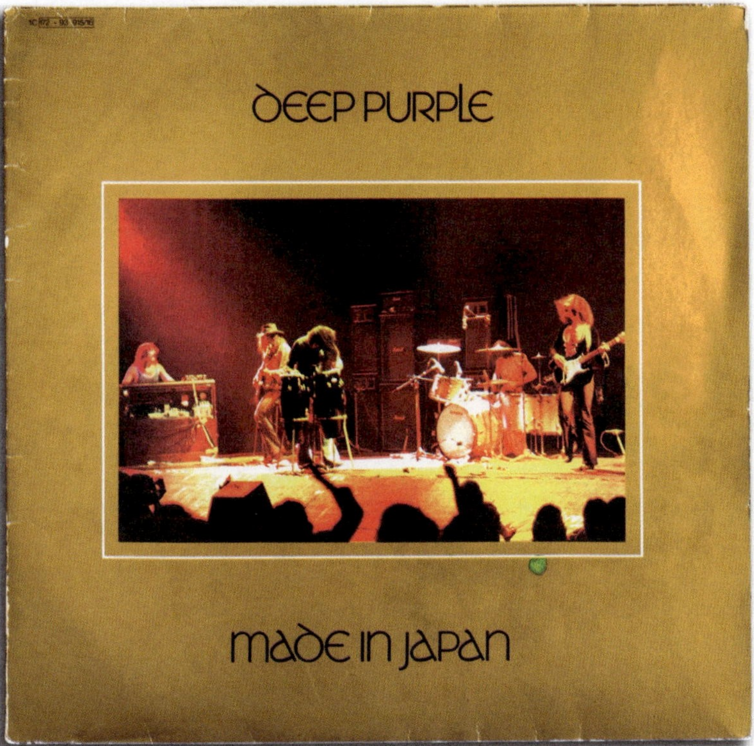

Deep Purple
Made In Japan
Purple Records, 1972
Roger Clover (Design)
Fin Costello (Photo)

08 JUL

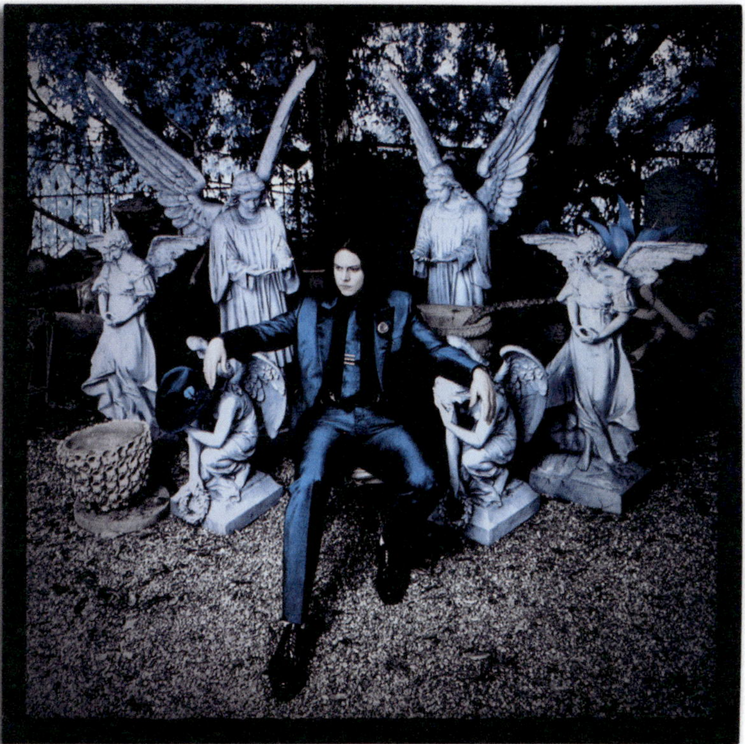

Jack White
Lazaretto
Third Man Records, 2014
Jack White & Nathanaio Strimpopulus (Design)
Mary Ellen Matthews (Photo)

* Jul 9th, 1975
John Anthony Gillis
Detroit (Michigan)

09 JUL

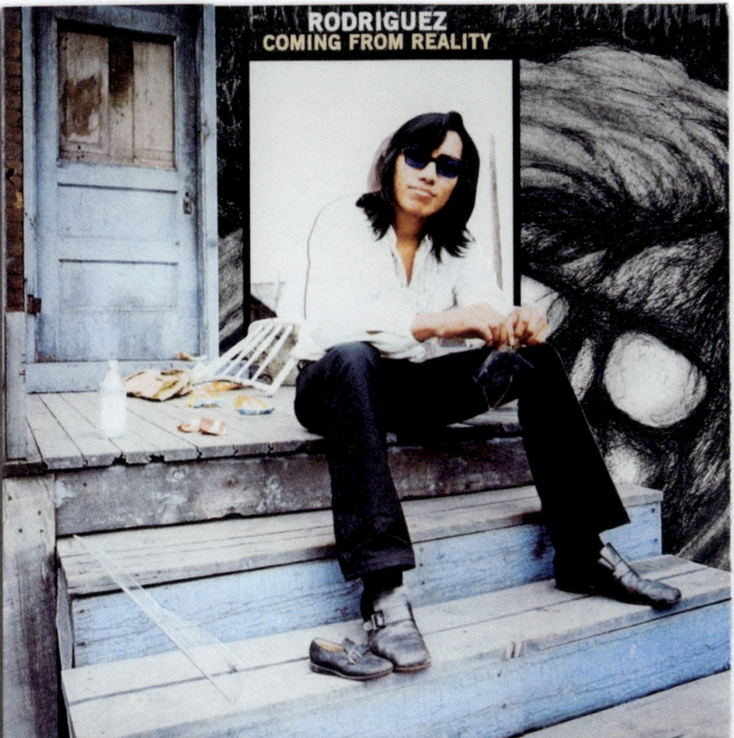

Rodriguez
Coming From Reality
Light in the Attic, 2009
Milton Sincoff (Design)
Hal Wilson (Photo)

* Jul 10th, 1942
Sixto Díaz Rodríguez
Detroit (Michigan)

10 JUL

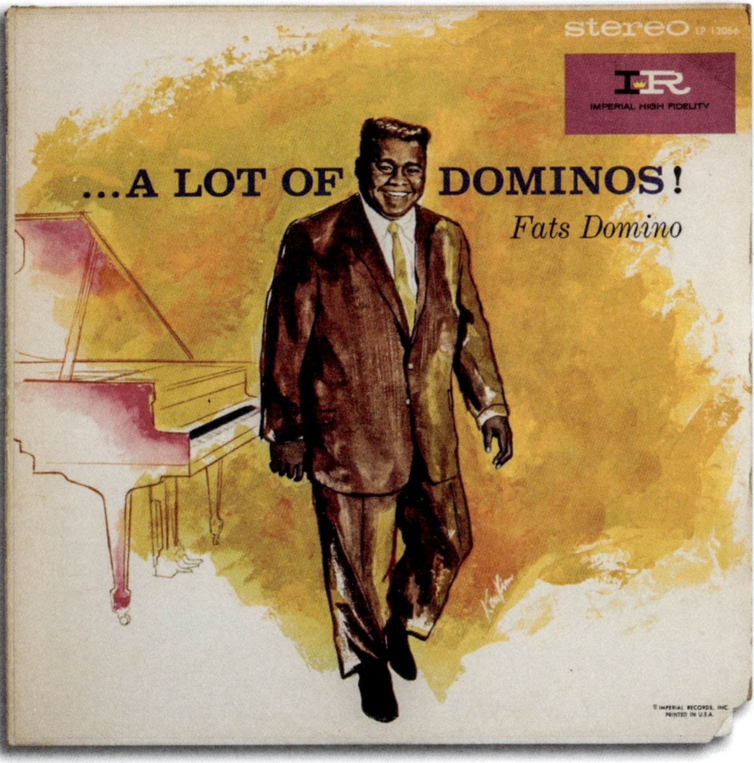

Fats Domino
...A Lot Of Dominos!
Imperial Records, 1960
Ken Kim (Illustration)

11 JUL

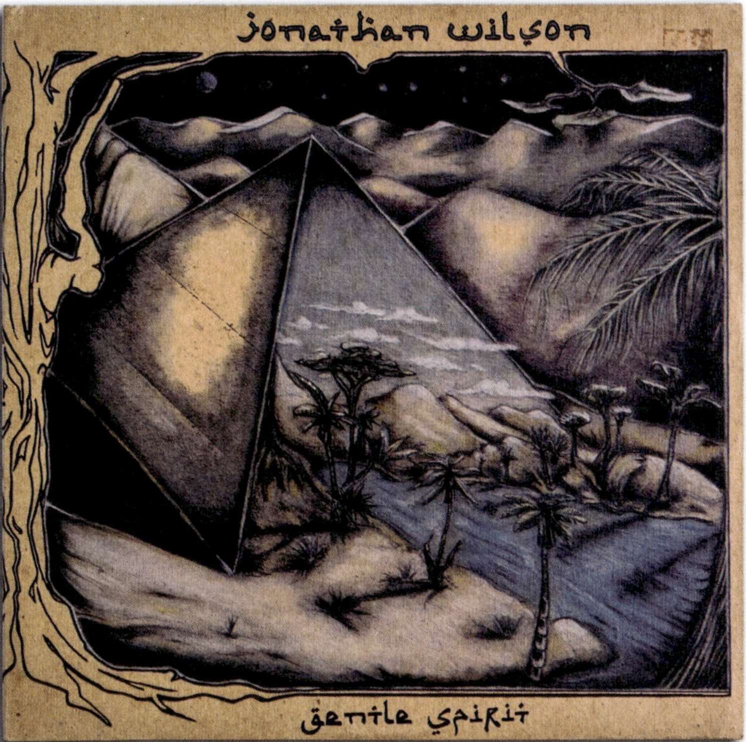

Jonathan Wilson
Gentle Spirit
Bella Union, 2011
Mike Sportes (Illustration)

12 JUL

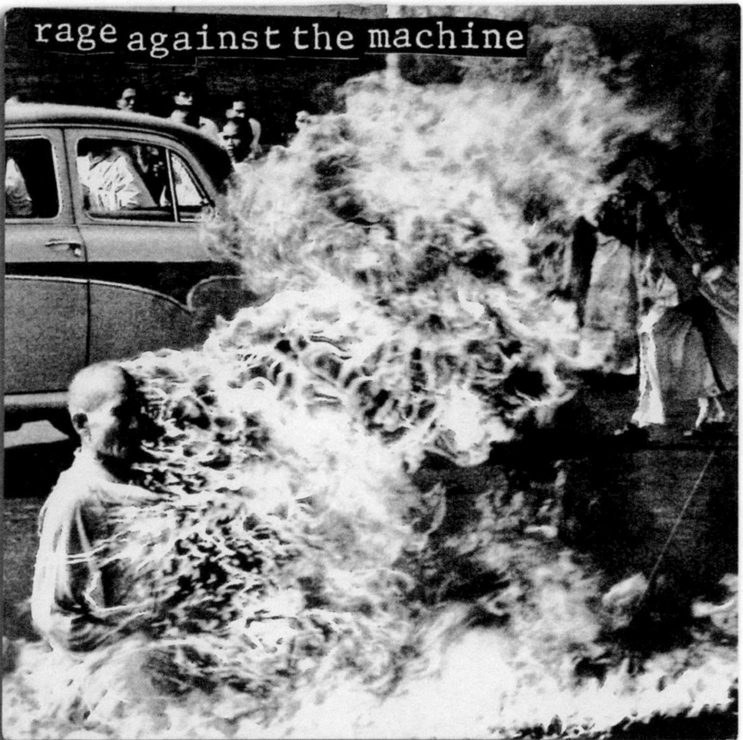

Rage Against The Machine
EPIC Records, 1992
Nicky Lindemann (Design)
Lindsey Price (Photo)

13 JUL

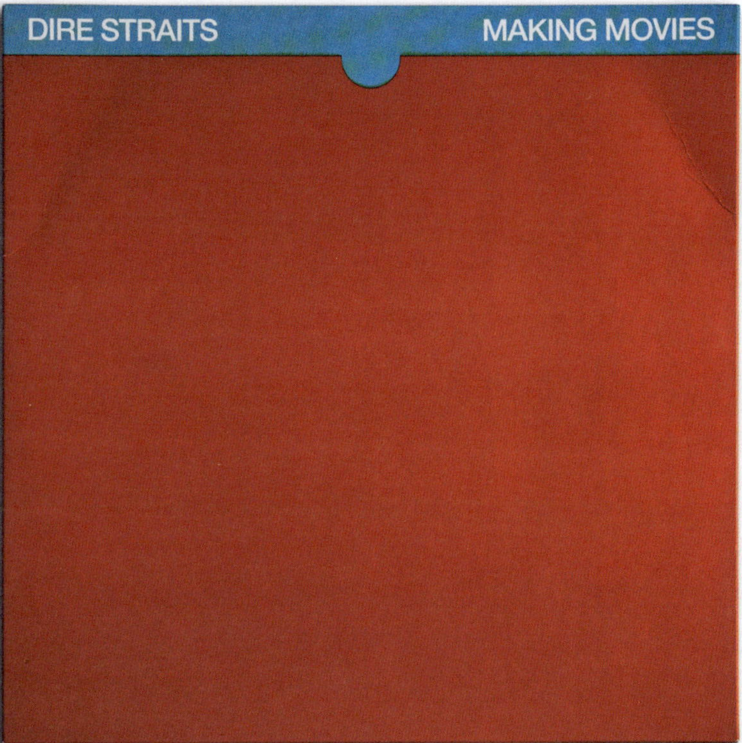

Dire Straits
Making Movies
Vertigo Records, 1980
Neil Terk (Design)

14 JUL

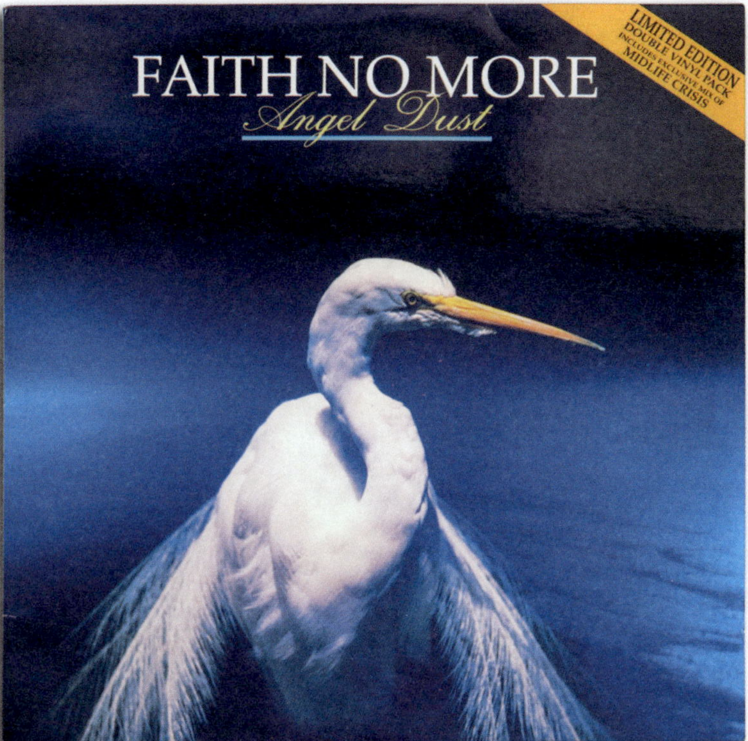

Faith No More
Angel Dust
Slash, 1992
Kim Champagne (Design)
Werner Krutein (Photo)

15 JUL

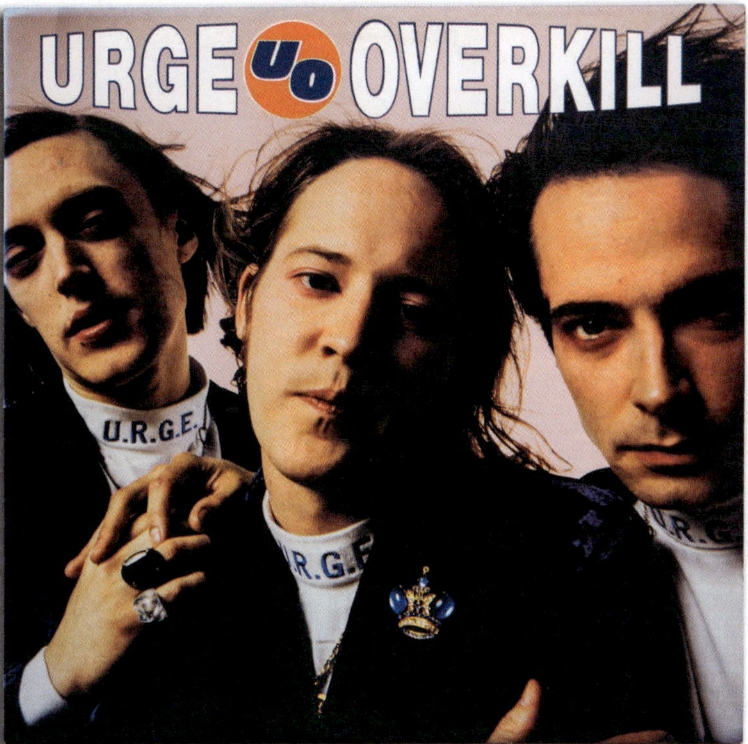

Urge Overkill
The Supersonic Storybook
Touch and Go, 1991
Daniel Clowes (Design)
Josh Miller (Photo)

16 JUL

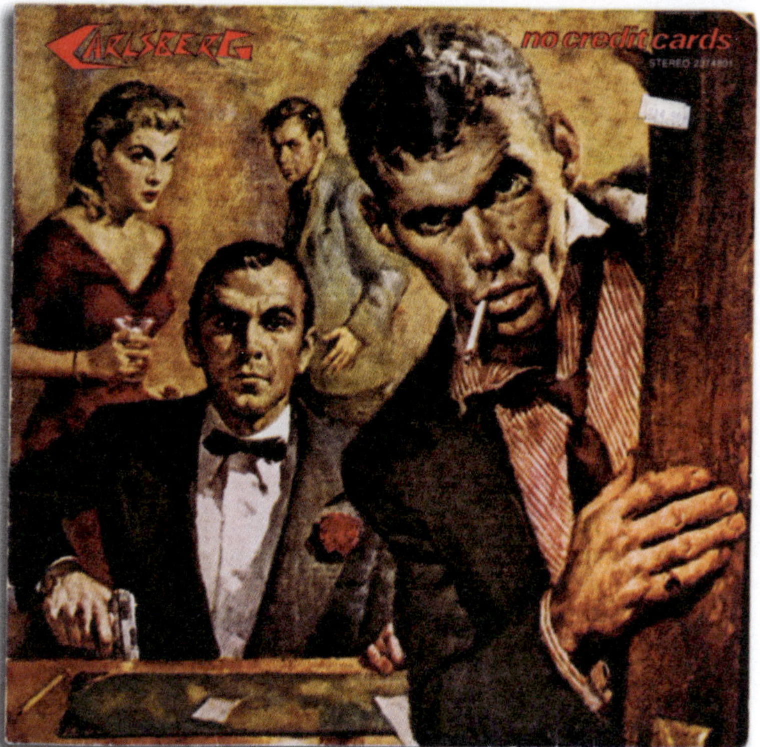

Carlsberg
No Credit Cards
GIP Records, 1979
Bart Terlaak (Design)
Meese (Illustration)

17 JUL

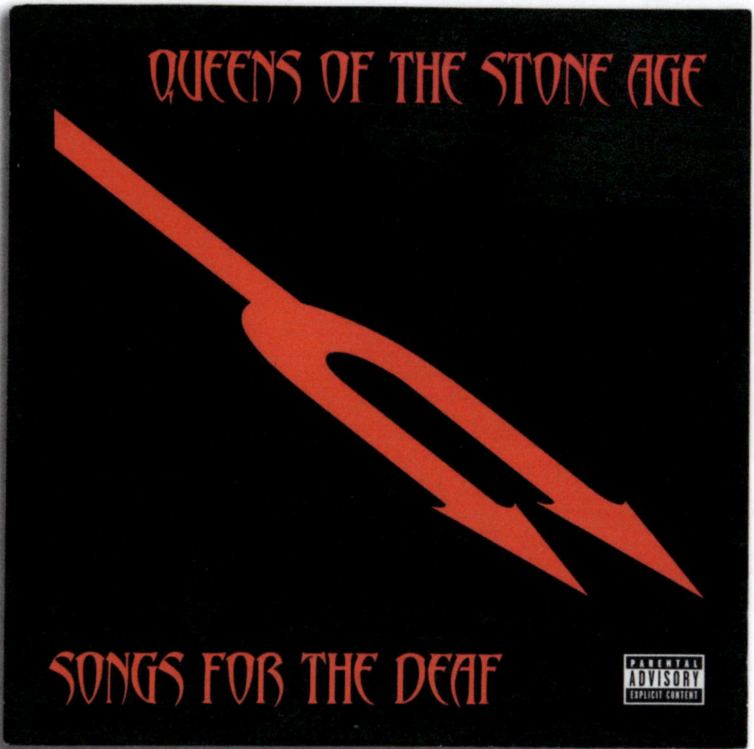

Queens Of The Stone Age
Songs Of The Deaf
Interscope Records, 2002
Patrick Hutchinson (Design)

18 JUL

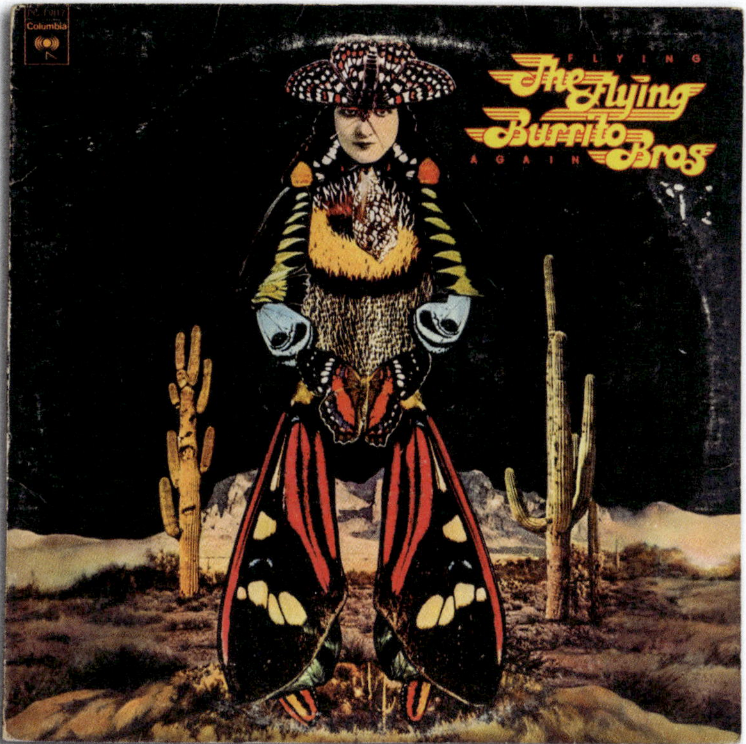

The Flying Burrito Bros
Flying Again
Columbia Records, 1975
Ron Caro (Design)
Lou Beach (Photo)

19 JUL

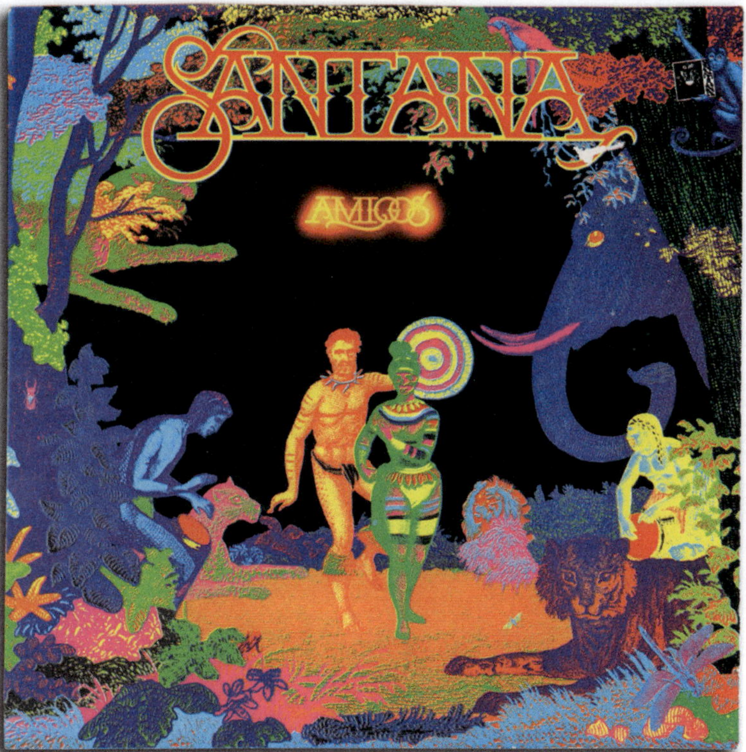

Santana
Amigos
CBS Records, 1976
Tadanori Yokoo (Design)

* Jul 20th, 1947
Carlos Santana
Autlán de Navarro (Mexico)

20 JUL

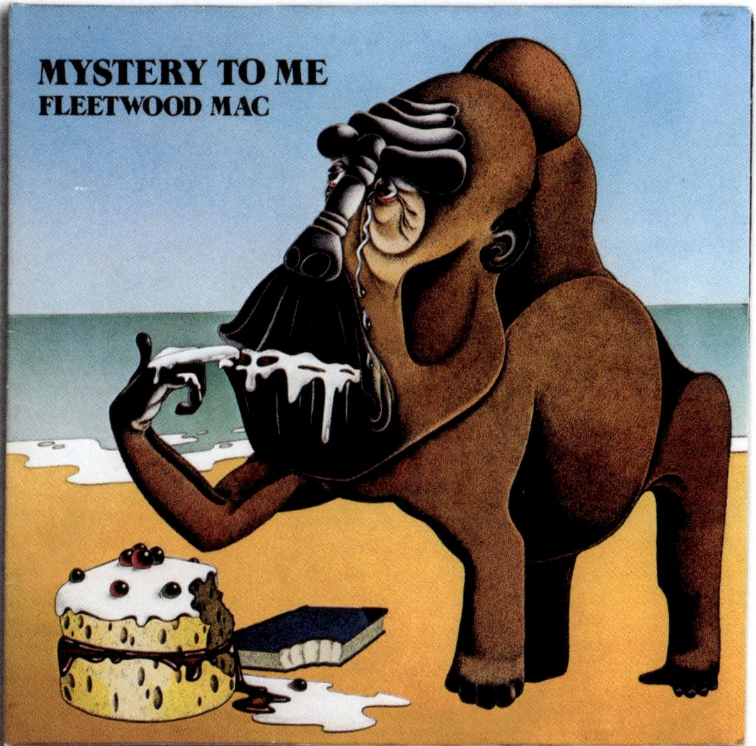

Fleetwood Mac
Mystery To Me
Reprise Records, 1973
Modula (Design)

21 JUL

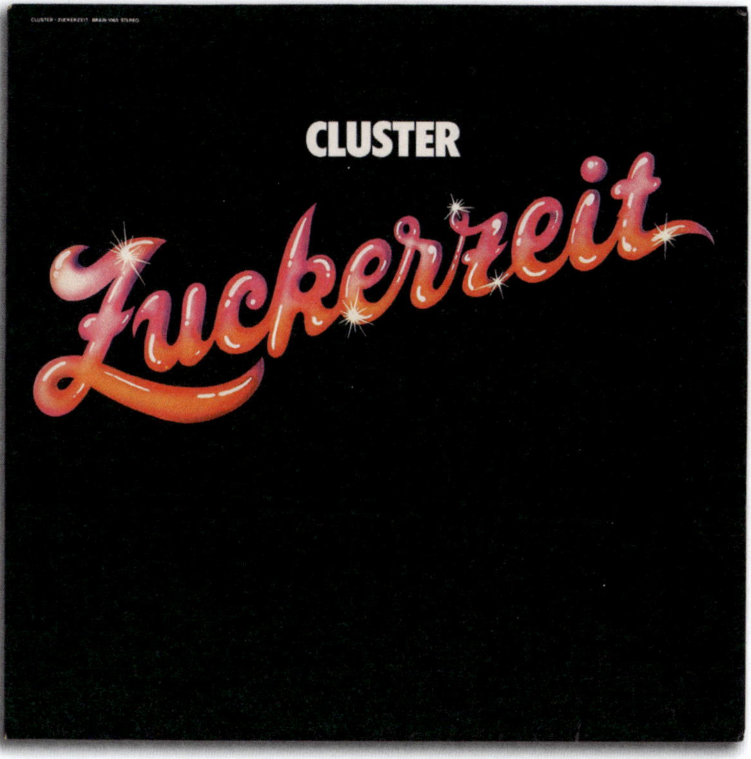

Cluster
Zuckerzeit
Brain Records, 1974
Stender (Design)

22 JUL

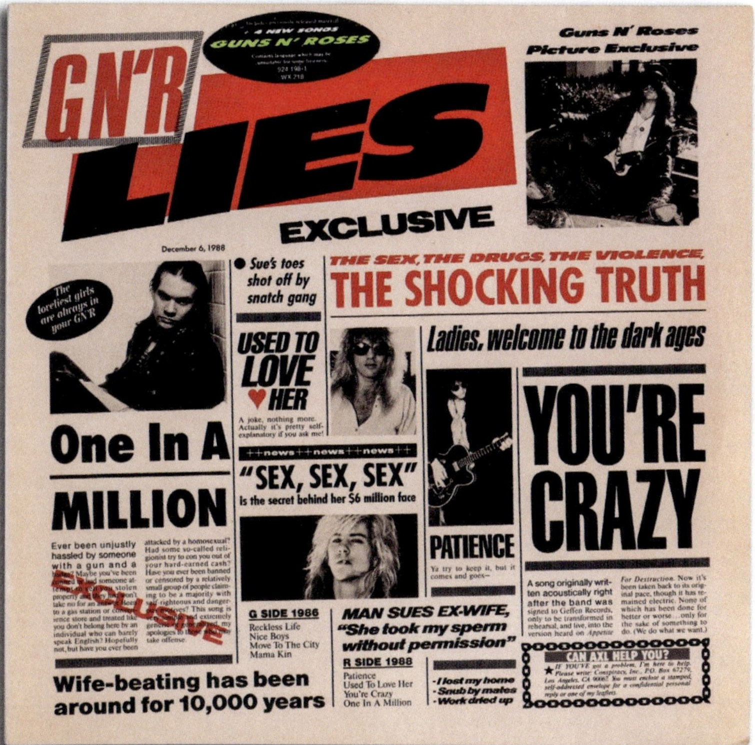

Guns N'Roses
G'N'R Lies
Geffen Records, 1986
Slash (Design)
Robert John (Photo)

23 JUL

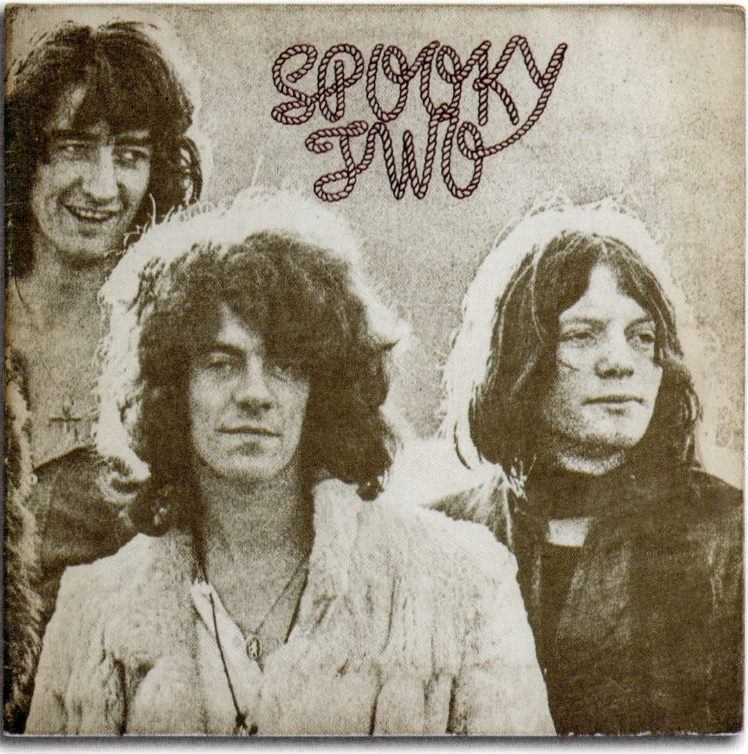

Spooky Tooth
Spooky Two
Island Records, 1969
Guy Stevens, Mike Sida (Design)
Ethan Russell (Photo)

24 JUL

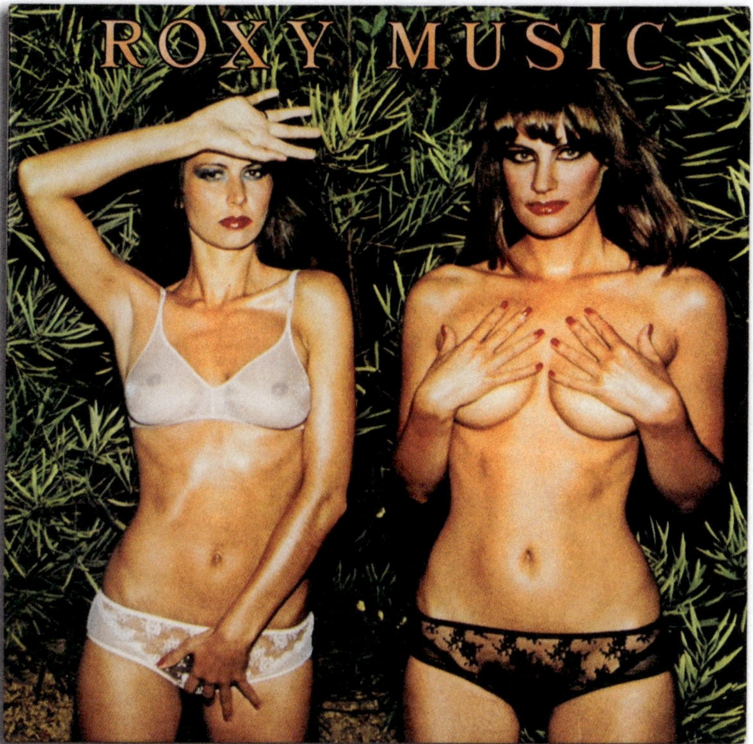

Roxy Music
Country Life
Island Records, 1974
Bob Bowkett (Design)
Eric Boman (Photo)

25 JUL

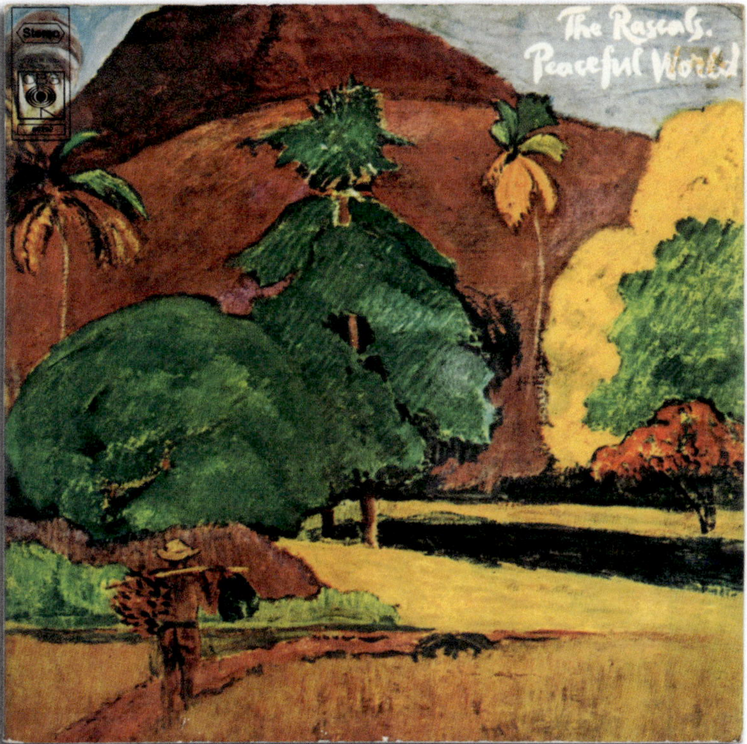

The Rascals
Peaceful World
Columbia Records, 1971
Paul Gauguin (Illustration)

26 JUL

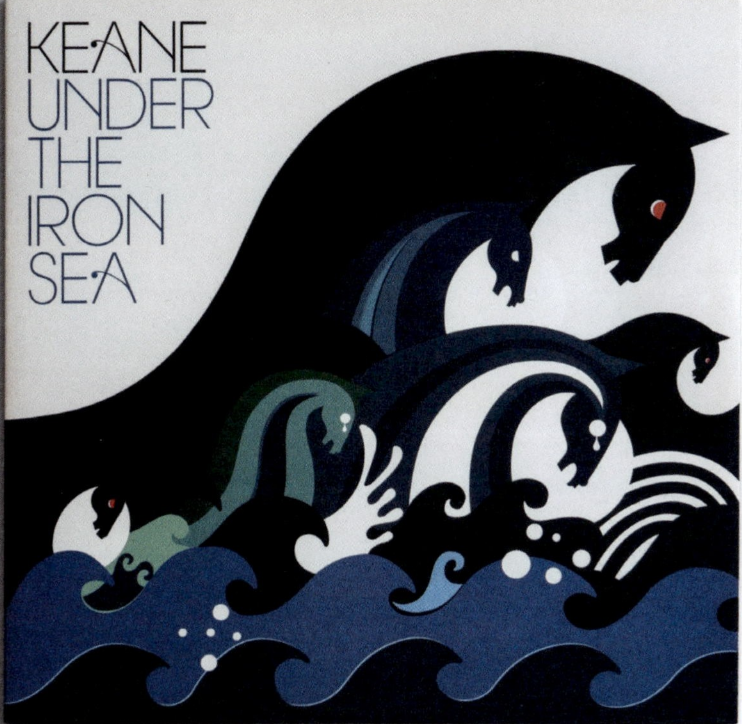

Keane
Under The Iron Sea
Island Records, 2006
Gerard Saint, Richard Andrews (Design)
Sanna Annuka (Illustration)

27 JUL

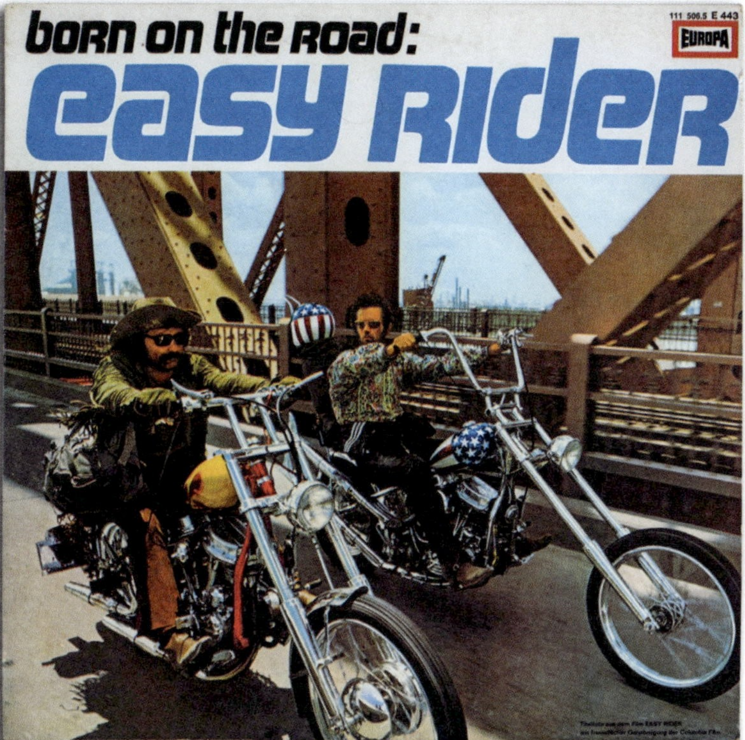

Various Artists – Soundtrack
Easy Rider
Europa, 1971
Cover Artists Unknown

28 JUL

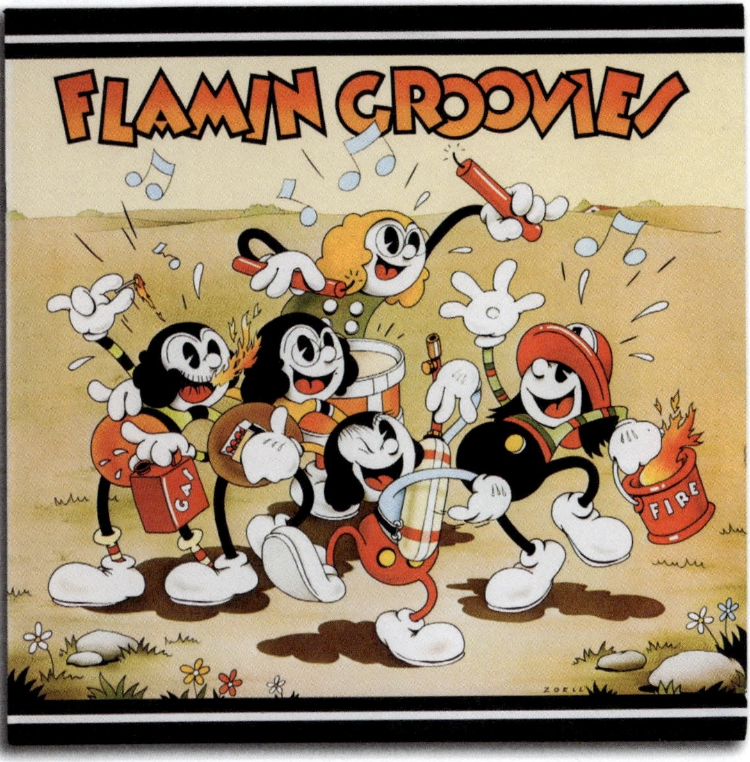

Flamin Groovies
Supersnazz
EPIC Records, 1969
Bob Zoell (Design)

29 JUL

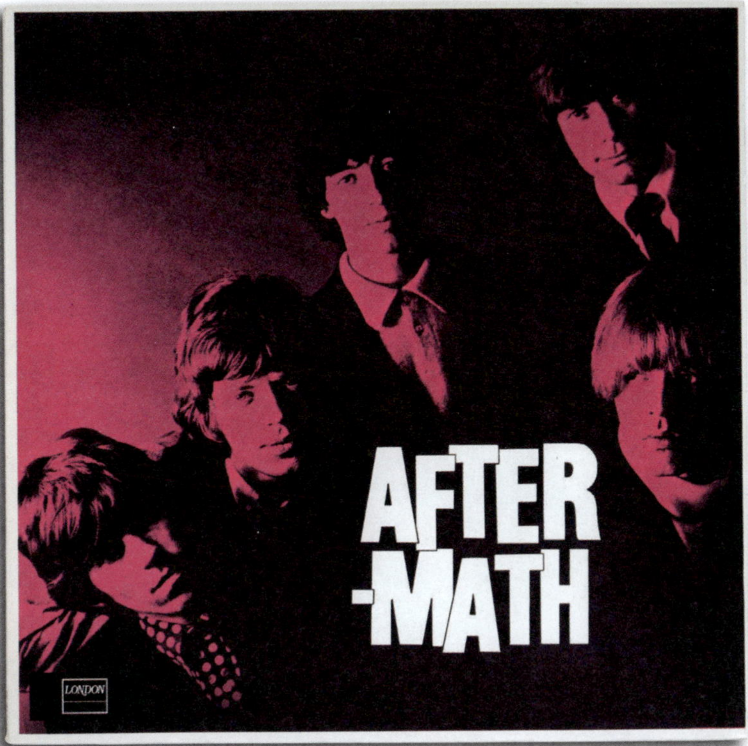

The Rolling Stones
Aftermath
Decca, 1966
Sandy Beach (Design)
Guy Webster & Jerrold Schatzberg (Photo)

30 JUL

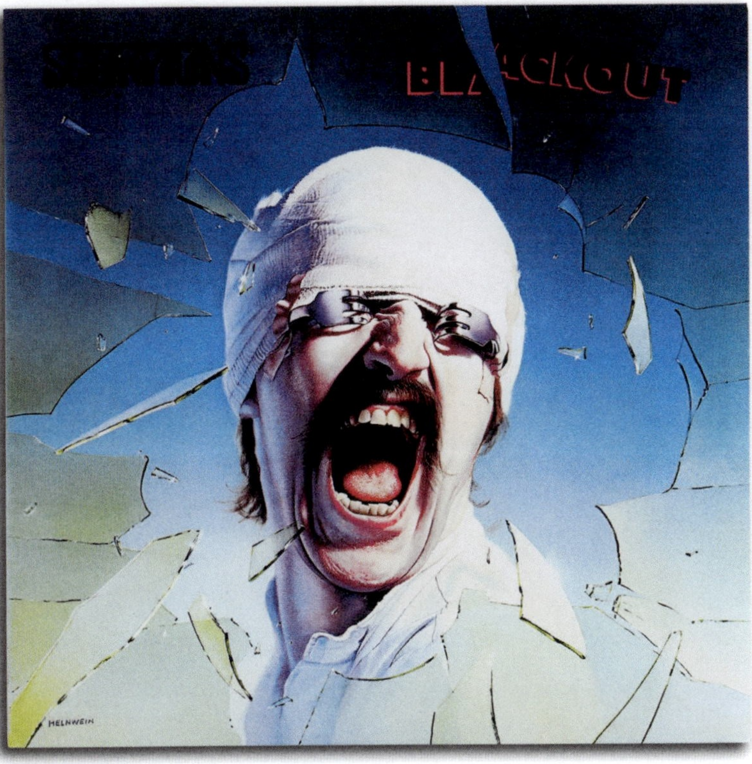

Scorpions
Blackout
Harvest, EMI Electrola, 1982
Gottfried Helnwein (Illustration)

31 JUL

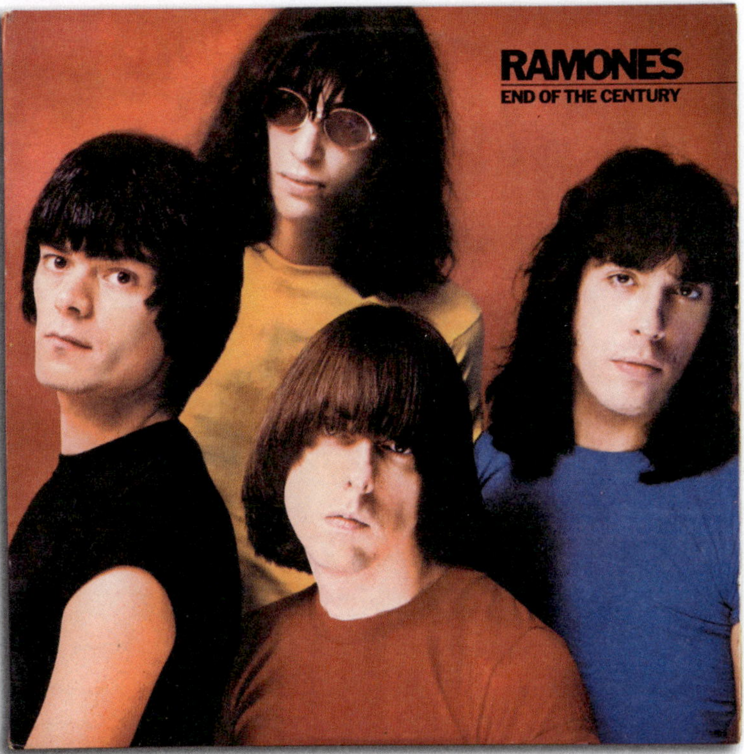

Ramones
End Of Century
Sire Records, 1980
John Gillespie (Design)
Mick Rock (Photo)

01 AUG

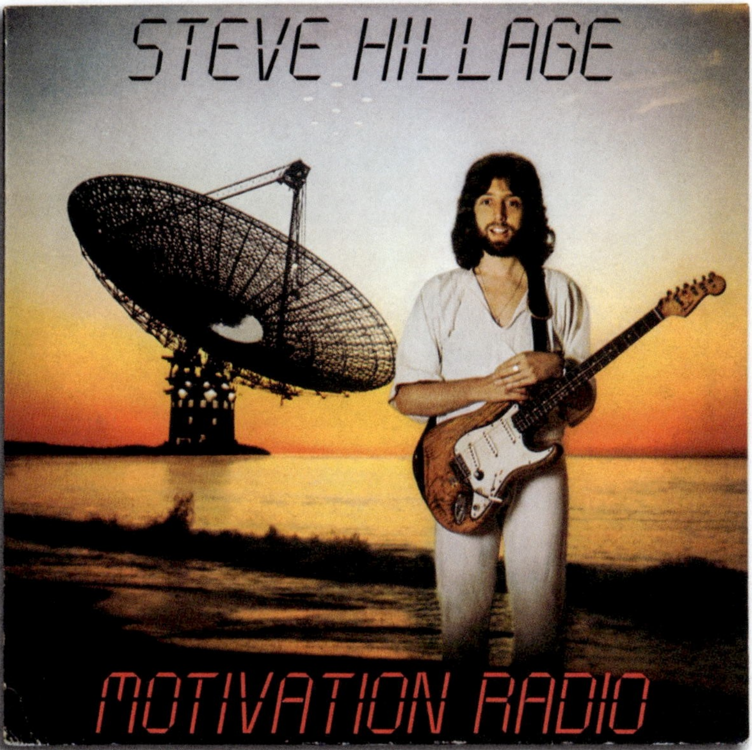

Steve Hillage
Motivation Radio
Virgin Records, 1977
Howard Carriker & Ted Staidle (Design)
Bob Cato (Photo)

* Aug 2nd, 195
Steve Hillage
London (UK)

02 AUG

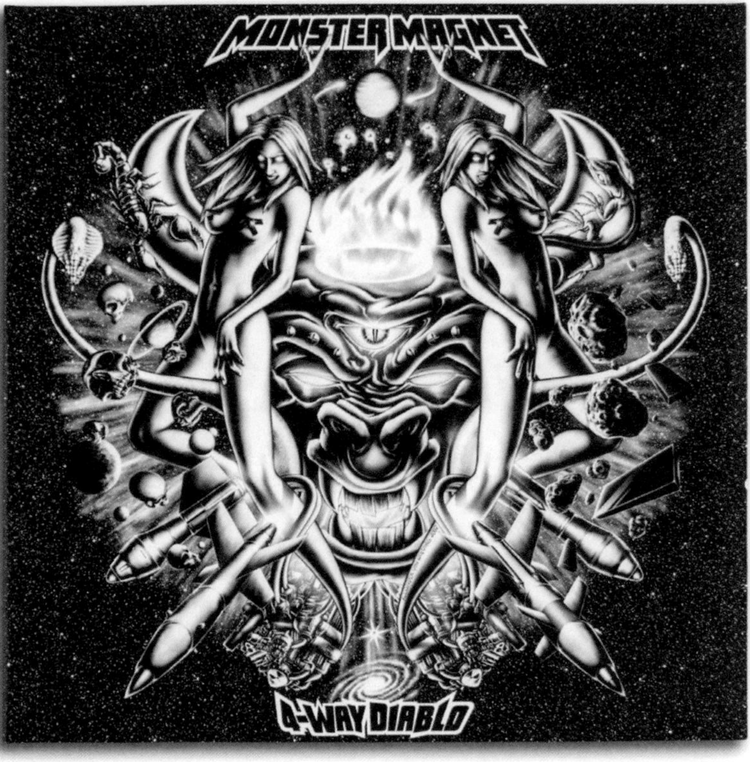

Monster Magnet
4-Way Diablo
Steamhammer, 2007
Alexander von Wieding (Design)

03 AUG

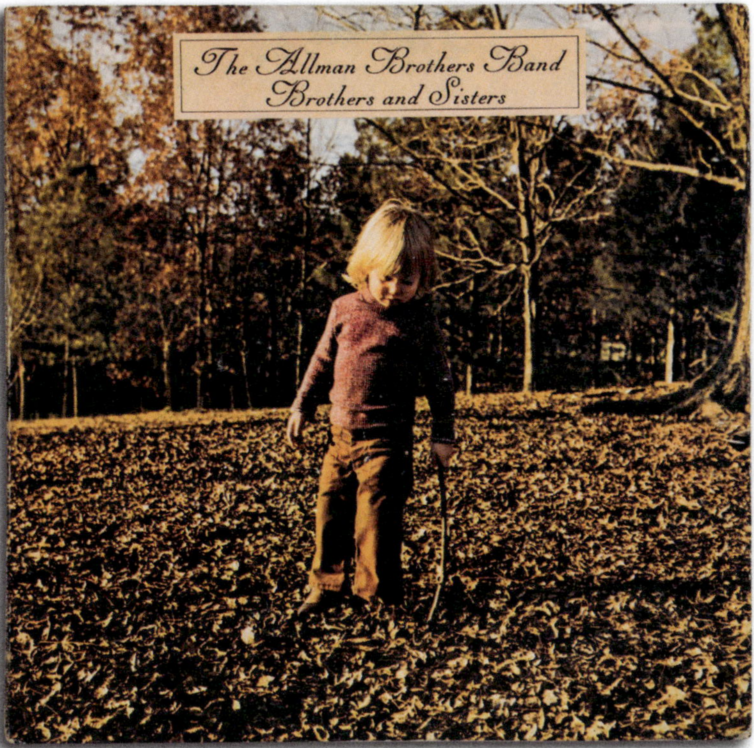

The Allman Brothers Band
Brothers And Sisters
Capricorn Records, 1973
Judi Reeve (Design)
Bo Meriwether, Dan Hudson Jr. (Photo)

04 AUG

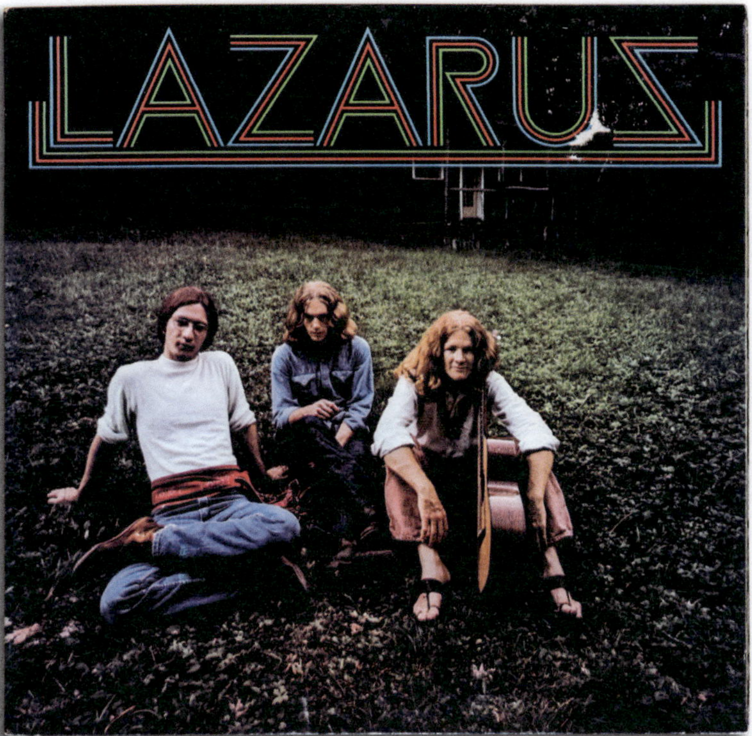

Lazarus
Bearsville Records, 1971
Milton Glaser (Design)
Benno Friedman (Photo)

05 AUG

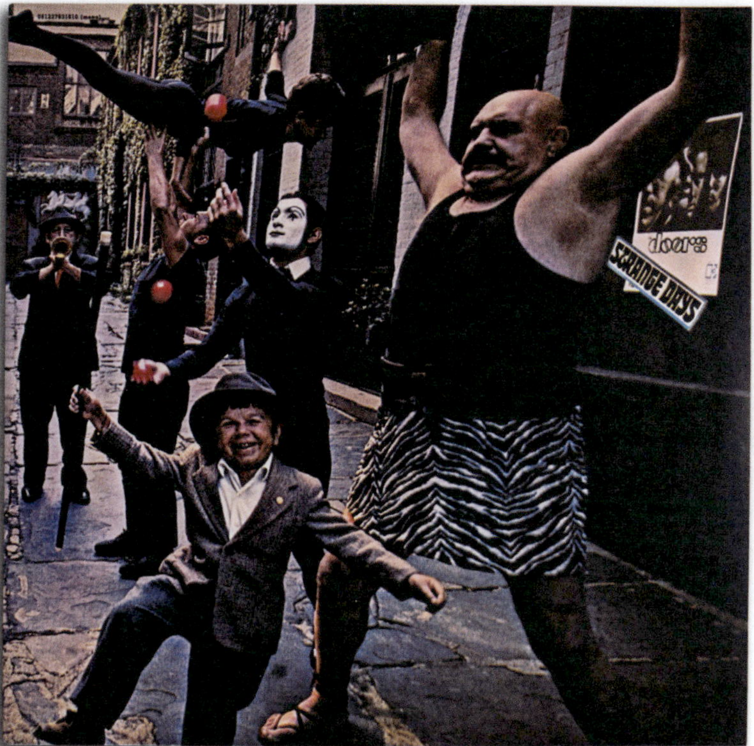

Doors
Strange Days
Elektra, 1967
William S. Harvey (Design)
Joel Brodsky (Photo)

06 AUG

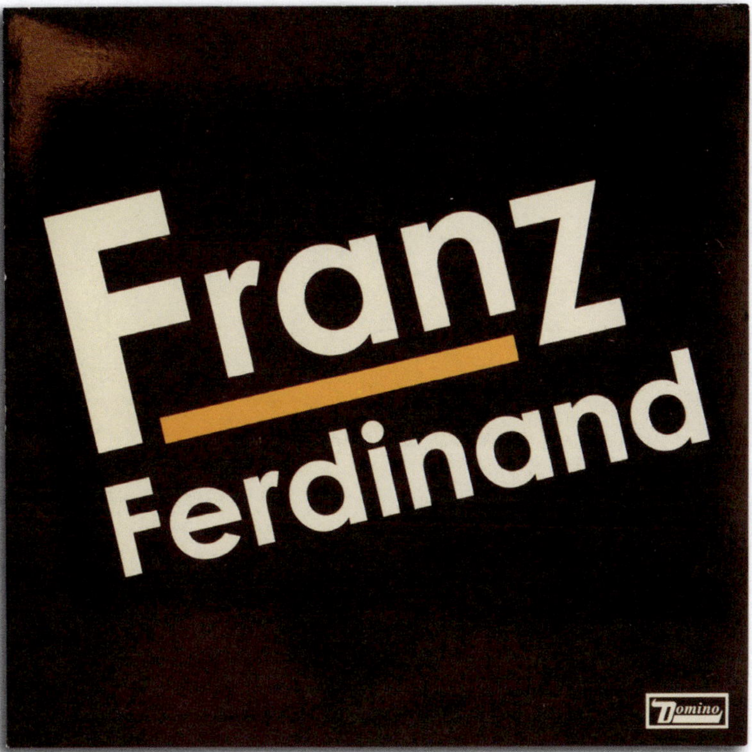

Franz Ferdinand
Domino, 2004
Vivian Lewis (Design)

07 AUG

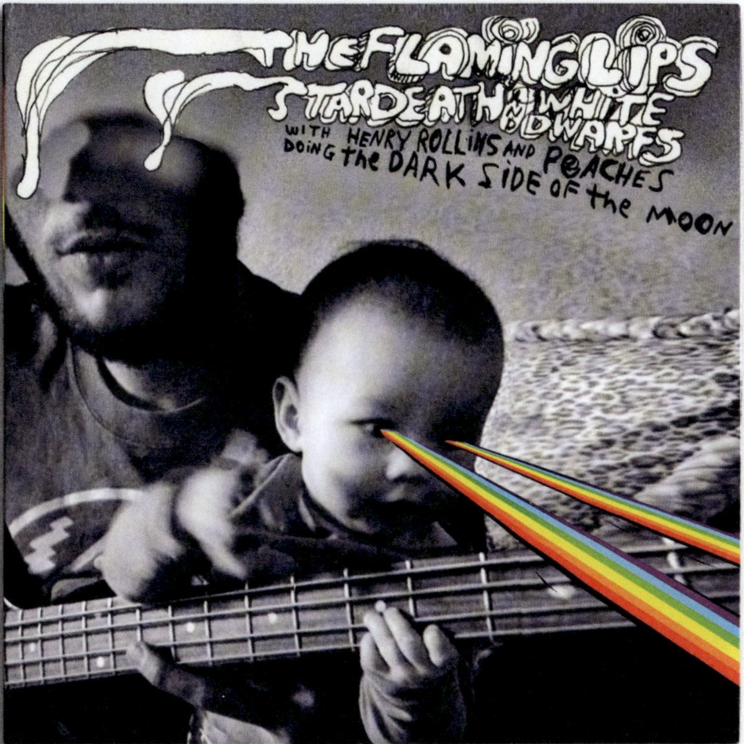

The Flaming Lips & Stradeath and White Dwarfs
The Dark Side Of The Moon
Warner Brothers, 2009
George Salisbury Who Is Particle (Design)
Jessica Joseph (Photo)

08 AUG

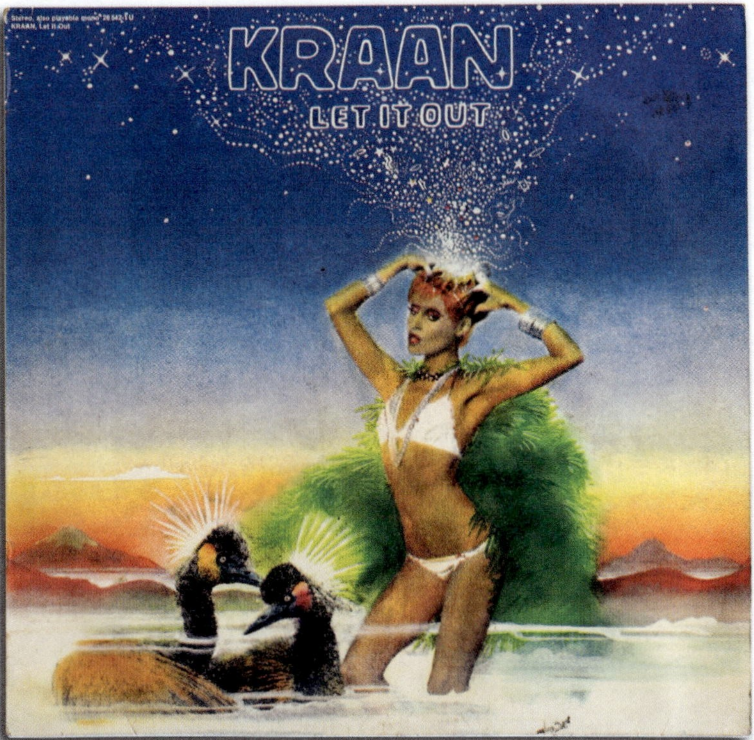

Kraan
Let It Out
Spiegelei, 1975
Peter Wolbrandt (Design)

09 AUG

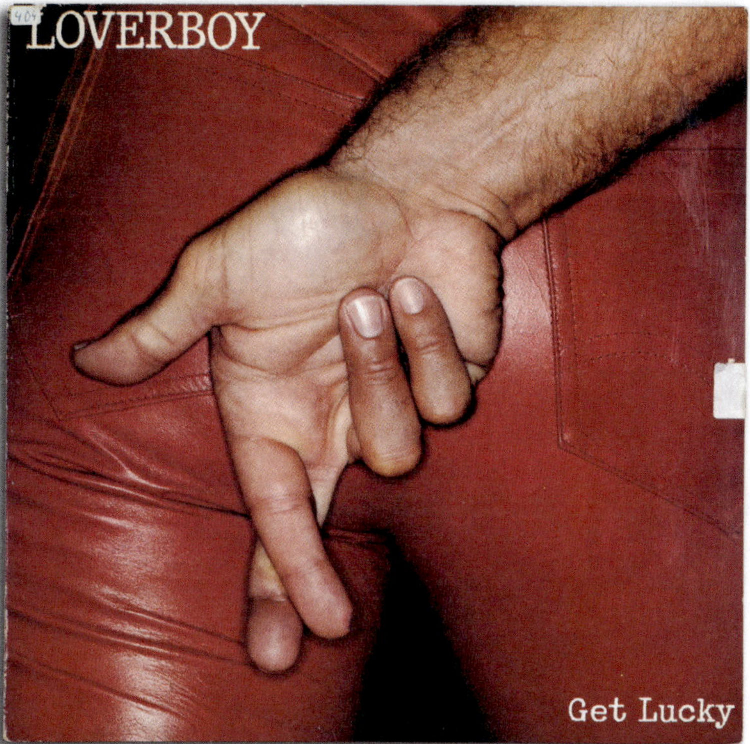

Loverboy
Get Lucky
Columbia Records, 1981
John Berg (Design)
David Kennedy (Photo)

10 AUG

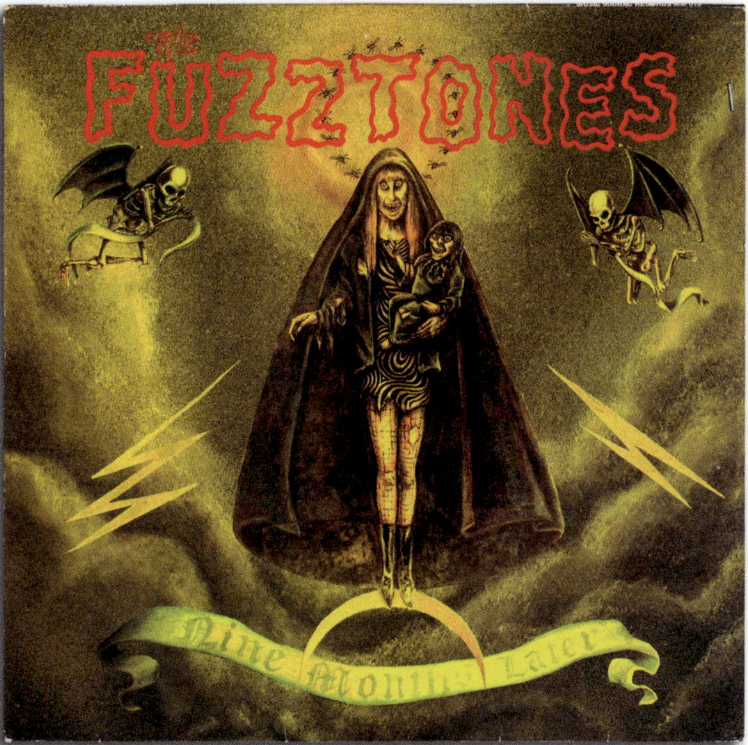

The Fuzztones
Nine Months Later
Music Maniac Records, 1988
Cover Artists Unknown

11 AUG

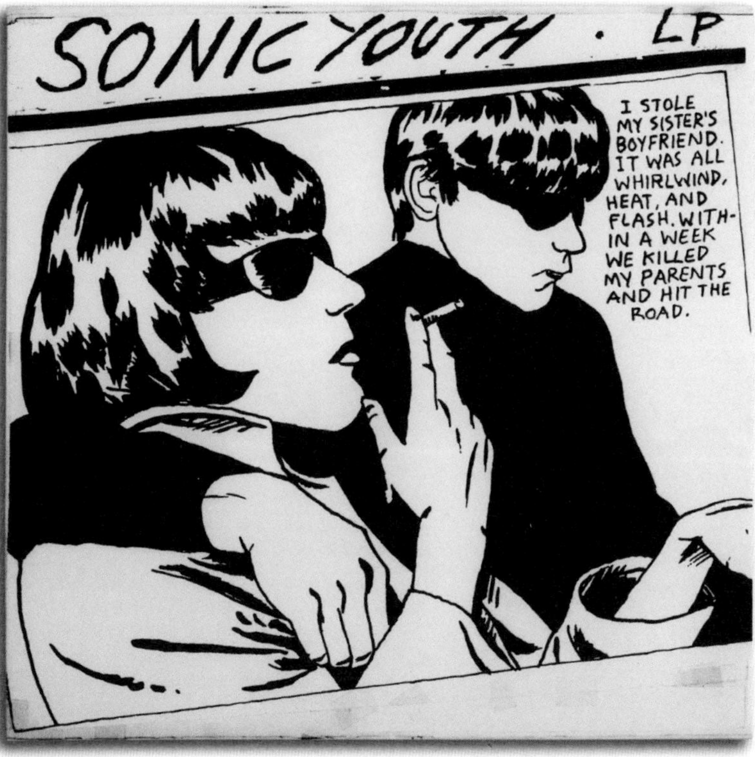

Sonic Youth
Goo
David Geffen Company, 1990
Kevin Reagan (Design)
Raymond Petticon (Illustration)

12 AUG

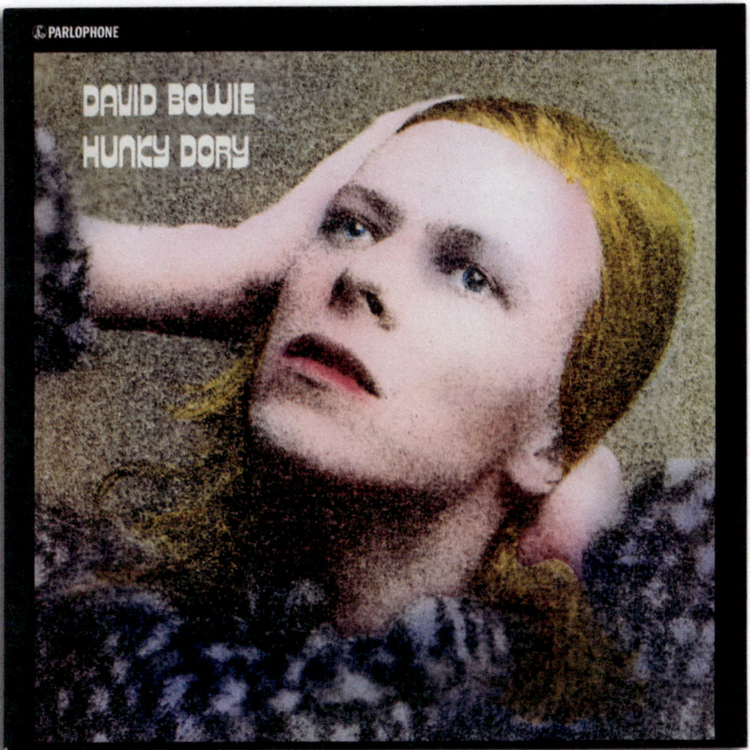

David Bowie
Hunky Dory
RCA Victor, 1973
George Underwood, Terry Pastor (Design)
Brian Ward (Photo)

13 AUG

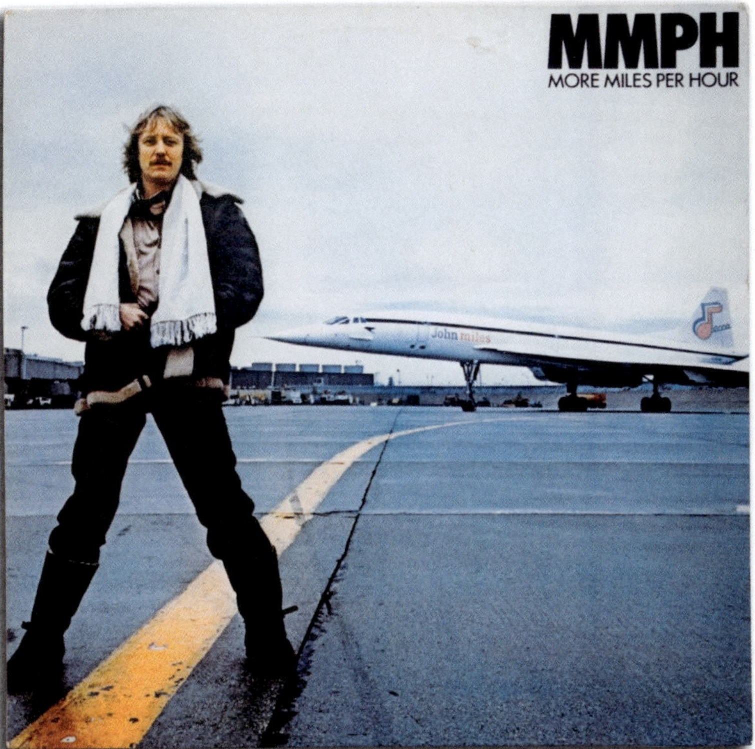

John Miles
More Miles Per Hour
Decca, 1979
Ashcroft, Hawkins (Design)
Terry O'Neill (Photo)

14 AUG

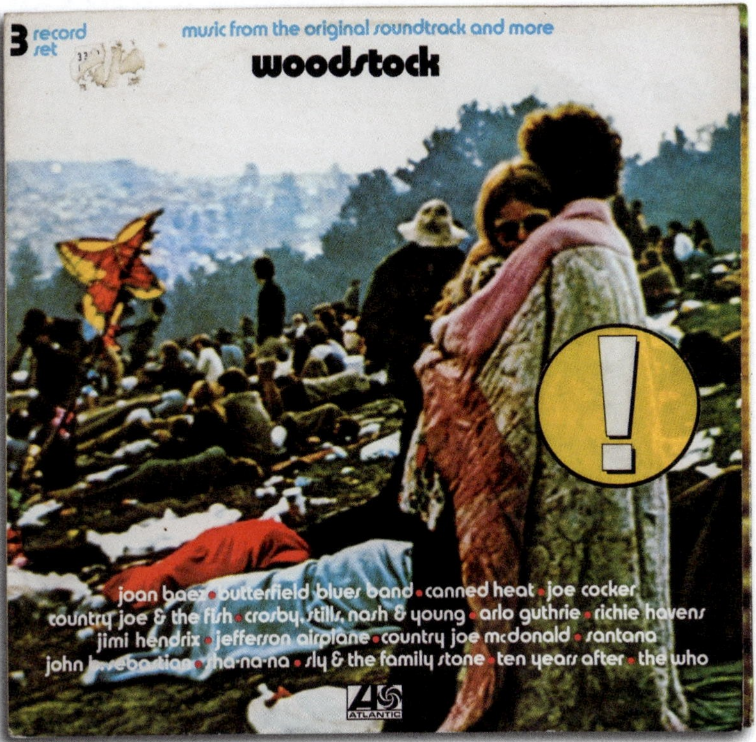

Various Artists – Soundtrack
Woodstock
Cotillion Records, 1970
Loring Eutemey (Design)
Magnum Photos (Photo)

Aug 15th–17th, 1969
Woodstock Festival
Bethel (New York)

15 AUG

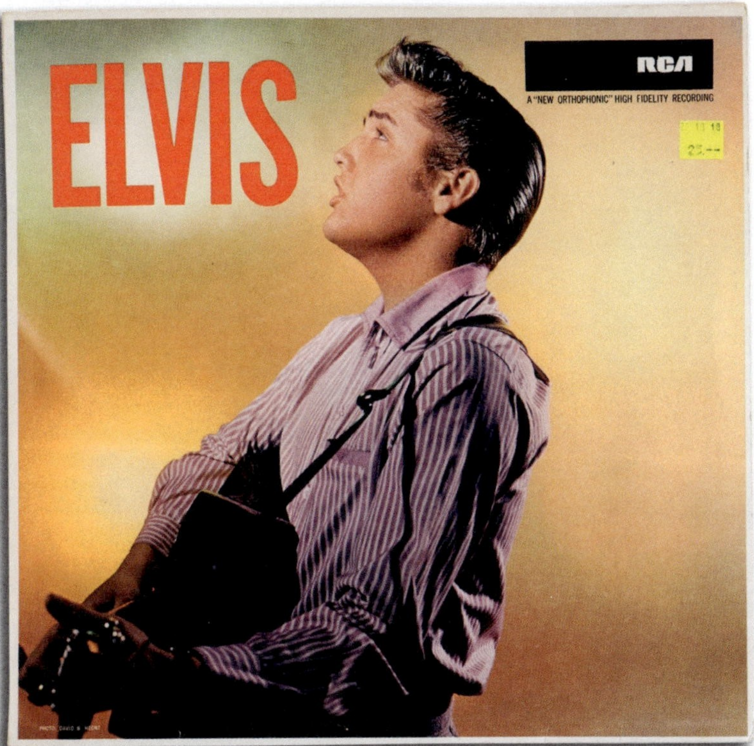

Elvis Presley
Elvis
RCA Victor, 1956
Cover Artists Unknown

† Aug 16th, 1977
Elvis Aaron Presley
Memphis (Tennessee)

16 AUG

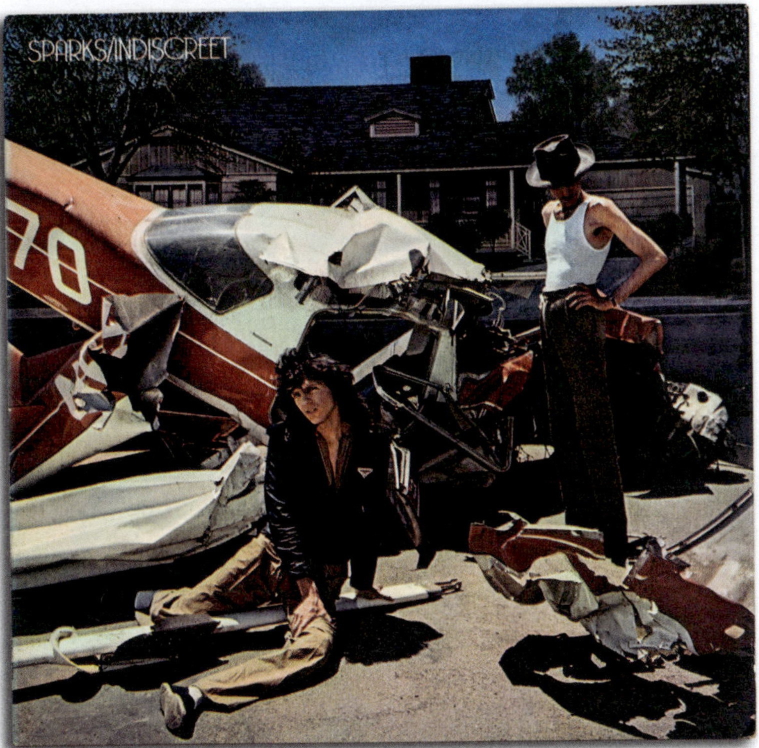

Sparks
Indiscreet
Island Records, 1975
Richard Creamer (Photo)

17 AUG

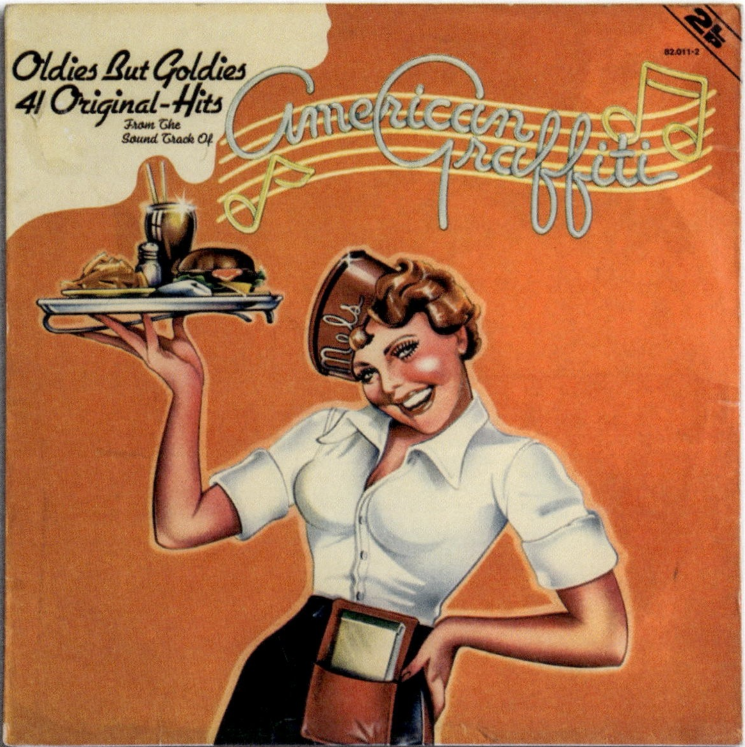

Various Artists – Soundtrack
American Graffiti
MCA Records, 1973
Cover Artists Unknown

18 AUG

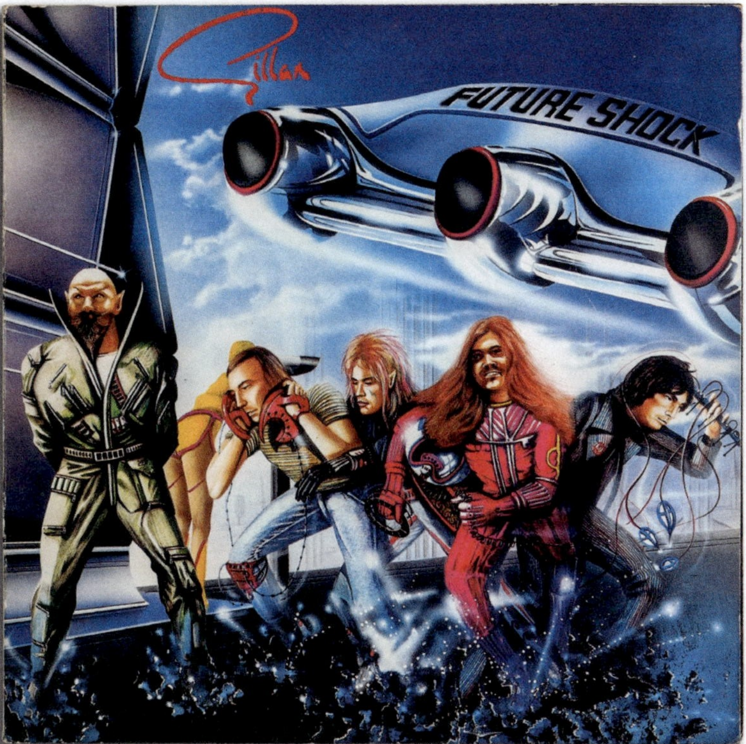

Gillan
Future Shock
Virgin Records, 1981
Alan Daniels, Angus McKie (Design)
Alan Daniels (Illustration)

* Aug 19th, 1845
Ian Gillan
Hounslow (Middlesex)

19 AUG

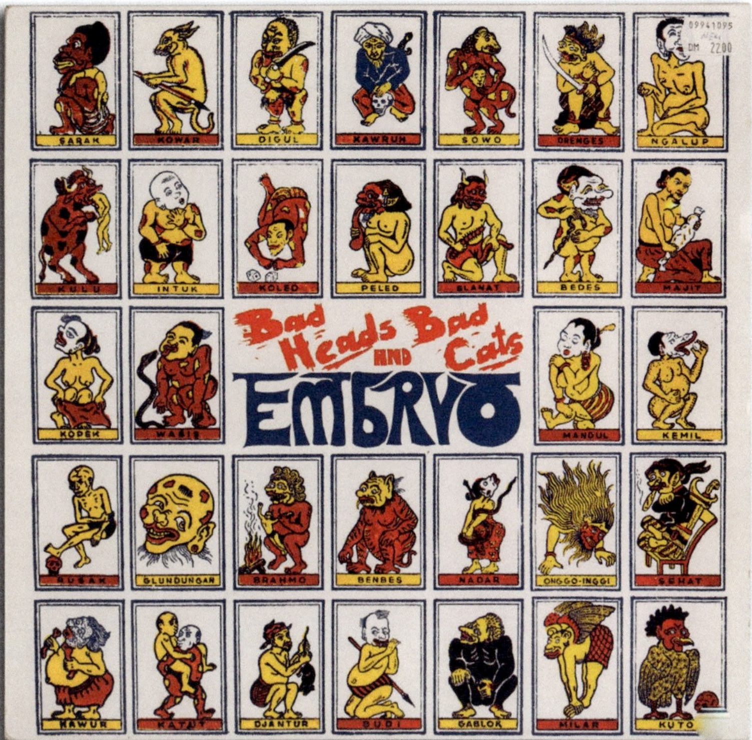

Embryo
Bad Heads And Bad Cats
April Records, 1976
Embryo (Design)

20 AUG

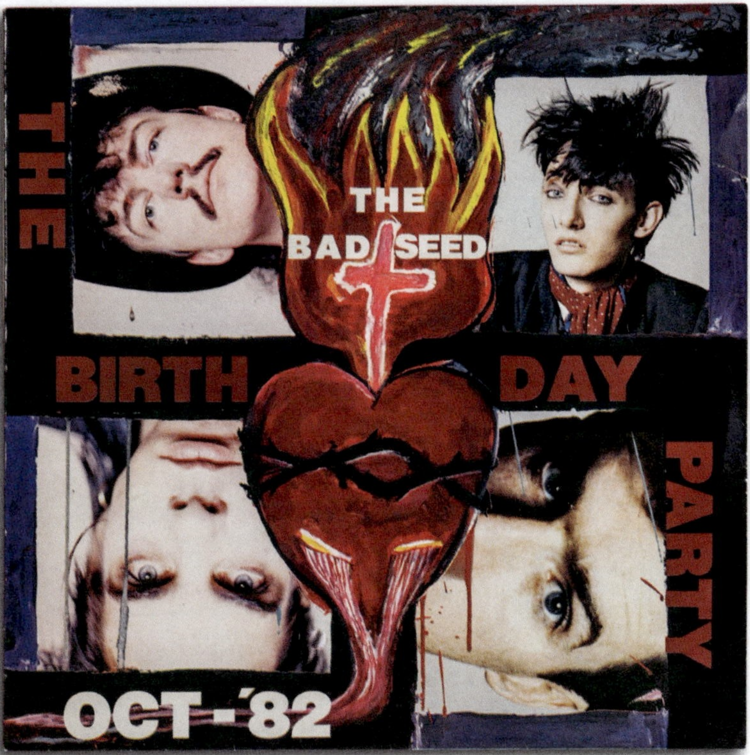

The Birthday Party
The Bad Seed
4AD, 1983
Laurence Stevens (Design)
Bleddyn Butcher (Photo)

21 AUG

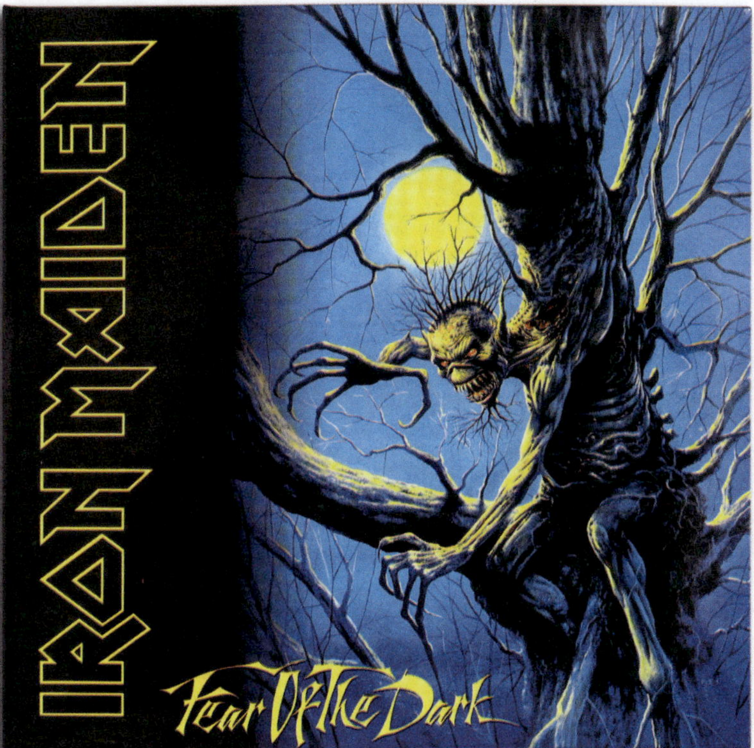

Iron Maiden
Fear Of The Dark
EMI, 1992
Melvyn Grant (Illustration)

22 AUG

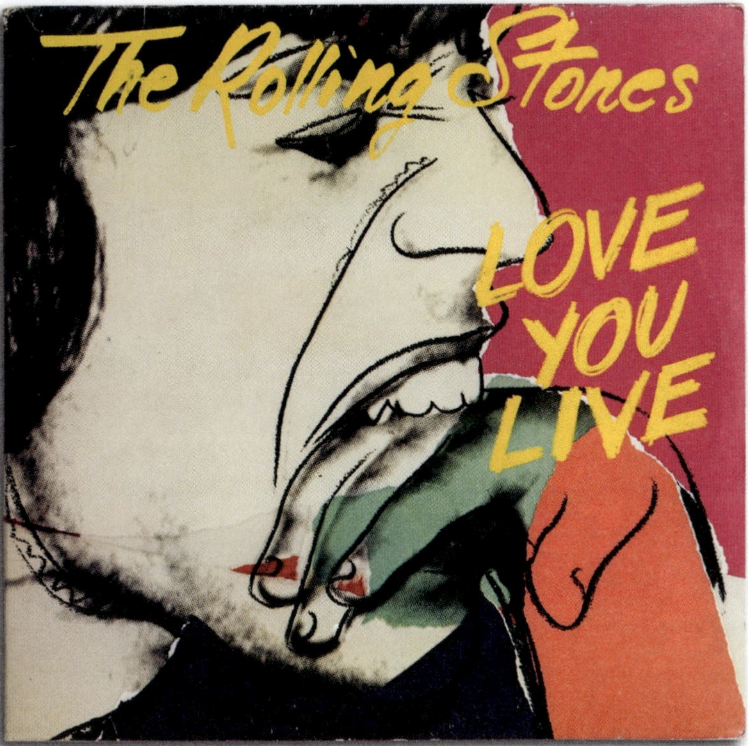

The Rolling Stones
Love You Will
Rolling Stones Records, 1977
Andy Warhol (Design)

23 AUG

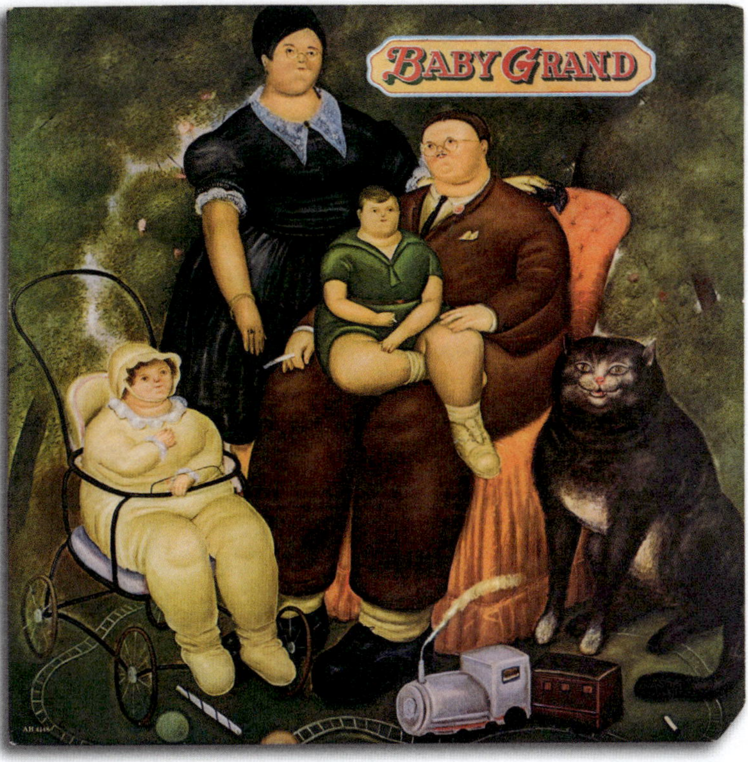

Baby Grand
Arista Records, 1977
Steve Feldman (Design)
Fernando Botero Angulo (Illustration)

24 AUG

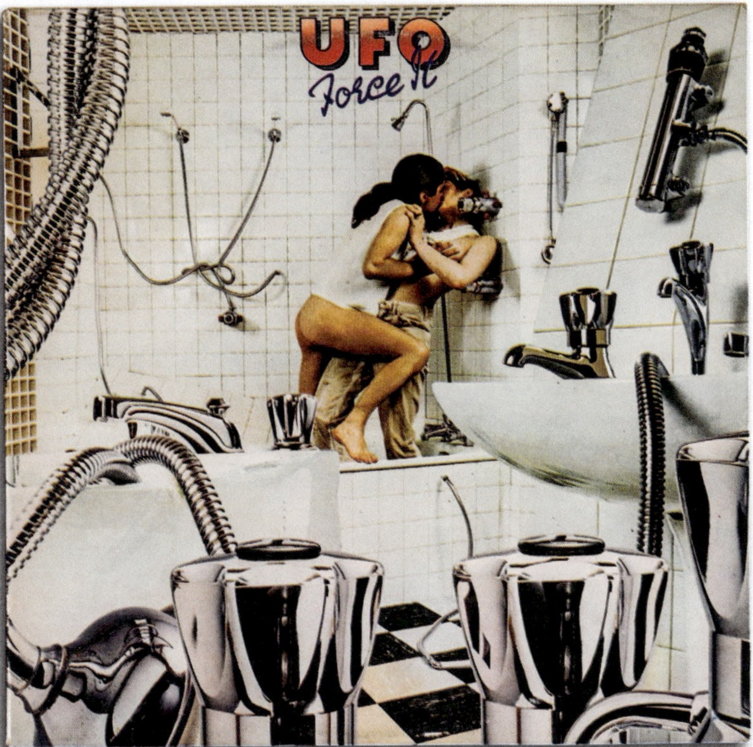

UFO
Force It
Chrysalis Records, 1975
Peter Christopherson (Design)
Hipgnosis (Photo)

25 AUG

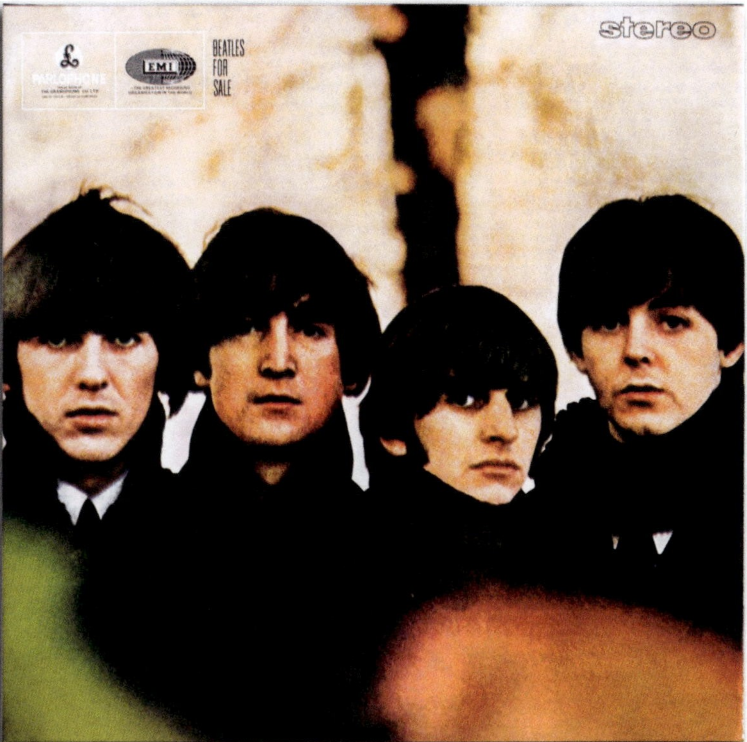

The Beatles
Beatles For Sale
Parlophone, 1964
Robert Freeman (Photo)

26 AUG

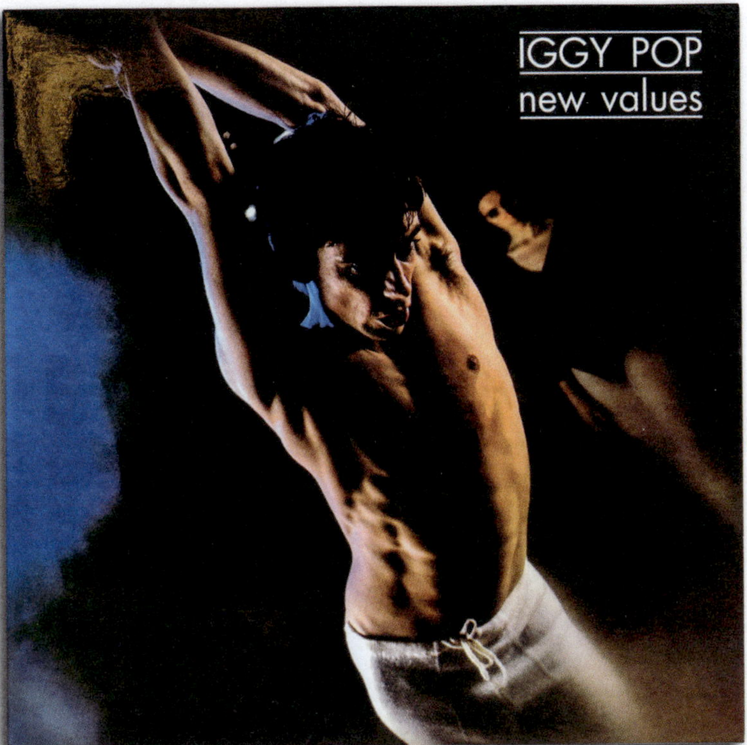

Iggy Pop
New Values
Arista, 1979
Paul Henry (Design)
Trevor Rogers (Photo)

27 AUG

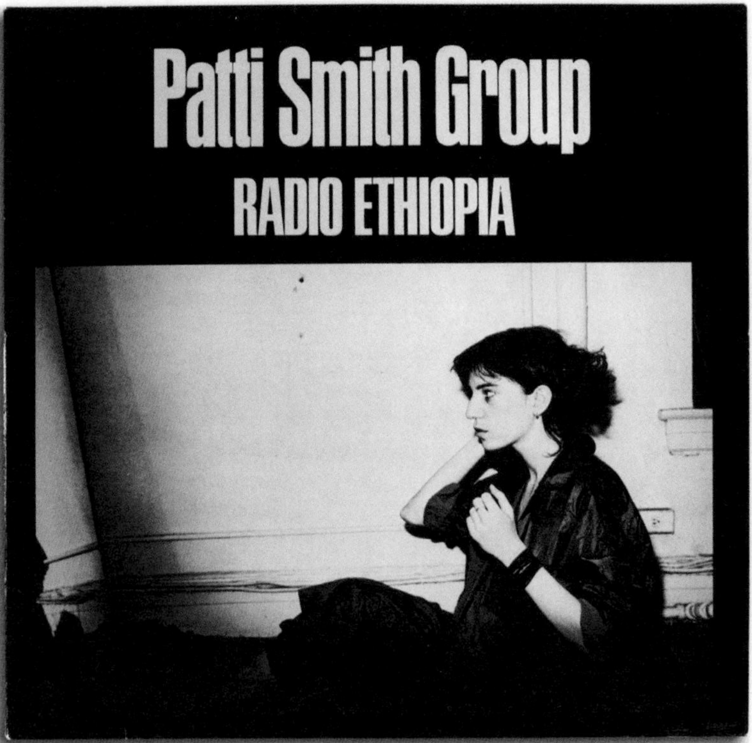

Patti Smith Group
Radio Ethopia
Arista Records, 1976
Patti Smith & Nancy Greenberg (Design)
Judy Linn (Photo)

28 AUG

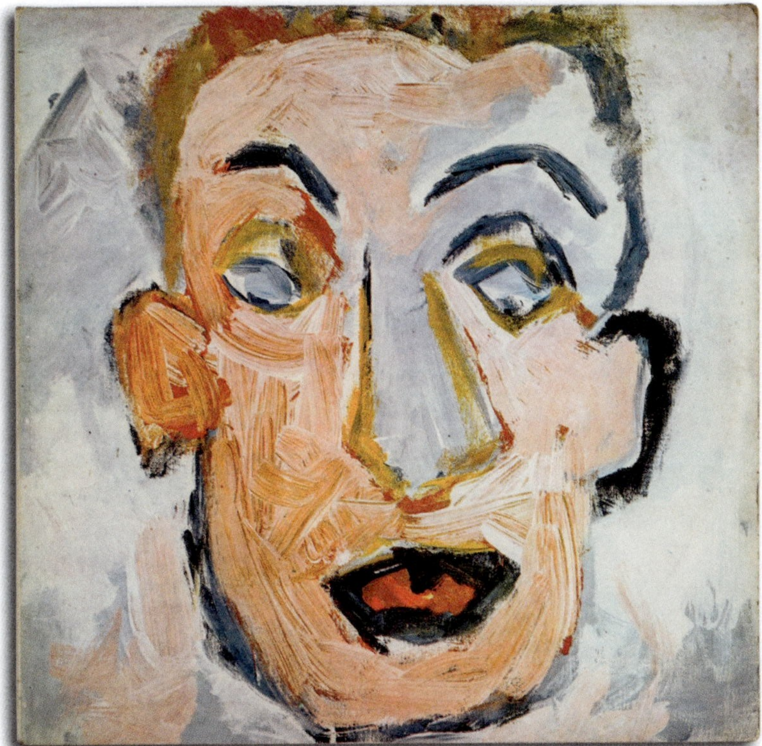

Bob Dylan
Self Portait
Columbia Records, 1970
Ron Coro (Design)
Bob Dylan (Illustration)

29 AUG

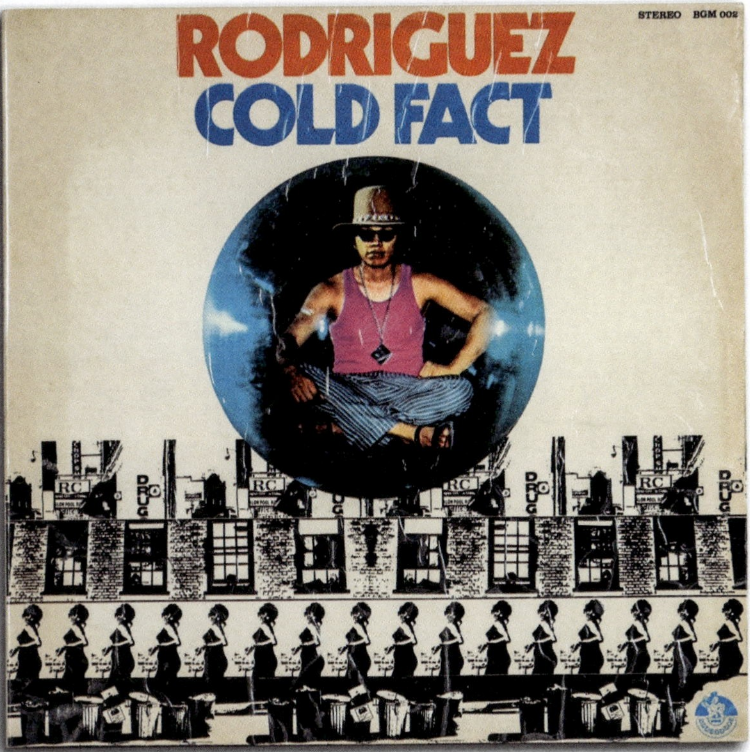

Rodriguez
Cold Fact
Sussex Records, 1970
Nancy Chester, See/ Her! & How! (Design)
Bob Flath of Ransier and Anderson (Photo)

30 AUG

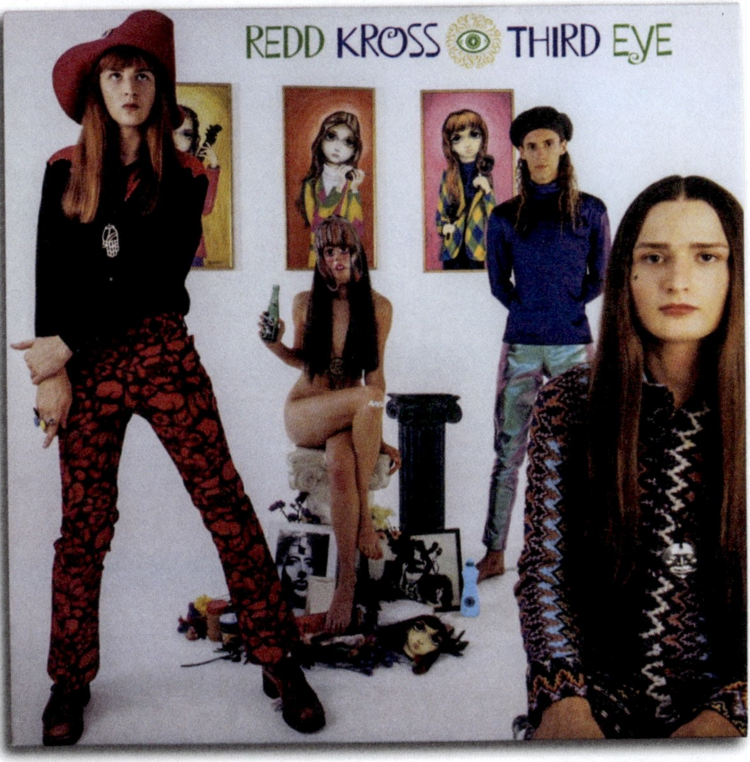

Redd Kross
Third Eye
Atlantic, 1990
Vicki Berndt (Design)
Mojgan B. Azimi (Photo)

31 AUG

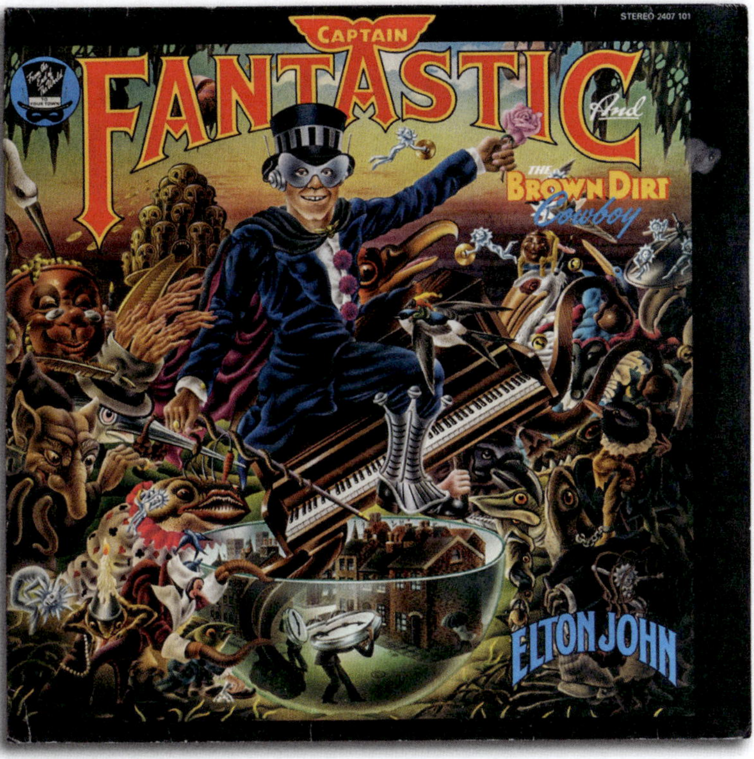

Elton John
Captain Fantastic And The Brown Dirt Cowboy
DJM Records, 1975
Bernie Taupin, David Larkham (Design)
Alan Aldrige (Illustration)

01 SEP

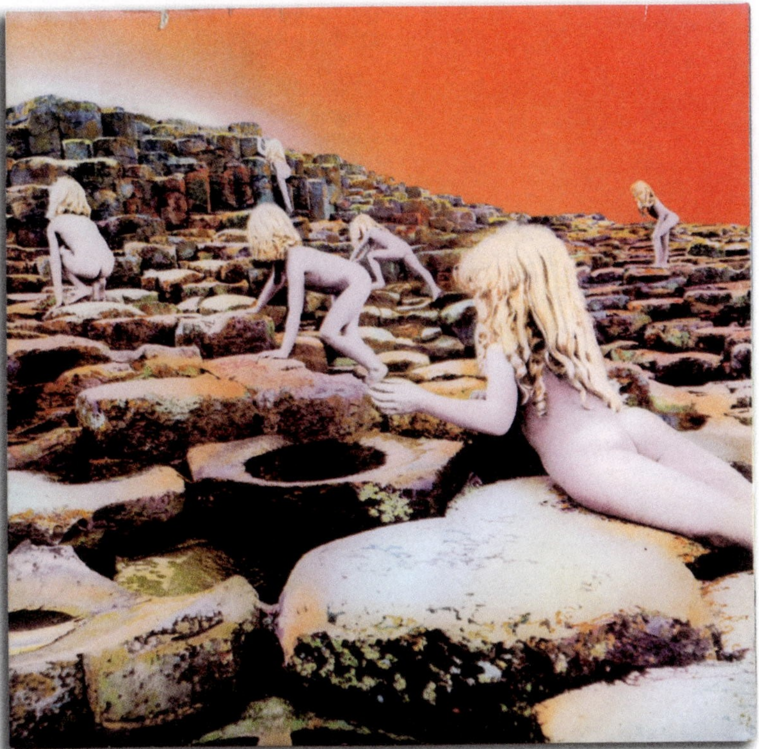

Led Zeppelin
Houses Of The Holy
Atlantic Records, 1973
Hipgnosis (Design)

02 SEP

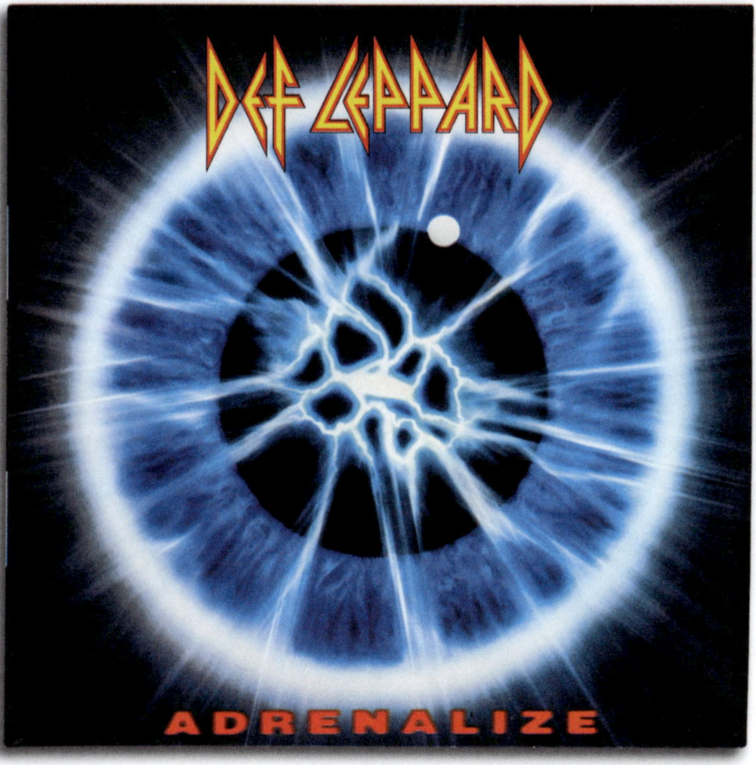

Def Leppard
Adrenalize
Bludgeon Riffola, 1992
Andie Airfix (Design)

03 SEP

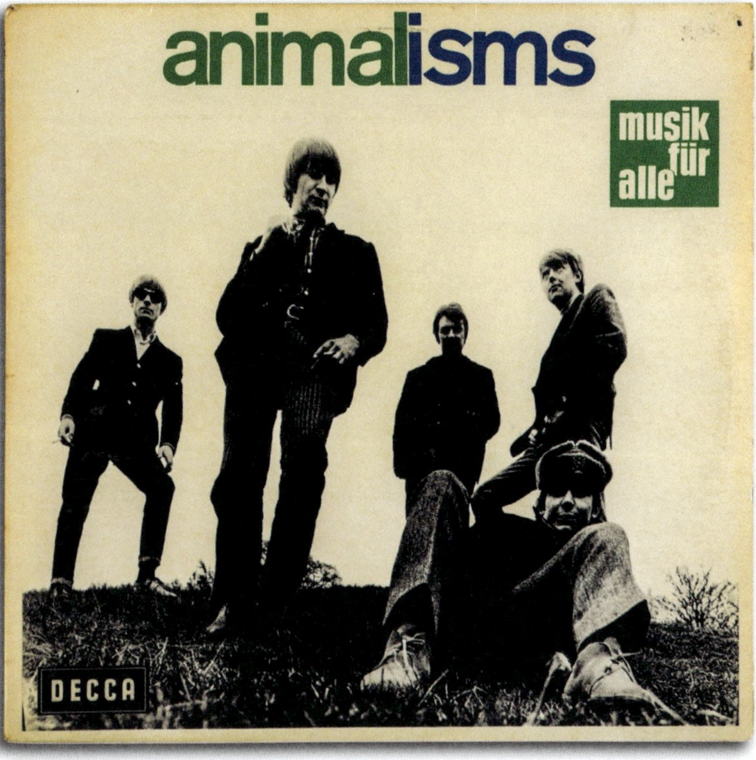

The Animals
Animalisms
Decca, 1966
Maintery (Design)

04 SEP

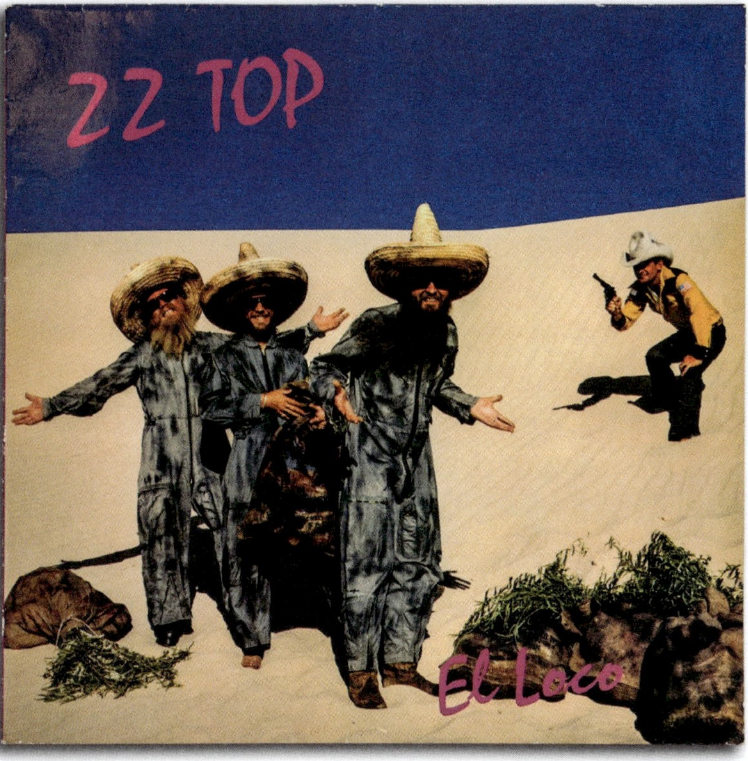

ZZ Top
El Loco
Warner Bros. Records, 1981
Dennis Ritter (Design)
Bob Alford (Photo)

05 SEP

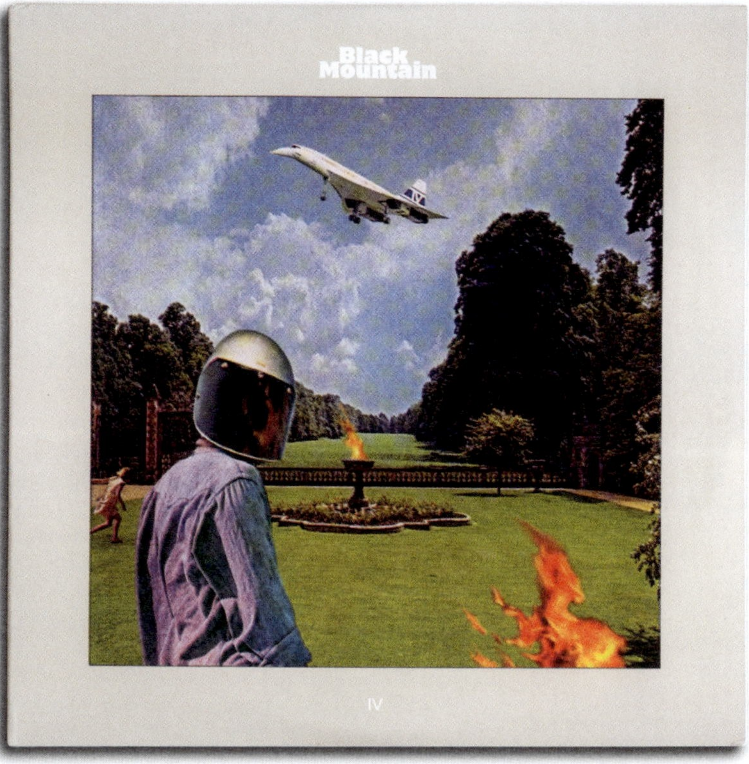

Black Mountain
IV
Jagjaguwar, 2016
Jeremy Schmidt (Design)

06 SEP

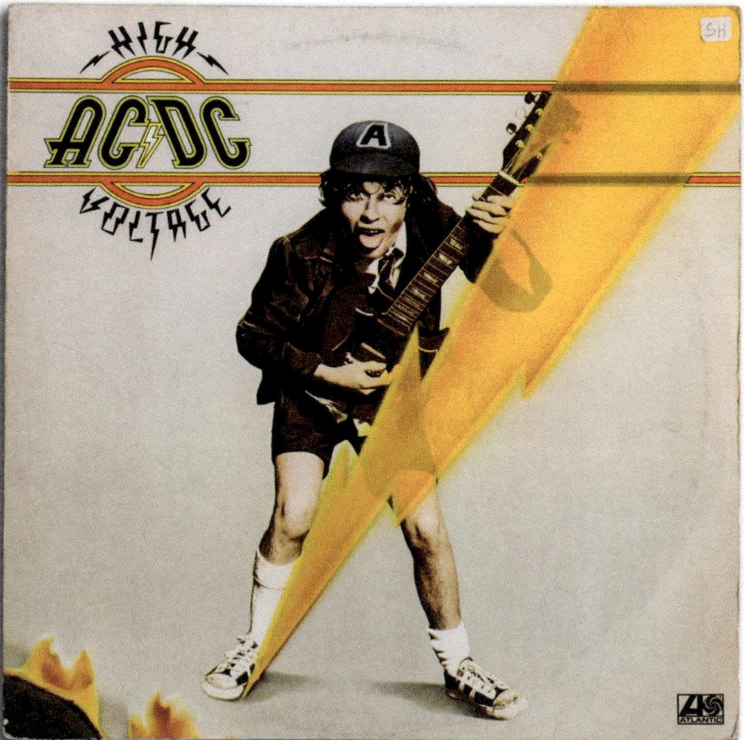

AC/DC
High Voltage
Atlantic Records, 1976
Michael Putland (Photo)

07 SEP

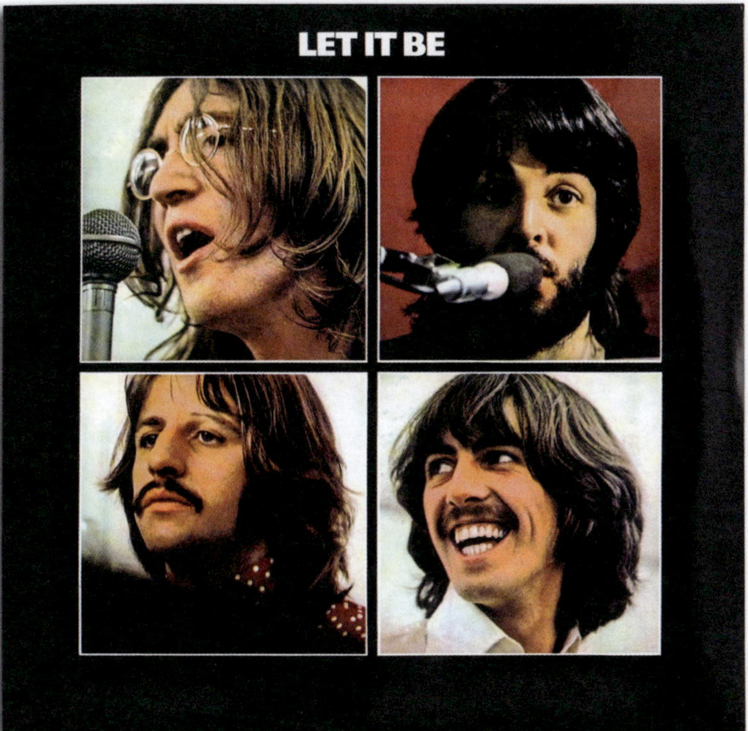

The Beatles
Let It Be
Apple Records, 1970
John Kosh (Design)
Ethan Russell (Photo)

08 SEP

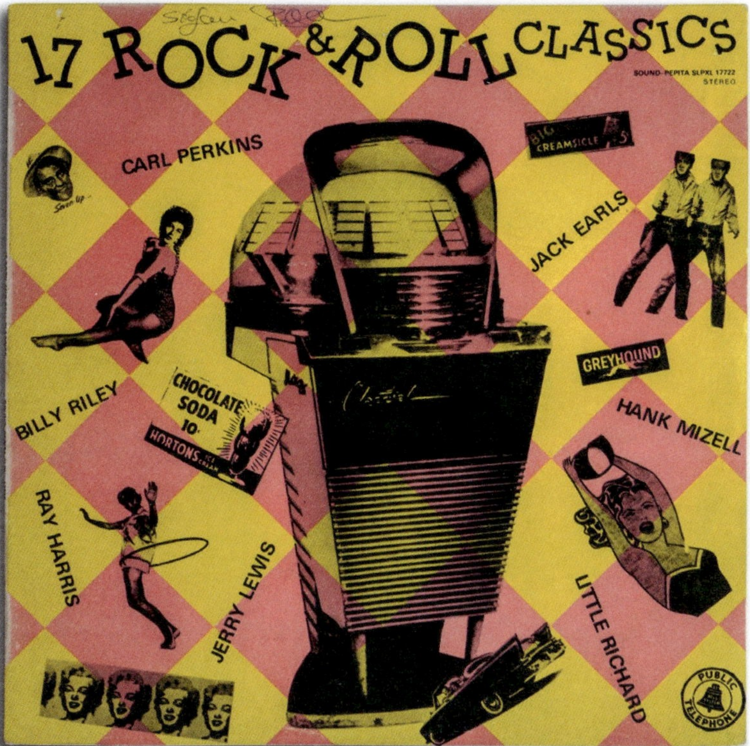

Various Artists
17 Rock & Roll Classics
Sound Pepita, 1982
Nagy Péter (Design)

09 SEP

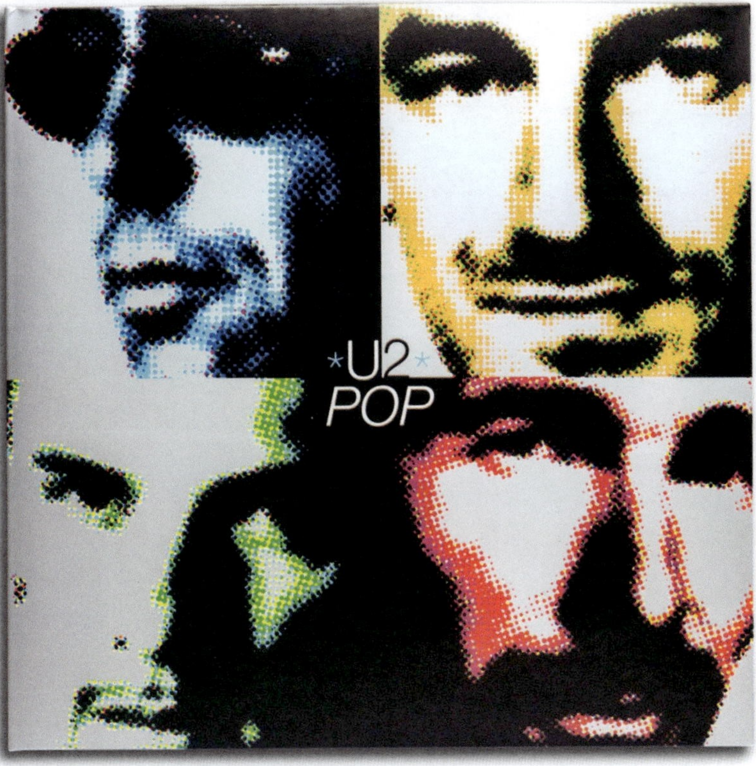

U2
Pop
Island Records, 1987
Mark Fisher (Design)
Anton Corbijn (Photo)

10 SEP

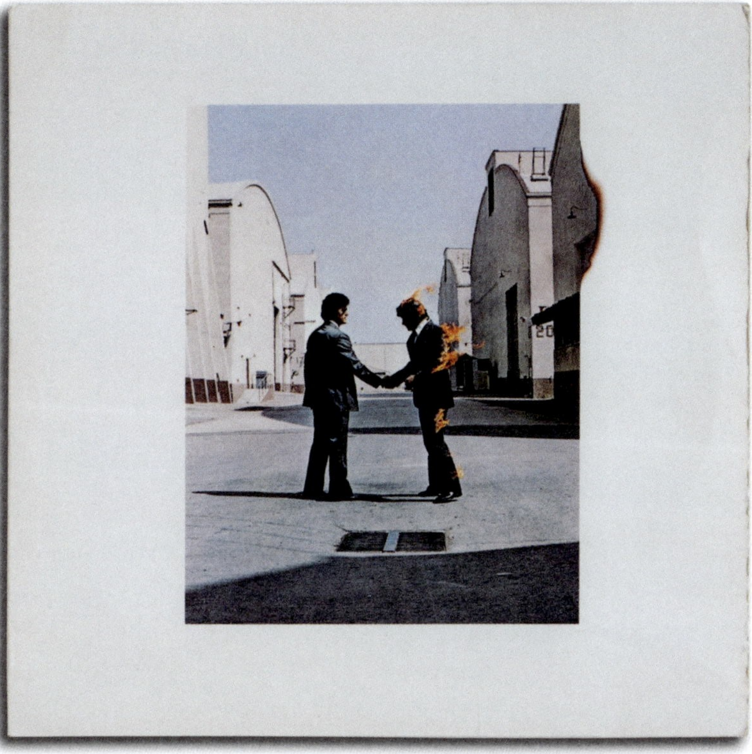

Pink Floyd
Wish You Were Here
EMI Electrola, 1975
Hipgnosis (Design)
Peter Christopherson (Photo)

11 SEP

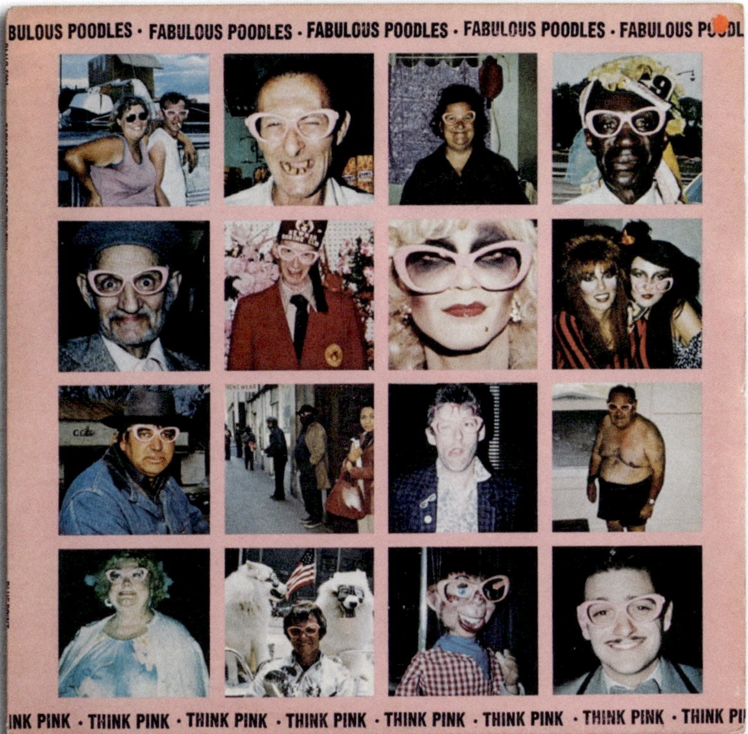

Fabulous Poodles
Think Pink
Blueprint, 1979
Mary Ann Morgenthaler (Design)
John Parsons (Photo)

12 SEP

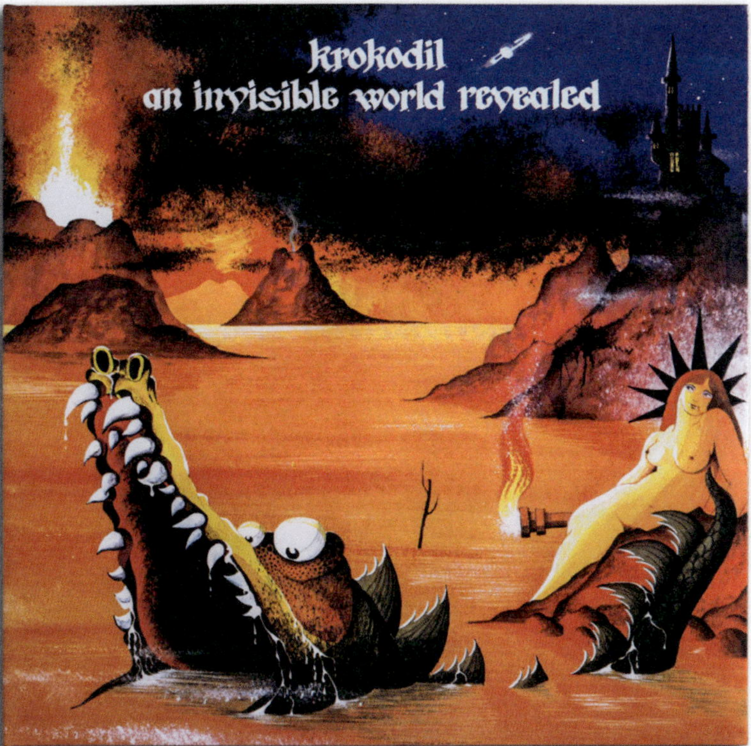

Krokodil
An Invisible World Revealed
Krokodil Records, 1971
Düde Dürst (Design)

13 SEP

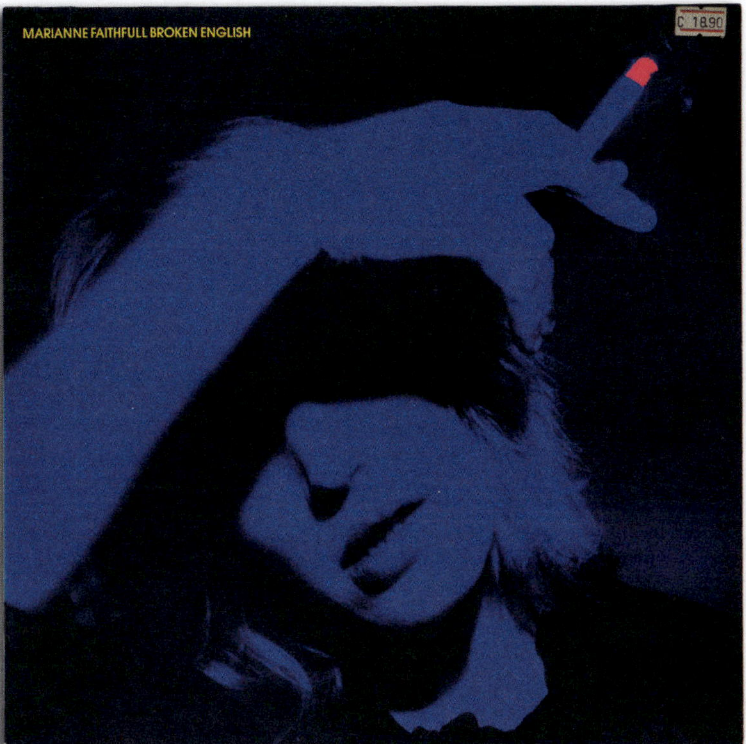

Marianne Faithfull
Broken English
Island Records, 1979
Dennis Morris (Photo)

14 SEP

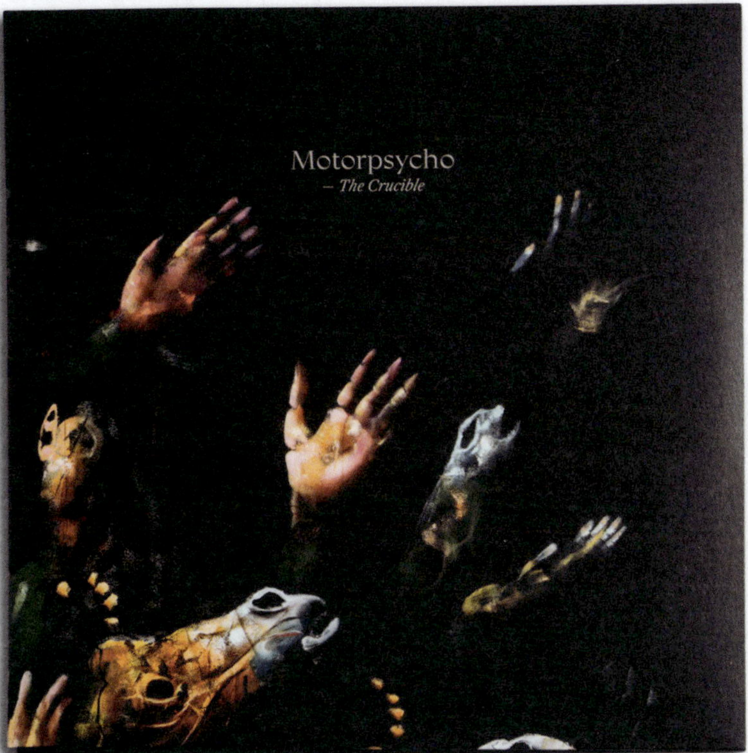

Motorpsycho
The Crucible
Stickman Records, 2019
Håvard Gjelseth (Design)
Håkon Gullvåg (Photo)

15 SEP

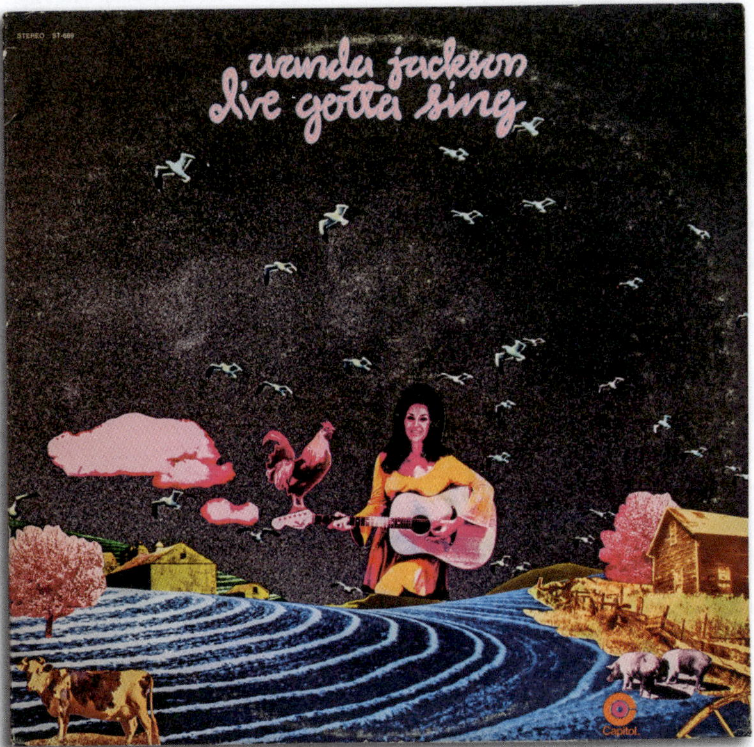

Wanda Jackson
I've Gotta Sing
Capitol Records, 1971
Roland Young (Design)
Pyramid Productions (Photo)

16 SEP

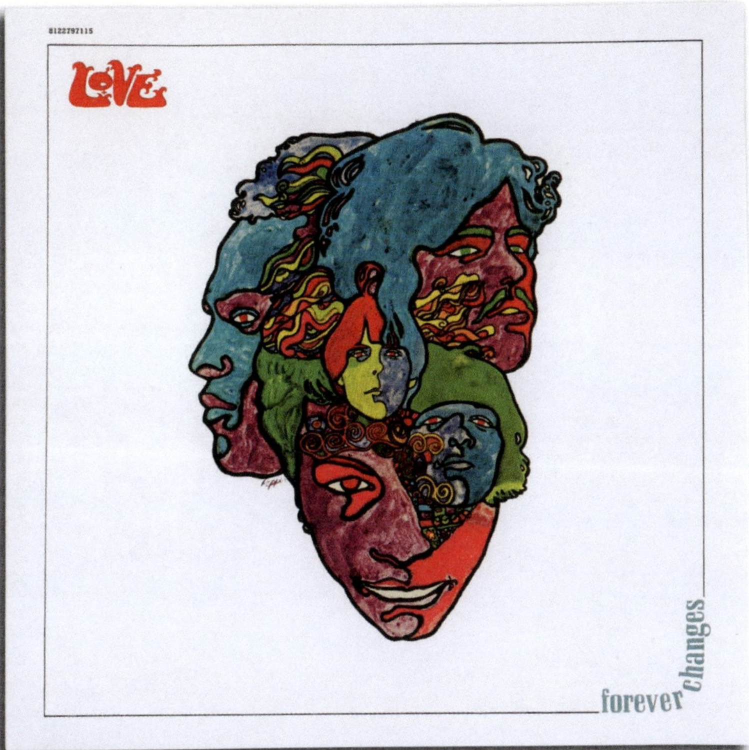

Love
Forever Changes
Elektra, 1967
William S. Harvey (Design)
Bob Pepper (Illustration)

17 SEP

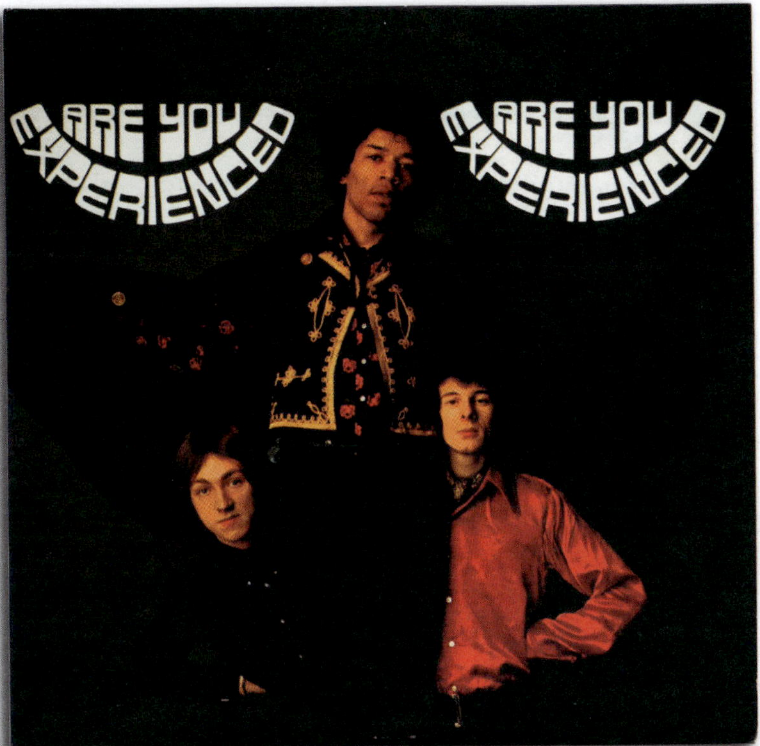

The Jimi Hendrix Experience
Are You Experienced
Polydor, 1967
Cover Artists Unknown

18 SEP

† Sep 18th, 1970
James Marshall "Jimi" Hendrix
London (UK)

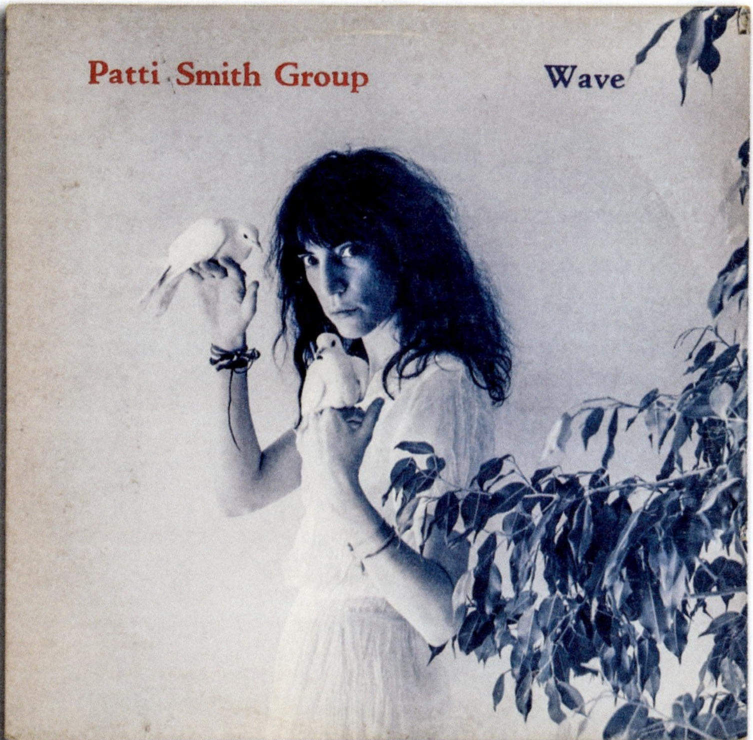

Patti Smith Group
Wave
Arista Records, 1979
Maud Gilman, Patti Smith (Design)
Robert Mapplethorpe (Photo)

19 SEP

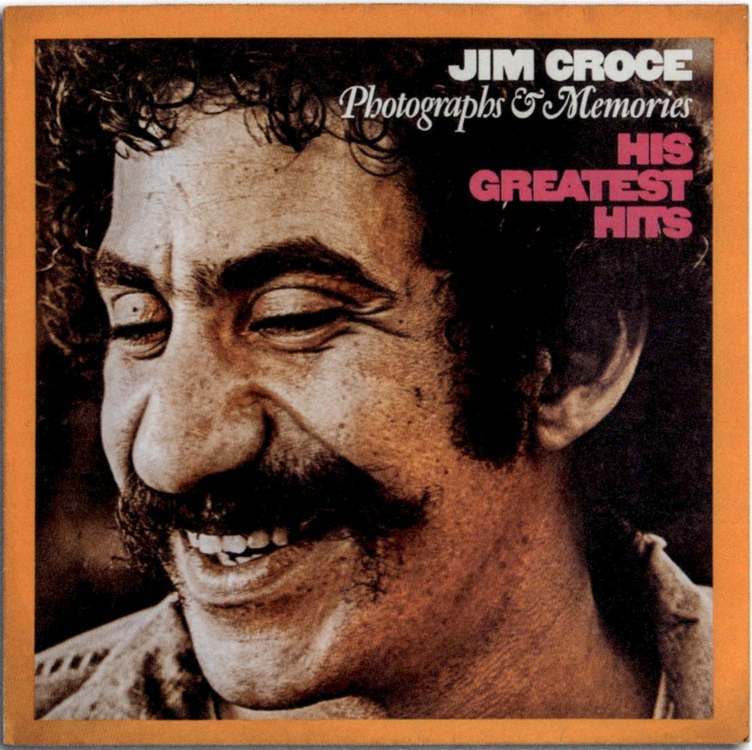

Jim Croce
Photographs & Memories
ABC Records, 1974
Robert L. Heimall (Design)
Benno Friedmann (Photo)

† Sep 20th, 1973
James Joseph Croce
Natchitoches (Louisiana)

20 SEP

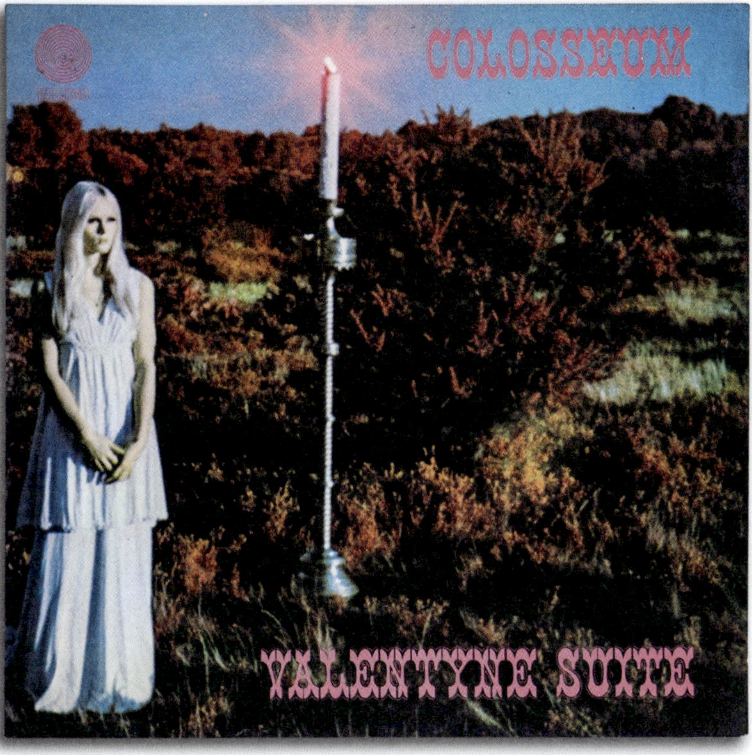

Colosseum
Valentyne Suite
Vertigo Records, 1969
Marcus Keef (Design)
Marcus Keef & Peter Smith (Photo)

21 SEP

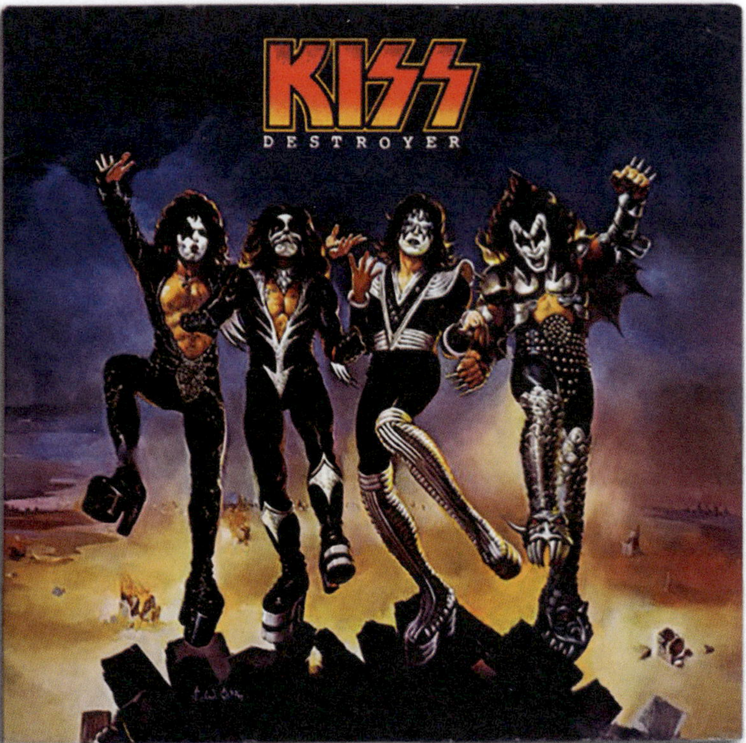

Kiss
Destroyer
Casablanca Records, 1976
Dennis Woloch (Design)
Ken Kelly (Illustration)

22 SEP

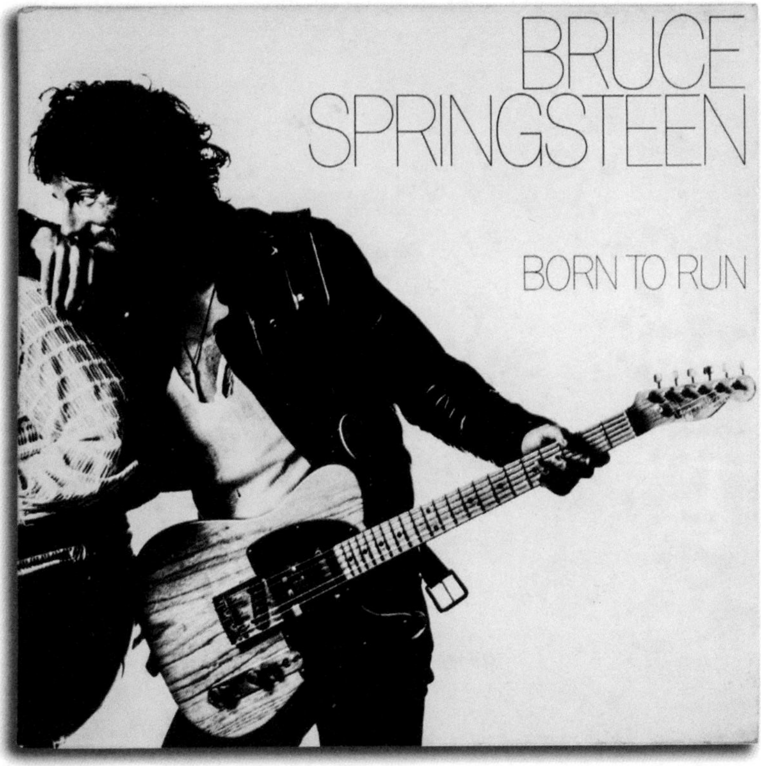

Bruce Springsteen
Born To Run
Colmbia, 1975
Andy Enge, John Berg (Design)
Eric Meola (Photo)

* Sep 23rd, 1949
Bruce Frederick Joseph Springsteen
Long Branch (New Jersey)

23 SEP

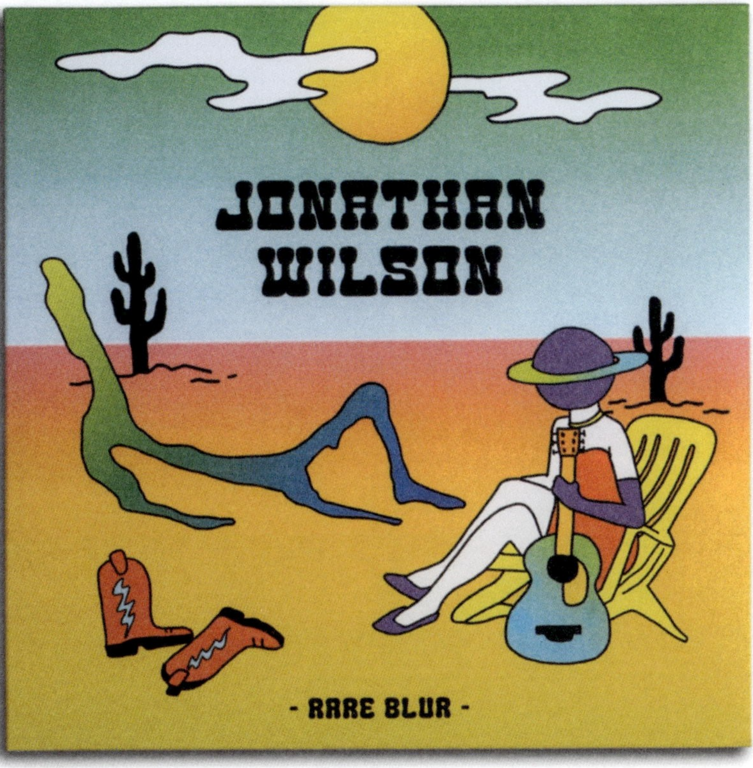

Jonathan Wison
Rare Blur
Bella Union, 2020
Cover Artists Unknown

24 SEP

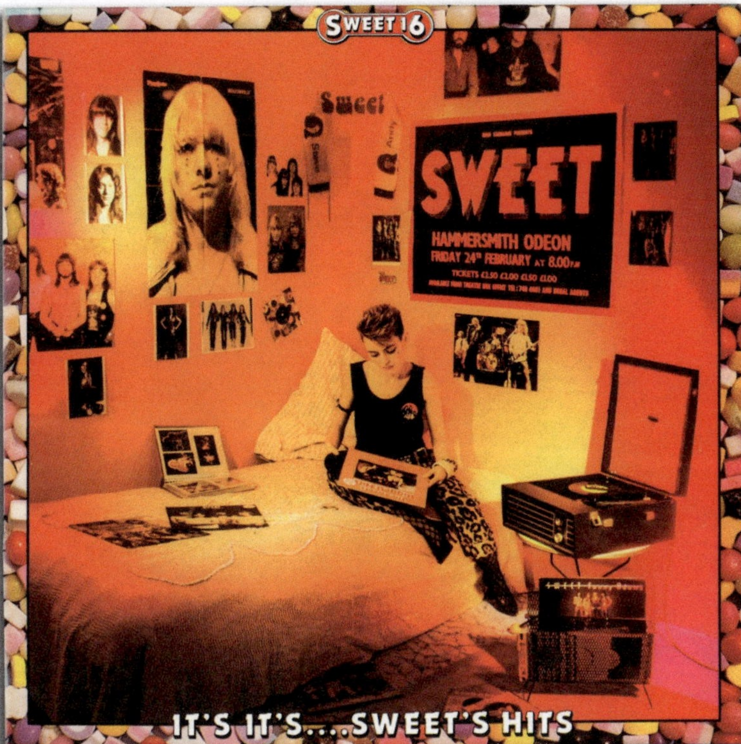

Sweet
Sweet 16: It's It's... Sweet's Hits
Anagram Records, 1985
Jim Phelan (Design)
Phil Ward (Photo)

25 SEP

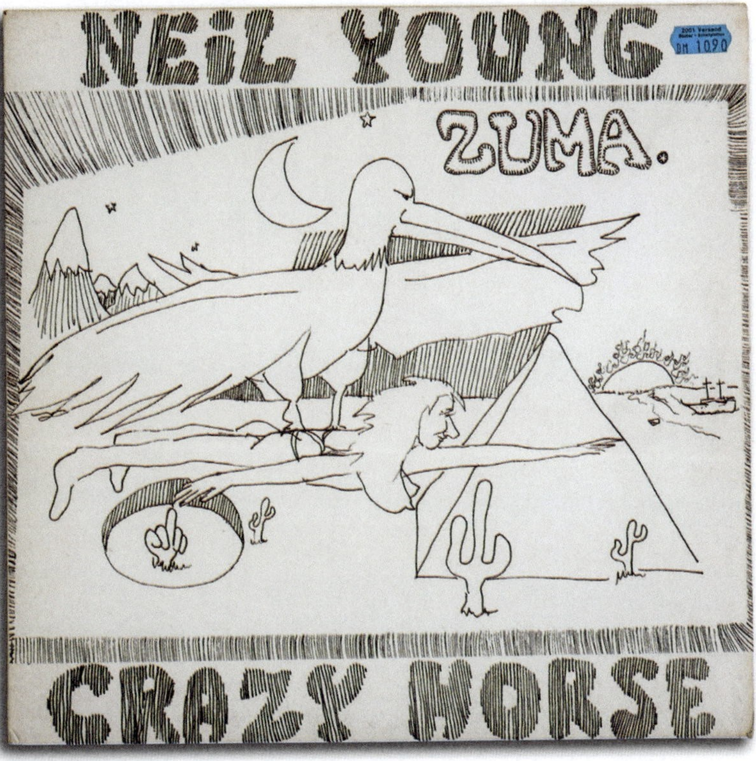

Neil Young With Crazy Horse
Zuma
Reprise Records, 1970
James Mazzeo (Illustration)

26 SEP

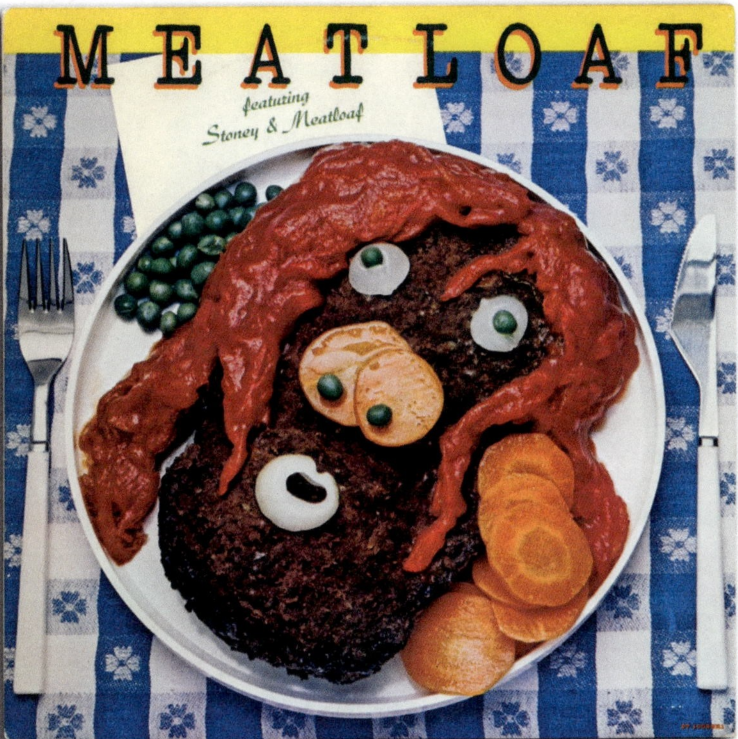

Meatloaf
Featuring Stoney & Meatloaf
Prodigal, 1978
Curtis McNair (Design)
John Dornes (Photo)

* Sep 27th, 1947
Marvin Lee Aday
Dallas (Texas)

27 SEP

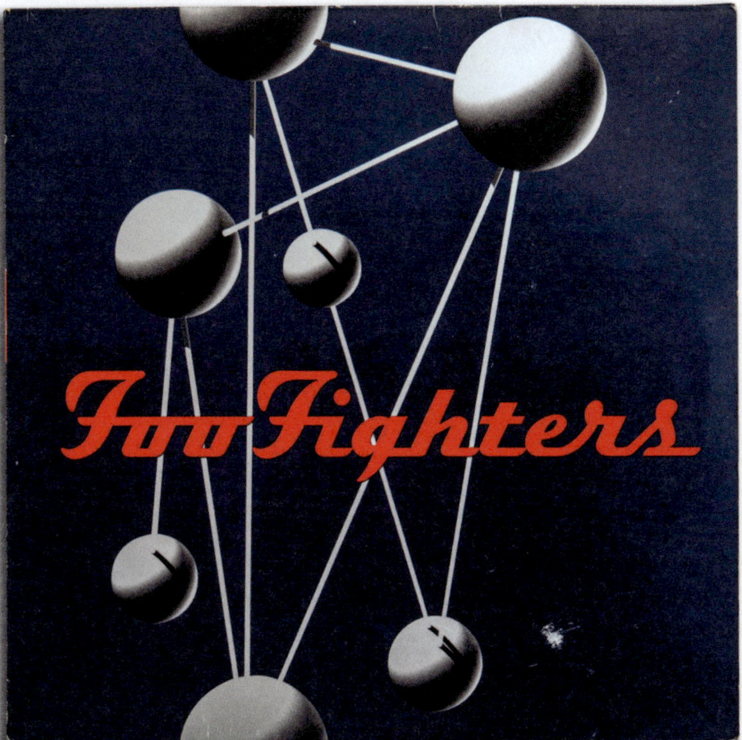

Foo Fighters
The Colour And The Shape
Capitol Records, 1997
Foo Fighters, Jeffery Fey, Tommy Steele (Design)
Andy Engel (Illustration)

28 SEP

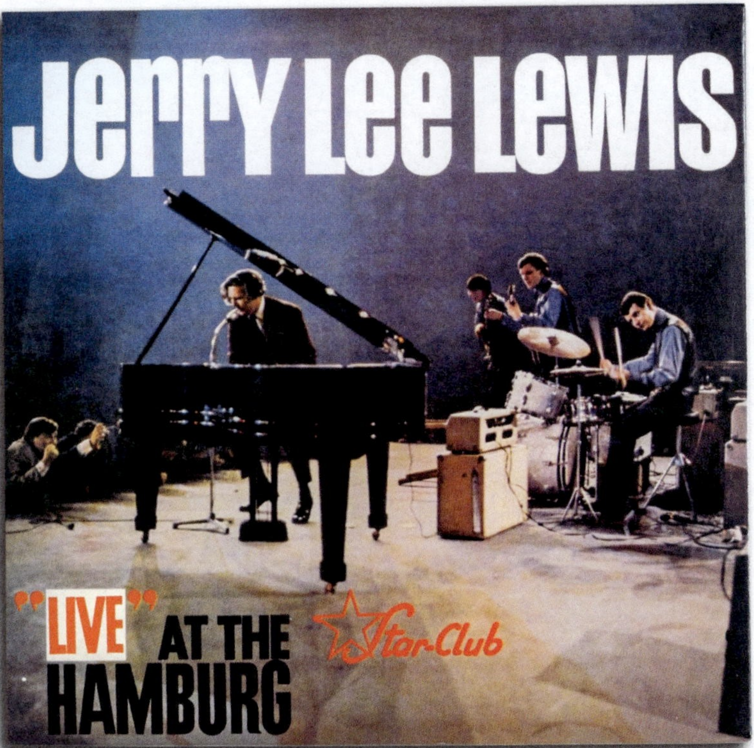

Jerry Lee Lewis
"Live" At The "Star Club" Hamburg
Philips, Bear Family Records, 1964
Ingrid Buhring (Photo)

29 SEP

* Sep 29th, 1935
Jerry Lee Lewis
Ferriday (L.A) (California)

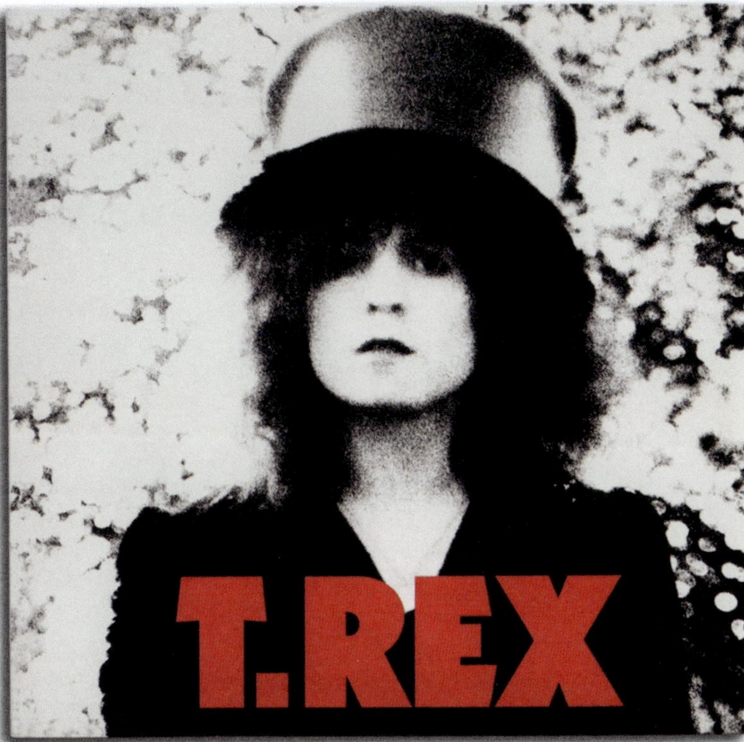

T. Rex
The Slider
EMI, 1972
Ringo Starr (Photo)

* Sep 30th, 1947
Marc Bolan
London (UK)

30 SEP

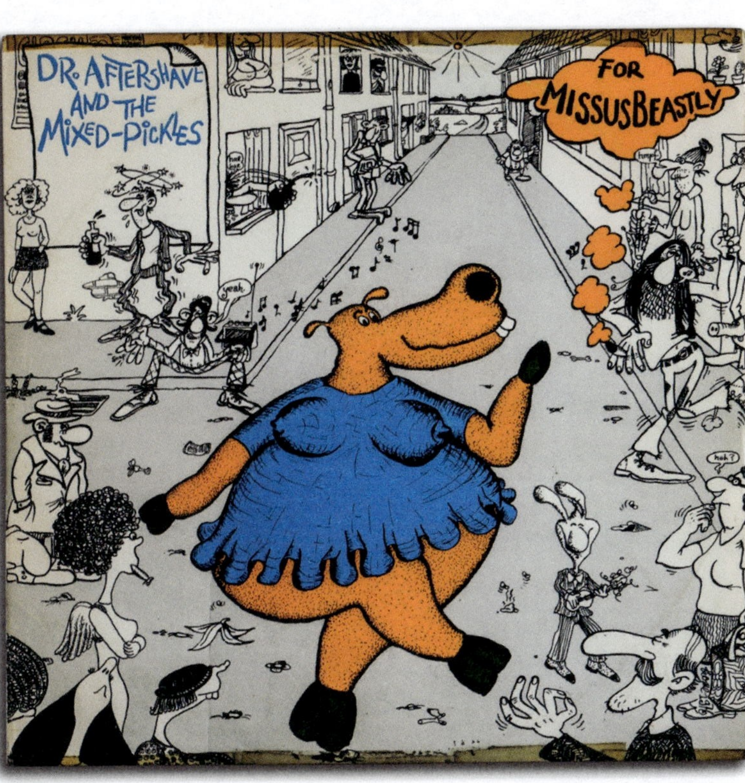

Dr. Aftershave and The Mixed-Pickles
For Missus Beastly
April Records, 1976
Axel Thomae, Klaus Strunck, Klaus Tiedemann (Design)

01 OCT

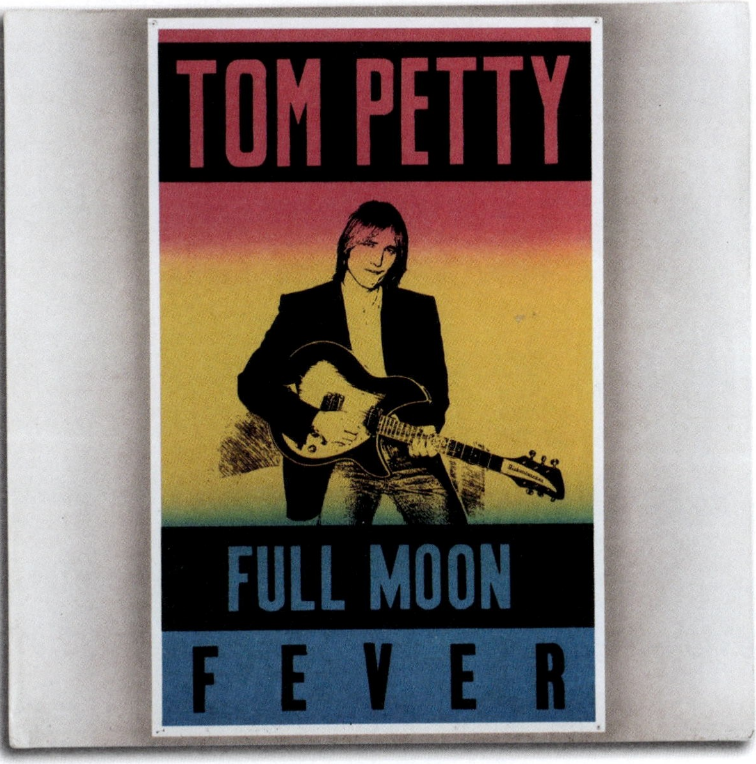

Tom Petty
Full Moon Fever
MCA Records, 1989
Awest & Tiny Bouchet (Design)
Aaron Rapoport (Photo)

† Oct 2nd, 2017
Thomas Earl "Tom" Petty
Santa Monica (California)

02 OCT

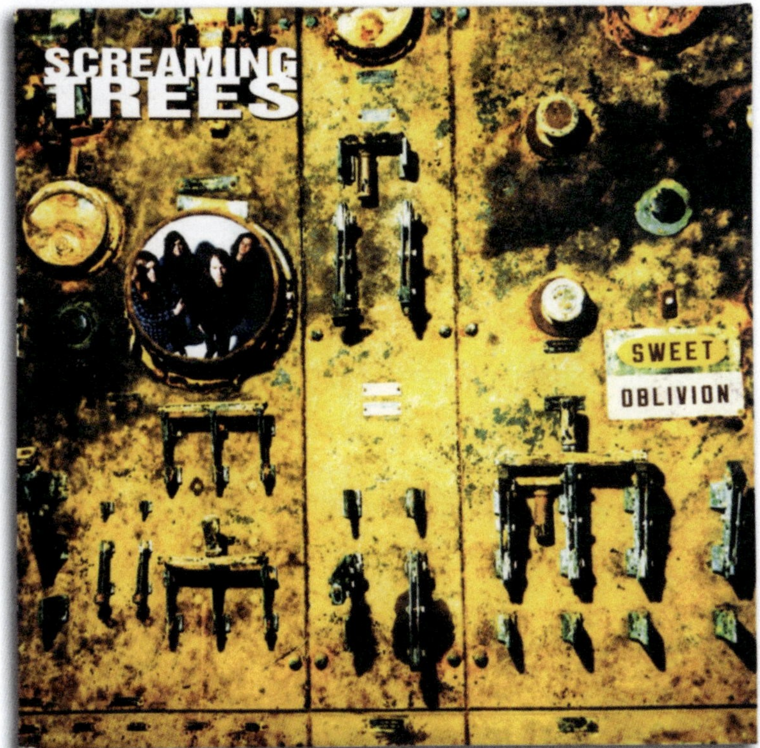

Screaming Trees
Sweet Oblivion
EPIC Records, 1992
David Coleman (Design)
Michael Lavine (Photo)

03 OCT

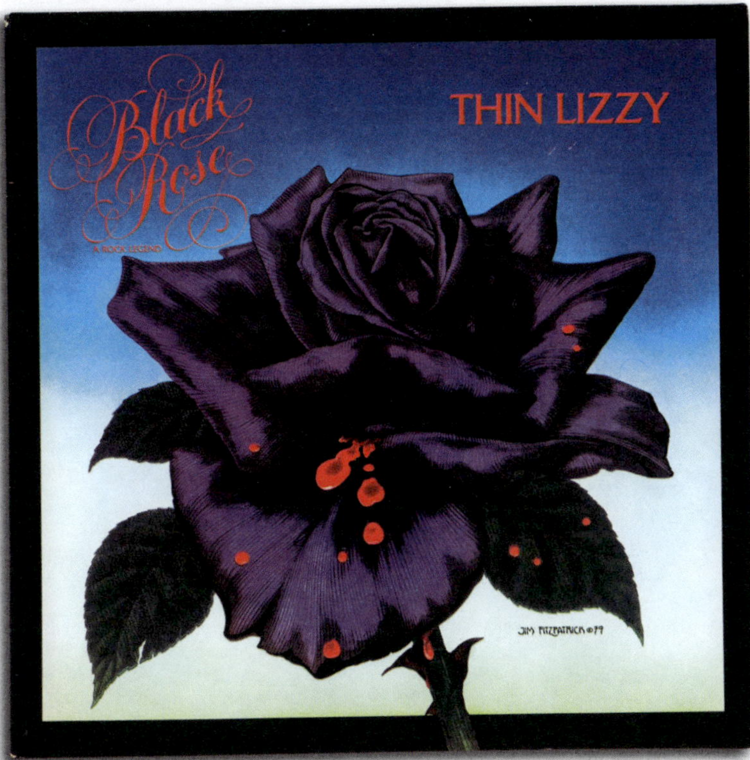

Thin Lizzy
Black Rose (A Rock Legend)
Vertigo, 1979
Jim Fitzpatrick (Illustration)

04 OCT

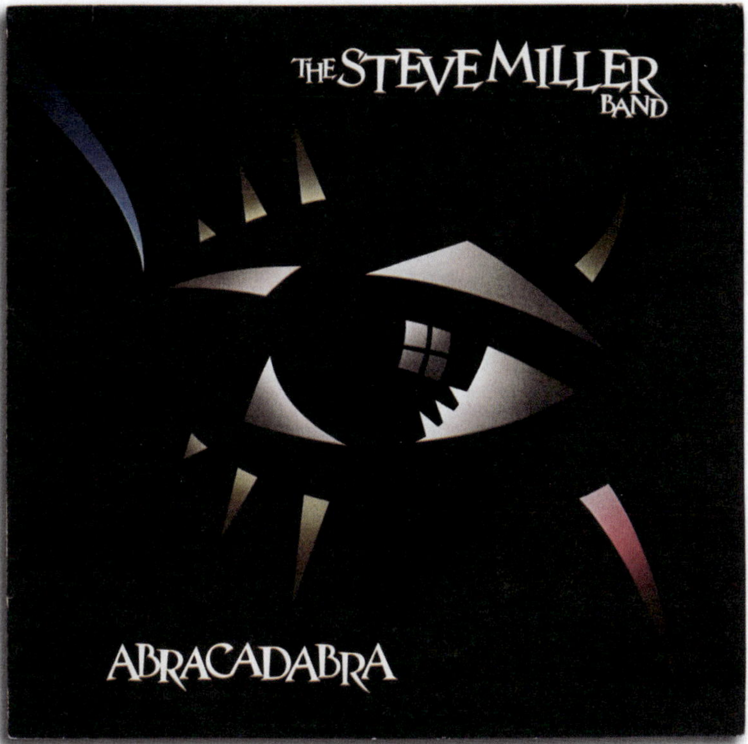

The Steve Miller Band
Abracadabra
Mercury Records, 1982
Tommy Steele (Design)

* Oct 5th, 1943
Steven Haworth Miller
Milwaukee (Wisconsin)

05 OCT

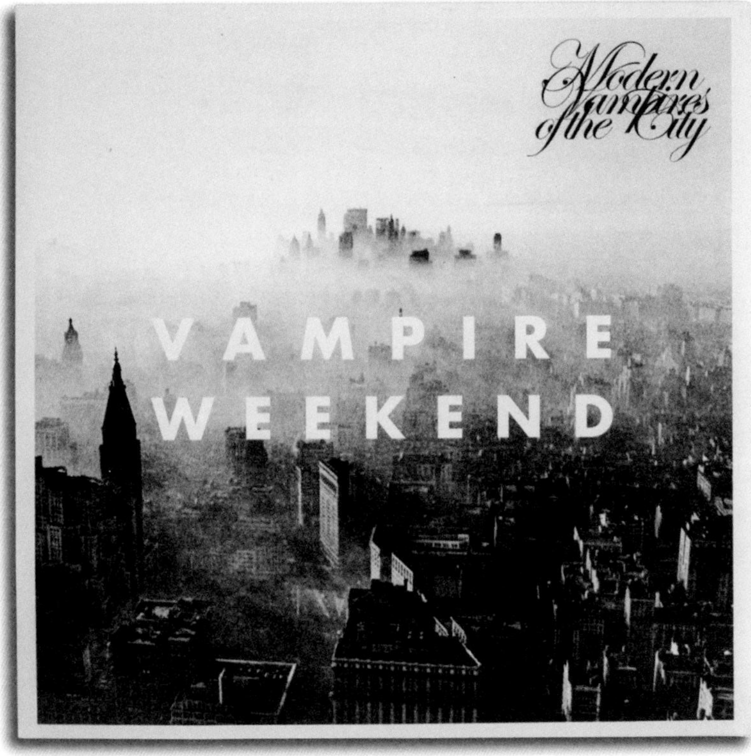

Vampire Weekend
Modern Vampires of The City
XL Recordings, 2013
Ezra Koenig, Rostam Batmanglij (Design)
Neal Boenzi (Photo)

06 OCT

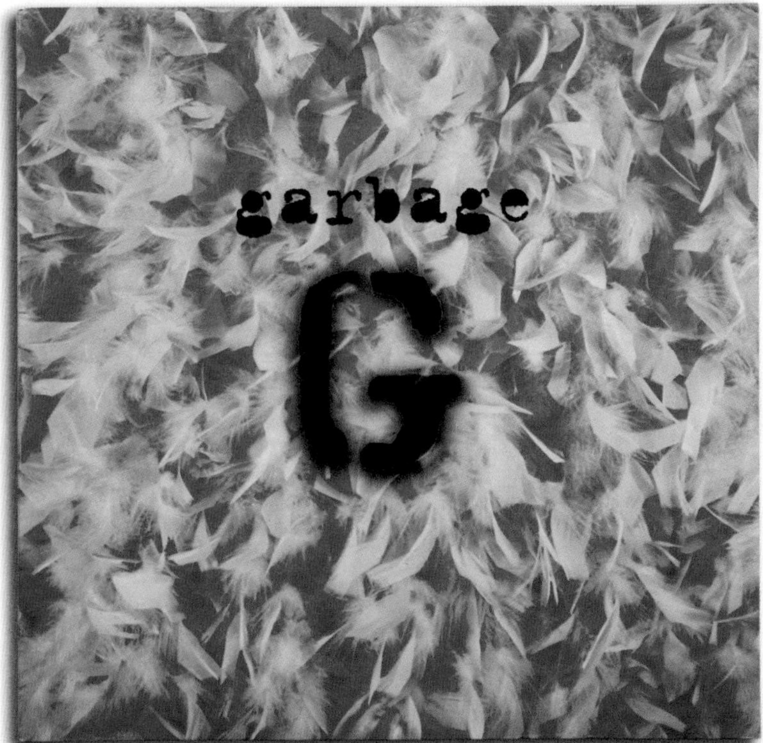

Garbage
Almo Sounds, 1995
Garbage, Janet Wolsborn (Design)
Stéphane Sednaoui (Photo)

07 OCT

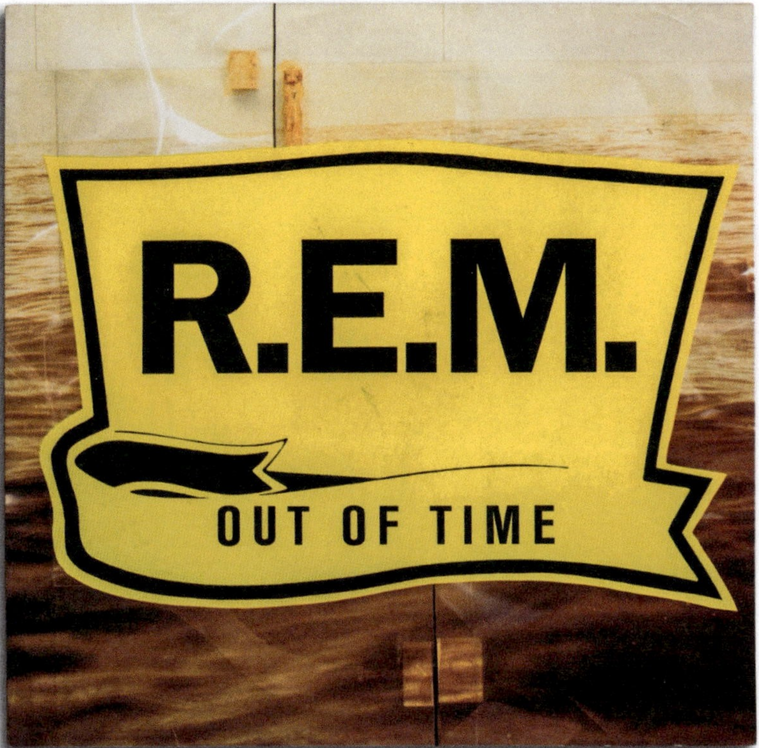

R.E.M
Out Of Time
Warner Bros. Records, 1991
Michael Stipe, Tom Recchion (Design)

08 OCT

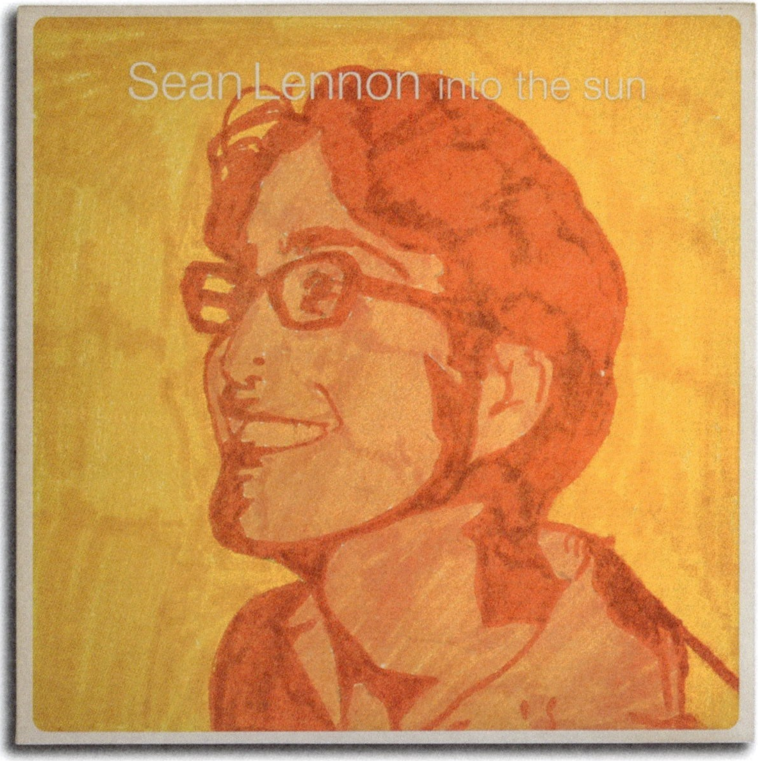

Sean Lennon
Into The Sun
Grand Royal, 1998
Mike Mill (Design)
Sean Lennon (Illustration)

* Oct 9th, 1975
Sean Lennon
New York City

09 OCT

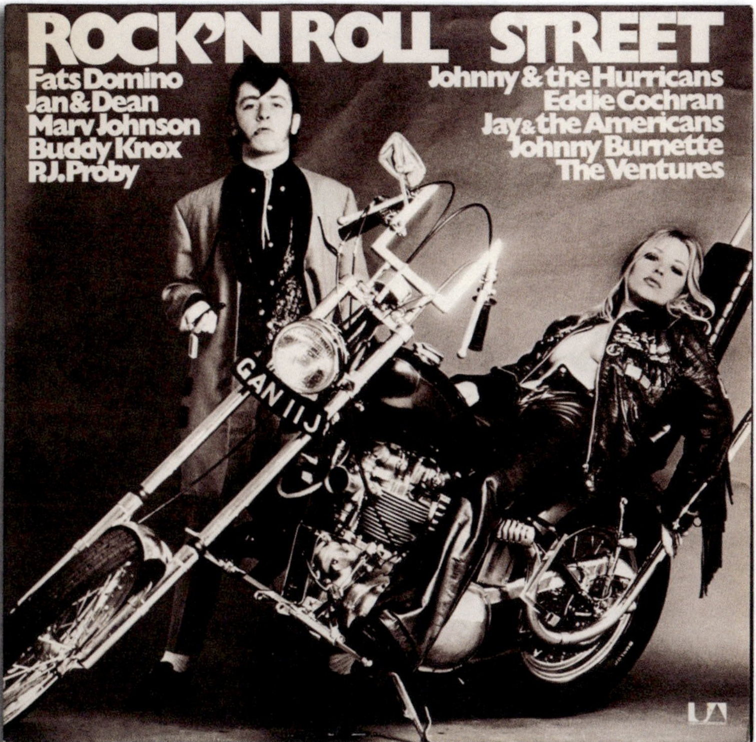

Various Artists
Rock'n Roll Street
United Artists Records, 1975
Ulrich Eichberger (Design)

10 OCT

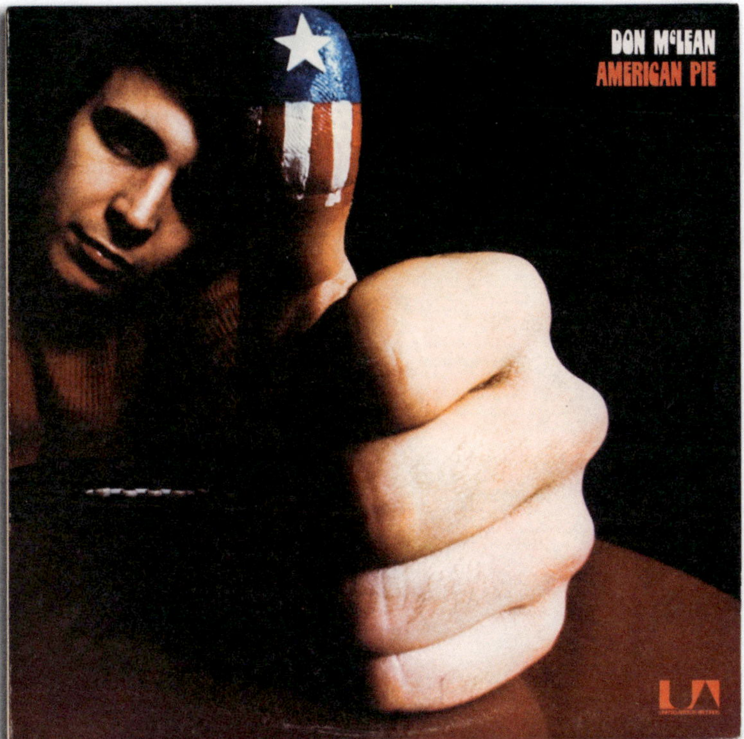

Don McLean
American Pie
United Artists Records, 1977
George Whiteman (Photo)

11 OCT

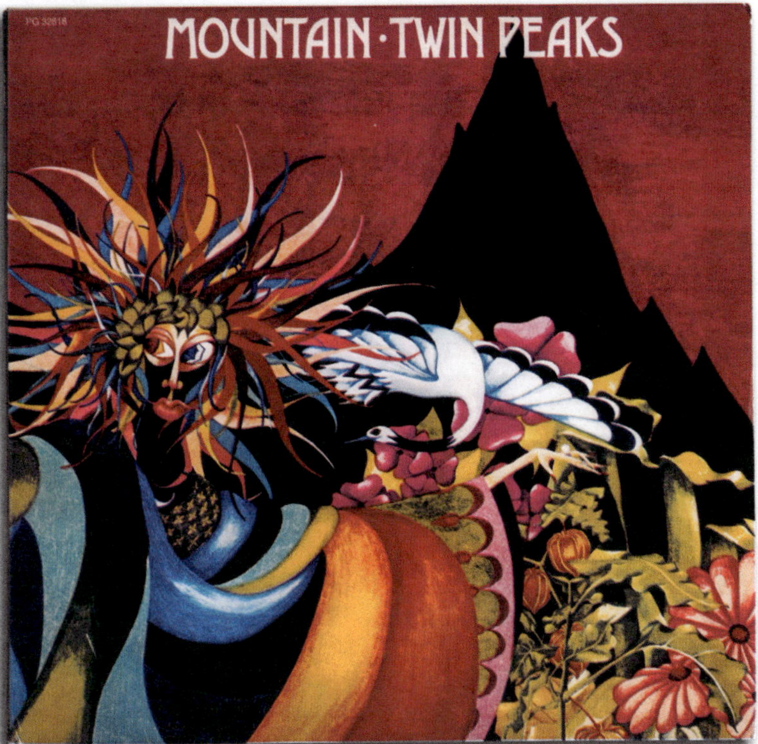

Mountain
Twin Peaks
Columbia Records, 1974
Gail Collins (Illustration)

12 OCT

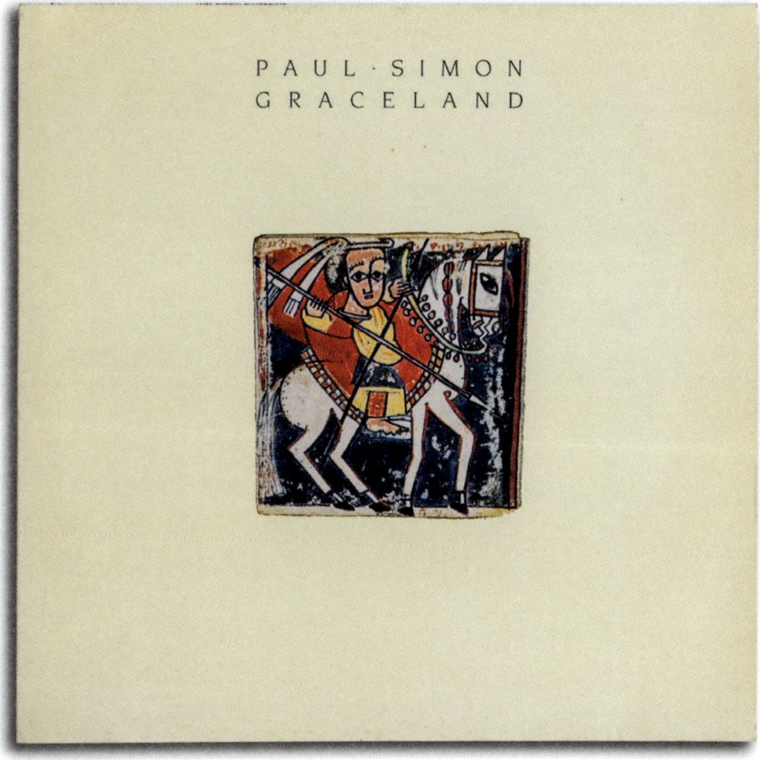

Paul Simon
Graceland
Warner Bros. Records, 1986
Jeffrey Kent Ayeroff, Jeri McManus (Design)
Mark Sexton (Photo)

* Oct 13th, 1941
Paul Frederic Simon
Newar (New Jersey)

13 OCT

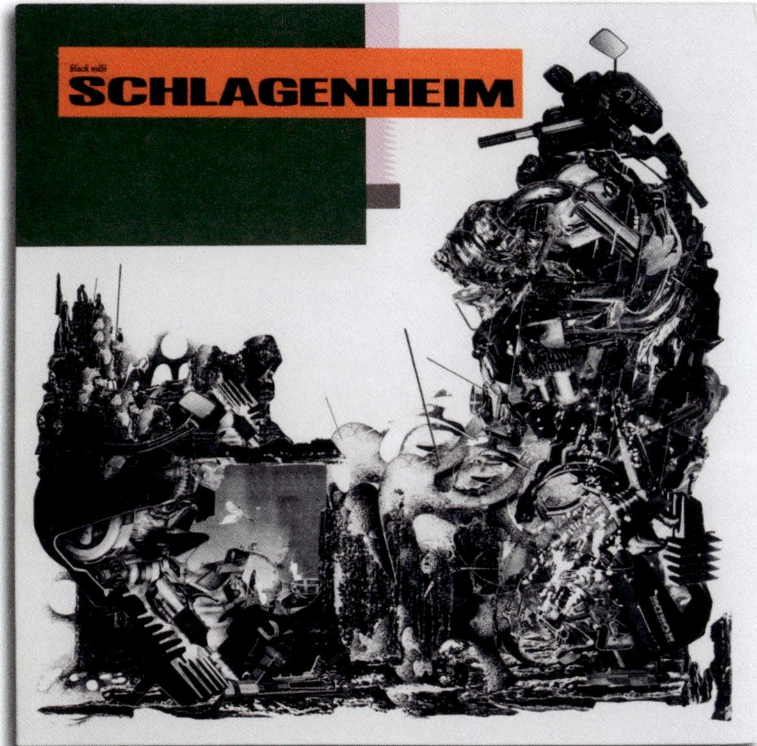

Black Midi
Schlagenheim
Rough Trade, 2019
David Rudnick (Design)

14 OCT

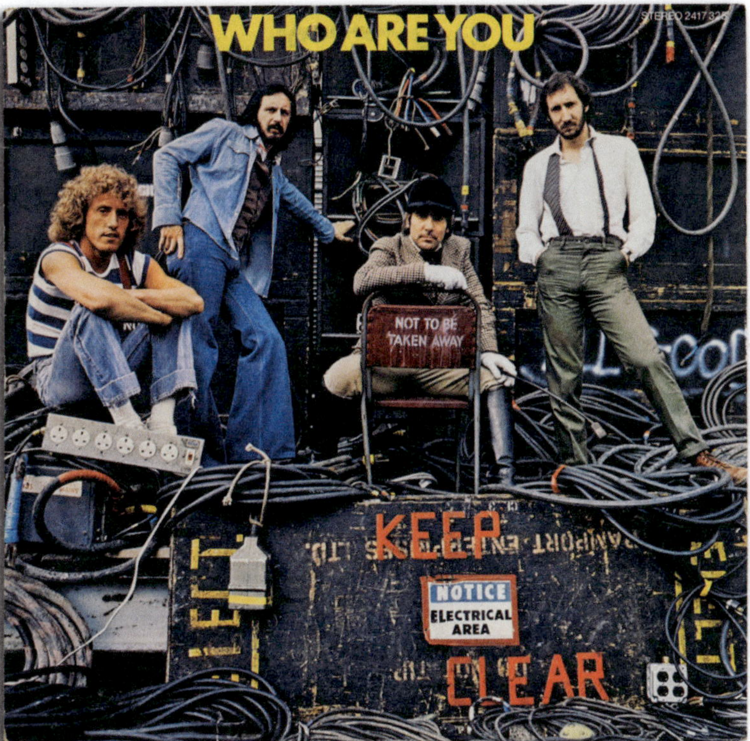

The Who
Who Are You
Polydor, 1978
Bill Smith (Design)
Terry O'Neill (Photo)

15 OCT

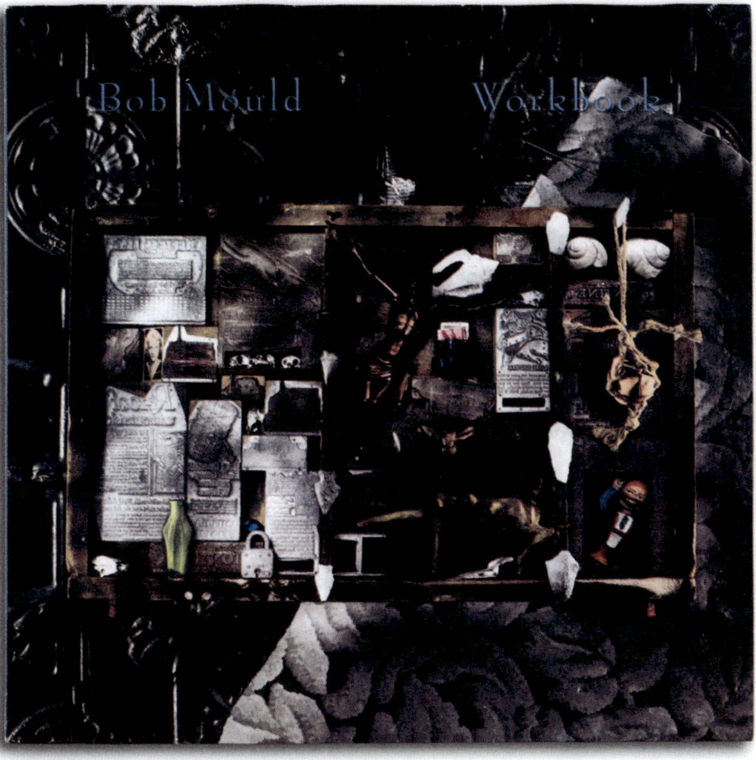

Bob Mould
Workbook
Virgin Records, 1989
Michael Covington (Design)
Marc Norberg (Photo)

* Oct 16th, 1960
Bob Mould
Malone (New York City)

16 OCT

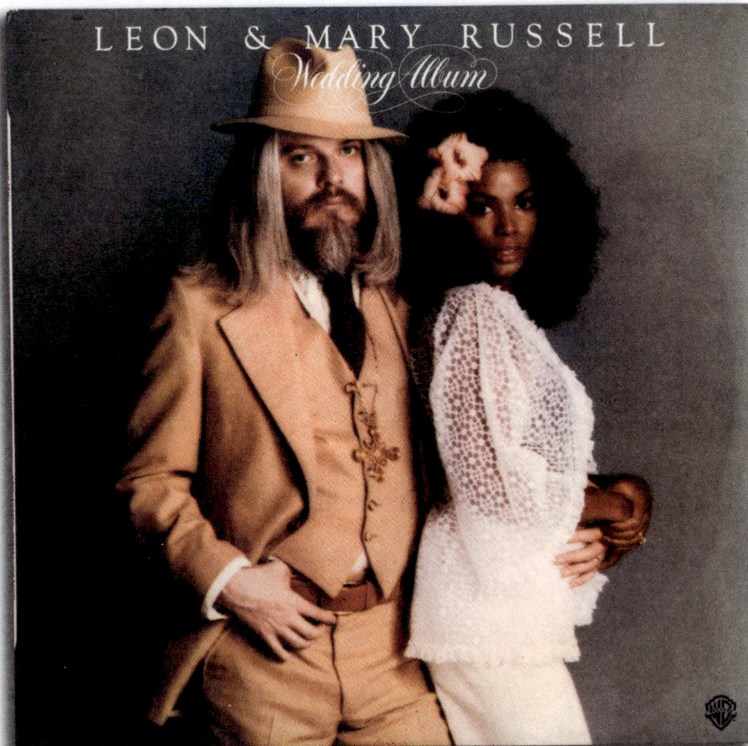

Leon & Mary Russell
Wedding Album
Paradise Records, 1976
Lockart (Design)
Greg Gorman (Photo)

17 OCT

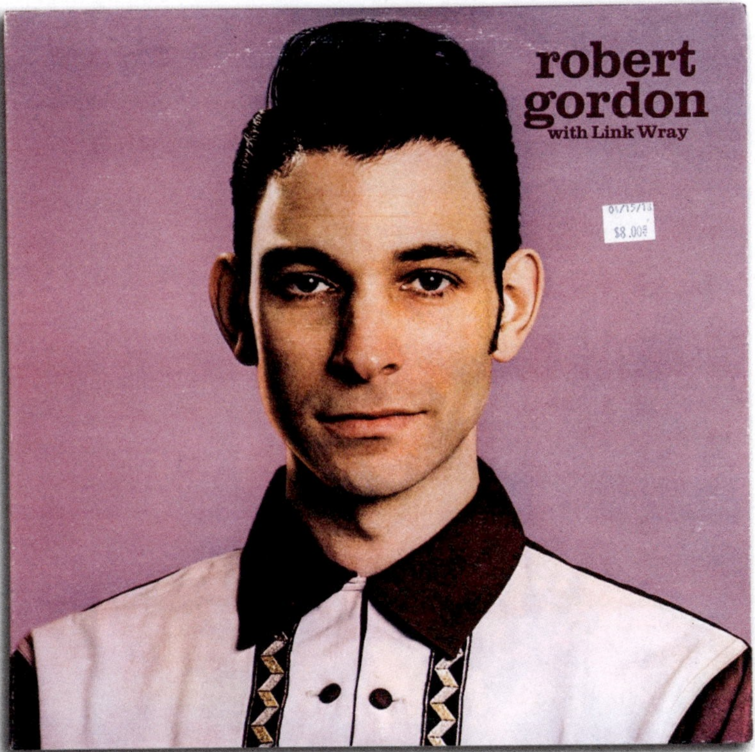

Robert Gordon With Link Wray
Private Stock Records, Ltd., 1977
Richard Mantel & Beverly Weinstein (Design)
Benno Friedmann (Photo)

18 OCT

† Oct 18th, 2022
Robert Ira Gordon
New York City

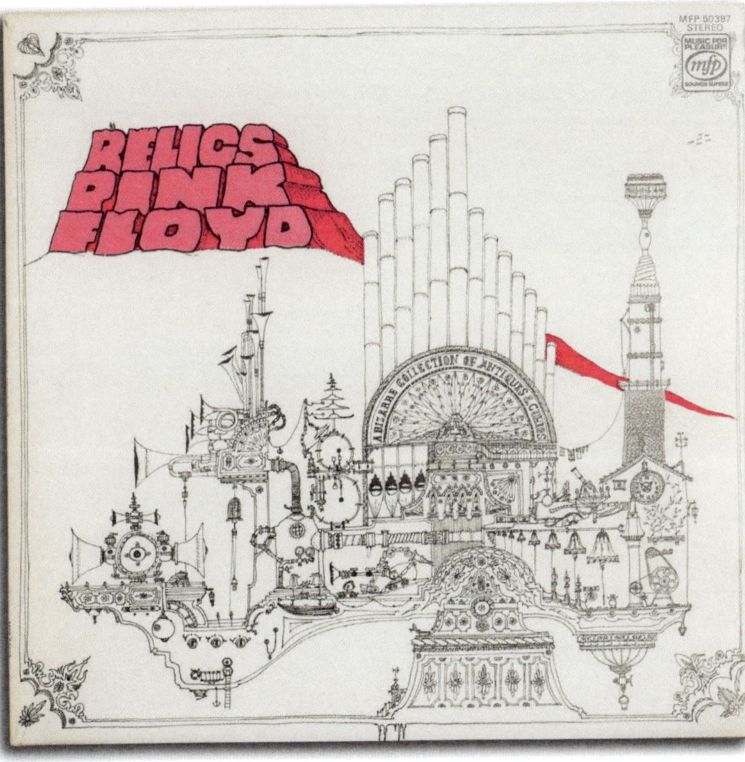

Pink Floyd
Relics "A Bizare Collection Of Antiques & Curios"
Music For Pleasure, 1971
Nick Mason (Illustration)

19 OCT

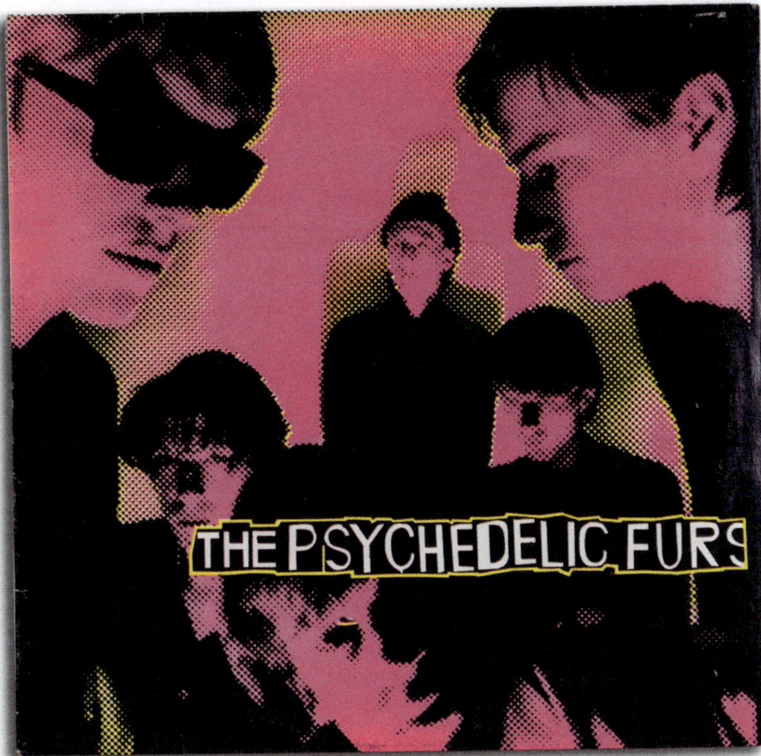

The Psychedelic Furs
CBS Records, 1980
Steven Newman (Design)
Paul Cox (Photo)

20 OCT

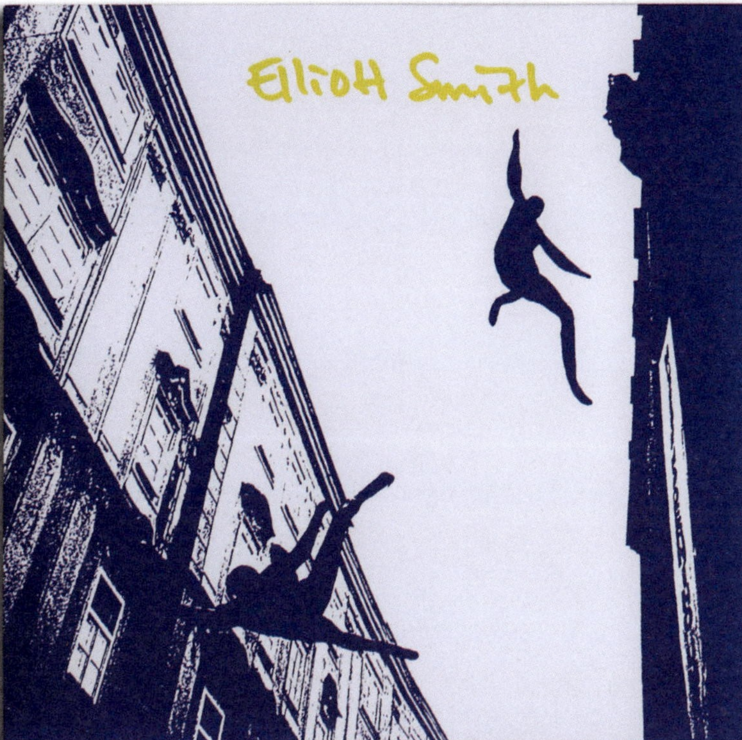

Elliot Smith
Kill Rock Stars, 1995
JJ Gonson (Photo)

† Oct 21st, 2003
Steven Paul Smith
Los Angeles (California)

21 OCT

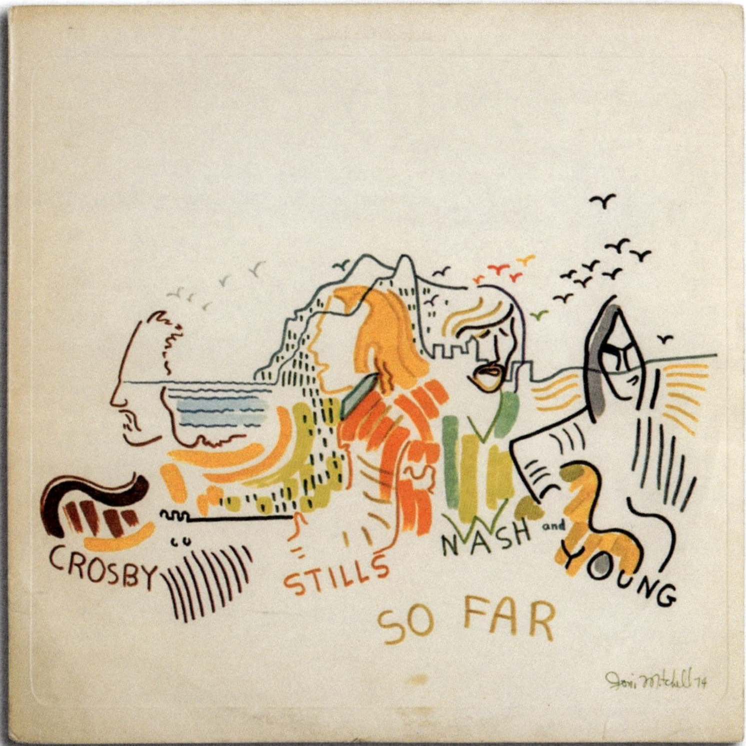

Crosby, Stills, Nash & Young
So Far
Atlantic Records, 1974
Gary Burden (Design)
Joni Mitchell (Illustration)

22 OCT

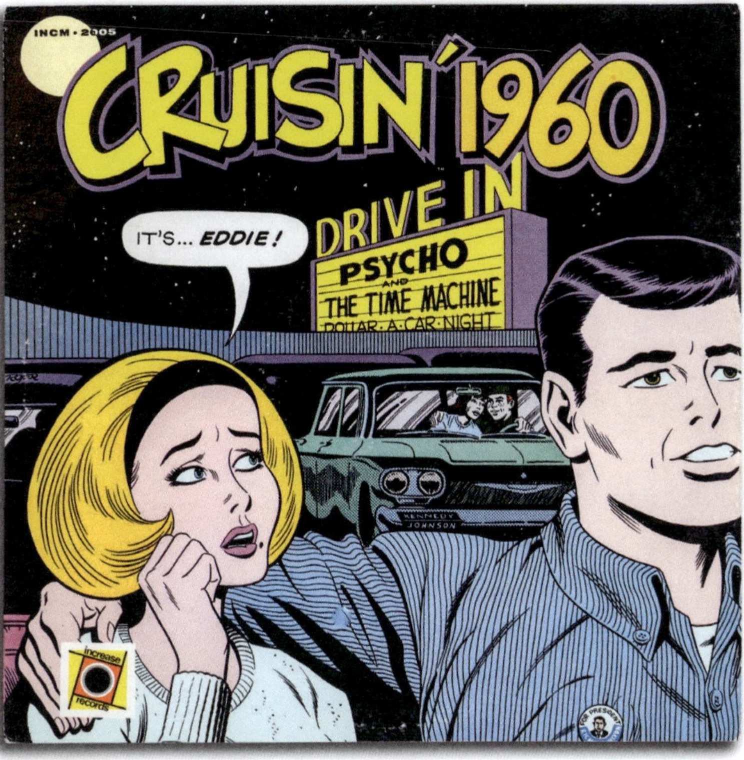

Various Artists
Cruisin' 1960
Increase Records, 1960
Mike Royer (Illustration)

23 OCT

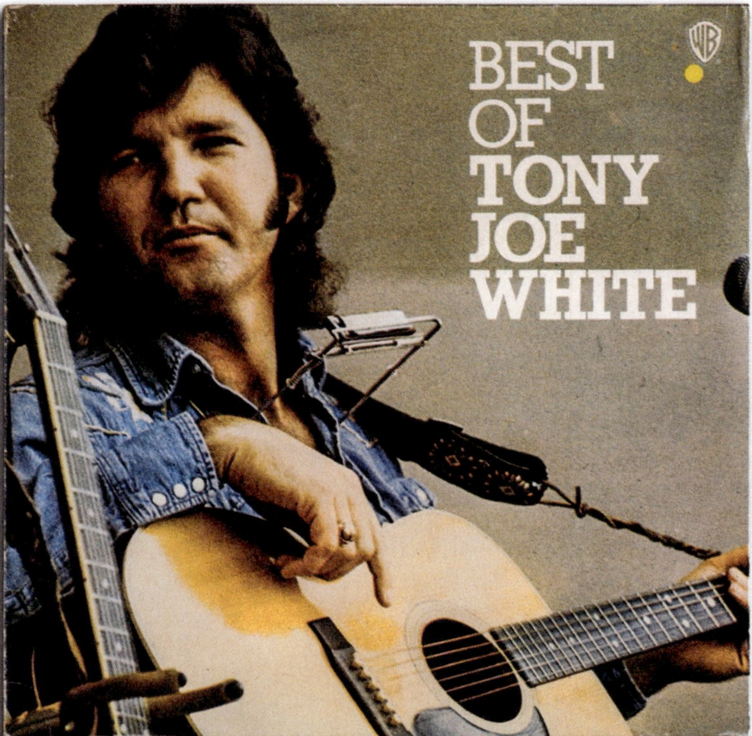

Tony Joe White
Best Of
Warner Bros. Records, 1975
Mike Putland (Photo)

† Oct 24th, 2018
Tony Joe White
Leiper's Fork (Tennessee)

24 OCT

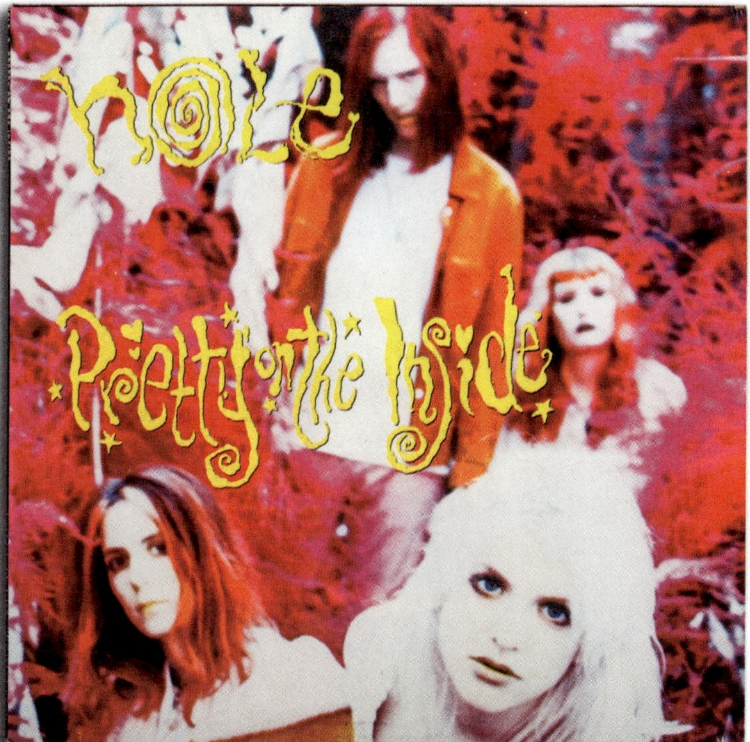

Hole
Pretty On The Inside
City Slang, 1991
Stephen Pizzurro (Design)
Vickie Berndt (Photo)

25 OCT

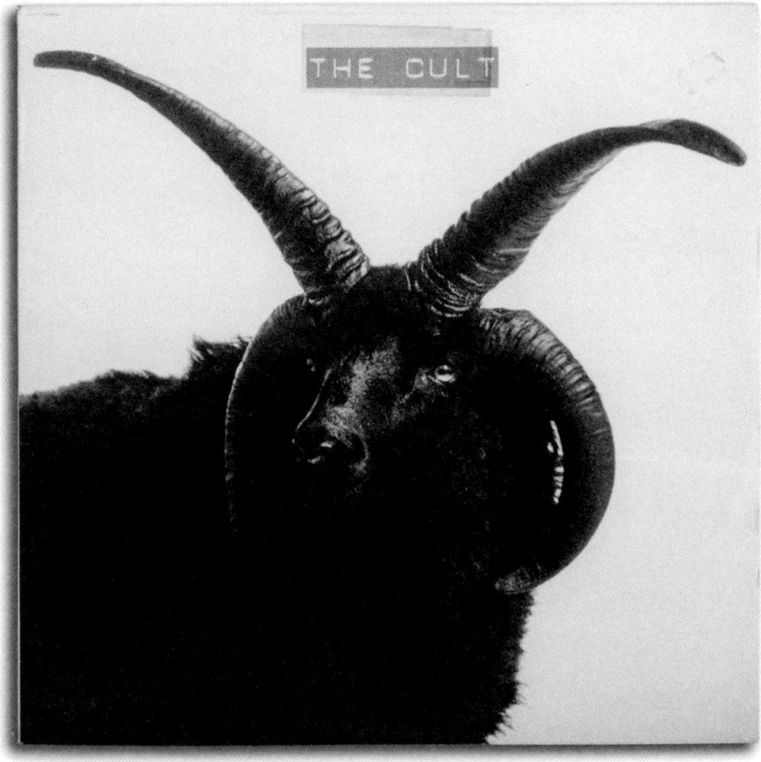

The Cult
Beggars Banquet, 1994
Ian Astbury, Kim Champagne (Design)
Peter Barlow (Photo)

26 OCT

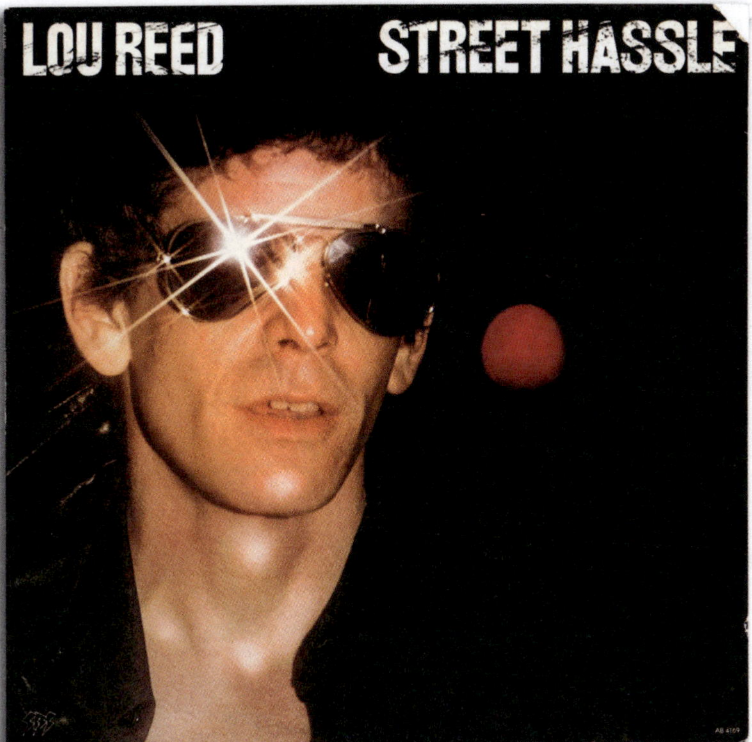

Lou Reed
Street Hassle
Arista, 1978
Mick Rock (Design)

† Oct 27th, 2013
Lou Reed
New York City

27 OCT

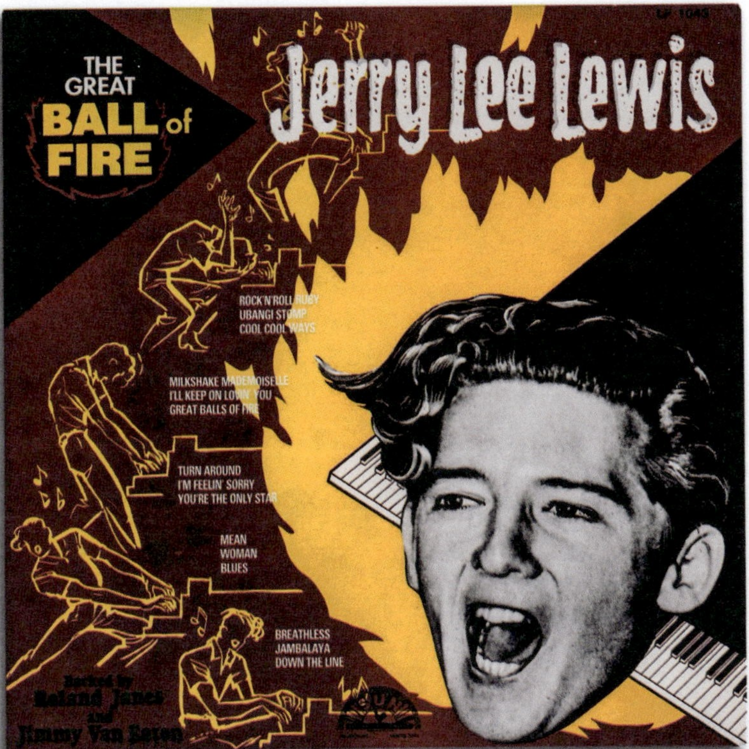

Jerry Lee Lewis
The Great Ball Of Fire
Sun Record Company, 1986
Cover Artists Unknown

† Oct 28th, 2022
Jerry Lee Lewis
DeSoto County (Mississippi)

28 OCT

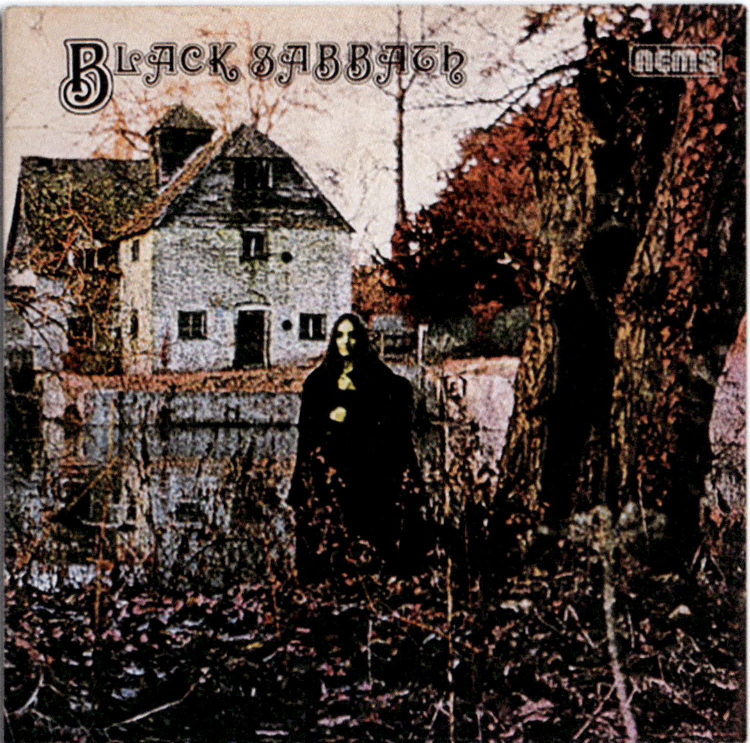

Black Sabbath
NEMS Records, 1976
Keef (Design)
Keef (Photo)

29 OCT

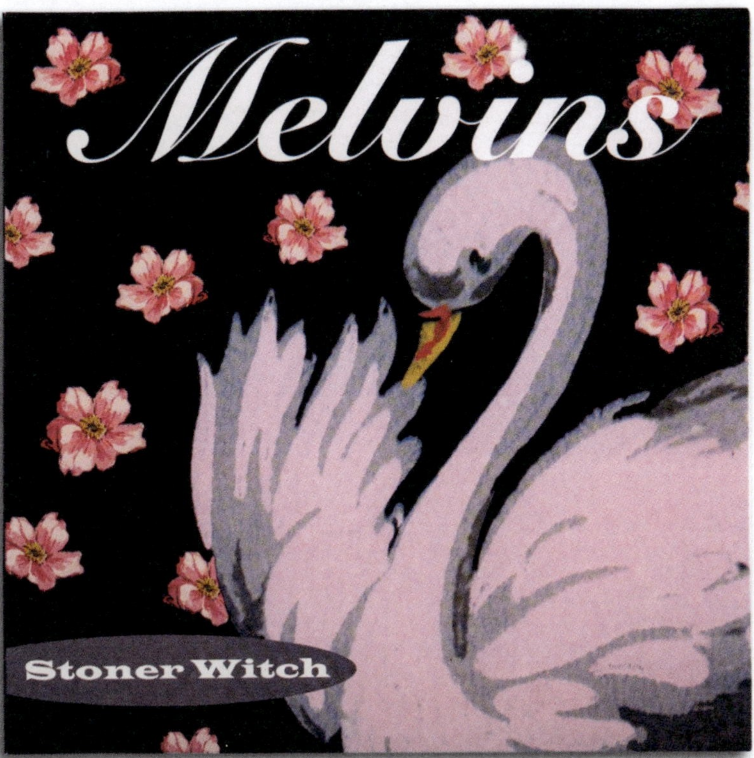

Melvins
Stoner Witch
Atlantic Records, 1994
Mackie Osborne (Design)

30 OCT

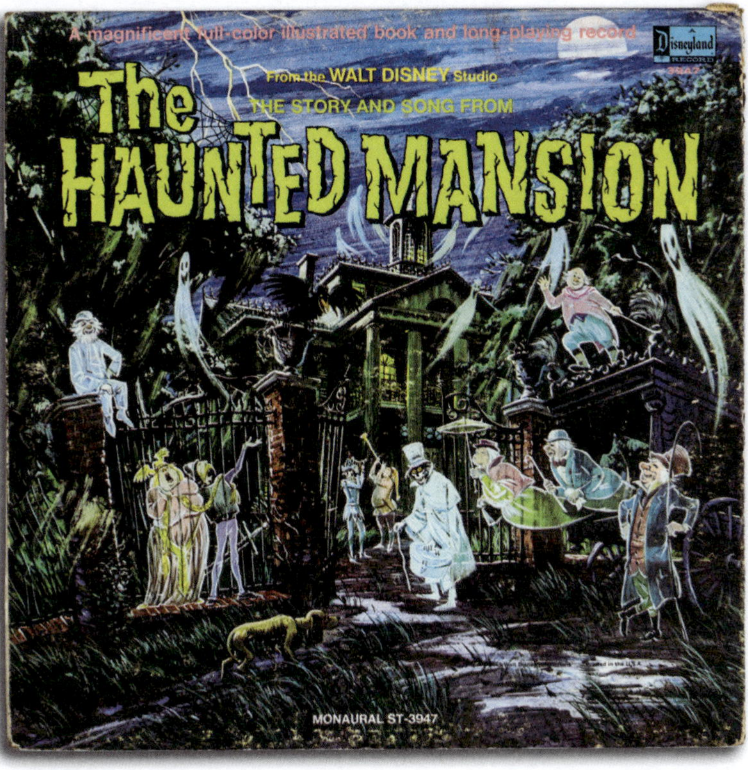

Walt Disney Studio
The Story And Song From The Haunted Mansion
Disneyland Record, 1969
Collin Capbell (Illustration)

31 OCT

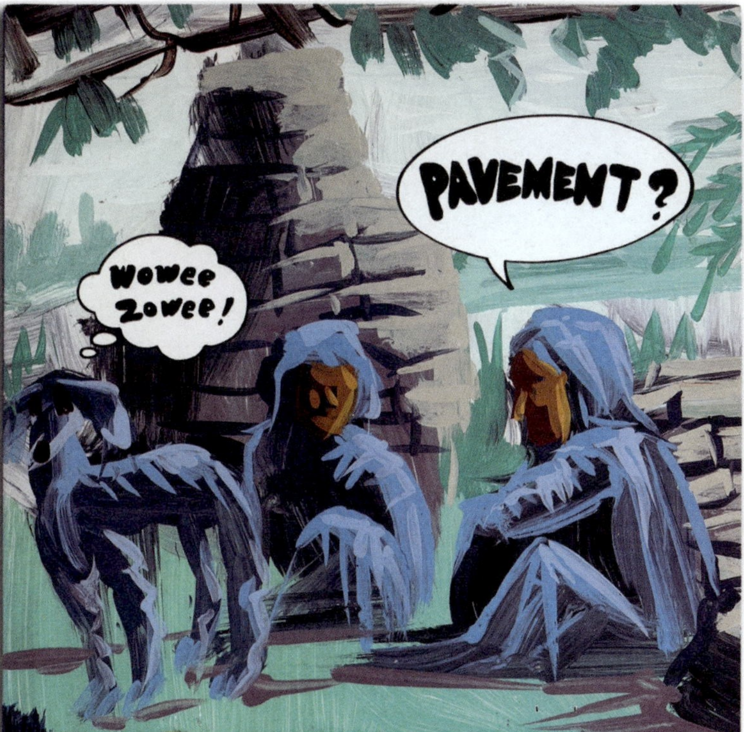

Pavement
Woge Zowee!
Big Cat, 1995
Steve Keene (Design)

01 NOV

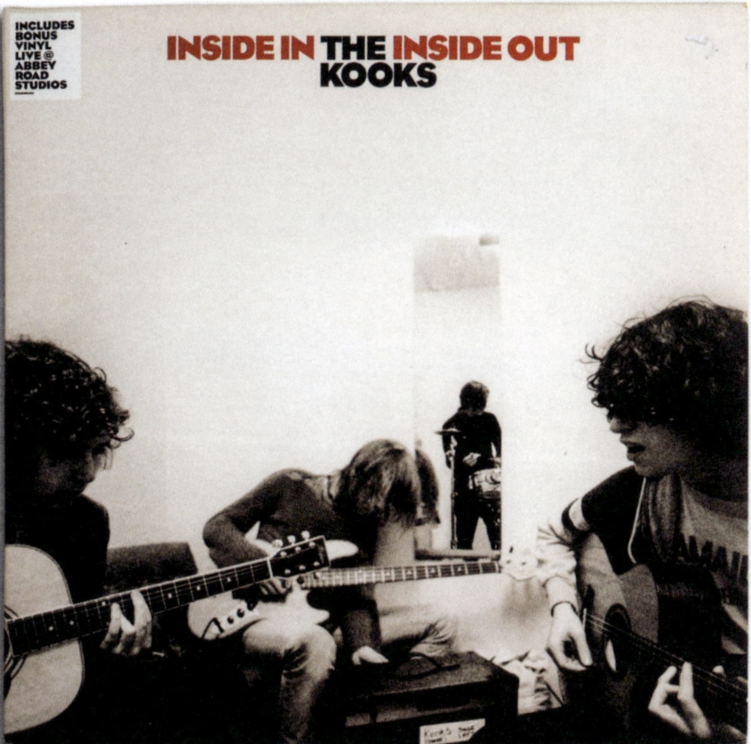

The Kooks
Inside In / Inside Out
Virgin Records, 2006
Andrew Murabito, The Kooks (Design)
Ben Parks (Photo)

02 NOV

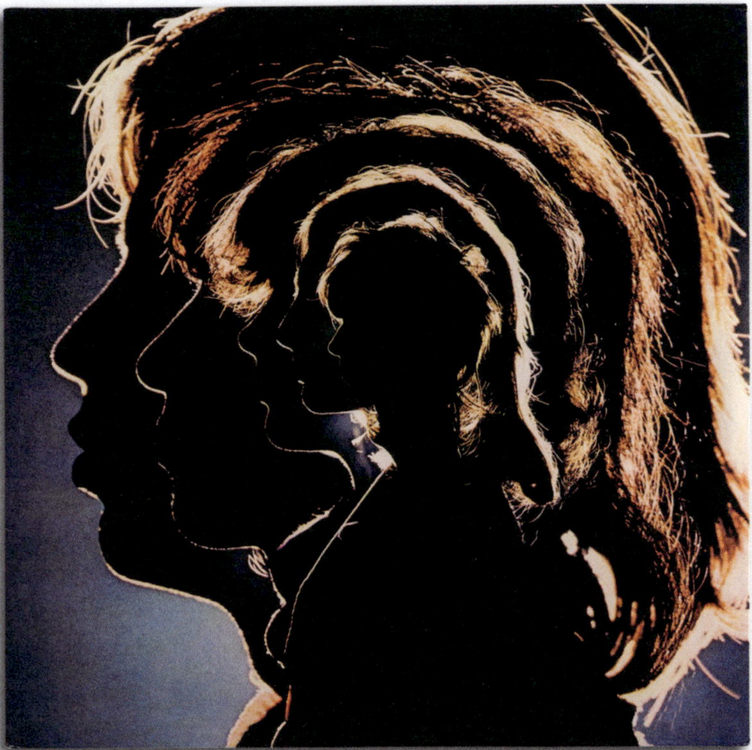

Rolling Stones
Hot Rocks
London Records, 1990
Michael Gross (Design)
Ron Raffaelli (Photo)

03 NOV

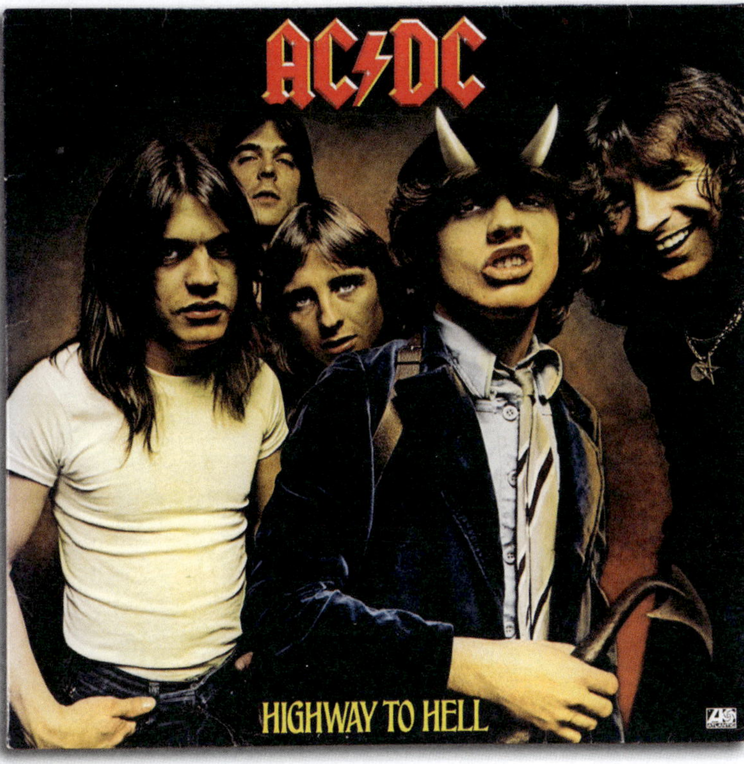

AC/DC
Highway to Hell
Atlantic Records, 1979
Bob Defrin (Design)
Jim Houghton (Photo)

04 NOV

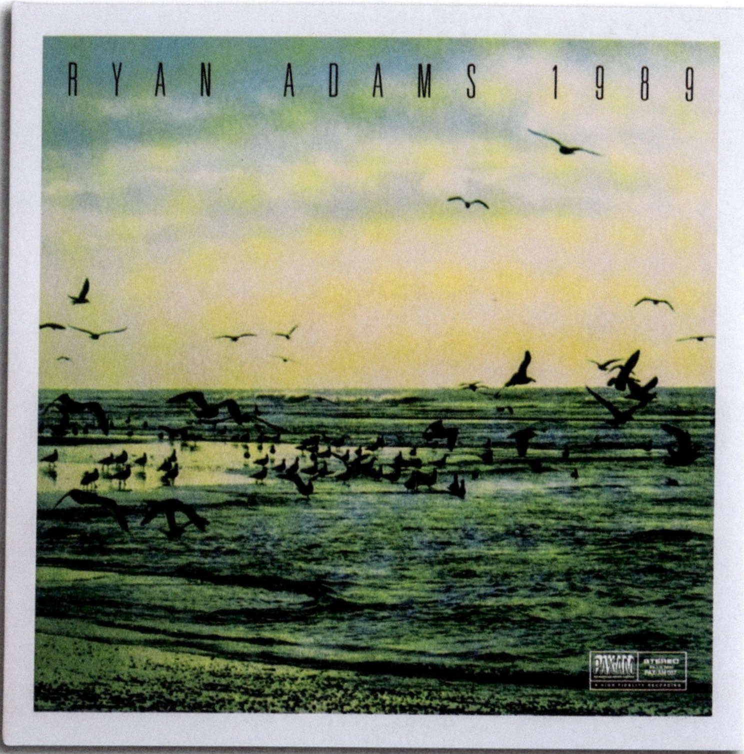

Ryan Adams
1989
Pax Americana Record Company, 2015
Andy West (Design)
Julia Brokaw (Photo)

* Nov 5th, 1974
David Ryan Adams
Jacksonville (North Carolina)

05 NOV

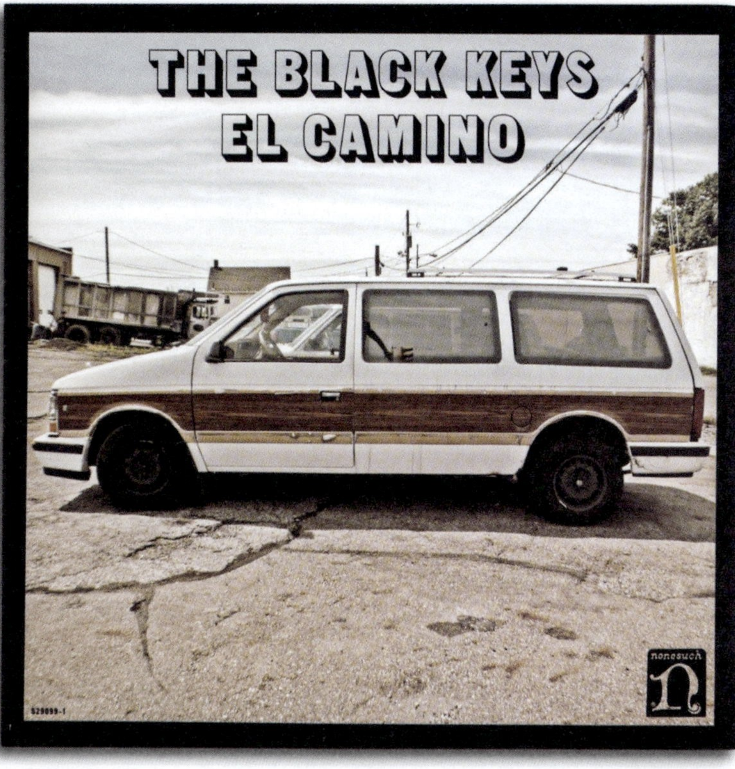

The Black Keys
El Camino
Nonesuch Records, 2011
Michael Carney (Design)
Michael Carney (Photo)

06 NOV

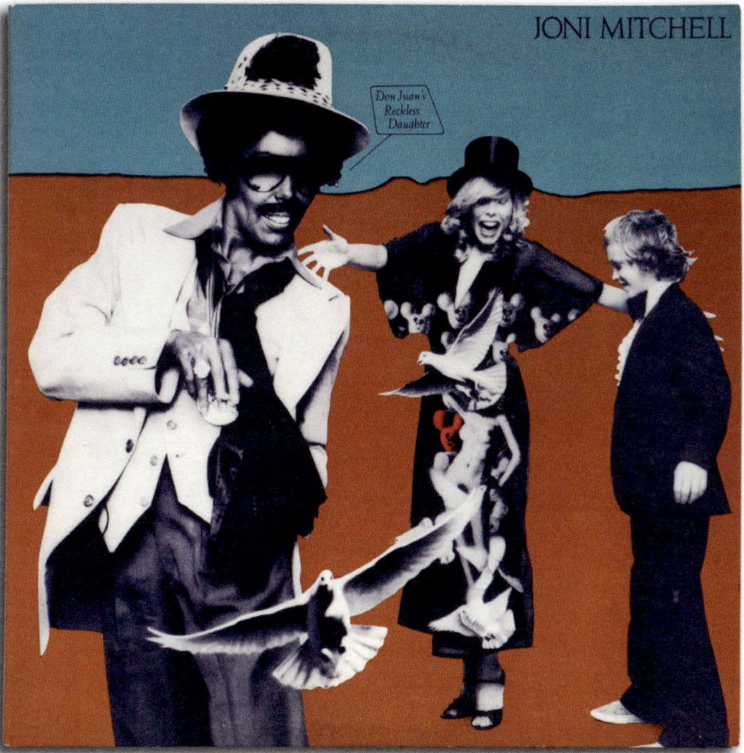

Joni Mitchell
Don Juan's Reckless Daughter
Asylum Records, 1977
Glen Christensen (Design)
Norman Seef (Photo)

07 NOV

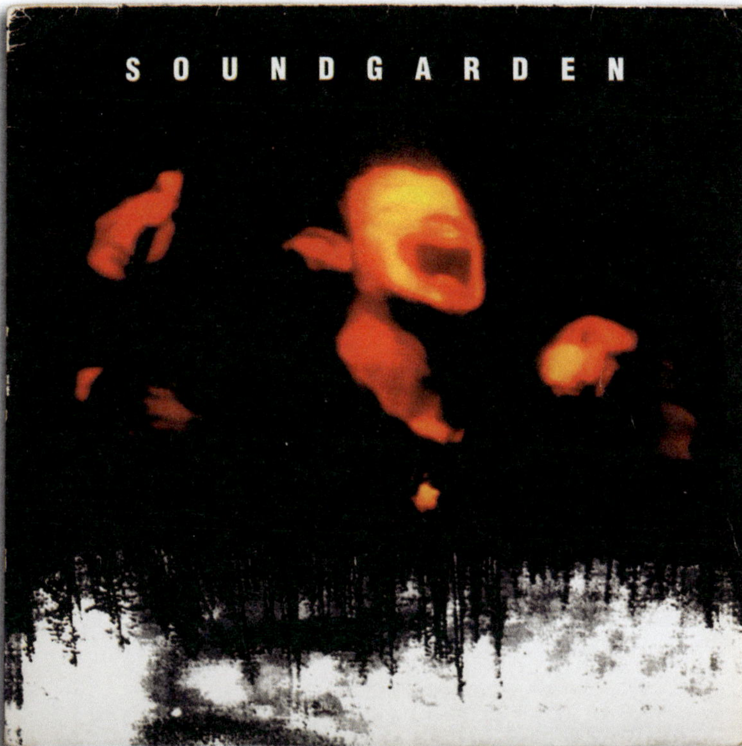

Soundgarden
Superunknown
A&M Records, 1994
Kelk (Design)

08 NOV

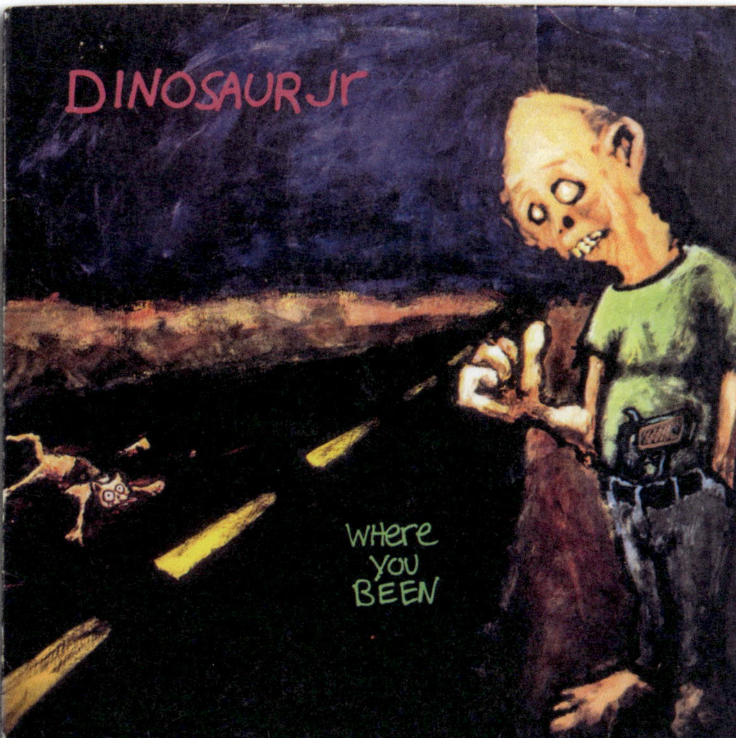

Dinosaur Jr.
Where You Been
Blanco Y Negro, 1993
Angry Johnny (Illustration)

09 NOV

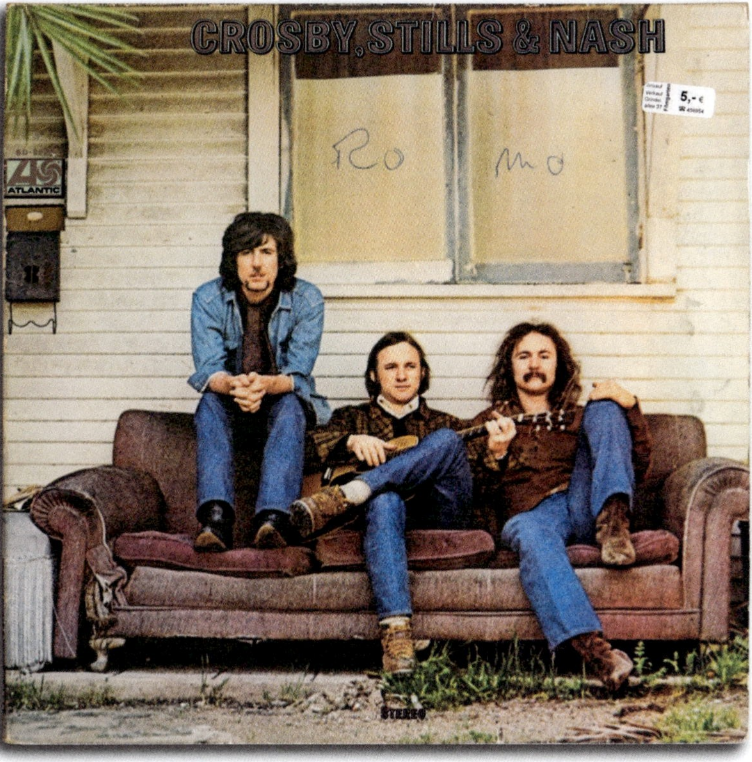

Crosby, Stills & Nash
Atlantic Records, 1969
Gary Burden (Design)
Henry Diltz (Photo)

10 NOV

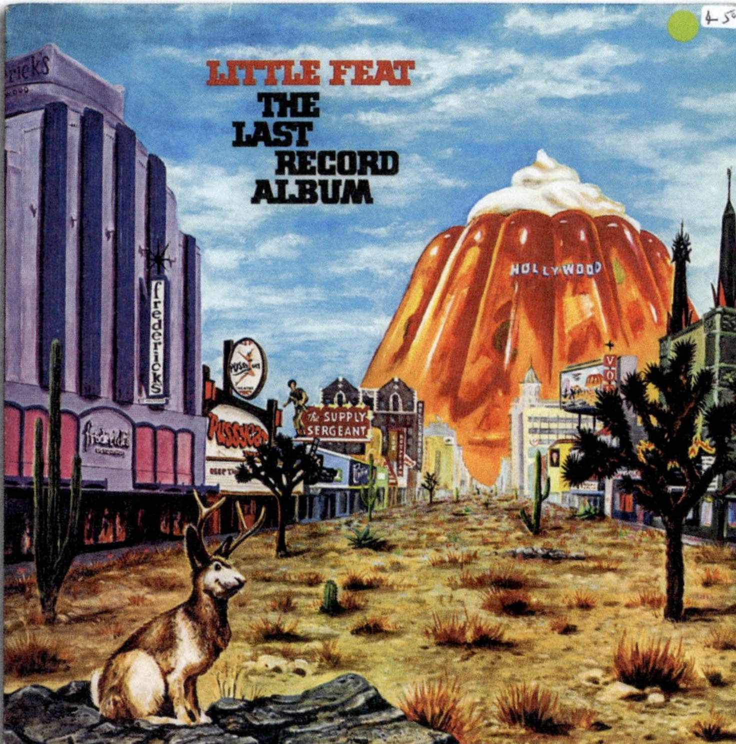

Little Feat
The Last Record Album
WEA Records, 1975
Neon Park (Design)
Neon Park (Illustration)

11 NOV

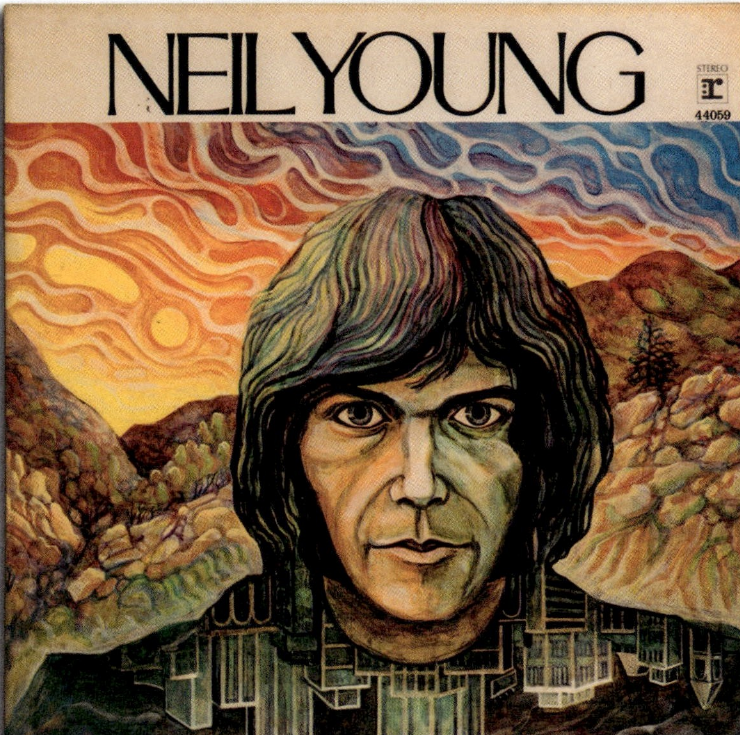

Neil Young
Reprise Records, 1971
Roland Diehl (Design)

* Nov 12th, 1945
Neil Young
Toronto (Canada)

12 NOV

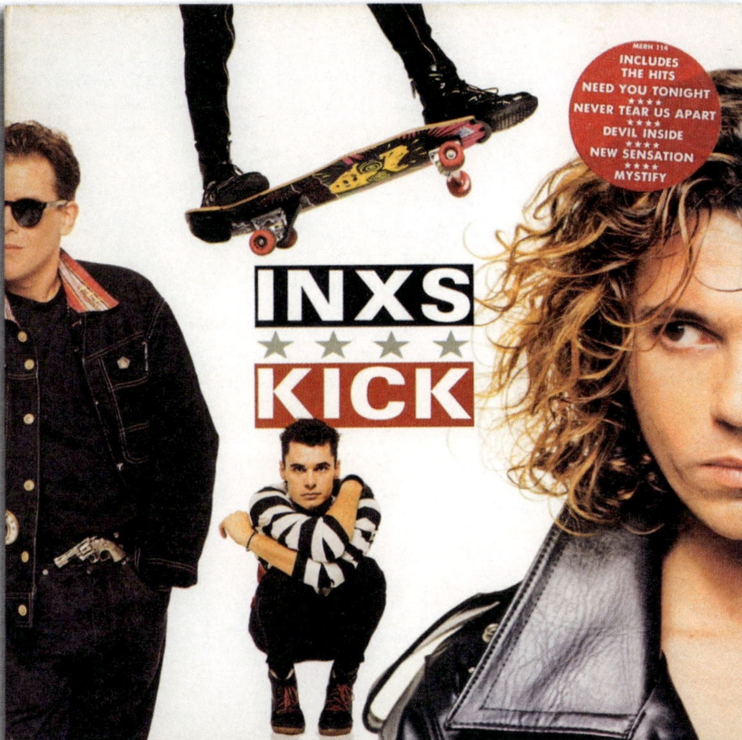

INXS
Kick
Mercury Records, 1987
Nick Egan (Design)
Grant Matthews (Photo)

13 NOV

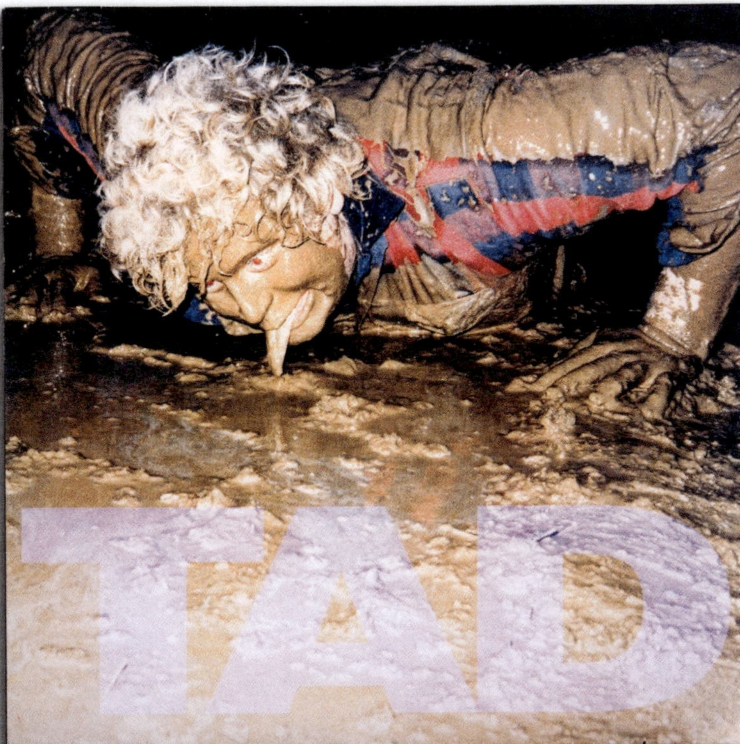

TAD
Salem
Sub Pop, 1992
Cover Artists Unknown

14 NOV

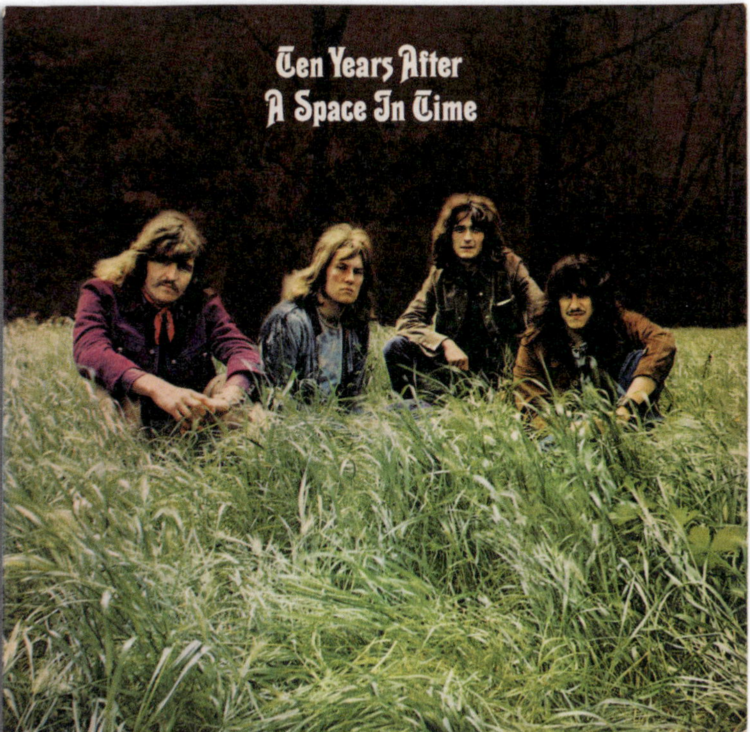

Ten Years After
A Space In Time
Chrysalis Records, 1971
Ed Caraeff (Photo)

15 NOV

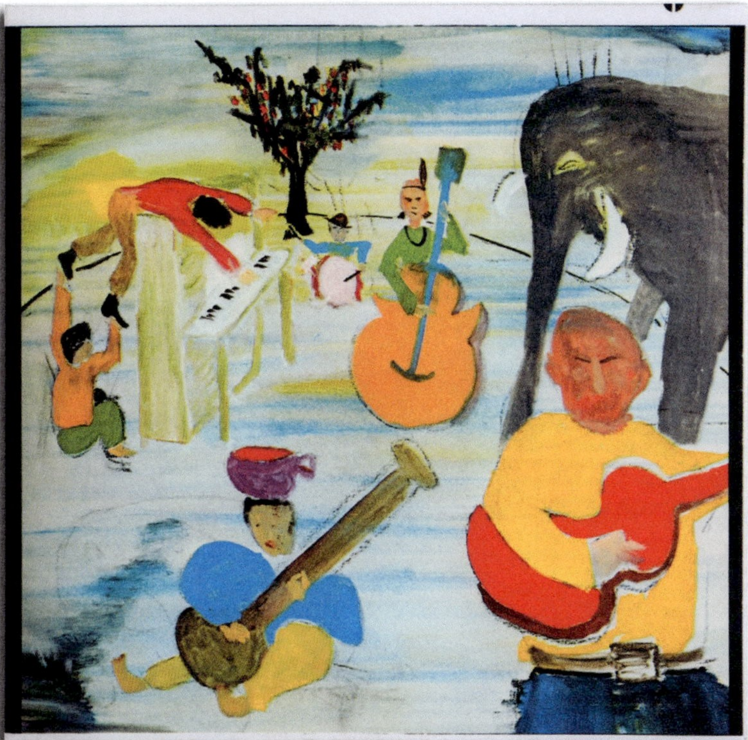

The Band
Music From The Big Pink
Capitol Records, 1968
Milton Glaser (Design)
Bob Dylan (Illustration)

16 NOV

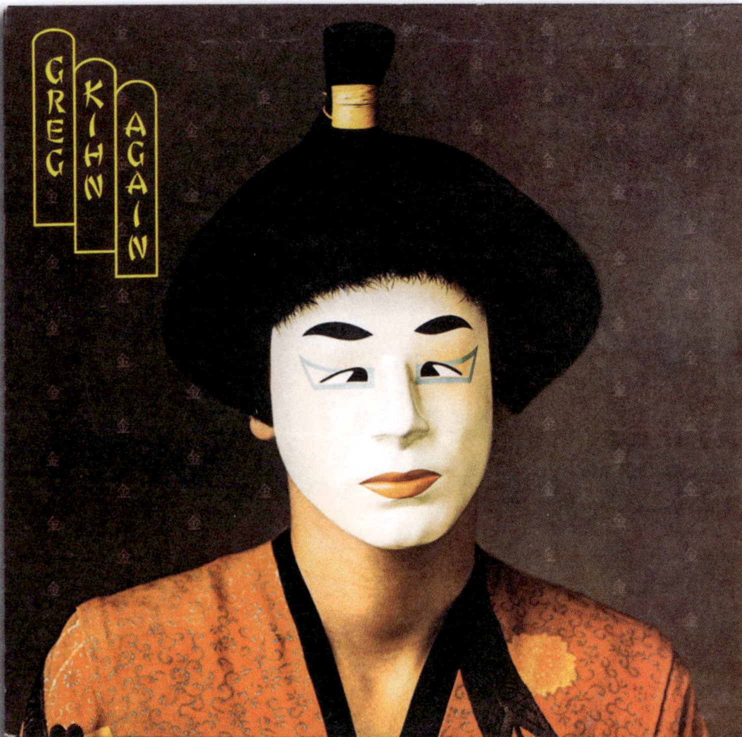

Greg Kihn
Greg Kihn Again
Beserkley, 1977
Jim Blodgett (Design)
John Jensen (Photo)

17 NOV

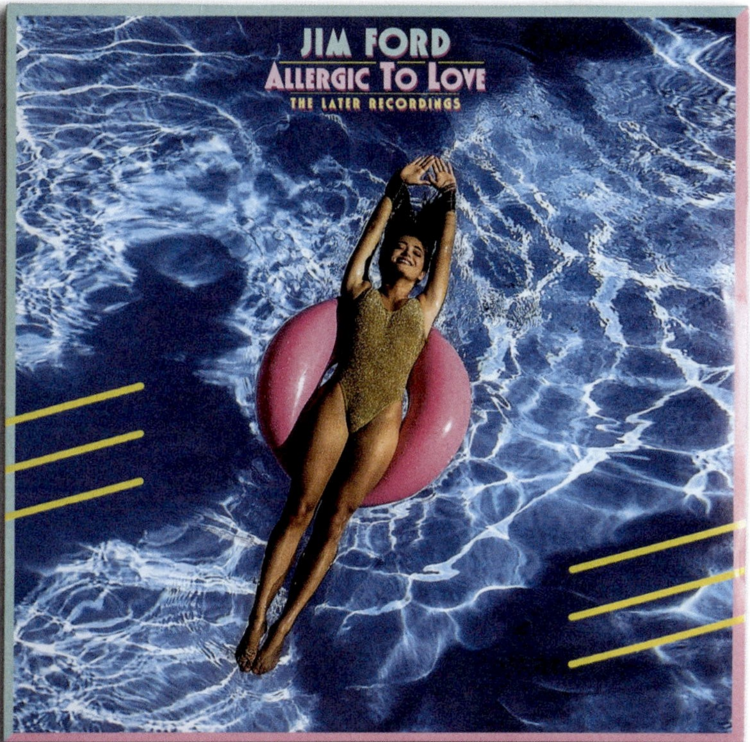

Jim Ford
Allergic To Love (The Later Recordings)
Bear Family Records, 2016
Michael Gerstenberger (Design)

18 NOV

† Nov 18th, 2007
Jim Ford, birth name James Henry Ford
Fort Bragg (California)

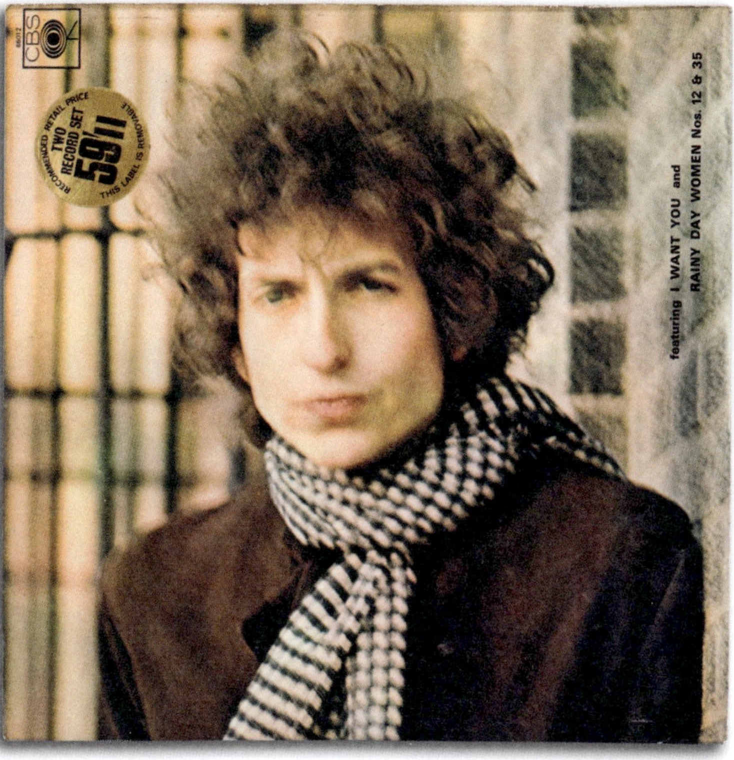

Bob Dylan
Blonde On Blonde
CBS Records, 1966
John A. Beck (Design)
Jerry Schatzberg (Photo)

19 NOV

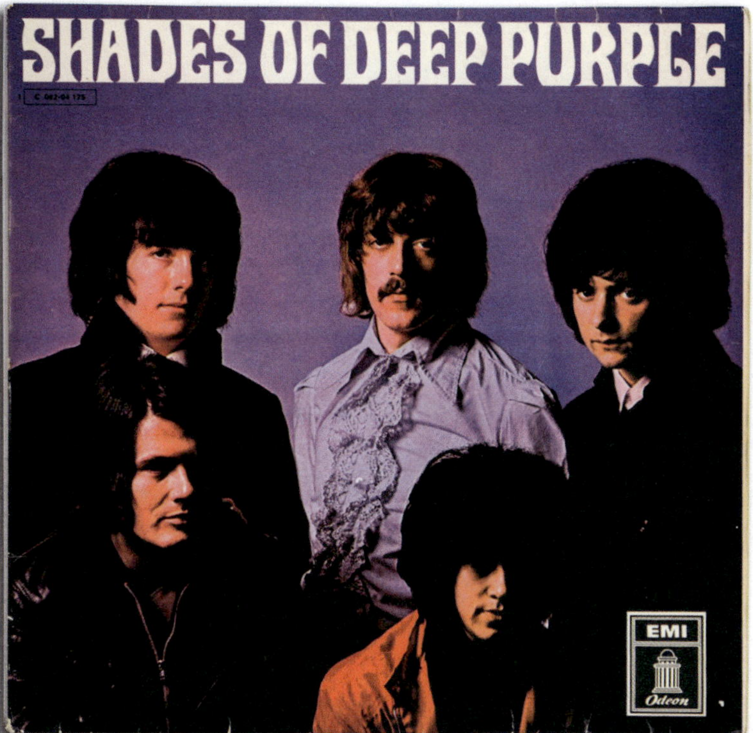

Deep Purple
Shades Of Deep Purple
EMI Records, 1968
Les Weisbrich (Design)

20 NOV

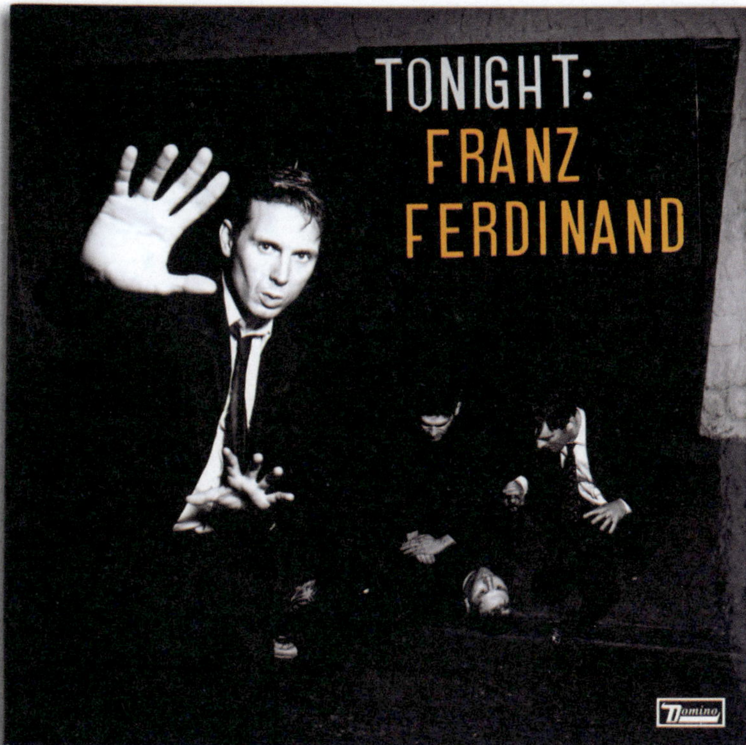

Franz Ferdinand
Tonight
Domino, 2009
Franz Ferdinand, Matthew Cooper (Design)
Søren Solkær Starbird (Photo)

21 NOV

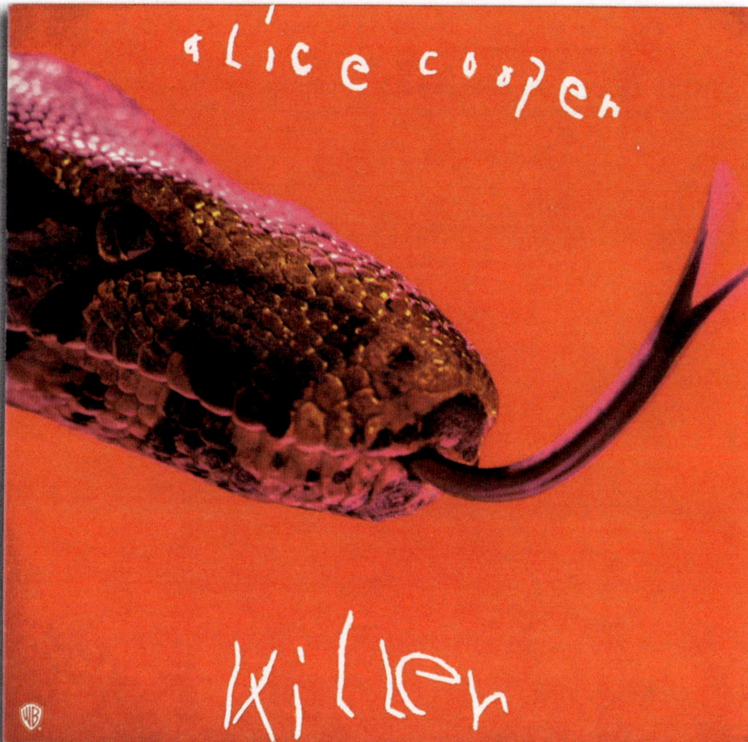

Alice Cooper
Killer
Warner Bros. Records, 1971
Alice Cooper (Design)
Pete Turner (Photo)

22 NOV

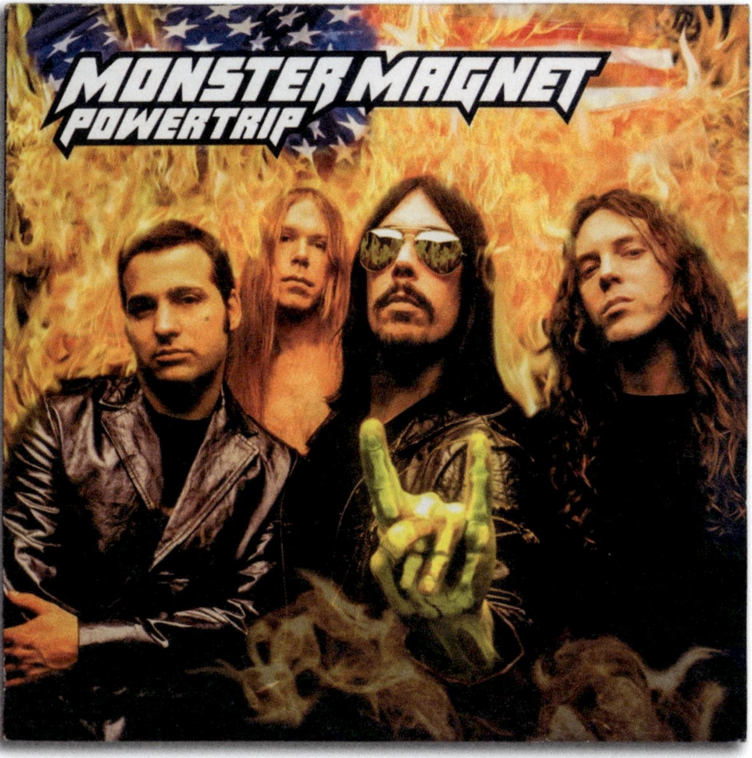

Monster Magnet
Powertrip
A&M Records, 1998
Larimie Garcia (Design)
John Eder (Photo)

23 NOV

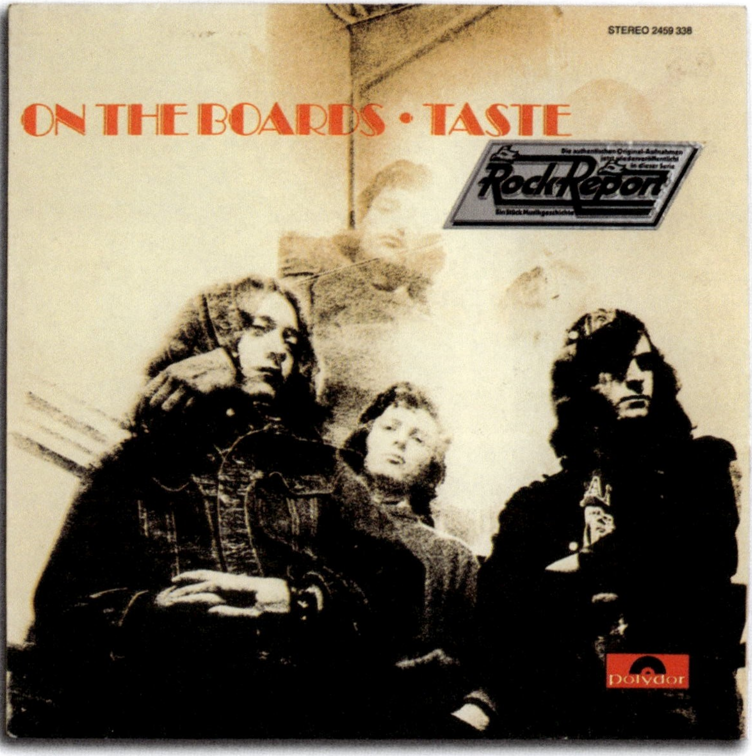

Taste
On The Boards
Polydor, 1970
Hamish Grimes (Design)
Monty Coles (Photo)

24 NOV

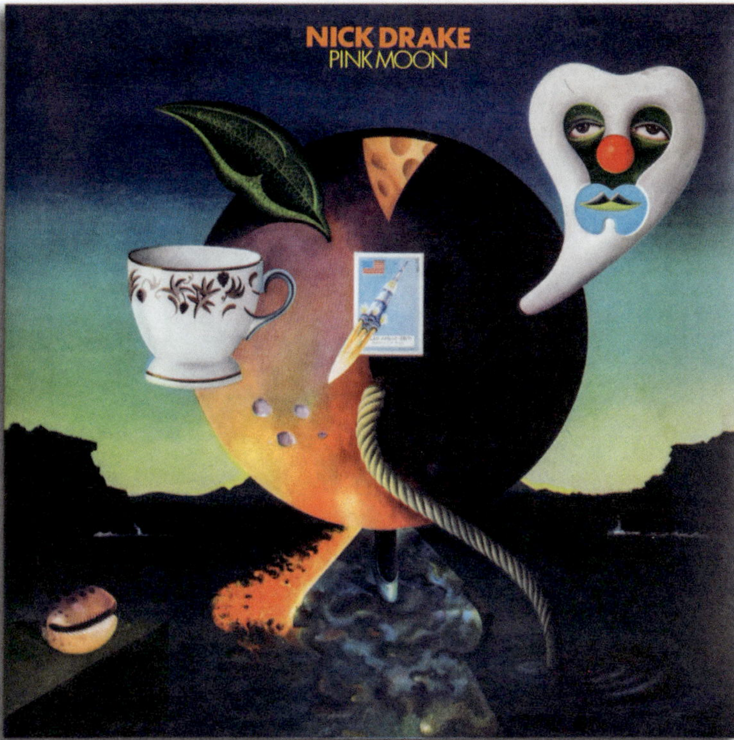

Nick Drake
Pink Moon
Island Records, 1972
Michael Trevithick (Illustration)

25 NOV

† Nov 25th, 1974
Nicholas Rodney Drake
Tanworth-in-Arden (UK)

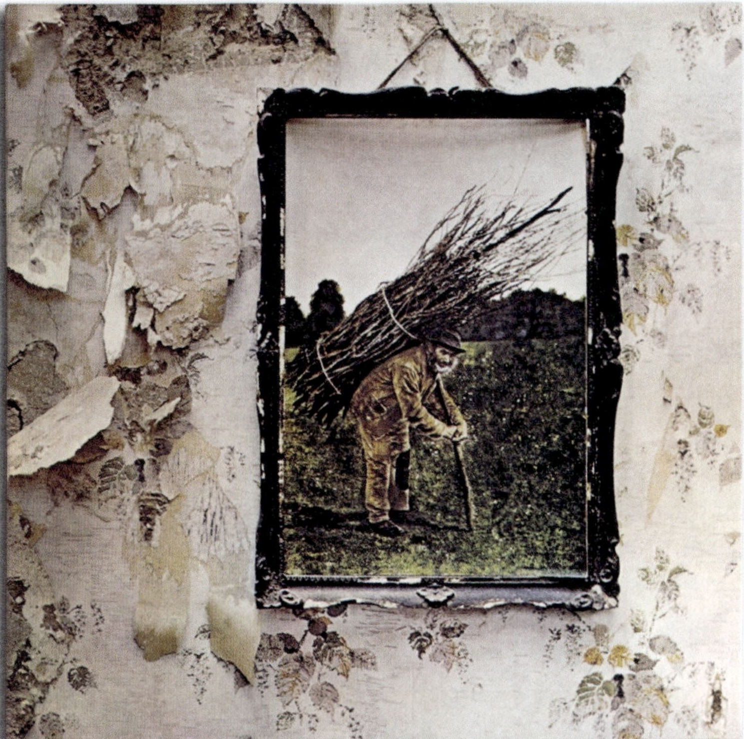

Led Zeppelin
Untitled
Atlantic Records, 1971
Barrington Colby M O M (Design)
Keith Morris (Photo)

26 NOV

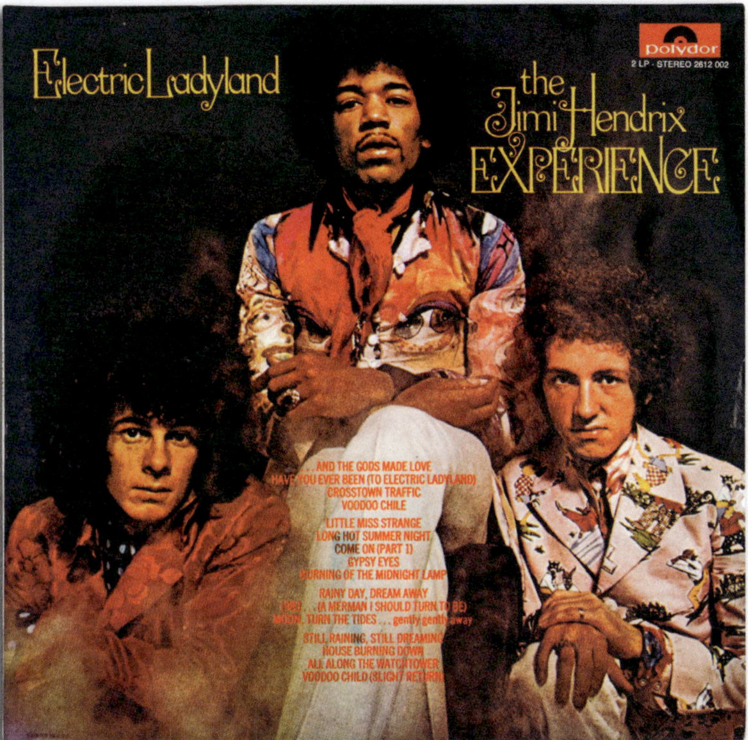

Jimi Hendrix
Electric Ladyland
Polydor, 1968
David King (Design)
David Montgomery (Photo)

* Nov 27th, 1942
John Allen Hendrix
Seattle (Washington)

27 NOV

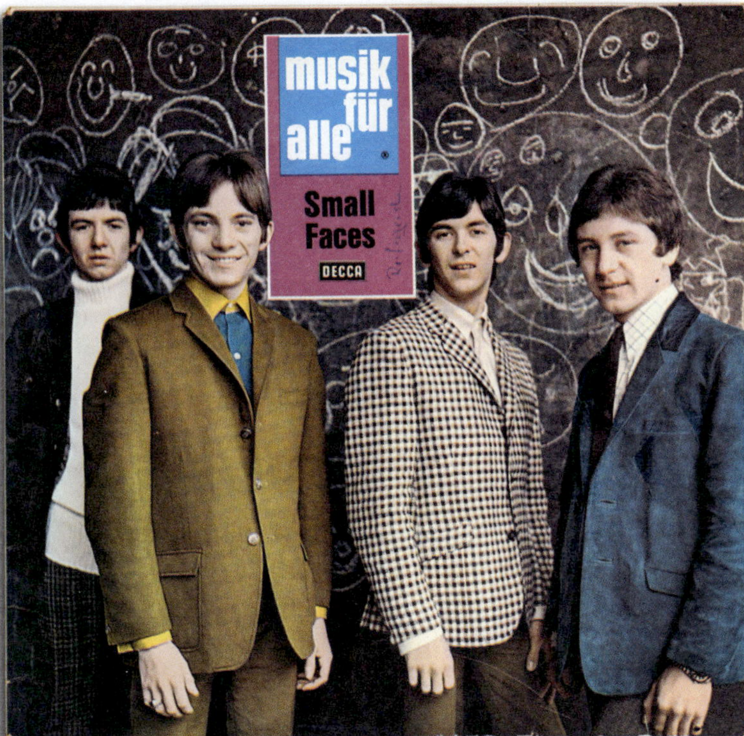

Small Faces
From The Beginning
Decca, 1967
The Whole Hog Design Co. Ltd. (Design)

28 NOV

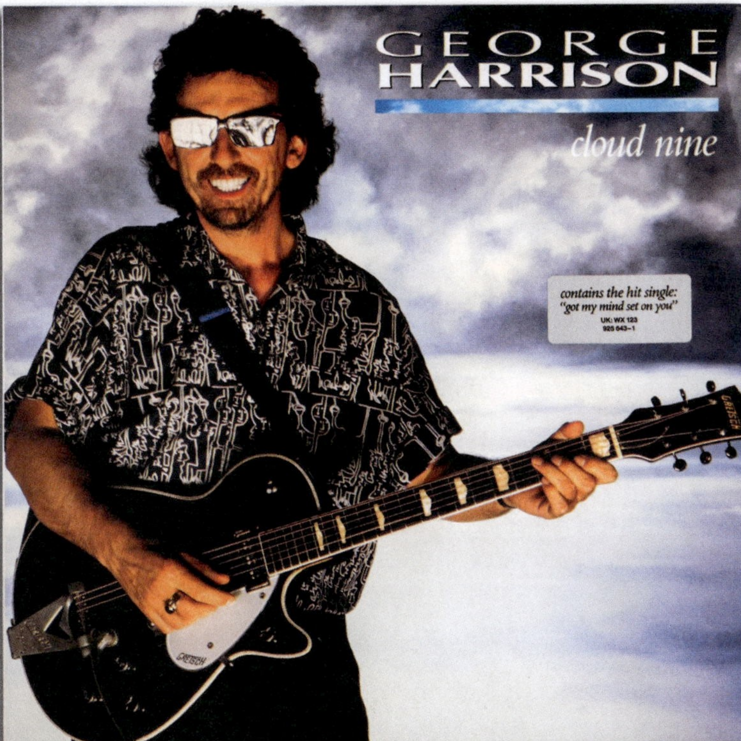

George Harrison
Cloud Nine
Dark Horse Records, 1987
David Costa (Design)
Gerd Mankowitz (Photo)

† Nov 29th, 2001
George Harrison
Bevery Hills (California)

29 NOV

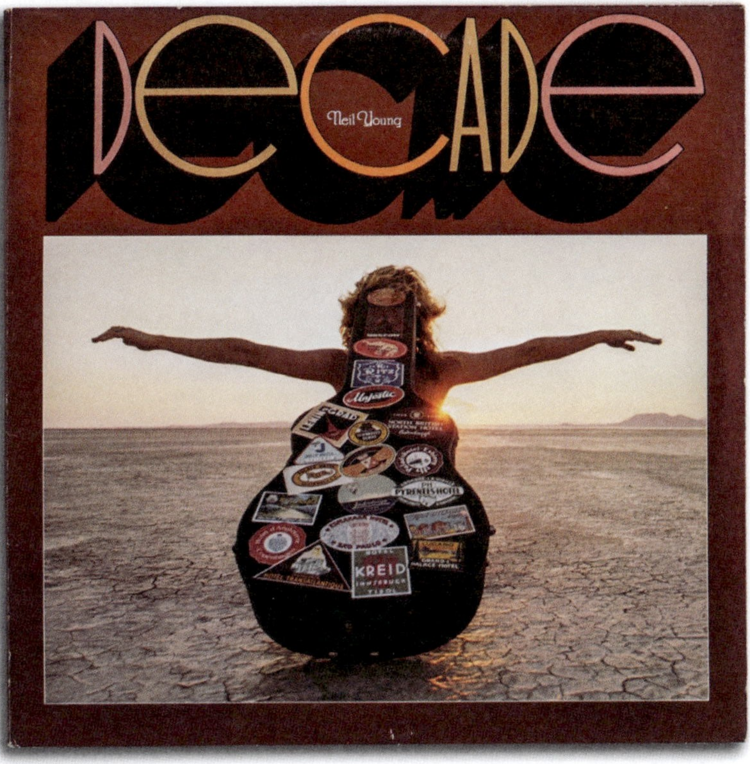

Neil Young
Decade
Reprise Records, 1970
Tommy Grekel (Design)
Gary Burden (Photo)

30 NOV

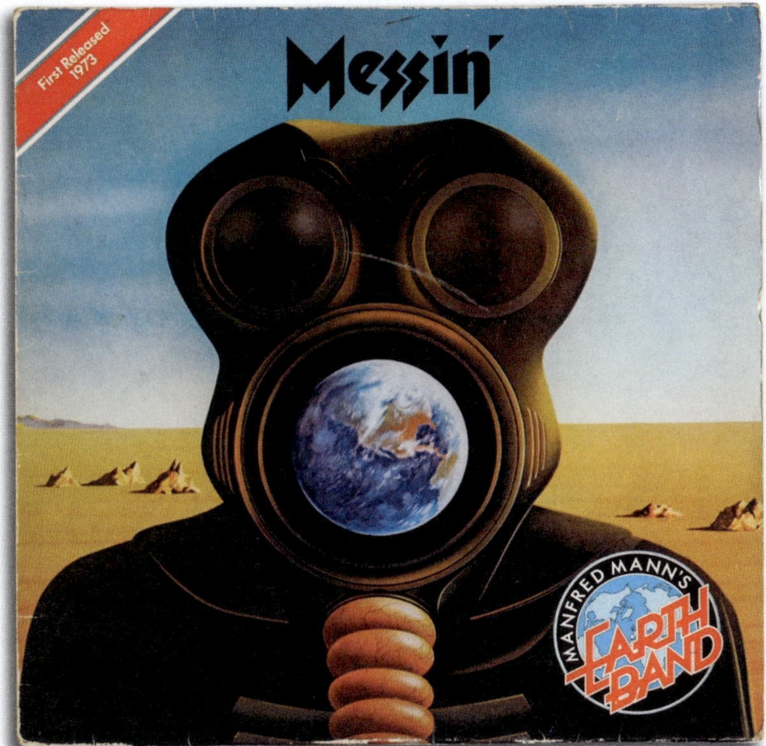

Manfred Mann's Earth Band
Messin'
Bronze, 1973
Peter Hignett (Design)
Peter Goodfellow (Illustration)

01 DEC

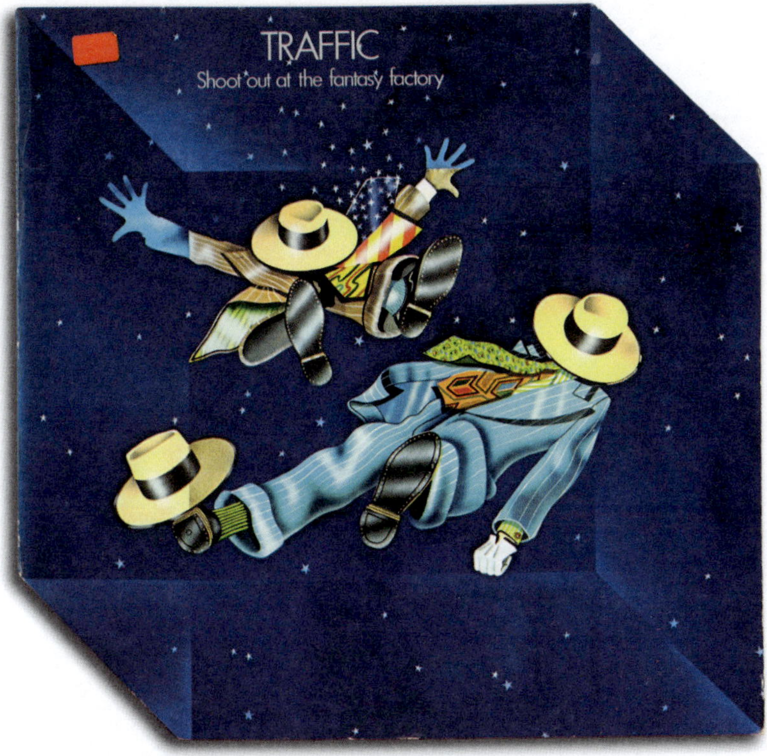

Traffic
Shoot Out At The Fantasy Factory
Island Records, 1973
Tony Wright (Illustration)

02 DEC

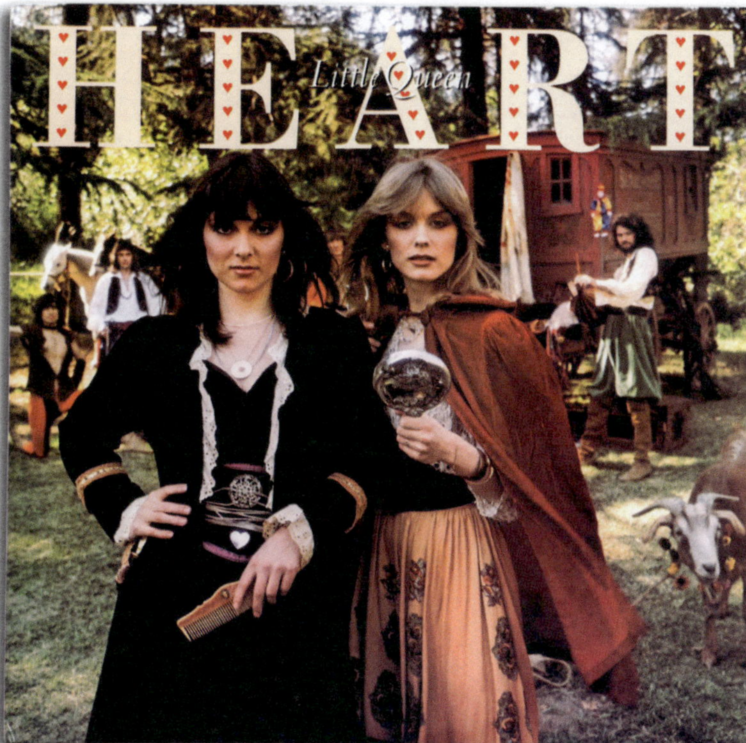

Heart
Little Queen
Portrait, 1977
Mike Doud (Design)
Bob Seidemann (Photo)

03 DEC

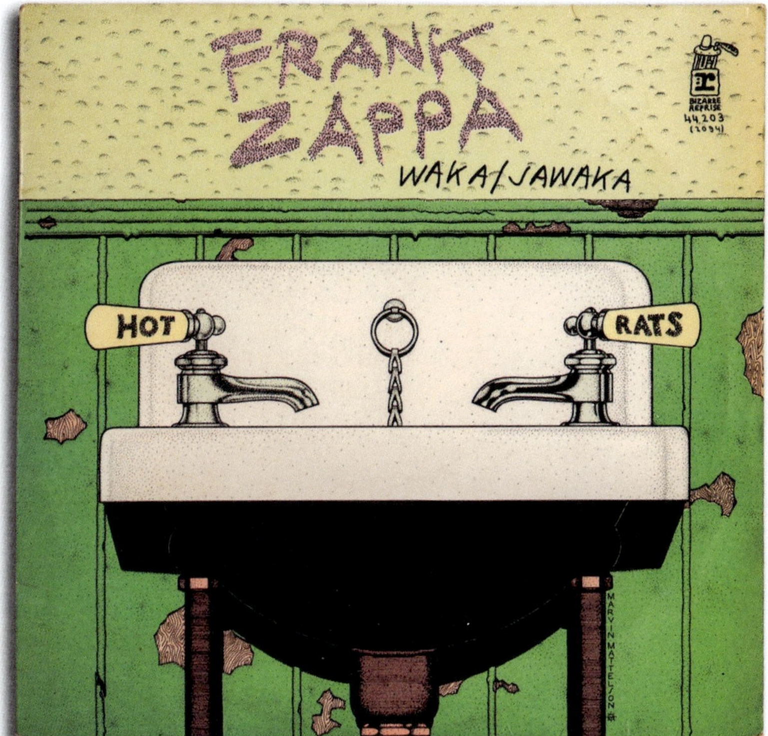

Frank Zappa
Wake/Jawaka
Reprise Records, 1972
Marvin Mattelson (Design)

† Dec 4th, 1993
Frank Vincent Zappa
Laurel Canyon (California)

04 DEC

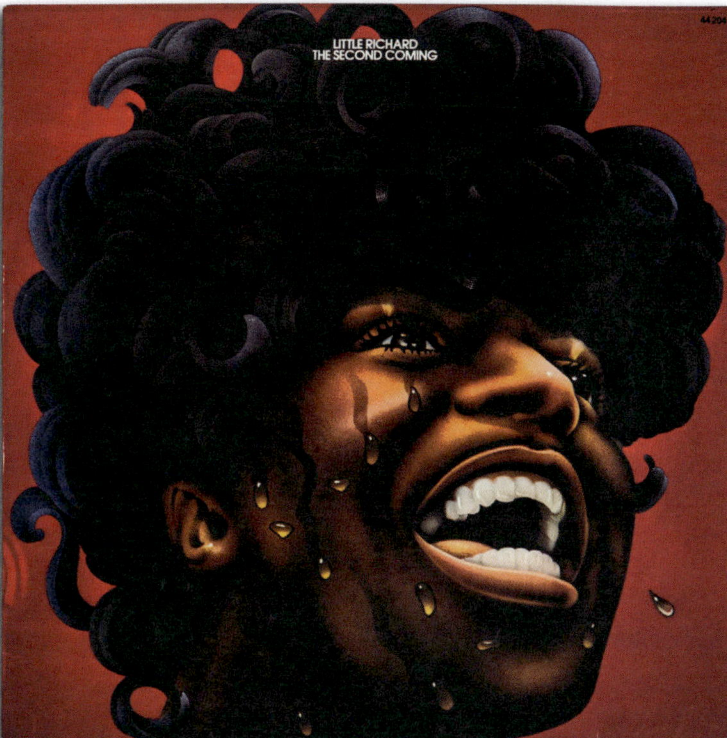

Little Richard
The Second Coming
Reprise Records, 1972
Ed Trasher (Design)
Dave Willardson (Illustration)

* Dec 5th, 1932
Little Richard
Macon (Georgia)

05 DEC

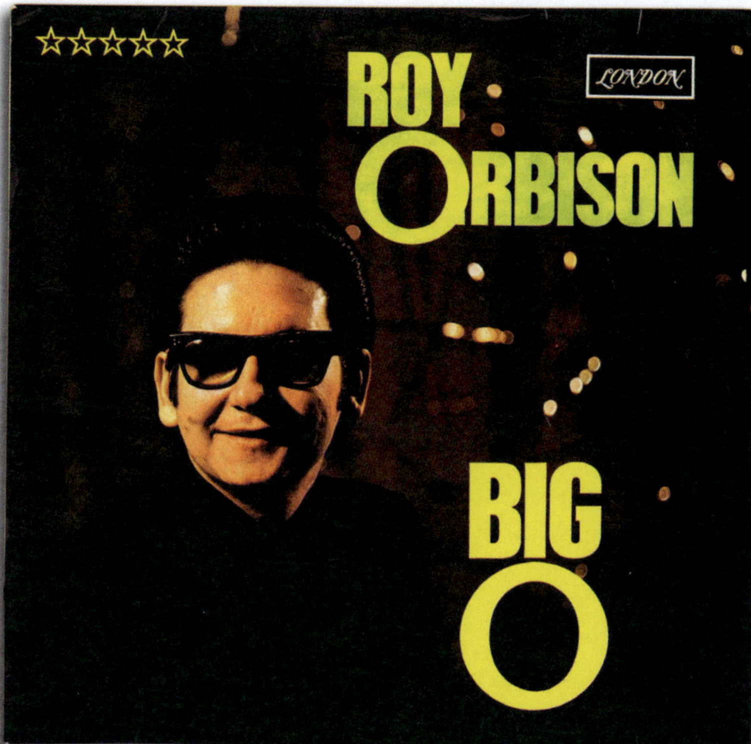

Roy Orbinson
Big O
London Records, 1970
Sidney Paice (Photo)

† Dec 6th, 1988
Roy Kelton Orbinson
Hendersonville (Tennessee)

06 DEC

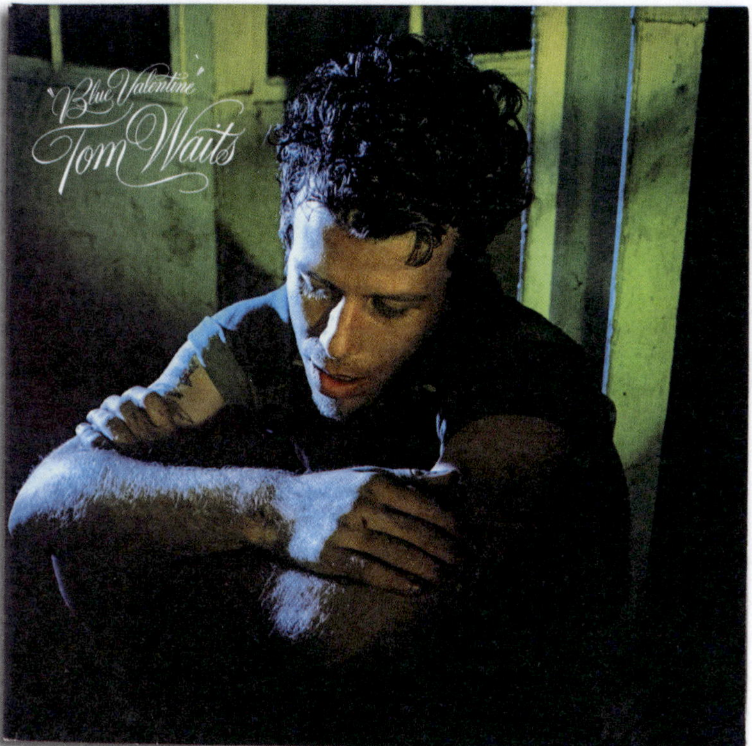

Tom Waits
Blue Valentine
Asylum Records, 1978
Ron Coro (Design)
Elliot Gilbert (Photo)

* Dec 7th, 1949
Thomas Alan "Tom" Waits
Pomona (California)

07 DEC

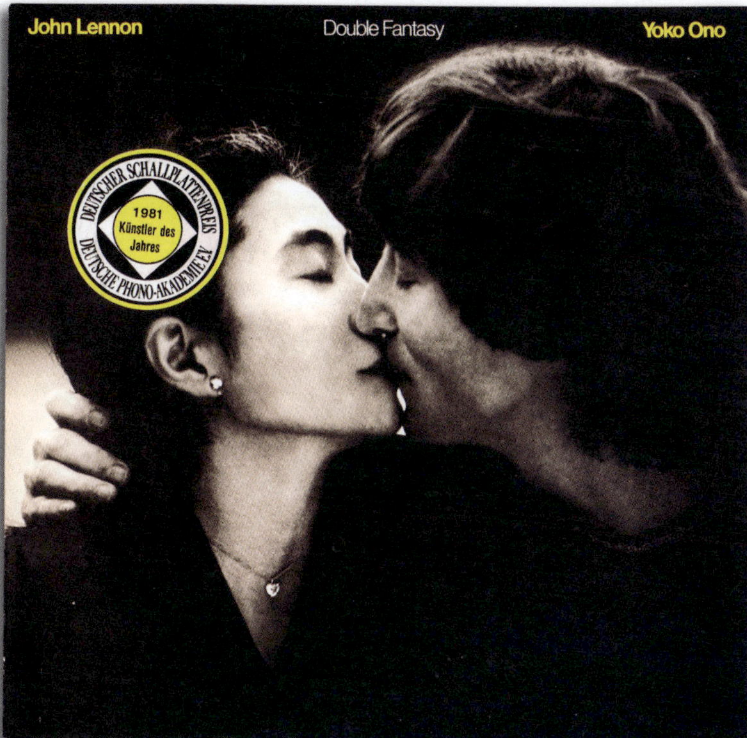

John Lennon & Yoko Ono
Double Fantasy
Geffen Records, 1980
Christopher Whorf / Art Hotel (Design)
Kishin Shinoyama (Photo)

† Dec 8th, 1980
John Winston Ono Lennon
New York City

08 DEC

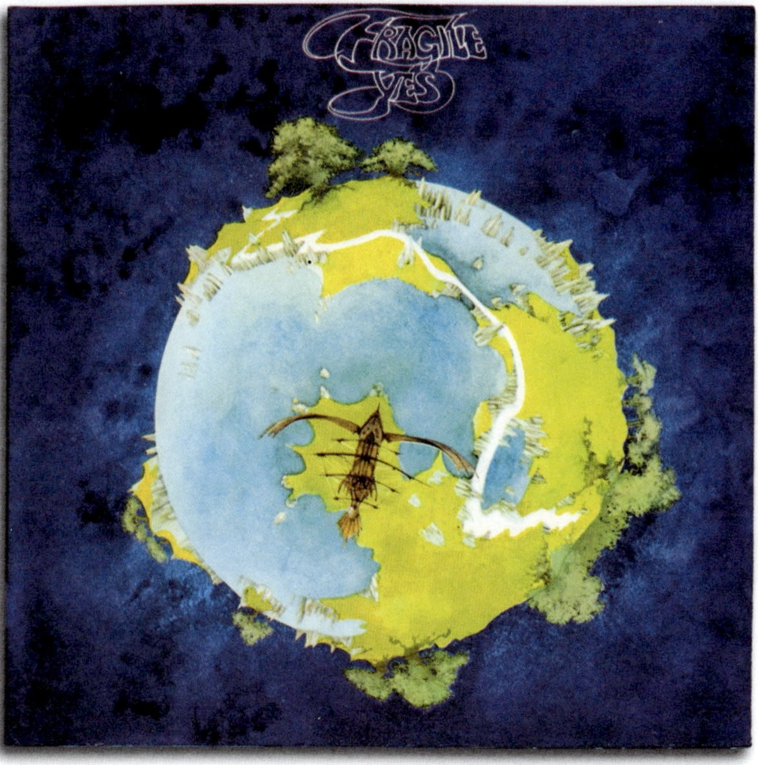

YES
Fragile
Atlantic, 1973
Roger Dean (Illustration)

09 DEC

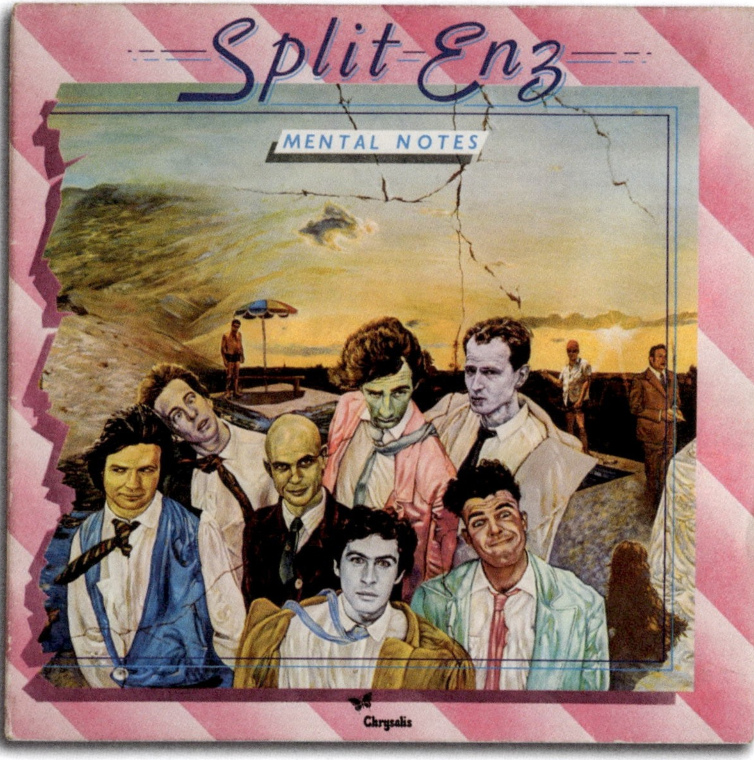

Split Enz
Mental Notes
Chrysalis Records, 1976
Graeme Webber (Design)

10 DEC

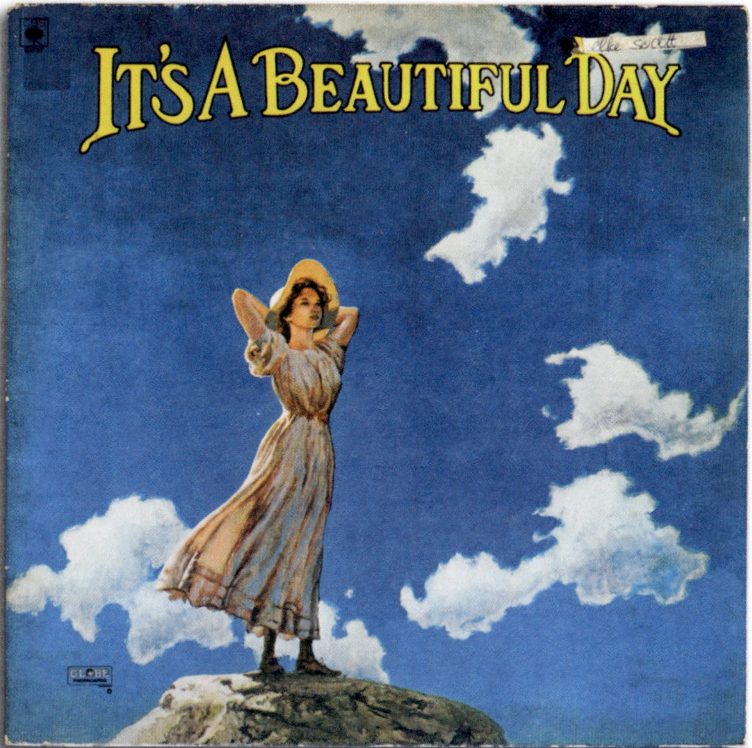

It's Beautiful Day
CBS, 1972
Globe Propaganda (Design)

11 DEC

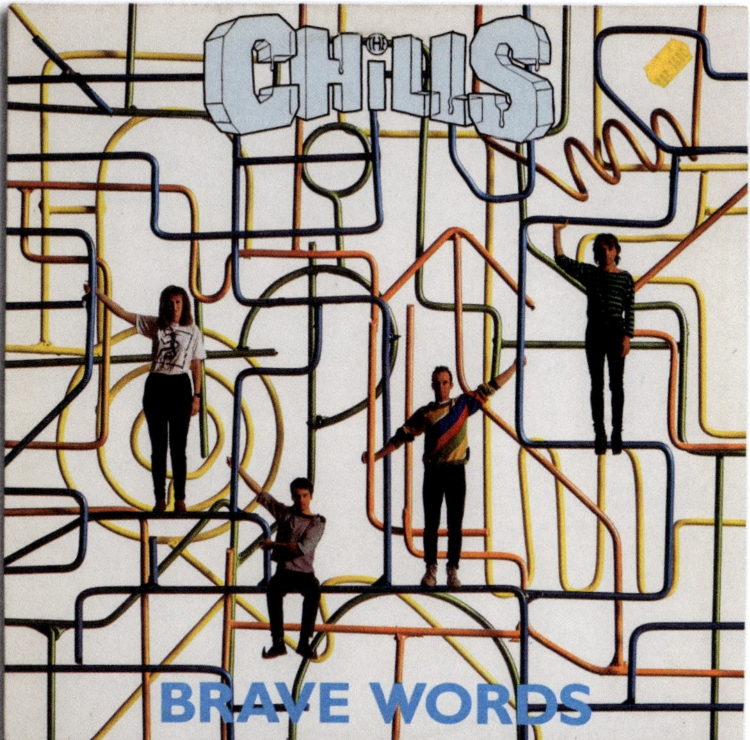

The Chills
Brave Words
Flying Nun Europe, 1987
Martin Philipps (Design)
World Travel (Photo)

12 DEC

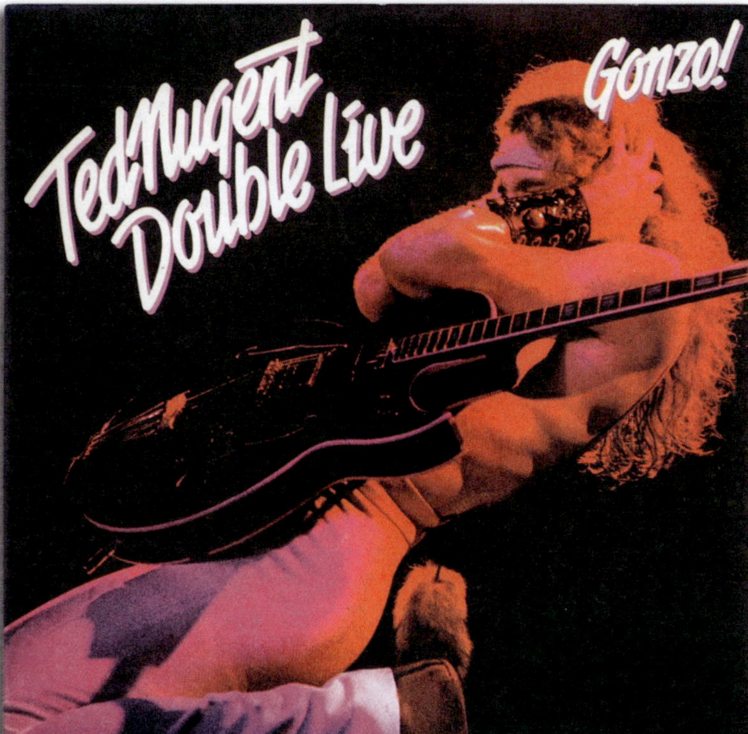

Ted Nugent
Double Live Gonzo!
EPIC Records, 1978
John Berg, Paula Scher (Design)
David Gahr (Photo)

* Dec 13th, 1948
Theodore Anthony „Ted“ Nugent
Detroit (Michigan)

13 DEC

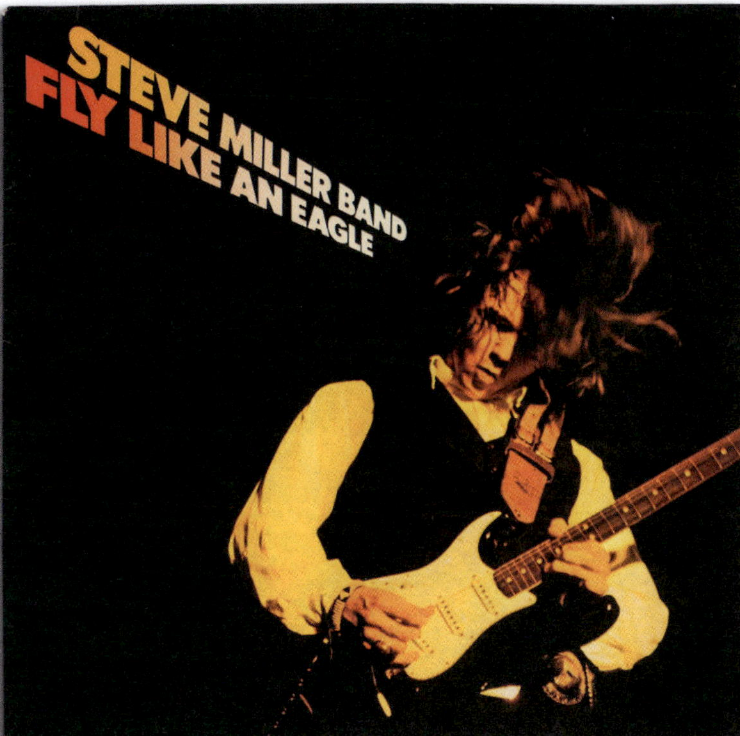

Steve Miller Band
Fly Like An Eagle
Phonogram, 1976
Casarini / Von Hamersveld (Design)
Susan McCardle (Photo)

14 DEC

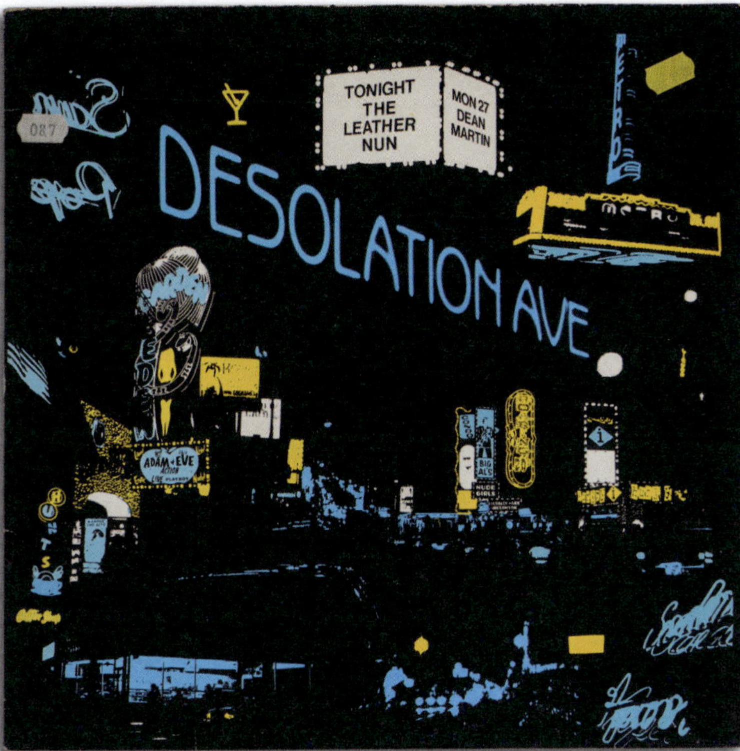

The Leather Nun
Desolation Ave
Wire Records, 1985
B. Aronsson (Design)
B. Aronsson (Photo)

15 DEC

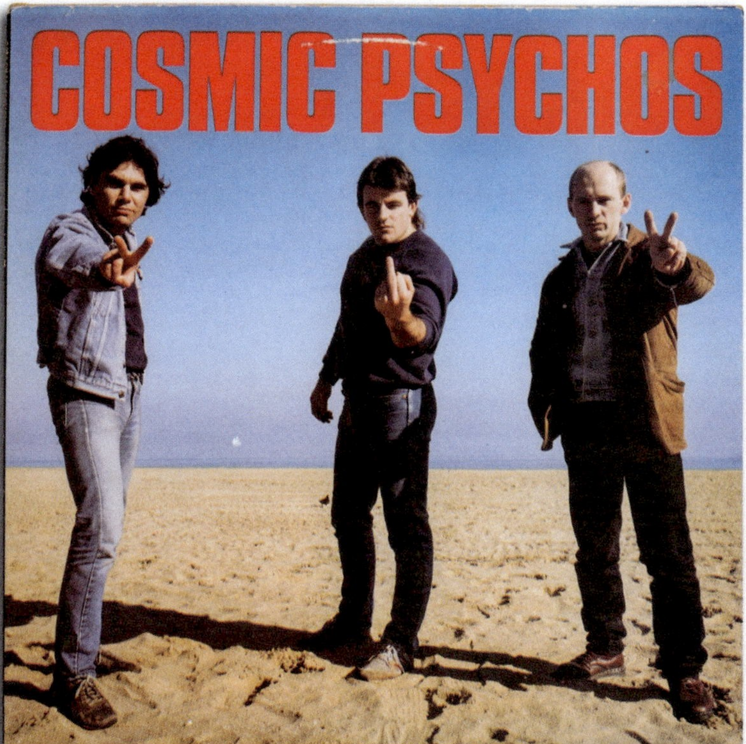

Cosmic Psychos
What Goes on Records, 1988
Ian Davidson (Design)
Ian Davidson (Photo)

16 DEC

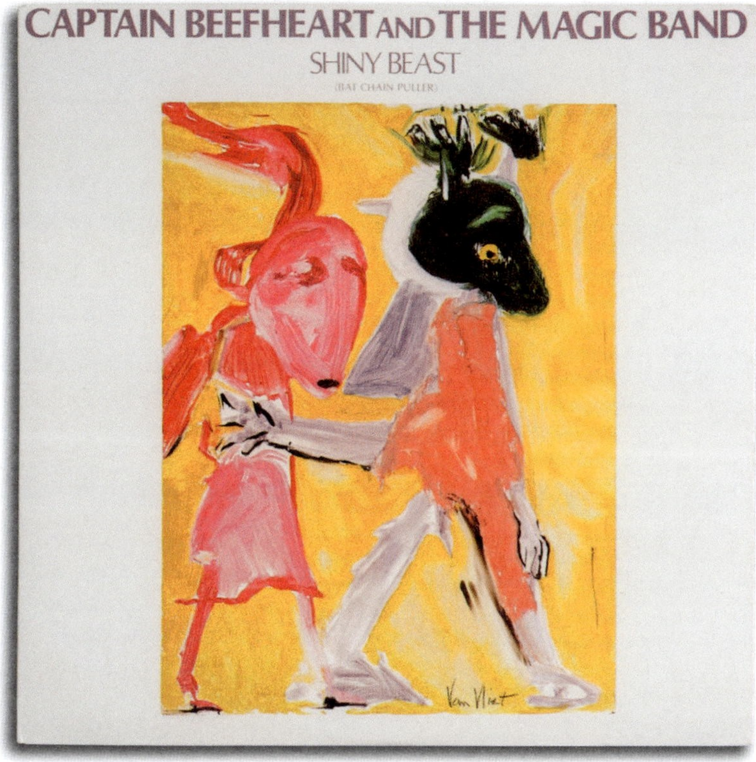

Captain Beefheart And The Magic Band
Shiny Beast
Warner Bros. Records, 1978
John Cabalka (Design)
Don Van Vliet (Illustration)

† Dec 17th, 2010
Don Glen Van Vliet
Arcata (California)

17 DEC

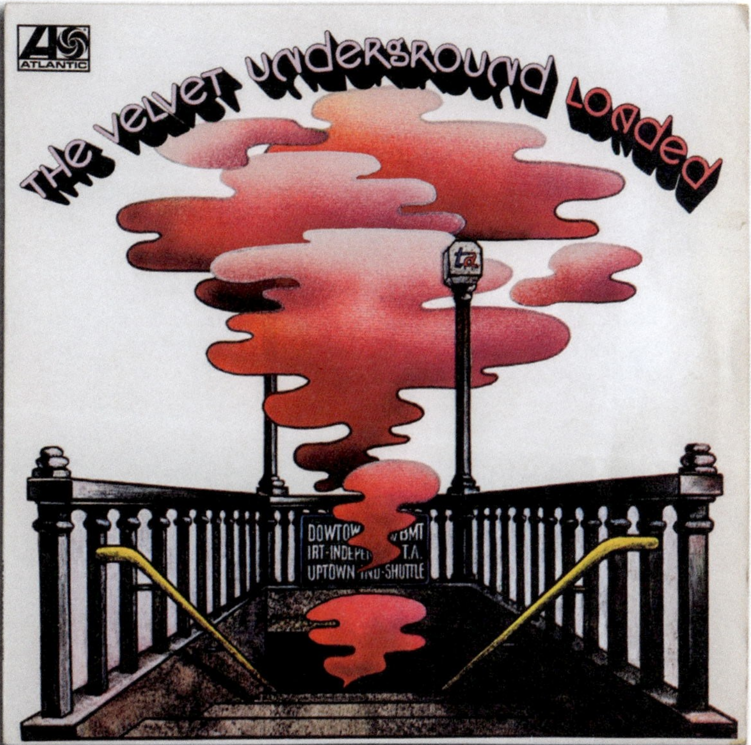

The Velvet Underground
Loaded
Atlantic Records, 1971
Stanislaw Zagorski (Illustration)

18 DEC

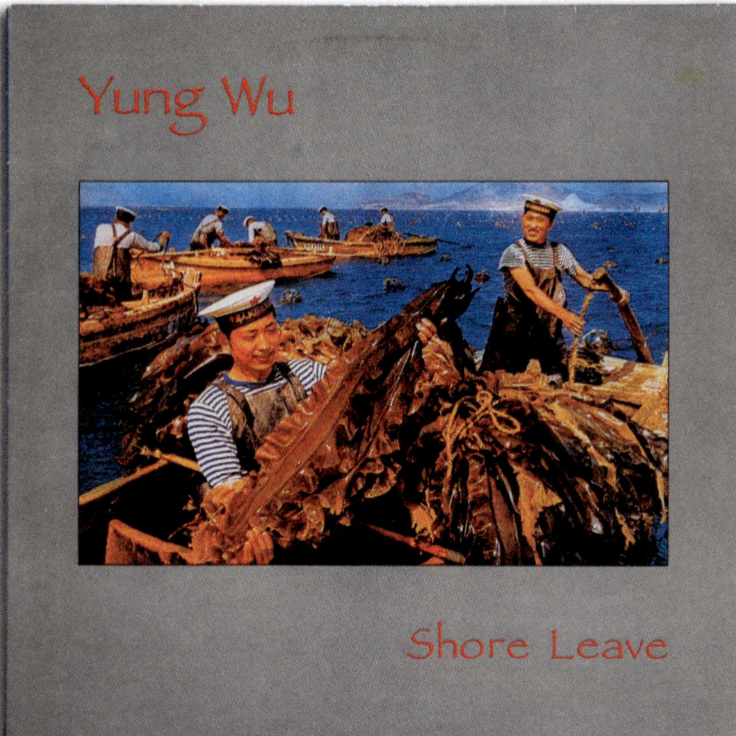

Yung Wu
Shore Leave
Megadisc, 1987
Glenn Mercer (Design)
New China Pictures (Photo)

19 DEC

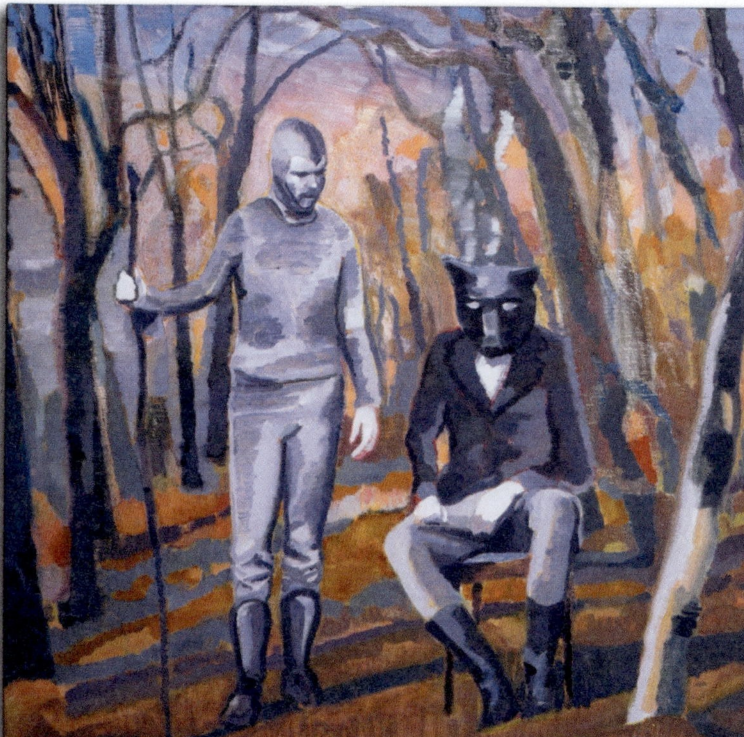

Midlake
The Trails Of Van Occupanther
Bella Union, 2016
Luke Jarvis (Design)
Brian Lotti (Illustration)

20 DEC

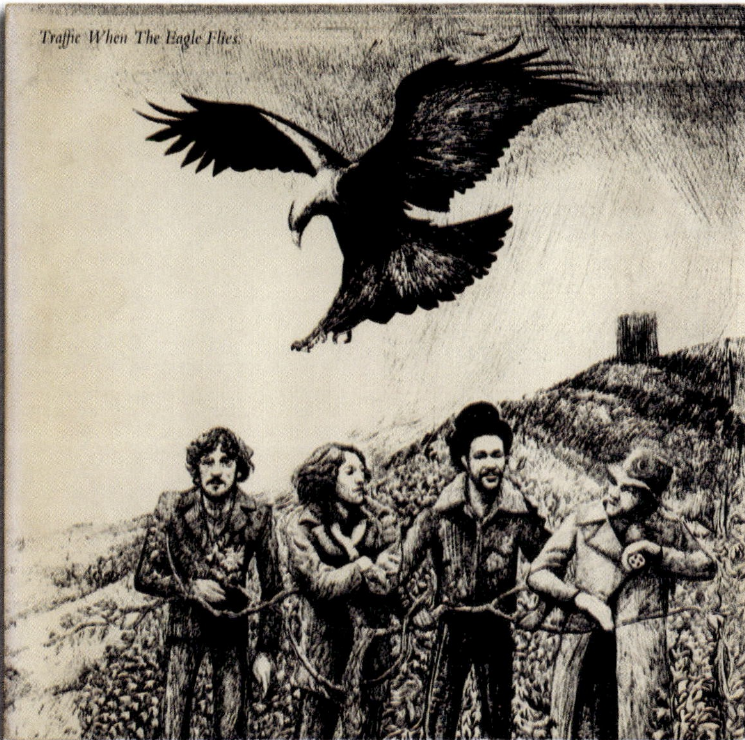

Traffic
When The Eagle Flies
Island Records, 1974
Martin Hughes (Design)

21 DEC

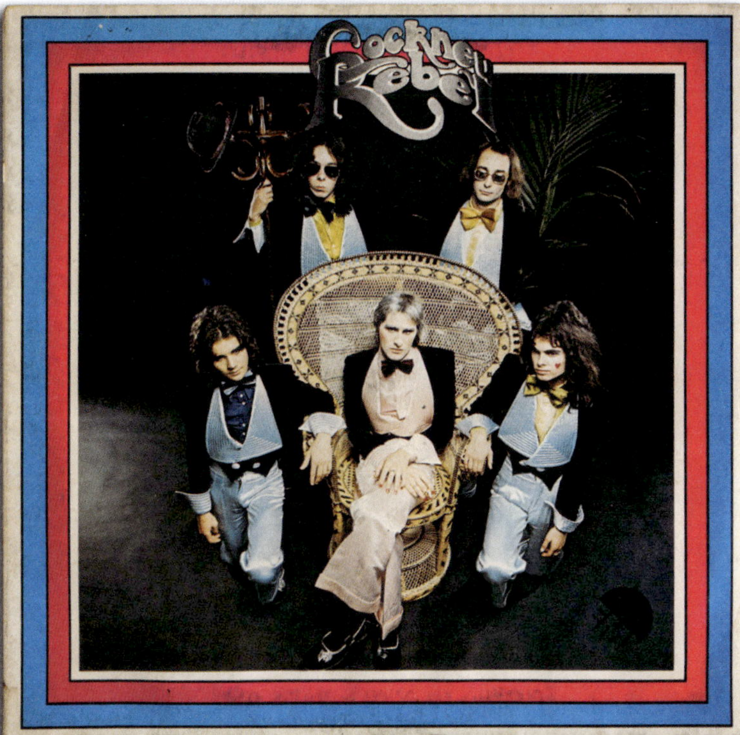

Cockney Rebel
The Human Menagerie
EMI Records, 1973
Star Trek Enterprises (Design)
Peter Vernon (Photo)

22 DEC

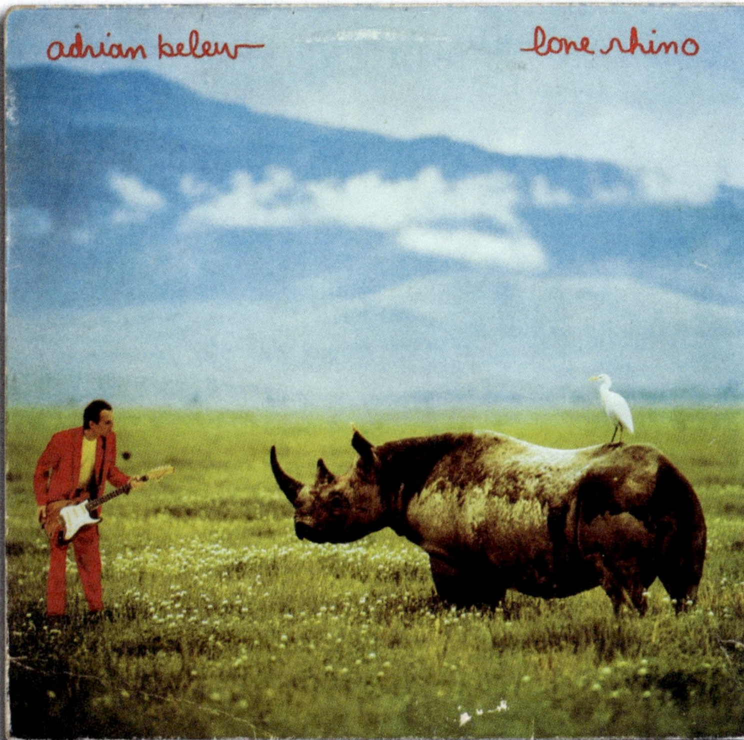

Adrian Belew
Lone Rhino
Island Records, 1982
Sukita & Koyo Tanaka (Photo)

23 DEC

* Dec 23rd, 1949
Robert Steven „Adrian“ Bele
Covington (Kentucky)

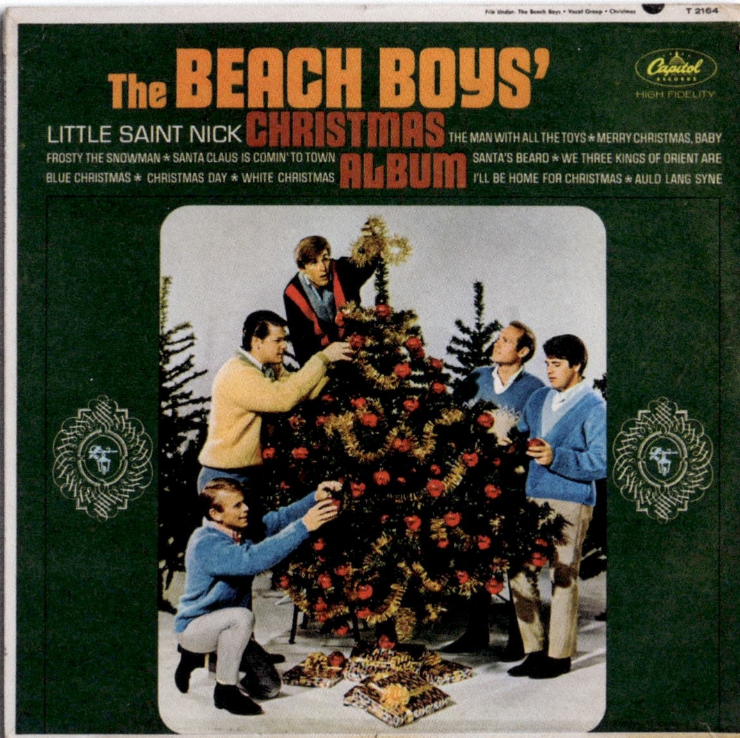

The Beach Boys
Christmas Album
Capitol Records, 1964
George Jerman, Capitol Photo Studio (Photo)

24 DEC

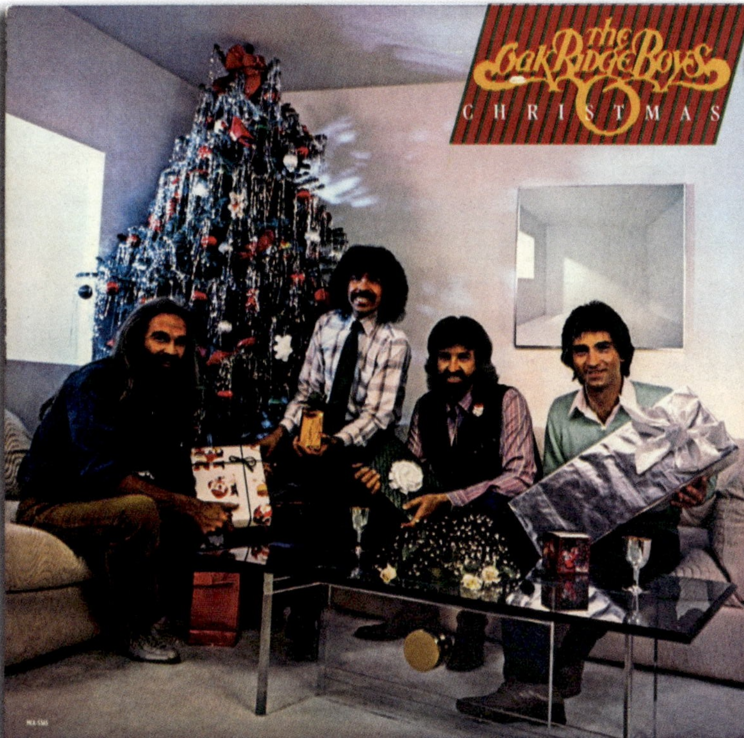

The Oak Ridge Boys
Christmas
MCA Records, 1982
Cover Artists Unknown

25 DEC

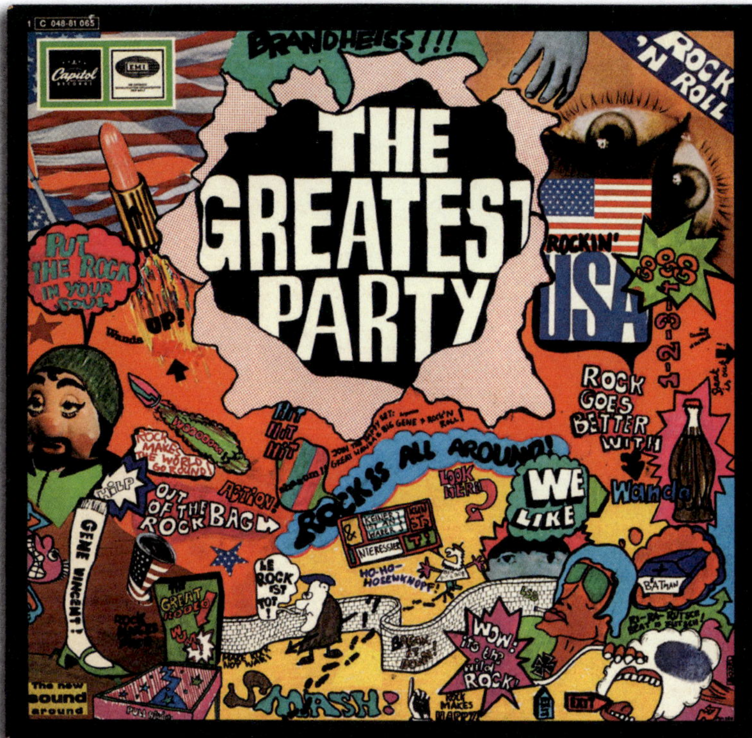

Gene Vincent & Wanda Jackson
The Greatest Party
Capitol Records, 1972
Cover Artists Unknown

26 DEC

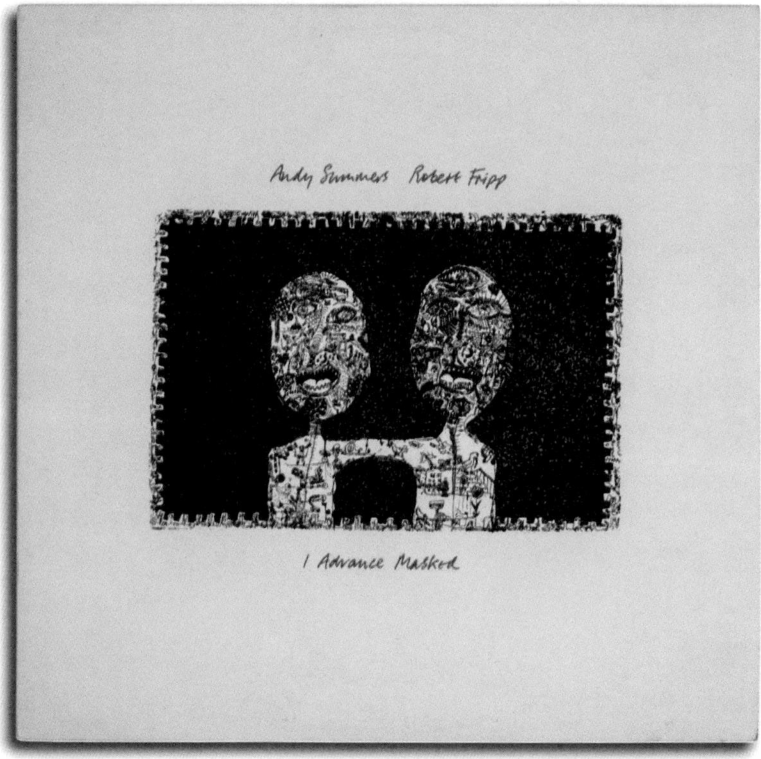

Robert Fripp & Andy Summers
I Advance Masked
A&M Records, 1982
Michael Ross, Andy Summers (Design)
Jimmi Rizzi (Illustration)

27 DEC

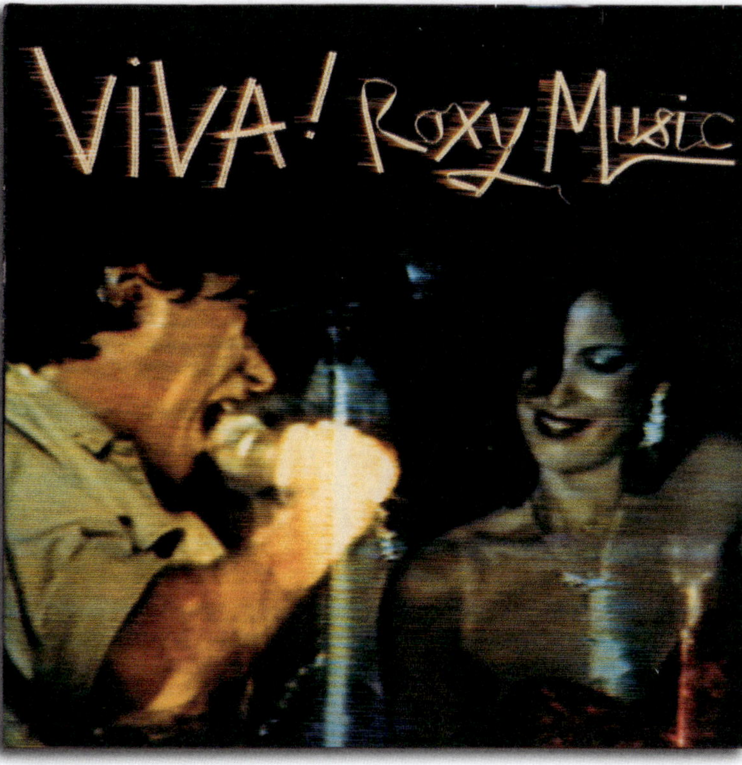

Roxy Music
Viva! Roxy Music
Island Records, 1976
Cover Artists Unknown

28 DEC

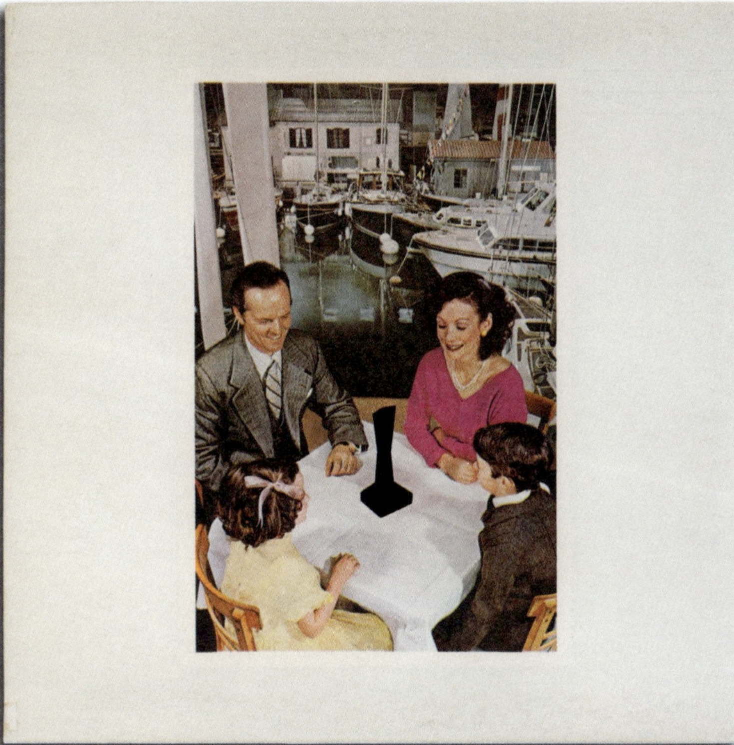

Led Zeppelin
Presence
Swan Song Records, 1976
Hipgnosis & Hardie (Design)
Andrew Zaeh (Photo)

29 DEC

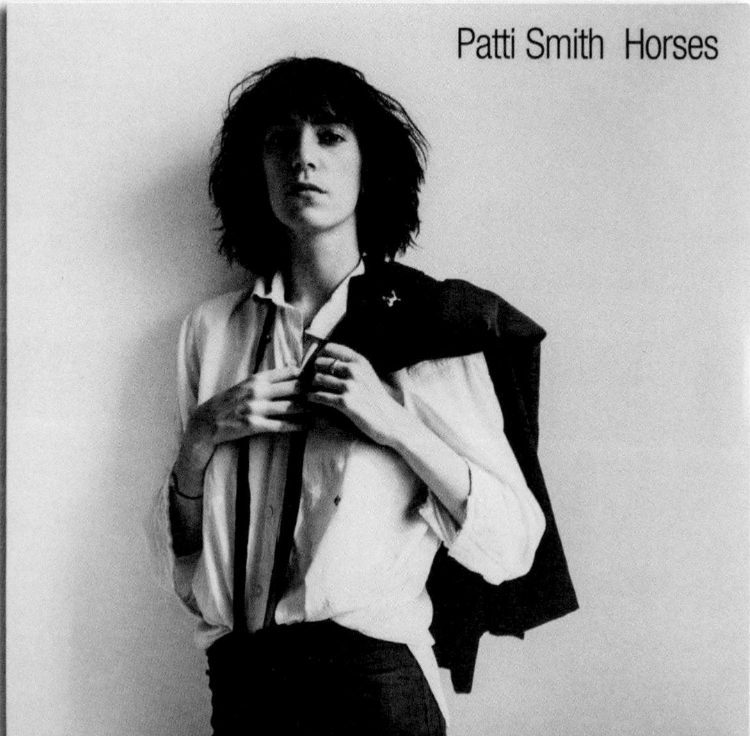

Patti Smith
Horses
Arista Records, 1975
Bob Heimall (Design)
Robert Mapplethorpe (Photo)

* Dec 30th, 1946
Patricia Lee „Patti“ Smith
Chicago (Illinois)

30 DEC

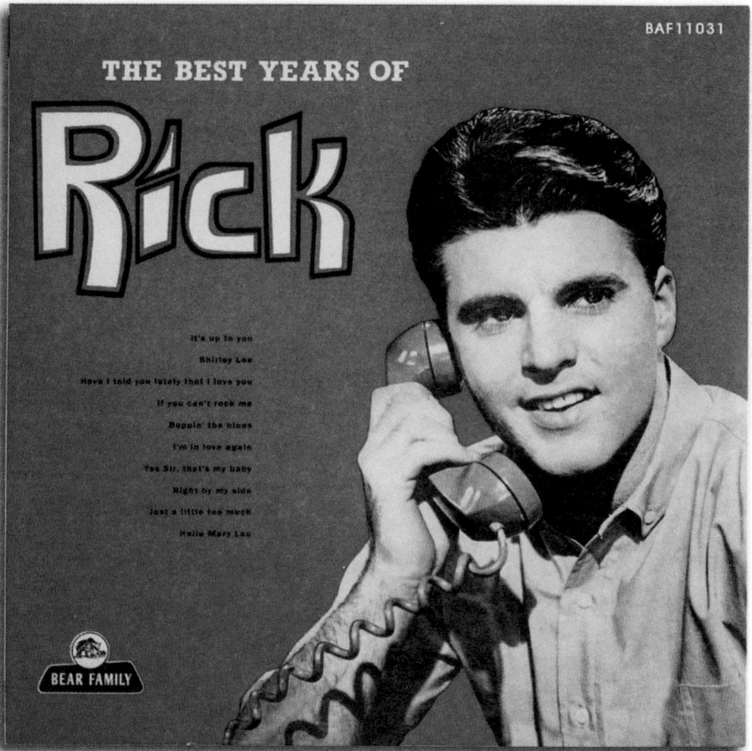

Ricky Nelson
The Best Years Of Rick
Imperial / Bear Family Prod. Ltd., 1961
Cover Artists Unknown

31 DEC

† Dec 31st, 1985
Ricky Nelson
Kalb (Texas)

Imprint

THE ART OF ROCK COVERS

Published by
Seltmann Publishers
Zillestr. 105A, 10585 Berlin, Germany
www.seltmannpublishers.com

Cover Selection & Background Research:
Bernd Jonkmanns

Thanks to Johnny Jonkmanns, Alf Burchardt and Gregor Lengler

Art Direction: Sandro Heindel and Stefan Küstner

We thank everyone involved for their unique artistic work
that made this project possible.

This project is an homage to the great and glorious decade of vinyl records and their wonderfully designed covers. With this project, we aim to showcase and preserve the covers as well as their high level of artistic power and profound meaningfulness. Every cover has been selected from personal vinyl collections and individually photographed.
If you have any questions or suggestions, please do not hesitate to contact us:
info@seltmannpublishers.com

Please note:
Not all artists or albums are available on streaming services,
so some albums may not be available

ISBN 978-3-949070-37-2